980.
LATI
D1762950

Latin
America:
A Political
Dictionary

Latin America: A Political Dictionary

Ernest E. Rossi
Jack C. Plano
Western Michigan University

ABC-CLIO
Santa Barbara, California
Denver, Colorado
Oxford, England

Copyright © 1992 by ABC-CLIO, Inc.

All rights reserved. No part of this publication may be reproduced, stored in a retrieval system, or transmitted, in any form or by any means, electronic, mechanical, photocopying, recording, or otherwise, except for the inclusion of brief quotations in a review, without prior permission in writing from the publishers.

Library of Congress Cataloging-in-Publication Data

Rossi, Ernest E.
   Latin America : a political dictionary / Ernest E. Rossi, Jack C. Plano.
      p.   cm. — (Clio dictionaries in political science)
   Rev. ed. of: The Latin American political dictionary. c1980
   Includes index.
   1. Latin America—Dictionaries.   2. Latin America—Politics and government—Dictionaries.
I. Plano, Jack C.   II. Rossi, Ernest E.
Latin American political dictionary.   III. Title.   IV. Series.
F1406.R67   1992   980′.003—dc20   92-28946

ISBN 9-87436-608-9 (cloth: alk. paper)
ISBN 9-87436-698-4 (pbk: alk. paper)

99 98 97 96 95 94 93 92   10 9 8 7 6 5 4 3 2 1 (cloth)
99 98 97 96 95 94 93 92   10 9 8 7 6 5 4 3 2 1 (pbk)

This is a revised edition of *The Latin American Political Dictionary,* copyright © 1980 by
   Ernest E. Rossi and Jack C. Plano.

ABC-CLIO, Inc.
130 Cremona Drive, P.O. Box 1911
Santa Barbara, California 93116-1911

This book is printed on acid-free paper ∞.
Manufactured in the United States of America

Contents

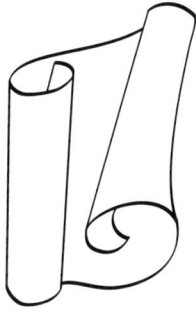

Preface	vii
1 – Geography, Population, and Social Structure	3
2 – Historical Perspective	21
3 – Political Culture and Ideology	43
4 – Revolution and Political Change	65
5 – Political Parties, Interest Groups, and Elections	85
6 – The Military	109
7 – Governmental Institutions and Processes	123
8 – Economic Modernization and Political Development	141
9 – Economic Integration	167
10 – International Law and Organization	183
11 – United States–Latin American Relations	197
Index	221

Preface

Latin America was not immune from the effects of momentous events that occurred throughout the world during the 1980s and early 1990s. To cite several examples pertaining to the region, in 1980 most Latin American nations were under some form of military rule, but by 1990 military governments had been set aside in favor of civilian ones; the foreign debt crisis drove many states to the edge of bankruptcy; a revolutionary government in Nicaragua was replaced with a conservative one by free elections; and state socialist and corporatist economic policies began to give way to free market policies and the sale of public enterprises to the private sector. These and other dramatic changes encouraged us to write a new edition of the previously entitled *Latin American Political Dictionary*, with many changes and additions. There are about 50 new major entries, an increase of over 20 percent from the first edition. Most entries, except for a few historical ones, have been expanded and updated using the most recent information. Many new individuals, political parties, organizations, and concepts have been identified or defined within major entries. These items may be quickly located by using the comprehensive index. While being selective, we have tried to incorporate important topics, issues, persons, and organizations so that this book can remain the useful teaching tool, learning tool, and reference source that was first published in 1980. It will continue to serve as a guide to the technical language for the Latin American region as well as a guide to the operation of Latin American political systems.

Precision in the use of language is the primary scientific tool of every intellectual discipline. This was, in both editions, our first consideration. Other objectives included producing a work that would enable students of Latin American politics, economics, sociology, geography, and history to acquire, easily and accurately, a knowledge of some of the most useful concepts that relate to that region of the world. The book concentrates on the Latin nations in the Americas and how the United States relates to them. We would like to emphasize, however, that efforts to include all terms were not exhaustive. Rather, we selected those concepts, events, institutions, strategies and theories that are most applicable to achieving an understanding of the Latin American region. The book thus places a major emphasis on helping students learn the basics, with the assumption that an ability to communicate in the technical language of Latin American politics will aid students in searching for knowledge in the field.

Several special features of this book are aimed at achieving these objectives. First, the entries have been systematically selected to complement the subject matter found in various textbooks that focus on Latin America. Second, a subject-matter chapter format makes the book useful as a teaching and learning tool. The topical organization of the chapters in the dictionary dovetail with those found in many books in the field so assignments can be coordinated by the instructor. Third, each entry, in addition to including an up-to-date definition, contains a paragraph entitled *Significance* wherein the term's historical importance and its current relevance are discussed and analyzed. Fourth, the book contains extensive cross-references that offer the reader access to additional information pertaining to a subject. A comprehensive index makes the book an effective reference tool as well as an effective teaching and learning device.

Politics and the field of political science probably suffer more than most disciplines from semantic confusion. This is especially true when students begin studies that focus on foreign regions generally unfamiliar to them. Providing help to those undertaking a first course in Latin American studies was one of our prime motivations. Comments from students and faculty about the book are greatly appreciated, and past comments have contributed to changes found in this new edition. We accept full responsibility, however, for any errors of commission as well as omission.

Latin America: A Political Dictionary is organized so that entries and supplementary data can be located in several ways. Entries are arranged alphabetically within subject-matter chapters. Terms relating to regional arrangements like the "Organization of American States" can be found under the rubric "Inter-American System" in the chapter "International Law and Organization." When doubtful about the appropriate chapter or rubric, consult the general index. Entry numbers for terms appear in the index in bold type; subsidiary concepts discussed within entries can be found in the index identified by entry numbers in regular type. For study purposes, numerous entries have also been subsumed under major topical headings in the index, giving the reader access to broad classes of related information.

The reader can also more fully explore a topic by using the extensive cross-references provided in most entries. These may lead to materials in the same chapter or may refer to other chapters. Entry numbers have been included in all cross-references for the convenience of the reader. A few concepts can be found as entries in more than one chapter, but in each case the definition and significance of the item is related to the subject matter of that chapter in which the entry appears.

The authors have designed the unique format of this book to offer the reader a variety of useful applications in the quest for information. These include its use as (1) a dictionary and reference guide to the language of the field of Latin American studies; (2) a study guide for the introductory course in Latin American politics; (3) a supplement to the *textbook* in such courses; (4) a source of review material for the student enrolled in advanced courses; and

(5) a social science aid for use in cognate fields such as international relations and international economics.

We acknowledge the important role of the many scholars whose articles and books have contributed to the enrichment of the language and illuminated the theories of the field of Latin American studies, but the special character of this work does not permit us to cite their contributions. We are grateful to and we also thank our students who have challenged and excited us over the years in a manner that contributed to the value of this work. Also, we express our thanks and appreciation to Jean E. Rossi who completed the computer typing of the manuscript with skill, dispatch, and good humor.

Ernest E. Rossi
Jack C. Plano
Western Michigan University

Latin America: A Political Dictionary

Geography, Population, and Social Structure

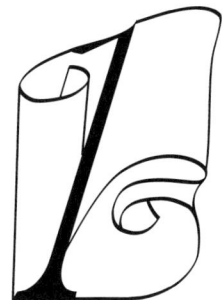

Creole (Criollo)　　　1

In the colonial period, a person of full Spanish ancestry born in the Americas. Creoles are distinguished from peninsulars *(peninsulares)*, or Spaniards who were born in the Iberian peninsula. Most important governmental, ecclesiastical, and military positions during the colonial period were held by peninsulars. For example, of the 170 viceroys, only 4 were creoles; of the 602 captains-general, governors, and presidents, only 14 were creoles; of the 606 archbishops and bishops, 105 were creoles. Many creoles were well educated and trained in the professions; some were wealthy large landholders or mine owners. They resented the special privileges, wealth, and social snobbery of the peninsulars, and they were embittered by the economic and political restrictions placed on them by colonial administrators. In Brazil, the situation was essentially the same as in Spanish America, except that Brazilian-born whites were known as *mazombos* and whites born in Portugal were known as *reinois*. *See also* CRÉOLE (62); PENINSULAR (15).

Significance
By the end of the eighteenth century, many creoles saw themselves as *americanos* rather than as Spaniards. They were attracted to the ideas of political independence, republicanism, and natural rights, and their hatred of the peninsulars united them politically. The municipal councils *(cabildos)* were dominated by creoles, and they used this position to support a break with Spain and to govern the colonies during the Wars of Independence. Creoles came into power after independence and, although they split into factions, they remained basically conservative in their approach to social reform. Creoles then replaced the peninsulars as the upper social class, and they used their power to increase their wealth and solidify their position against Indians and *mestizos*.

Demographic Cycle 2

The sequence of changes in the size and composition of a society's population as it is affected by technological change. The demographic cycle evolves through three stages. The first stage is characterized by a preindustrial base, with a near equilibrium between births and deaths producing a relatively stable population. Both birth and death rates are very high, the infant mortality rate is high, life expectancy is about 30 years, and population increase is slow but steady. The second stage of the demographic cycle is transitional and involves continued high birthrates, a sharp decline in death rates and, as a result, a veritable population explosion. In this stage, infant mortality rates fall dramatically, resulting in a biologically young population. The third stage of the demographic cycle is ushered in as industrialization and technological advancements tend to substantially reduce the birthrate while the death rate continues its decline begun during the second stage. *See also* POPULATION (17).

Significance

The impact of the demographic cycle on Latin America is probably greater than on any other region in the world. Most Latin states have moved into the second stage and are caught up with the greatest population surge ever experienced on the globe. Some societies, for example, have doubled their populations during the brief span of 17 years. Countries with the highest growth rates include Colombia, Costa Rica, Ecuador, El Salvador, Honduras, Mexico, Paraguay, Peru, and Venezuela, all of which have had annual rates of growth that exceeded 3 percent. Argentina, Cuba, and Uruguay have the lowest growth rates in Latin America and have annual growth rates of considerably less than 2 percent. Because industrial development and general modernization proceed at an uneven pace within states, most Latin countries have geographical areas or regions that reflect all three of the major stages of the demographic cycle. Areas that still typify the first stage of extremely high birth and death rates, however, are becoming rare. Although the population growth rate for the region has declined in recent years, the population explosion has tended to create a major problem: Evidence from developed countries indicates that industrialization tends to bring the high growth rate under control, but achieving major economic growth in societies where populations are doubling in several decades remains an unfulfilled challenge for most Latin societies.

Ejido 3

An agricultural landholding community in Mexico. Ejidos were originally communal lands of Mexican Indian villages; a few of these still remain. Most ejidos, however, were created by the great land reforms enacted since the mid-1930s. In a typical *ejido*, woodland and meadows are used in common, but cropland is divided into parcels and distributed to the *ejidatarios* (members of an *ejido*). A few *ejidos* are operated as cooperatives in which the cropland is farmed jointly and profits are shared by the *ejidatarios*. An *ejido* differs from a state farm in that the land is nationalized in state farms and peasants become agricultural laborers who work for a wage. An *ejido* that has been parceled among its members differs from a privately owned family farm because, although *ejido* parcels are worked by families and may be inherited, *ejido* land may not be sold, mortgaged, leased, or alienated in any way. Most *ejidos* operated as cooperatives have not been successful, and the *ejidatarios* have suffered from state policies and corrupt *ejido* managers. Some parceled *ejidos* are more productive than traditional haciendas, but generally *ejido* plots are small, poor techniques are used, mechanization has not been adopted, and production is low. For the most part, *ejido* peasants practice subsistence agriculture. *See also* LAND REFORM (10); MEXICAN REVOLUTION (37).

Significance
Over 45 million hectares, or almost 50 percent of Mexican croplands, are in the *ejido* system, and about a third of the population depends on it for its livelihood. Although production is not satisfactory, the *ejido* system is one of the major social achievements of the Mexican Revolution, and any attempt to change it by forced consolidations would undoubtedly disturb the political stability of the nation. Since the 1940s, the Mexican government has favored the medium-sized, privately owned farm because it is more productive. Despite the great land reforms that have taken place in Mexico since the 1930s, a population explosion has produced more landless peasants today than there were in 1910. Pressures on the government to break up large farms sometimes take the form of squatters (called *paracaidistas,* or parachutists) who invade and occupy desirable croplands. These attempts have usually been repulsed by the Mexican government, which finds itself faced by a dilemma. As the leader of the continuing Mexican Revolution, the government must defend and support the revolutionary principle of land reform. On the other hand, government leaders believe that if most of the remaining privately held farms were redistributed to *ejidos*, agricultural production would fall and the revolutionary goals of national development and economic independence would be set back.

Élite [4]

The upper social class in Haiti that historically governed the nation. The *élite,* who constitute about 5 percent of the population of Haiti, are mulattoes and a few wealthy blacks. They live in Port-au-Prince, speak French, practice Catholicism, value French culture and style, are well educated and wealthy, and display an elegant deportment. The *élite* are sharply differentiated from the illiterate rural masses, almost 90 percent of the people, who live in abject poverty, speak *Créole,* and practice Voodoo. The small urban working class (about 6 percent) is similar to the peasants in these matters. The new urban middle class (from 2 to 4 percent) is black, educated, and French speaking. It has been affected by black nationalist and black consciousness movements, but it is not cohesive, however, and is uncertain of its position in Haitian society. *See also* CRÉOLE (62).

Significance
The *élite* were the dominant part of the unofficial two-caste system that developed in Haiti after independence was achieved in 1804. Unlike the traditional upper class of Spanish America, the *élite* were not a landed gentry and have always lived in urban areas. Following independence and the freeing of the slaves, all farmland was divided into small plots and given to former slaves. The *élite* inherited the social and psychological position of the French colonials. They were attracted to the professions, looked down on manual labor, and avoided industry and commerce. Their political and economic position declined after the black middle-class physician, François Duvalier, took power in 1957. Although his son, Jean-Claude Duvalier, who succeeded him in 1971, married a mulatto woman from the business community, he failed to reconcile the interests of the mulatto *élite* and black

groups. Military interventions, political violence, and unstable governments that followed his overthrow in 1986 have reinforced the uncertain position of the *élite*.

Geographical Factors: Climate [5]

The impact of weather conditions on the political, economic, social, and military power of nations. In Latin America, climate changes dramatically from east to west, from north to south, and between lower and higher altitudes. The Andes mountain range, which runs the length of the South American continent from Venezuela to the southern tip of Chile, has a substantial impact on weather conditions for most of the continental countries. The west coast changes from lush growth supported by heavy rains north of the equator to desert land in Peru and Chile south of the equator. The Andes, cold and snowcapped, support life in a few valleys protected by surrounding peaks and in the Altiplano (high plateau) in Bolivia. Proceeding east from the Andes along the Amazon's headwaters from Colombia to Bolivia is la montaña, the forested eastern border valleys of the Andes and the eastern plains. The Amazon Basin is a vast jungle, and its climate is determined by the fact that it is barely above sea level. The high temperatures in the Amazon Basin and heavy rains in the region inhibit agriculture and make it mostly unfit for human habitation. Farther south, a vast treeless plain known as the pampa stretches across southern Brazil and most of Argentina, enjoying moderate temperatures and rainfall sufficient to support large-scale ranching operations. *See also* GEOGRAPHICAL FACTORS: LOCATION (6); GEOGRAPHICAL FACTORS: TOPOGRAPHY (7).

Significance
The climatic conditions of a state or region are determined mainly by its temperature, topography, precipitation, location, and wind patterns. Moderate or temperate climatic conditions typically encourage developments that strengthen national power, such as those found in Argentina and in southern Brazil. Adverse conditions can be overcome, but a greater investment in human effort and resources is required, which makes developmental progress more difficult to achieve. The South American continent's great climatic diversity results not only from its topographical features but also from its vastness, stretching about 4,500 miles from north to south and 3,000 miles from east to west. Because the equator traverses the northern portion of the continent, encompassing snowcapped peaks and humid lowlands, Latin culture is influenced by the immediacy of climatic changes. Most of South America lies within the equatorial zone—from a latitude of 30 degrees north of the equator to 30 degrees south. Thus, it more closely resembles sub-Sahara Africa climatically than the United States or Europe. Climate is one of the most important geographical factors because it directly affects growing food and performing work. For example, the highland Indians over the centuries made blood and lung physiological adaptations to living in the thin air of the mountains. When they were transported by the Spaniards to work on plantations in the humid tropical coastal lowlands, they could not perform effectively and thousands died. Subsequently Africans were imported as slaves to work on the coastal plantations.

Geographical Factors: Location [6]

The relationship between physical position on the globe and a nation's or region's economic, political, social, and military power. The location of Latin America in the Western Hemisphere has meant closer and more direct ties with the United States than with Europe after the colonies gained independence. The Panama Canal has promoted closer relationships by providing a more proximate linking of the great cities of the eastern and western coastal regions of the two continents. Mexico and the Caribbean countries, which include the island nations, Central America, and Venezuela, have tended to be subject to greater external pressures than the rest of the continental countries, especially because of political, economic, and military pressures emanating from the United States. Those states located in the southern portions of the continent—Argentina, Bolivia, Brazil, Chile, Paraguay, and Uruguay—are particularly affected by the great distances to both Europe and the United States. The policies and actions of many smaller Latin states are also influenced because of their location next to powerful neighbors, such as the case of the states of Bolivia, Paraguay, and Uruguay that are located proximate to Argentina, Brazil, and Chile. *See also* GEOGRAPHICAL FACTORS: CLIMATE (5); GEOGRAPHICAL FACTORS: TOPOGRAPHY (7).

Significance
The location of Latin America has been a powerful geographical factor influencing and often determining political and economic outcomes. Independence was secured and maintained in part because of the great distance between Europe and South America. The efforts of the United States to establish hegemony and its interventions in Mexico and the Caribbean region were encouraged by the factor of location. The great distance separating the southern states of the continent from the United States and Europe has encouraged attitudes and policies promoting economic, political, and military independence. Also, the great distance over which primary commodities must be shipped to reach the markets of the industrialized states of Europe and Asia has reduced the competitiveness of Latin American products and encouraged closer economic ties with the United States. Development programs have suffered as a result of high transportation costs. The strategic connection between location and foreign policy has increasingly given rise to geopolitical considerations of policy on the part of Latin decision makers. Location, however, does not create power but it does facilitate or, conversely, tend to discourage its growth and use. For example, Brazil has the capacity to become a great power on the global political/military scene because of its size, large population, resources, and economic potential, but its location tends to militate against this occurring.

Geographical Factors: Topography   7

The effect of the physical features of a state or a region on its economic, political, social, and military power. Topography includes such elements as mountain ranges, plains, river systems, rainforests, deserts, and marshlands. Latin America includes a great variety of topographical features, all of which tend to affect or influence the power position of the states involved. The most impressive feature is the mountain chain *(cordillera)* that extends from northern Mexico to the southernmost regions of Argentina and Chile, with peaks ranging up to 23,000 feet. Another mountain chain runs along much of the eastern coastal area. The South American continent has four major river systems: the Amazon (Brazil), the Rio de la Plata (Argentina), the Orinoco (Venezuela), and the Rio Magdalena (Colombia). The Amazon Basin, the largest river system in the world, is a tangled mass of rainforests, impenetrable jungles, and a series of tributary rivers that together cover an area greater than that of the continental United States. Much of the region from Peru to central Chile is covered by the Atacama Desert, a rainless and barren coastal region. In Argentina, a treeless, flat *pampa* provides grazing lands for cattle, and another treeless plain called the *llanos* is found in the Orinoco valley in Venezuela. Parts of Bolivia, Paraguay, and Argentina are covered by the Gran Chaco, a vast region of plains, savannahs, scrub forests, lakes, and swamps. *See also* GEOGRAPHICAL FACTORS: CLIMATE (5); GEOGRAPHICAL FACTORS: LOCATION (6); RAINFOREST DILEMMA (19).

Significance
In Latin America as elsewhere, topography has affected the nature and quality of life, the location of concentrations of population, the stability of political boundaries, the level of technology, the type of agriculture, and cultural similarities and differences. For example, topographical features have tended to isolate many communities and have contributed to localism and regionalism in Latin American politics. Military security and fears of attack by neighboring states are often related to topographical features. Since Central America is an isthmus, it has been subjected to much attention by major naval powers and by private businesses interested in building canals and railroads there, especially in Nicaragua and Panama. On the South American continent, many of the major urban areas—Buenos Aires, Callao, Caracas, Guayaquil, Lima, Montevideo, Rio de Janeiro, Santiago, São Paulo, and Valparaiso—are clustered along the eastern and western coasts, mostly where the major river systems reach the sea. Few roads exist in some areas, and in many regions the only access to the interior is by boat. Surrounded by mountains, jungles, and vast river systems, the interior of the continent is mostly unpopulated because ingress and egress is difficult. In the Caribbean area, populations are dispersed on islands and in a variety of Central American republics. As a result many of the people of Latin America tend to be isolated from the rest of the world and from each other as well.

Haciendas | 8 |
Large estates that constituted the chief economic and social unit that functioned in the rural areas of most Latin American countries until recent times. The typically absentee owners are known as *hacendados*. They often live in the capital city or in Europe, occasionally visiting the hacienda. A manager runs the hacienda, presiding over hundreds of underpaid and often-abused peons. The peasants live with their families in huts on the hacienda and receive minor benefits, such as low pay, credit from the hacienda store, a small plot of ground for their families to work, and, in some cases, a small church or visits from a priest. Most haciendas are engaged in agriculture, but some, especially in Argentina, are largely ranching operations. Haciendas can be distinguished from large plantations that use wage labor to produce cash crops, especially for export, and do not constitute a self-sufficient socioeconomic system as does the hacienda. In Brazil, haciendas are called *fazendas*. *See also* LATIFUNDIA SYSTEM (LATIFUNDISMO) (11).

Significance
The roots of the hacienda originated in colonial times when Spanish royalty endowed their faithful military officers with *encomiendas* or grants that conveyed rights over certain land areas and the Indians living on them. The hacienda system that later evolved has been the main object of land reform in Latin America, but with little success in most cases. The hacienda system is economically inefficient, but it is based on tradition and social unity so that change is difficult. Agricultural experts have often advocated that the haciendas

not be broken up into small plots through land reform but rather turned into cooperatives or state-run enterprises utilizing modern farming methods and machinery. In many Latin countries, the best land remains in the hands of the *hacendados,* and the great majority of the people are essentially landless.

Imperial City [9]

A city patterned after the Spanish-Moorish capital cities of the Iberian peninsula that reflect the style, power, and attributes of the political center of an empire. In Latin America, the imperial-style capital city dominates the political, economic, social, and cultural life of most nations. Only a few of these capital cities were built on the ruins of captured Indian communities, such as Mexico City. Most Latin capitals were erected on new sites, laid out in a rectangular plan, and patterned on the empire model, with Lima a prime example. In colonial times, capital cities became the center of political and economic power, high culture, and elegant living. Upper classes viewed the city as the desirable place to live and, by the second century of the conquest, the landed oligarchy had largely moved to the city and adopted its ways and intermarried with the urban elite. Unlike the capital cities of northern Europe and the North American colonies, which were primarily commercial centers dominated by the middle classes, Latin American capital cities reflected the style, grace, power, and values of the upper social classes. This combination of physical setting and socioeconomic power characterized the capital cities of Latin America throughout the colonial period and the first 100 years of independence. In the twentieth century, the population of the capital cities rose dramatically as they became great commercial, industrial, and transportation centers as well.

See also SLUM NEIGHBORHOODS (20); URBANIZATION (22).

Significance
With few exceptions in Latin America, the imperial-style capital city is the largest city in a country. The city is the center of fine arts and higher education, the residence of wealthy and powerful people, the base of intellectual movements, and the leading industrial and commercial center. The political consequences arising from the expansion of capital cities have imposed extra burdens on national governments. The striking contrast between the beauty and elegance of the central core and wealthy residential areas with the backwardness of provincial towns and the abject poverty of peasant villages has provided an additional cause for rural protest movements. The location in a capital of prestigious universities with large and politically active student bodies—often of a radical bent—exacerbates the political problems of conservative governments. The symbolic value of the city as the seat of government makes it a natural target for revolutionary groups. Because of governmental centralization the capture and control of a capital city often marks the successful completion of a revolution against established authority.

Land Reform [10]

Major changes in the ownership and utilization of agricultural land. Land reform, also called agrarian reform, is primarily directed at large estates held as private property *(latifundio),* which may be farmed as plantations, by tenant sharecroppers, or as traditional haciendas. In land reform, the land is confiscated or purchased under the authority of public law and then collectivized or redistributed to new owners. Squatters who seize land illegally may force a government to legally recognize their actions. The distributions and institutions created under land reform legislation are of several types, which include: (1) state farms, where large estates are kept intact, titles are transferred to the state, and the peasants become agricultural laborers who work for a wage; (2) cooperatives, in which the land is redistributed to a community whose members farm the land in common and share the proceeds; (3) family farms, where large estates are subdivided and redistributed to individual families, who are entitled to purchase their portion and pay for it over a long period of time. Some cooperatives may be managed like large farms and placed under supervision of a public agency, but in many cases portions of communal land are redistributed among peasants as private plots. Some land reform measures are largely symbolic because only unused or undesirable land is purchased from large estates, which profit from the transaction. Other land reform acts involve only a transfer of title, which may be sufficient to satisfy the political pressures of the time, but are not concerned with agricultural production. When this occurs, the latifundia system is often transferred into a minifundia system and agricultural production falls. Because of the small size of their plots, peasants are forced to practice subsistence agriculture. A complete or integrated land reform program changes the land tenure system, establishes agricultural credit institutions and extension services, promotes the adoption of modern farming techniques, and helps organize the marketing of agricultural products. The government may also build irrigation projects and roads and open new lands for settlements. *See also* EJIDO (3); LATIFUNDIA SYSTEM (LATIFUNDISMO) (11); MINIFUNDIA SYSTEM (MINIFUNDISMO) (14).

Significance
Land reform legislation has been enacted by most Latin American nations, but it is often symbolic, piecemeal, and ineffective. Dramatic changes in land tenure systems have taken place in countries where major social revolutions have occurred—Mexico, Bolivia, and Cuba. In Mexico, a substantial portion of agricultural land has been redistributed to *ejidos* (landholding communities), but the economic and social expectations of this revolution have not been fully realized. *Ejidos* were generally given poor land, and most cropland has been distributed to families in small plots that may not be sold. Production is low and peasants practice a form of subsistence agriculture. A growing population and increase in the number of landless peasants have put pressures on the Mexican government for redistribution of the better middle-sized farms still in private hands. In Bolivia, the broad goals of the revolution to end the feudal system and to incorporate the Indian into national life were more successfully achieved. The agrarian reform of 1953 broke up the large estates, redistributed land to peasants as private property, opened new lands to colonization, and promoted changes in land use. In some regions of Bolivia, the changes have been only partially successful, but there has been a great increase in production in other areas. In Cuba, the Castro government transformed the large sugar plantations, which were mostly owned by a few U.S. companies, into state farms *(granjas del pueblo)* and enacted a broad range of rural social welfare programs. State agricultural policy, however, has been largely unsuccessful. Castro first attempted to diversify agriculture, which lowered production, and then shifted to an exceptionally high concentration on producing sugar, which seriously dislocated the economy. In Peru, the military made a revolution in the property system after 1968, and turned large estates into cooperatives. Workers on collectivized coastal plantations benefited from

the reform, but the results in the highlands were not successful and subsequent governments reprivatized many cooperatives. Other nations, such as Venezuela and Colombia, have instituted land reforms of a more modest nature. In Chile, land reform began in 1960 under the conservative president, Jorge Alessandri; was expanded by the Christian Democrat, Eduardo Frei; and was intensified by the Socialist government of Salvador Allende. When the military assumed power in 1973, it returned much of the expropriated lands to former owners, dismantled the collectivist structures (cooperatives), and permitted peasants to purchase land that was previously held by cooperatives. In the 1980s, land reform continued to be a major issue in Latin America as population pressures increased and revolutionary movements promised land redistributions to peasants.

Latifundia System (Latifundismo) | 11 |

A pattern of land ownership based on large-scale plantations owned by local gentry, absentee landlords, and domestic or foreign corporations. In a latifundia system, large numbers of peons or agricultural workers live and work on plantations or haciendas under semi-feudal arrangements. Latifundia, first developed by the ancient Romans, took root in the Iberian peninsula and was transferred to the New World when Spain and Portugal established their colonial empires. The system remained the predominant form of economic, social, and political organization in the post-independence period. Latifundia estates are generally called haciendas, although they are known as *estancias* in Argentina and Uruguay and as *fazendas* in Brazil, and they also take the form of large plantations that use hired workers and produce cash crops for export. *See also* HACIENDA (8); LAND REFORM (10); MINIFUNDIA SYSTEM (MINIFUNDISMO) (14).

Significance
The latifundia system contributes much to an understanding of the contemporary life and problems of Latin America. It established a model for elite behavior and class structure that typifies much of the urban as well as rural scene. Agriculture is dominated by latifundia, with about 65 percent of total farm acreage in Latin America in huge landed estates. Although minifundia (extremely small farms) constitute a majority of the farms, they aggregate only a small percentage of the total acreage under cultivation. Because agricultural jobs are the principal type of employment in many Latin American states, control of the land often translates into political power. Many observers regard the latifundia system as a major obstacle to political, economic, and social modernization. The failure of land reform movements to break up and redistribute the large plantations or convert them into huge cooperatives remains in the 1990s a major factor contributing to political instability and the threat of revolution in the less-industrialized nations.

Latin America | 12 |

The name most commonly given to the group of 20 republics of the Western Hemisphere that were former colonies of Spain, Portugal, and France. By extension, but less often, the term "Latin America" is used to refer to all territory in the Western Hemisphere south of the United States, thus including the present and former possessions of Great Britain, the Netherlands, France, and the United States. The traditional Latin states are: Argentina, Bolivia, Brazil, Chile, Colombia, Costa Rica, Cuba, the Dominican Republic, Ecuador, El Salvador, Guatemala, Haiti, Honduras, Mexico, Nicaragua, Panama, Paraguay, Peru, Uruguay, and Venezuela. The Commonwealth of Puerto Rico, formerly a Spanish colony but since 1898 a nonindependent political entity of the United States, is often included with the independent Latin republics as part of Latin America. *See also* AMERICANISMO (49); THIRD WORLD (229).

Significance
The term "Latin America" was coined by French writers in the nineteenth century as a way to promote French leadership of the Catholic and Latin world against other linguistic groups. Although it is not geographically precise and implies a single ethnic group or culture not found throughout the entire region, it has been preferred over the term "Hispanic America," which was promoted by Spanish and Spanish-American writers but was rejected by Brazilians. "Ibero-America" and "Indo-Hispanic America" as well as other expressions also have not taken hold. "Latin America" is widely used by Latin Americans, and it is also used officially by international organizations, such as the Latin American Free Trade Association (LAFTA) and the United Nations Economic Commission for Latin America (ECLA). Following the practice of Latin American writers, many English-language scholars when writing on Latin American themes prefer not to use the word "American" to describe something pertaining exclusively to the United States or its citizens, even though the full name of the country is the United States of America and its attributes and nationals are properly called American. Most Latins, including Mexicans, refer to citizens of the United States as North Americans, even though this expression geographically includes Mexico. Less often, a citizen or characteristic of the United States is referred to as *estadounidense* in Spanish (literally, United States-er), but this expression has no English equivalent. English writers therefore have tended to use United States as an adjective or possessive, a practice that grates on the ears of those who cherish the English language. A happier situation prevails with respect to Brazil, where the term "Luso-Brazilian" or less often "Luso-American" (after Lusitania, an ancient name for Portugal) is used exclusively to stress the Portuguese influence in Brazil. Despite the imprecision of the term "Latin America," it can justifiably be used with respect to the 20 republics because these states see themselves as different from the Anglo cultures of North America. Latins have experienced a similar 300-year history of colonial rule, share a common religion, use a Romance language as their official language, have similar economic, social, and political institutions, have been greatly influenced by Latin European culture, and often act as a bloc in world affairs and international organizations.

Migration 13
The movement of people from one nation or region to another. Migration to Latin America from Europe, particularly to the southern cone of South America, reached a peak in the period from 1870 to 1910, and these areas of the continent are more ethnically European than most other Latin states. With few exceptions, migration from one Latin country to another has not been very substantial. There have been territorial incursions across Latin boundaries in the twentieth century that have caused political problems, but they have not resulted in any major net changes in population. Two important migrations of Latin Americans have taken place in recent decades: (1) the internal migration from rural areas of the nation to urban centers; and (2) the external Latin migration to the United States. These migrations have been directly related to the Latin American population explosion, political unrest, and the inability of

many Latins to find suitable employment in their home communities. According to the Demographic Center of the Economic Commission for Latin America and the Caribbean (ECLAC), Argentina, Venezuela, Costa Rica, Canada, and the United States have received the most Latin American migrants in recent decades. *See also* IMMIGRATION REFORM AND CONTROL ACT OF 1986 (260); SLUM NEIGHBORHOODS (20); URBANIZATION (22).

Significance
Substantial internal migration from rural to urban areas has taken place in every Latin nation. In many countries the rate of urbanization is high and shantytowns surround the central cities as rural poverty is transferred to urban centers. This migration is of such massive proportions that the governments cannot regulate it properly, and the rural migrants often are unemployed, undernourished, and live in squalid shacks without public services. Latin migration to the United States is primarily from Mexico, Cuba, Puerto Rico, and the Caribbean region, including the British West Indies. Except for the Cubans, who are mainly middle-class political refugees from the communist system, most of these migrants are from lower classes. Many of them have entered the United States illegally and are known as undocumented aliens, or *sin papeles* (without papers). Most Cubans, who entered under special refugee arrangements, and all Puerto Ricans because they are citizens of the United States, have entered the United States under the law. Almost a million persons are apprehended yearly by U.S. officials and deported as illegal aliens. Unlike the *bracero* (laborer) program of the 1950s whereby Mexican migratory farm workers were admitted under the law, today illegal Mexican aliens (derisively called wetbacks) cross the border in huge numbers. These persons are often exploited by labor contractors and employers and take the least desirable jobs. The Mexican government does not discourage this movement because the migrants provide a partial relief from population pressures and because the migrants' remittances aid Mexican families that have remained behind. The U.S. government has found it difficult to stop the flow of undocumented migrants, and it recognizes that migrants are willing to accept jobs that most U.S. citizens reject. The U.S. government, under pressure from Mexican Americans *(Chicanos)* to grant an "amnesty" to undocumented migrants, included such a provision in the Immigration Reform and Control Act of 1986, which states that aliens who entered the United States illegally prior to 1 January 1982 are eligible for amnesty, residential status, and eventually, for U.S. citizenship. The law also provides that employers may be legally punished if they hire illegal immigrants. More than 20 million persons of Hispanic-American descent now live in the United States, and this ethnic-cultural group is the fastest-growing one because of its high birthrate and continuing large-scale migration. The increasing Latinization of many sections of the United States is a social phenomenon that will have major economic, cultural, and political consequences in the future. According to current projections, for example, Hispanic Americans may soon outnumber the black population, and bilingual education will become more common.

Minifundia System (Minifundismo) | 14 |

An agricultural system of extremely small farms averaging less than 20 hectares (a hectare is about 2.5 acres). *Minifundios* constitute about three-fourths of all farms in Latin America, but they aggregate less than 4 percent of the total acreage under cultivation. The minifundia system often exists side-by-side with the latifundia (giant plantation or hacienda) system. The typical *minifundio* is farmed by a single family or an extended family group. *See also* HACIENDA (8); LAND REFORM (10); LATIFUNDIA SYSTEM (LATIFUNDISMO) (11).

Significance
The minifundia system exists typically where inheritance laws divide property among the heirs rather than providing for primogeniture or inheritance of all property by the eldest son. In some countries it is the result of homestead laws, and in others it is the product of land reform programs. Although *minifundios* help to support many families on a subsistence level, they are fundamentally uneconomic in that they produce few surpluses to provide food for the exploding populations of the region. Some states have attempted major land reform programs in which *minifundios* and *latifundios* have been converted by the government into massive agro-industrial plantations operated as cooperatives.

Peninsular [15]

In the colonial period, a Spanish colonist who was born in the Iberian peninsula. Peninsulars *(peninsulares)* were the dominant social class in the Spanish colonies and were distinguished from creoles *(criollos)*, who were persons of full Spanish ancestry born in the Americas. Although both were part of the colonial elite, peninsulars were considered by the Crown and themselves to be superior to creoles. Peninsulars held virtually all the high posts in the colonial administration, the church, and the military. Of the 170 Spanish viceroys, 166 were peninsulars. The four creole viceroys were sons of peninsular officials. Peninsulars also received *fueros* (special privileges) that exempted them from certain laws and taxes and from the jurisdiction of the regular courts. They were often of noble birth and looked down on creoles, even though many creoles were wealthy. In Brazil, peninsulars were known as *reinois* and creoles as *mazombos,* and the relationships between the two groups were about the same. *See also* CREOLE (CRIOLLO) (1); FUERO (33).

Significance
Peninsulars were resented by creoles, not only for their wealth, privileges, and high posts, but also for their superior airs. This creole hatred of the peninsulars and what they represented was an important factor that ultimately led to the break with Spain. Although a few peninsulars in some countries supported the move to independence, they were displaced by creoles at the close of the Wars of Independence. Peninsular support for independence was strongest in Mexico and weakest in South America, where many of them were killed.

Peonage [16]

A system of debt-incurred quasi-slavery in which the worker (peon) was required to provide labor to the employer or creditor. Debt peonage, involving mainly Indians, resulted when the peon: (1) contracted debts in a company-owned store; (2) secured a loan from the landlord; or (3) purchased a small plot of land. The peon then was required to work a certain number of days without pay to remove his debt, or his debt would be subtracted from his wages. The peon was seldom able to pay off his obligation, and his debt was usually inherited by his children. This system, enforced by local police, resulted in peons being tied to a hacienda or plantation as virtual slaves. Although debt peonage was made illegal in the 1920s and 1930s, it continued to be practiced in some localities. The term "peon" is also often used to refer to any poor or homeless peasant. *See also* HACIENDA (8).

Significance
Debt peonage was prevalent in the nineteenth and early twentieth centuries in the rural areas of countries with large Indian populations, especially Mexico, Guatemala, Ecuador, Bolivia, and Peru. This form of involuntary servitude replaced the forced labor systems (slavery and *repartimiento*) of the early colonial period. It provided a large and disciplined labor force needed by the expanding agricultural sector in the nineteenth century. Cash crop plantations and traditional haciendas, both of which expanded after independence, relied on this form of forced labor. Because peons were at the mercy of the landlords and suffered greatly, debt peonage contributed to the rise of rural protest movements, popular revolts, and demands for land reform. In Mexico, where over 90 percent of the rural population suffered from the system, debt peonage finally disappeared with the great land reforms begun by President Lázaro Cárdenas in 1936.

Population 17
An aggregate of individuals who inhabit a country or region and who contribute to its domestic and foreign power position. The population factor of a state relates to such considerations as geographic location, economic status, the nature of the political system, the indigenous characteristics of the people, and their social system. In Latin America as elsewhere, both quantitative and qualitative population characteristics are important considerations in the determination of domestic and foreign policy. Population totals and densities vary greatly among the many countries of Latin America. Brazil, with over 140 million people, is the most populous state, with Panama the least populated mainland country (about 2 million). Totals for all of Latin America were about 20 million in 1800, 60 million in 1900, and an estimated 350 million in 1980. If present growth trends continue, Latin America's population will be about 540 million by the year 2000. Densities also vary greatly among Latin nations and within countries between the rural and urbanized regions. Other states with large populations include Mexico (over 80 million), Argentina (over 32 million), Colombia (over 32 million), Peru (over 20 million), and Venezuela (17 million). El Salvador is one of the world's most densely populated countries. Latin nations with the highest population growth rates are Bolivia, Costa Rica, Ecuador, Guatemala, Honduras, Mexico, Nicaragua, Paraguay, Peru, and Venezuela. Uruguay, Cuba, and Argentina have the lowest growth rates. Population pressures resulting from rapid growth have produced large-scale unemployment and much internal and subregional conflict in many countries of the region. This in turn has resulted in greatly increased migration as millions move to find a place where they can survive. *See also* DEMOGRAPHIC CYCLE (2); MIGRATION (13); URBANIZATION (22).

Significance
Latin America more than any other region of the world faces a massive problem of population growth that is aptly referred to as a population explosion. The region encompasses a vast land area, but much of it is sparsely populated and for the most part unsuited to support a larger population. Massive mountain ranges, rainforests and jungles, and deserts and plains cover much of the continental area. In most countries, except for Argentina, heavy population densities contribute to high levels of poverty, disease, illiteracy, and mass frustrations and tensions. Such conditions are more conducive to producing revolutionary upheavals than steady growth and modernization. Population control, viewed

as a *sine qua non* by demographers and developmentalists alike, is difficult to achieve because of the powerful role played by the Catholic church in Latin America and because the entire region is caught up in the high growth rates characteristic of the second stage of the demographic cycle. Paradoxically, Latin countries are caught in an enigmatic position. Their exploding populations can only be brought under control by following the example of Western modernization, but progress that drastically reduces birthrates is extremely difficult when populations double within a few decades.

Racial Group (18)

The classification of people according to genetically transmitted physical characteristics, such as skin color, hair, and facial features. All major racial groups and various mixtures exist in Latin America. In the colonial period, Spaniards were known as *peninsulares* (peninsulars) and American-born whites *(blancos)* were called *criollos* (creoles). An *indio* (Indian) is a person native to the Western Hemisphere, and *negro* (black) a person native to Africa. Mixtures of these races soon occurred. The most common group on the continent is *mestizo* (known as *ladino* in Guatemala, *cholo* in Peru, and *mameluco* in Brazil), a person of mixed white and Indian parentage or ancestry. Mulattoes are the offspring of white and black parents, and *zambos* come from Indian and black parents. Persons who originated in the Indian subcontinent in Asia and their offspring are known as East Indians to distinguish them from native American Indians, who are referred to as "Amerinds" by scholars. "East Indian" is a racial classification for many such persons, who, along with blacks, live in the West Indies (Caribbean islands). A *turco* is a person whose origin is the Middle East, a group that includes Turks, Lebanese, and Syrians, but not Jews. A substantial number of Orientals from the Far East are found in Latin America. *See also* BLACK LEGEND (23); CREOLE (CRIOLLO) (1); ÉLITE (4); NEGRITUDE (71); PENINSULAR (15).

Significance

The variety of racial groups found in Latin America, including Western Hemisphere Indians, is the result of historic migrations and miscegenation (racial interbreeding). During the colonial period a complex caste system was created in Spanish America that recognized 16 or more kinds of racial mixtures, known as *las castas*. The concept of race is biological and sociocultural, and the history of the region is a complex one of discrimination and separation but also of miscegenation and integration. The theory of the racial superiority of the white race was challenged by Latin intellectuals in the nativist movement called *indigenismo*. They promoted the role of the Indian in Latin life and argued that Latin culture is continuous with Indian culture. The end product of miscegenation would be a "cosmic race" *(raza cosmica)*, a superior type that combined white, Indian, and black elements. A recent use of the term *la raza* (the race) by Latins refers to the ethnic and cultural condition of being Latin American and expresses a type of pride in that condition. Where *mestizos* exist in great numbers and have succeeded in making a revolution, as in Mexico, discrimination has been greatly reduced and pride in the Indian heritage has been fostered. In Brazil, racial integration has been more successful although not complete, and higher social status is associated with a lighter skin color. The Castro Revolution in Cuba has nearly eliminated racism among the masses, but the leadership of the system is mostly white. Because of the extensive mixture of races in Latin America and the traditional Latin acceptance of racial differences, fewer problems of racial discrimination exist in the region than in the United States and some European countries.

Rainforest Dilemma [19]

Issues relating to the attempts to preserve the complex ecosystem covering the Amazon Basin and its threatened destruction as a result of efforts to convert the tropical forests into farmland and ranchland. A number of Latin American states are caught up in the rainforest dilemma, but it is particularly a Brazilian problem. *See also* GEOGRAPHICAL FACTORS: TOPOGRAPHY (7).

Significance
Attempts to turn rainforests into farmland and ranchland have created scorched and barren land, thereby destroying rare species of plants and animals, displacing native peoples, and greatly increasing the amount of carbon dioxide and other gasses threatening to turn the Earth into a gigantic greenhouse. In this way, the sun's heat is trapped, resulting in a gradual but potentially disastrous warming of the earth's climate. Moreover, the burning decreases global photosynthesis, by which plants and trees remove carbon dioxide from the air and convert it into oxygen. Each year, an estimated 25 million acres of rainforests are destroyed in the world, with over 12 million acres slashed and burned in the Amazon region. Huge fires creating global cloud conditions result from the burning of millions of trees each year. Rainforest soils, however, are unsuited for growing food crops, and within a few years farmers must abandon their land and again move deeper into the rainforest. In the past, much of this activity has been regarded as development progress, with most financing provided by multilateral development banks predominantly under the control of the United States and other First World countries. Political pressures, however, have recently led to the creation of environmental departments in many of these banks, including the largest, the World Bank. Offers to forgive some of Brazil's international debt in exchange for limiting developmental policies in the Amazon have been rejected by Brazil as an invasion of its sovereignty. Recently, however, the Brazilian and Ecuadorian governments have adopted policies aimed at reducing the pressures on their rainforests by limiting the freedom to exploit them and by reducing or eliminating the subsidies that encouraged rainforest destruction in the past.

Slum Neighborhoods [20]

Squalid urban housing, squatter settlements, and shantytowns. Urban slum neighborhoods are variously called *barriadas* (Peru), *ranchos* (Venezuela), *callampas* (Chile), *villas miserias* (Argentina), *tugurios* (Colombia), and *favelas* (Brazil). Some governments, as in Peru, refer to larger slum neighborhoods or districts as *pueblos jovenes* (young towns). Shacks and huts in slum areas are built of waste materials: planks, corrugated sheets, flattened tin cans, and straw mats. They are usually constructed on less desirable lands, such as steep hillsides, riverbanks, along railroad tracks, and near swamps and dumps. Slum neighborhoods often house thousands of people, and public services (sewerage, running water, electricity, and paved streets) are usually lacking. In older squatter communities, houses have been upgraded and built of brick or cement block, some public utilities are in place, schools have been constructed, and neighborhood associations provide a type of informal government. The building of slum neighborhoods usually involves an illegal seizure of land, as groups of families invade unused public or private land and overnight lay out streets and erect makeshift structures. Many residents are rural migrants and are primarily Indians, *mestizos*, blacks, or mulattoes. A substantial number of urban dwellers live in slum neighborhoods. The *barriadas* and *pueblos jovenes* of Lima house a half-million to a million people, or one-fourth of the city, and the *favelas* of Rio de Janeiro are inhabited by nearly one-third of the city's population, or almost a million persons. The same pattern exists in many other urban centers of Latin America. *See also* IMPERIAL CITY (9); URBANIZATION (22).

Significance
Urban slum neighborhoods began to develop in the 1930s, mushroomed in the 1950s, and are still growing. The causes of these developments are traced to large-scale rural migration to the cities and the rapid population growth that characterizes most Latin American countries. The shantytowns grew as migrants encountered a housing shortage, unsteady employment, inability to pay rents, a high cost of housing construction, and the need to live close to jobs within the city. Social conditions within the slums vary. Many areas display typical social ills, such as a low standard of living, malnutrition, disease, high level of crime, and prostitution. In other slum neighborhoods, however, family ties are strong, residents constantly upgrade their dwellings, two-story houses are built, children are sent to school, and neighborhood associations control the buying, selling, and building of huts and seek clear title to the land. Despite miserable living conditions in many slums, most of the residents of these areas have not been attracted to radical, revolutionary, or urban guerrilla movements. This may be because the living conditions of the slums, and the expectations and hopes that urban life arouses, represent an improvement in the lives of many rural migrants.

Southern Cone [21]
The southern portion of South America, which comprises the three republics of Argentina, Chile, and Uruguay. The three Southern Cone countries are distinguished from most of Latin America by having socioeconomic characteristics that typify a modern society. They are highly urbanized and have a low rate of population growth, low infant mortality rate, and higher longevity rates. The middle- and working-class sectors of society are larger and the agricultural population is smaller than those in most other Latin countries. Along with southern Brazil, these nations received large numbers of European immigrants prior to World War II, especially from Spain and Italy. Political parties that have European roots, such as the Liberal, Socialist, and Christian Democratic parties, are strong in the area. In 1990 Argentina and Brazil, building on past proposals for economic integration, decided to establish a common market to be in place by 1994. Uruguay and Paraguay later joined the Southern Cone Common Market, which is known by its acronym MERCOSUR.

Significance
The term "Southern Cone" is useful in comparing the three southernmost republics with the rest of Latin America. The contrasts that were readily apparent in the earlier part of this century between the Southern Cone and the rest of Latin America are decreasing, however, as other nations develop. Although the socioeconomic similarities among the three republics still continue, their political evolution has been different. With the coming of Peronism, Argentina developed more political instability and militarism than did the stronger democracies of Chile and Uruguay. But, like most of Latin America, the Southern Cone experienced the same high level of militarism and authoritarianism in the

mid-1960s to late 1980s. They returned to their democratic traditions in the 1990s.

Urbanization 22

The increase in area or population of a city or town, and the process by which a rural area becomes a large population center. The rate of urbanization in Latin America has accelerated in recent decades and greatly exceeds the rate of rural population growth. From 1950 to 1975, the percentage of people living in urban areas rose from 39 percent to 57 percent. This migration from rural areas to large metropolitan areas has continued to increase in recent years. The most urbanized countries are: Argentina, 85 percent urban; Uruguay, 85 percent; Venezuela, 78 percent; Chile, 82 percent; Brazil, 71 percent; Colombia, 70 percent; Mexico, 68 percent; and Peru, 67 percent. Major metropolitan centers have expanded, and 15 cities have over 1 million residents. Capital cities contain from 10 to 50 percent or more of each nation's population. Current projections suggest that by the year 2000 Mexico City will be the largest city in the world, with a population of 26 million. *See also* IMPERIAL CITY (9); POPULATION (17); SLUM NEIGHBORHOODS (20).

Significance
The process of urbanization in Latin America has continued since the post-independence period. During the nineteenth century capital cities and port cities became manufacturing centers, and landless peasants and other lower classes seeking employment were attracted to the cities. The rapid growth of urban areas in the mid-twentieth century is linked to industrialization, high population growth rates, and vast internal migrations that can be traced to rural poverty. Some Latin American cities and suburbs are today in danger of collapsing under the weight of unchecked urbanization. This growth has strained the ability of cities to provide employment, housing, and public services for their burgeoning populations. The larger cities are ringed and pockmarked by urban slums and shantytowns within view of, and in contrast to, the modernized high-rise apartment buildings, commercial skyscrapers, and dramatic, international-style architecture. The miserable living conditions and paucity of jobs for unskilled and illiterate migrants from rural areas have made cities a potential breeding ground for radical groups. Attempts to exploit this discontent by urban guerrilla and revolutionary groups have been largely unsuccessful. Both the subproletariat and the employed working class, however, have been effectively mobilized on some occasions by populist, caesaristic, and demagogic political leaders.

Historical Perspective

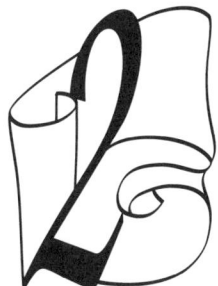

Black Legend 23

A critical interpretation of the Spanish conquest and colonization of the New World that attributed all manner of cruelty, evil, bigotry, and exploitation to the Spaniards. A mixture of fact and myth, the Black Legend *(la leyenda negra)* became the standard interpretation among Spain's enemies of Spanish-American history and Spanish national character. *See also* CONQUEST (28).

Significance
The Black Legend was circulated in Europe by enemies of Spain who drew their information from Spanish missionaries who had criticized the harsh treatment of Indians in the New World. One of the most vigorous critics was Bartolomé de las Casas (1474–1566), a Spanish colonist who had profited in the colonies but who later became a priest, a bishop, and a staunch defender of the Indians. He was named Protector of the Indians in 1516, and for over 40 years he fought hard but mostly unsuccessfully to end their abuse and enslavement. His many polemical tracts and histories, which exaggerated the abuse of Indians, became the foundation on which the Black Legend rested. His works were widely circulated in England, Holland, and France. Later, leaders of the Latin American independence movements also used the Black Legend to justify their revolutions against Spain. The term "Black Legend" was coined by Spanish writers who derided the prejudice of Spain's critics, and who in turn often posed a lesser-known "White Legend" that stressed the great achievements and the civilizing and Christianizing purposes of the conquest. In the twentieth century, most interpretations of the history of Spanish America have been more objective.

Central American Federation 24

The union of the provinces of Guatemala, Honduras, El Salvador, Nicaragua, Costa Rica, and Chiapas in a federal republic from 1823 to 1838. The Central American provinces of the Captaincy-General of Guatemala attained independence from Spain in 1821 and for a brief time were part of the Mexican empire of Agustín de Iturbide. Upon his fall in 1823, an assembly proclaimed independence from Mexico and established a loose federal system known as the United Provinces of Central America. The union was immediately beset with factional, sectional, sectarian, and personal rivalries. The first president, Salvadoran Manuel José Arce, was installed in office by liberals and moderates. He made concessions to conservatives and royalists and intervened in provincial affairs. Uprisings occurred, and Arce was forced out of office in 1829. He was succeeded by the liberal Honduran leader, Francisco Morazán, who instituted a far-ranging program of liberal reform that included many anticlerical measures. More provincial revolts occurred, territory was lost to bordering states, and the federal capital was moved to San Salvador from Guatemala City in 1835. An outbreak of cholera gave support to a religious-based and *caudillo*-led revolution under the Guatemalan Rafael Carrera. Morazán was defeated and the federation disintegrated into its constituent parts in 1838. Subsequent efforts by Morazán to reestablish the federation failed and he was executed in 1842. The breakup of the union was followed by a period of conservative reaction, political anarchy, and foreign intervention in Central America. *See also* FEDERALISM (167).

Significance
The Central American Federation was troubled throughout its brief existence by many insurmountable problems. The previous unity under Spanish colonial rule and a common indigenous culture were insufficient to overcome poor communications, financial problems, fear of Guatemalan hegemony, federal-state rivalry, social unrest, and partisan warfare. Complete federal control over the territory was never fully established. Chiapas, a former part of the Captaincy-General of Guatemala, was lost to Mexico, and Great Britain retained control over Belize. Although two-thirds of the 1.5 million people were Indian and about a third were *mestizo*, the governmental system was controlled by creoles and a rigid class system prevailed. Not every province had the same ethnic mix, however, since Guatemala was predominantly Indian and Costa Rica was largely white. The federation was the second nation in the Western Hemisphere to abolish black slavery; Haiti was the first. The anticlerical laws, however, went too far for churchmen and conservatives who rallied superstitious peasants against Morazán's regime in the wake of a cholera epidemic. Although the Central American Federation was a failure, the federal ideal has resurfaced several times in Central America, but with no success. Yet the economic, geographic, social, and political conditions of the region would seem to call for more cooperation and integration among the five Central American states and Panama. The Organization of Central American States (ODECA) and the Central American Common Market (CACM) are recent illustrations of this cooperation and the continuing efforts to achieve greater integration.

Chaco War [25]
A major conflict fought between Bolivia and Paraguay from 1932 to 1935 for possession of the territory called the Chaco Boreal. A desolate lowland region of scrub woodlands, arid desert, and swamps, the Chaco Boreal is that part of the Gran Chaco that lies north of Argentina and west of Brazil. Bolivia and Paraguay both laid claim to the territory since gaining their independence in the 1820s, but

the territory was largely ignored by Bolivia for many years and was only sparsely settled by Paraguay. The immediate causes of the war were: (1) Bolivia's mistaken belief that the region possessed vast oil resources; (2) Bolivia's desire to secure a waterway outlet to the Atlantic via the Paraguay River; (3) Paraguay's wish to keep territory it had settled; and (4) the desire of both nations to redeem their national honor and to compensate themselves for territory lost in nineteenth-century wars. Following frontier skirmishes in 1927, a full-scale war broke out in 1932. Although larger and well armed, Bolivia fared badly in the fighting. The conscripted Indian soldiers from the highlands could not adapt as well as the Paraguayans to the climate of the lowlands. Both sides suffered greatly from disease, exposure to the harsh environment, and from the fighting. There were over 60,000 Bolivian and 40,000 Paraguayan deaths and a total of 250,000 casualties. The truce of 1935 came after both sides were exhausted, at which time Paraguay was in possession of most of the disputed territory. The peace treaty of 1938 gave Paraguay about 75 percent of the Chaco Boreal, and Bolivia was granted rights to a port and passage rights through Paraguay to the sea. *See also* PARAGUAYAN WAR (38).

Significance
The Chaco War was the bloodiest South American war in the twentieth century, and the conflict had important economic, social, and political consequences in each country. Both sides were burdened with large debts, economic development was set back, xenophobic nationalism grew, and political unrest and government instability resulted. Paraguay retained most of the disputed territory, but the Paraguayan people were dissatisfied with the peace settlement. The next few decades witnessed a continuation of political instability, a succession of military governments, and the rise of the Febrerista movement. The political consequences for vanquished Bolivia were more pronounced as new political forces were unleashed. The war opened vistas for the Indian soldier, who became nationalized and politicized. The "Chaco generation" of veterans organized peasant leagues, labor unions, and new reformist and revolutionary political parties. These forces quickened the pace of modernization and helped bring about the Bolivian Revolution of 1952.

Científicos 26
The common name (scientists) for a group of government officials in the Porfirio Díaz regime in Mexico who believed it was possible to solve social and economic problems by applying scientific methods. The *científicos*, who were followers of the Positivist school of philosophy, were influential in the period from 1890 to 1911. *See also* PORFIRIATO (39); POSITIVISM (76).

Significance
Científicos were few in number but very influential in the last two decades of the Díaz regime. They were creoles who came from the wealthy middle class who accepted Díaz's dictatorship as the necessary means to provide the political stability that could foster the economic development of Mexico. They promoted honest and efficient government administration, educational reform, conservative fiscal policies, economic modernization and industrialization, and massive foreign investment. These policies helped modernize the economy but also tended to concentrate wealth and land in the hands of a few. Foreign business interests came to own and operate public utilities and most of Mexican industrial, mining, and petroleum enterprises. In addition,

the policies hurt the urban working class and the great mass of Indian peasants. Many Mexicans objected to the control over the economy exercised by foreign interests. As a result, the *científicos* became unpopular and their policies contributed to the growth of revolutionary forces. They were removed from power when the Mexican Revolution forced Díaz out of office in 1911.

Colonial Government 27

The institutions and processes by which Spain and Portugal governed their colonies in the Americas. The source for all authority in Spanish colonial government was the Crown, and the colonies were the personal possessions of the Spanish monarch. Before the establishment of a full system of colonial government, the title *adelantado* was given to explorers and conquerors in the early sixteenth century. *Adelantados* possessed broad military, civil, and judicial powers and were equivalent to colonial governors. In 1524, the Council of the Indies was chartered and was granted supreme legislative, executive, and judicial authority over the colonies. The viceroy was the highest official in the colonies, possessing supreme civil and military authority in his territory. A captain-general, only nominally subject to the viceroy, held similar powers for a smaller-sized territory. Less important regions were called *presidencias* and were headed by a *presidente* who possessed civil authority. The *audiencia*, composed of *oidores* (judges), was the highest court, but it was also a council of state with administrative powers. It acted as a check on the viceroy. Provincial government was headed by a *corregidor* (corrector or protector) with supreme authority within his district, including towns. *Corregidores de indios* had authority over Indian towns (*pueblos*) and the power to protect Indians from abuse by colonists. Municipal government included a *cabildo* (town council) of 12 *regidores* (councilmen), who were closely supervised by the *corregidor*. On occasion a *cabildo abierto* (open council) was authorized, in which nonmembers were permitted to express their views on important matters. A host of other officials with specialized functions were spread throughout a vast bureaucracy. At the close of a royal official's term of office, a judicial and administrative review of his actions was undertaken by a *residencia*. Officials were also subject to a *visita* (investigation) by a *visitador* (investigator) at unannounced times. In Portuguese America, a similar system of government was created after an initial period of experimentation. In order to encourage the development of the vast territory of Brazil, the colony was divided into 12 *capitanias* (captaincies) ruled by hereditary *donatarios* (donataries), who were granted broad powers to colonize and develop their territories. The donatary system was not successful, and a governor-general was appointed for Brazil in 1549. *See also* CREOLE (CRIOLLO) (1); PENINSULAR (15).

Significance
The system of colonial government in Spanish America was subject to much abuse. Officials often purchased their position, residencias were bribed, and nepotism, graft, and corruption were common. Higher positions in the system were held by peninsulars (Spaniards) of noble birth who looked down on the creoles (white colonists). The bureaucracy was overstaffed, indifferent to royal authority, and acted arbitrarily towards colonists and Indians. Creoles participated only at the cabildo level, but this experience became important when they assumed authority during the Wars of Independence. The colonial system of government in Brazil operated in much the same fashion, although it

was less harsh. Many features of colonial government were carried over to the independence period, such as centralism, bureaucratism, and corruption, and they persist in modern times.

Conquest 28

The defeat and subjugation of most of the native peoples of the Western Hemisphere by Spain. The Spanish Conquest began with the island of Hispaniola soon after the discovery of the West Indies by Christopher Columbus in 1492 and was generally completed by 1545. Although the *conquistadores* had few soldiers, they soon subjugated the 20 million Indians who were living in advanced civilizations. The Aztecs in Mexico were defeated in 1521, the Maya in Central America in 1525, the great Inca empire in Peru by 1535, the Chibcha Indians in northern South America by 1538, and the Maya in the Yucatan peninsula by 1545. Less advanced Indian tribes in remote areas of Central America, southern South America, and northeast South America were more difficult to bring under control, and in some places they were not subdued until the nineteenth century. The relative speed and ease of the Spanish Conquest was a remarkable military achievement that has greatly interested historians. The major factors that are believed to have contributed to the Conquest are: (1) the superior military technology of the Spaniards, which included cannon and muskets, crossbows, and steel swords and armor; (2) the horse, which the Spaniards used to great advantage and which at first amazed or frightened Indian fighters; (3) Spanish military tactics, cunning, and treacherous acts, which Indians could not understand or cope with; (4) the ability of the Spaniards to make allies of subjugated tribes and use them against dominant tribes; (5) the religion of the Aztecs, which caused their leaders to believe that Hernán Cortés was their fair-haired god who had promised to return from the sea; and (6) the civil war among the Incas, which Spaniards exploited to great advantage. *See also* CONQUISTADOR (29); RECONQUEST (40).

Significance
Considering the few Spaniards involved, the Conquest stands out as a remarkable example of imperialistic expansion. It opened up vast territories that Spain settled and exploited through a colonial system that lasted over 300 years. By living off the wealth of the New World, Spain became a great power and the monarchy was strengthened. But this in turn contributed to Spain's decline because its mercantilist system of exploitation retarded its own economic development. The native Indian population in 1500, estimated to be about 20 to 25 million, was reduced to about one-half that number by 1600 as a result of disease, overwork, killing, lack of food, and dislocations. Caribbean tribes and other lowland Indians who were at the hunting and fishing stages of development died out, but agricultural Indians in the highland areas survived. Tribes that were part of highland empires; had hereditary monarchs; made tributary payments to ruling tribes; had forced labor systems, rigid class systems, and state religion found it easier to adapt to Spanish rule. The Conquest enabled the Spaniards to transplant their political, economic, and social system throughout much of the New World, and it is this culture, in some places modified by traditional Indian or African traits, that generally characterizes the region today.

Conquistador 29

A Spanish conqueror of Indian civilizations and tribes in the Americas during the first half of the sixteenth century. *Conquistadores* received their authority from the Spanish Crown or its representative in the New World and were authorized to subdue and Christianize Indians, to establish settlements, and at times to act as governors. Their conquest of the more civilized parts of the New World was achieved within a 50-year period, using only a few Spanish soldiers. The outstanding *conquistadores* were Vasco Núñez de Balboa (1475–1517), who founded a colony on the isthmus of Panama and discovered the Pacific Ocean on 15 September 1513; Hernán Cortés (1485–1547), who conquered the Aztec empire in 1521; Diego de Almagro (1475–1538), who subdued the Maya in Guatemala in 1525; Francisco Pizarro, (1475–1547), who completed his conquest of the Incan empire in 1535; and Gonzalo Jiménez de Quesada (c. 1499–1579), who overcame the Chibchas in northern Colombia in 1538. *See also* CONQUEST (28).

Significance
The *conquistadores* were a group of daring and courageous men who displayed remarkable energy and resourcefulness and endured many hardships to achieve their aims. Driven by ambition and greed, they were also ruthless and cruel, using treachery and deceit against Indians and each other. The *conquistadores* were often in rebellion against Spanish authority, and a sizable percentage of them were killed by other *conquistadores*, were executed or imprisoned by Spanish authorities, or died penniless and out of favor. Yet the military achievements of these men seem to be unmatched by other conquerors. Cortés set out to retake the Aztec capital of Tenochtitlán with only 1,300 Spanish soldiers; Almagro had only 420 Spaniards; Pizarro began his campaign with 168 men and had only 1,200 Spaniards when he finally took Peru; and Quesada set out to conquer the Chibchas with only 166 Spaniards. In these and other expeditions, the *conquistadores* were able to enlist the help of Indian tribes. They succeeded in taking control of over 20 million Indians and bestowing a great colonial empire on Spain.

Cristero Rebellion | 30 |

A rural Mexican revolt of militant Catholics that occurred during the period from 1926 to 1929, following the enforcement of anticlerical laws by the revolutionary Mexican government. The *cristeros,* who were named after their battle cry, *"¡Viva el Cristo Rey!"* ("Long live Christ the King!"), were active in several western and northern states. Armed bands of peasant guerrillas attacked federal officials and institutions and in turn were ruthlessly crushed by federal troops. Atrocities were committed by both sides. *See also* ANTI-CLERICALISM (50); CHURCH-STATE RELATIONS (109).

Significance
The *Cristero* Rebellion was a violent episode in the continuing struggle between church and state in Mexico. Upon taking power in 1924, President Plutarco Elías Calles was determined to limit the power of the church and rigorously enforced various anticlerical provisions of the 1917 constitution. Catholic bishops further inflamed matters when they published a manifesto denouncing the anticlerical provisions of the constitution. Calles limited the number of priests, closed church schools and convents, expelled foreign priests and some bishops, required priests to register, prohibited priests from wearing clerical habits in public, and nationalized church property. The church responded by suspending all public religious services for three years. Urban Catholic laymen called for a national economic boycott, and the *cristeros* took up arms. Under subsequent presidents an uneasy truce existed, but the government had

clearly established its supremacy in the struggle between church and state.

Encomienda ⬜31

A legal device adopted in 1503 by which the Spanish Crown assigned rights over Indians in the Spanish American colonies to deserving military leaders and other Spaniards. Through the *encomienda* (from *encomendar*, "to entrust"), the beneficiaries of the system, *encomenderos*, were permitted to exploit Indian labor but were vested with a responsibility in return to take care of the Indian's physical and spiritual wellbeing. The system was aimed at moderating the early brutal treatment of Indians through the system of *repartimiento* (from *repartir*, "to divide up"), that had permitted colonists to seize Indians at will and place them in slavery working the fields and the mines. *See also* PEONAGE (16).

Significance
Although the *encomienda* system was conceived by the Spanish monarchy to perform a civilizing role in the colonies, the plantation owners and mine operators who exploited Indian labor placed little emphasis on their responsibilities to those who had been entrusted to their care. In addition, the system led to the seizure of Indian lands as the *encomenderos* brought the inhabitants of those lands under their control. In time, the *encomienda* degenerated to the point that most of the Indians caught up in the system were virtual slaves, with no recognized rights. Angered by these abuses, the Crown and the church attempted to rectify the situation to protect the Indians. Successive efforts by Spanish kings to abolish the *encomienda* during the sixteenth and seventeenth centuries failed, and the system was not ended until the last part of the eighteenth century. In many places, the system of debt peonage replaced the forced labor system of the *encomienda*. The hapless state of the Indian population in many countries of Latin America today—landless and poverty-stricken—is partly due to the economic, cultural, and social impact of the *encomienda* system over a period of three centuries.

Filibuster ⬜32

In Latin America, a freebooter, buccaneer, or military adventurer. Originally, a Dutch word for freebooter, the term "filibuster" was used in the seventeenth century in reference to buccaneers who raided Spanish colonies. In the nineteenth century, the term was applied to irregular military adventurers and soldiers of fortune who launched invasions against various Latin American nations. In U.S. politics, the term refers to the use of obstructionist tactics by a minority to delay or prevent the passage of legislation, especially in the U.S. Senate. *See also* WALKER FILIBUSTER (45).

Significance
Filibusters were a feature of Latin American politics in the nineteenth century when countries were weak and suffered from civil wars. Filibustering expeditions were launched from U.S. territory against Mexico, Cuba, and Central America. The best-known filibusters were Narciso López, a Venezuelan who had settled in Cuba, and William Walker, a citizen of the United States. Having failed in a revolt against Spanish authority in Cuba in 1848, López twice invaded the island with sizeable expeditions composed mostly of North Americans. He failed to arouse popular support in Cuba on both attempts and was captured and executed on his second expedition in 1851. William Walker invaded Mexico in 1853 but failed in his effort to establish a separate republic in Lower California and Sonora. He did

succeed in controlling Nicaragua from 1855 to 1857, but was captured and executed while on another attempt to conquer Central America in 1860. Some filibusters were strongly supported in the southern part of the United States by proslavery forces who wanted to bring slaveholding Central American and Caribbean nations into the U.S. federation.

Fuero ☐ 33

A special exemption or privilege granted to members of the nobility, the clergy, the military, and government officials in Spanish America. *Fueros* included exemption from certain taxes, immunity from imprisonment for debt, preference in public office, and special courts with civil and criminal jurisdiction. *Fueros* were abolished in Spain in 1820, but they were continued in Latin America well beyond independence from Spain. *See also* REFORMA, LA (41).

Significance
Fueros were resented by creoles (American-born whites) in the colonial period because most high offices in government, the military, and the church were held by *peninsulares* (native-born Spaniards) who enjoyed these privileges. By the late eighteenth century, creoles were taken into the officer corps and received the benefits of the *fuero militar*, special military tribunals. As more creoles filled privileged positions, they came into conflict with the liberal leaders of independence who wanted to abolish the *fueros*. The struggle against special military and ecclesiastical courts continued in the nineteenth century and was part of the liberal reform and anticlerical movements of the time. This controversy was especially bitter in Mexico. The Juárez Law of 1855 eliminated the jurisdiction of ecclesiastical and military tribunals in civil cases, and this contributed to the outbreak of a civil war from 1858 to 1861 in which the military and clergy were allied against the liberals.

Gran Colombia ☐ 34

The common name for the political union of the present states of Colombia, Ecuador, Panama, and Venezuela from 1819 to 1830. Gran Colombia (officially the Republic of Colombia) was established by Simón Bolívar after the defeat of Spanish forces in northern South America in the Wars of Independence. Disagreements over the form of government among independence leaders, particularly between Bolívar and Francisco de Paula Santander, and opposition to Bolívar's dictatorial rule led to the disintegration of Gran Colombia. In 1830, Ecuador and Venezuela proclaimed themselves independent republics. Colombia proper, under various federalist and centralist constitutions, was called the Republic of New Granada (1830–1857 and 1861–1863), the Granadine Confederation (1857–1861), the United States of Colombia (1863–1886), and the Republic of Colombia (since 1866). Panama broke away from Colombia in 1903. *See also* VIOLENCIA, LA (105); THOUSAND DAY WAR (43).

Significance
Gran Colombia was an example of the turbulent political history of Colombia, which has been marked by violent disagreements over the issues of centralism versus federalism, clericalism versus anticlericalism, and elite rule versus social reform. The Conservative and Liberal parties developed early in Colombia and divided over these major questions. The nineteenth century was a period of intense partisanship between Liberal and Conservative forces, which often broke out into brutal violence and civil wars. This partisan and violent tradition continued in the twentieth century even though most of the earlier issues had been

resolved. The history of Gran Colombia and its successor states shows the futility of Bolívar's goal to establish a political union of all Spanish areas of South America.

Liberators 35

The men who inspired and led Latin Americans during the early nineteenth century in the Wars of Independence against Spain. The liberators were creoles—colonists born in the Americas—who were influenced by the doctrines of nationalism, republicanism, and natural rights. They raised and trained armies and often defeated larger royalist forces by brilliant maneuvering. The most outstanding among the independence leaders was the Liberator—Simón Bolívar (1783–1830), a Venezuelan who freed Venezuela, Colombia, Ecuador, and Peru. José de San Martín (1778–1850), an Argentine, helped free Argentina in 1813, raised and trained a new army, crossed the Andes, and defeated royalist forces in Chile in 1817. He also helped raise a navy, invaded Peru, and occupied Lima, but he retired from the field of battle in order that Bolívar might complete the conquest of Peru. Bernardo O'Higgins (1778–1842), a Chilean, joined San Martín and helped defeat the royalists at the battle of Chacabuco in 1817. Antonio José de Sucre (1795–1830), a Venezuelan, fought with Bolívar and won the final battle of Ayacucho in 1824 against a royalist force nearly twice the size of his army. Although not liberators in the strict sense, two priest-patriots are recognized as national heroes in Mexico. Miguel Hidalgo y Costilla (1753–1811)—whose cry of Dolores *(grito de Dolores)* on 16 September 1810 in the town of Dolores began the Mexican War of Independence—raised a large peasant army but was defeated and executed. José María Morelos (1765–1815) continued the struggle against royalist forces after Hidalgo's death. He fought well for two years, declared the independence of Mexico, and drafted a revolutionary constitution at Chilpancingo, but he was finally defeated and executed. Of the many foreigners who helped the Latin patriots, the most outstanding was Thomas Alexander Cochrane (1775–1860), a Scottish naval officer who had been dismissed from the British navy. He commanded the Chilean navy, established naval supremacy on the west coast of South America, and transported San Martín's forces to Peru in 1818. Later, in 1823, he helped to protect the independence of Brazil. *See also* WARS OF INDEPENDENCE (48).

Significance
The liberators and patriots are honored today throughout Latin America as national heroes. They inspired and mobilized substantial forces, devised brilliant strategies, and defeated larger royalist armies. Bolívar's freeing of vast territories and San Martín's strategic moves highlighted their many achievements. San Martín's actions in attacking Peru by sea and crossing the Andes (considered to be a feat greater than Hannibal's crossing of the Alps) rank with the greatest achievements in military history. Yet although the liberators were brilliant fighters, they failed as governors. Bolívar, for example, was unable to keep greater Colombia from breaking up into several states, and when he failed to convince Latin Americans to adopt his plan for a Pan-American federation, he resigned as president of Colombia and left the continent convinced that Latins were ungovernable. San Martín was not welcomed back to Argentina after he left the field of battle, and he spent the last years of his life in Europe. Only in recent years have his efforts been fully appreciated. O'Higgins was forced to resign as the military dictator of Chile and left the country.

Sucre, a Venezuelan, was forced to resign as president of Bolivia, the country he liberated, and two years later he was assassinated in Colombia. Thus the heroes of Latin American independence all came to a sad end. This was quite unlike the leaders of U.S. independence, such as George Washington, John Adams, and Thomas Jefferson, who continued to serve the nation successfully after independence was achieved.

Maximilian Affair — 36

The installation by the French of the Austrian Archduke Maximilian as the Emperor of Mexico from 1864 to 1867. Maximilian, the brother of Emperor Franz Josef of Austria, was placed on the Mexican throne by Emperor Napoleon III of France at the invitation of conservative, clerical, and royalist Mexican groups. Napoleon had intervened in Mexico in 1862 against the liberal government of Benito Juárez, ostensibly for the purpose of collecting debts the Juárez government had refused to pay. Liberal forces defeated French troops at Puebla on 5 May 1862 (Cinco de Mayo), but a reinforced French army drove the liberal government from Mexico City in 1863. Maximilian decided to accept the Mexican crown after being convinced by a conservative delegation that the Mexican people desired a monarchy and had approved him in a plebiscite. Under his brief tenure, Maximilian emulated Mexican ways, tried to be a ruler for all the people, and supported some of the liberal anticlerical policies. He was opposed by the liberals, however, and he could maintain himself in power only with the support of French troops. At the close of the Civil War in the United States, Juárez received an increasing amount of war supplies and volunteers, and the U.S. government pressured Napoleon to leave Mexico. Most of the French troops, now needed to defend France against the rising power of Prussia, were withdrawn by the end of 1866. Maximilian refused to leave Mexico; he was defeated in battle and executed in 1867. *See also* REFORMA, LA (41).

Significance
The Maximilian Affair shows the extent to which the Mexican political system in the mid-nineteenth century was influenced by foreign powers that were called into play by local Mexican forces. Conservative, clerical, and royalist groups in Mexico, who opposed the liberal reforms of the Juárez government, believed it was necessary to reinstitute the monarchy in order to regain their privileges. Napoleon used these desires to further his ambition to establish a French empire of Catholic and Latin states. The United States preferred Juárez, but, involved in its own civil war, did little to aid him until the war was over. The United States then reasserted the principle of the Monroe Doctrine, which opposed any extension of the European system in the Americas. Although conservative Mexican forces were dishonored by the Maximilian Affair, they returned to power when General Porfirio Díaz overthrew the liberal regime in 1876. The Fifth of May, Cinco de Mayo, is celebrated as a national holiday in Mexico. One of the rare instances of a Mexican defeat of foreign forces, it also symbolizes the victory of the principle of nonintervention.

Mexican Revolution — 37

The political upheaval that began in 1910 and resulted in major political, economic, and social changes in Mexico. The term "Mexican Revolution" can be narrowly defined as the overthrow of the Porfirio Díaz regime in 1911, but it more broadly encompasses the continuing process of political and socioeconomic change. The causes of the revolution are usually attributed to: (1) the impoverished condition and exploitation of Indians, peasants, and urban workers; (2) the domination of Mexico's natural resources by large landowners and foreign investors; (3) the economic policies of the government that favored foreigners and the landed oligarchy and that hurt the growing *mestizo* middle class; (4) President Díaz's practice of continuing himself in office and his fraudulent reelection of 1910; (5) the repressive dictatorship that tolerated no opposition and brutally crushed revolts; and (6) strikes, political agitation, peasant revolts, economic recession, rising prices, and other events and conditions that spread hostility to Díaz and won support for rebel groups. The revolution proceeded through several stages starting in October 1910. In the first stage, Francisco Madero, in the Plan of San Luis Potosí, called for a revolt against Díaz, the restoration of the liberal Constitution of 1857, the return of illegally seized lands to the Indians, and the implementation of the principles of "effective suffrage and no reelection." Díaz fell in May 1911, and Madero was elected president. Madero ruled ineffectively, was overthrown by General Victoriano Huerta, and was assassinated in 1913. A major civil war followed in which there was much destruction of life and property. From 1913 to 1914, the counterrevolutionary government of General Huerta prevailed, but he was defeated by the constitutionalist forces of Generals Venustiano Carranza and Álvaro Obregón. The civil war continued until 1920 as various revolutionary forces fought each other for control of the nation. Ultimately, the violent period ended when the irregular forces of the bandit-general Pancho Villa and the peasant army of agrarian reformer Emiliano Zapata were defeated by Carranza and Obregón. A period of consolidation followed during which Obregón and Plutarco Elias Calles introduced modest social reforms, organized an official revolutionary political party (later renamed the Institutional Revolutionary Party or PRI), introduced strong anticlerical measures, and suppressed the revolt of militant Catholics known as the *cristeros*. In 1934, President Lázaro Cárdenas initiated a period of radical reform and gave meaning to the economic and social provisions of the Constitution of 1917. He nationalized the railroads and other enterprises; broke up large estates and gave the land to peasant agricultural communities *(ejidos);* supported labor organizations against industrialists; enacted labor, social, and educational reforms; and expropriated the holdings of foreign oil companies. The period of the "institutionalized revolution" is variously dated from 1940 or 1946 and continues to the present day. It is a period of political stability in which the nation has been demilitarized and the government is operated by civilian politicians who control the dominant political party, the PRI, in a system of limited party competition. The period has been marked by industrial expansion, rapid economic growth, foreign investment, and intermittent economic and social reforms in which liberal, innovative presidents alternate with conservative, consolidating presidents. *See also* CRISTERO REBELLION (30); EJIDO (3); INSTITUTIONAL REVOLUTIONARY PARTY (PRI) (120); MEXICAN CONSTITUTION OF 1917 (172); PORFIRIATO (39); VERACRUZ OCCUPATION (283).

Significance

The Mexican Revolution was the first major social revolution in the twentieth century antedating both the Russian and Chinese revolutions. A fundamental political, economic, and social transformation occurred in Mexico, marked by massive land reform, nationalization of economic enterprises, and the adoption of many social welfare programs. The Mexican Constitution of 1917, which was a direct product of the revolution, has influenced constitutional development throughout Latin America. The revolution led to the creation of the PRI, the most successful of Latin American national revolutionary parties. Militarism and banditry were brought under control, political stability was instituted, and economic modernization was promoted. Debt peonage was abolished, and the *mestizo* rose to dominate the political and economic life of the nation. The revolution also inspired a cultural rejuvenation in the fine arts, stimulated feelings of national pride in the Mexican people, reduced U.S. intervention in Mexican affairs, and contributed to the economic independence of the nation. Leftist critics of the Mexican government, however, argue that the revolution has been frozen at the level of the new middle class, and that the *ejido* peasant, farm laborer, and urban worker have received little benefit. They assert that the PRI, labor leaders, industrial and commercial interests, and foreign investors control and profit from the system. Conservative and leftist political party leaders charge that corruption is widespread and that meaningful political competition is not permitted. Supporters of the PRI government, however, point out that great economic and social progress has occurred. They assert that the accelerated pace of modernization and recent political and economic liberalization policies have established the base on which the goals of the revolution may be more fully achieved during the closing decade of the twentieth century.

Paraguayan War <u>38</u>
A major conflict from 1864 to 1870 between Paraguay on one side and Brazil, Argentina, and Uruguay on the other. Also known as the War of the Triple Alliance, the Paraguayan War was apparently set off by the ambitions of the Paraguayan dictator, Francisco Solano López, who had built a large army and wanted to make Paraguay a great power in the River Plate region. The war's more remote causes were the rivalry among Paraguay, Argentina, and Brazil; the unsettled boundaries of Paraguay; and the competition for influence in Uruguay. Paraguay initiated the conflict against Brazil when Brazil intervened in a Uruguayan civil war in favor of the Colorado party; Paraguay sided with the Uruguayan Blanco party government. Paraguay attacked Argentina when it refused permission for Paraguayan military forces to cross its territory to attack Brazil. Uruguay, now with a Colorado government, joined Brazil and Argentina in a triple alliance against Paraguay. The war, which was fought mostly on Paraguayan soil, dragged on for years and was bitterly contested. Asunción was taken in December 1868, but the war continued until mid-1870 when Lopez was killed. Under the terms of the peace settlement, Paraguay lost about 50,000 square miles of land to Brazil and Argentina and was required to pay heavy reparations. Allied forces under Brazilian command remained in Paraguay until 1876. *See also* CHACO WAR (25).

Significance
The Paraguayan War was the bloodiest and cruelest war in Latin American history. Although the war contributed to the national unification of each of the three victorious allies, the people of Paraguay were nearly annihilated. Almost all Paraguayan men between the ages of 12 and 60 were killed; the population was reduced from about 525,000 to 222,000; and only 28,000 adult men, mostly old, survived. The lack of males led to a continuing condition of promiscuity, illegitimacy, and *de*

facto polygamy. The Paraguayan economy was wrecked by the war, and the country was reduced to primitive conditions. A long period of political anarchy followed in which the country was ruled by a succession of *caudillos* and petty dictators. It took over 60 years for the nation, aided by large-scale immigration, to recover. Soon thereafter, however, the bitter nationalist and irredentist feelings that remained gave support to another territorial conflict against Bolivia in the Chaco War from 1932 to 1935. The Paraguayan War was carried to a senseless extreme, and most historians attribute it to the militaristic and expansionistic policies of the megalomanic dictator, Solano López, who fancied himself to be another Napoleon III. Paraguayans refute this interpretation and point out that the Paraguayan people, including women and children, fought until the bitter end to defend their country. Paraguayans today consider López to be a national hero who symbolizes the courage of small countries that steadfastly defend their vital interests against powerful states.

Porfiriato [39]

The regime of General Porfirio Díaz that ruled Mexico from 1876 to 1911. The *porfiriato* was a period of centralized political control, economic development, and material prosperity for the upper classes. Díaz, a general who had supported liberal causes during *La Reforma,* took power in 1876 and ran a conservative dictatorship during which he was "elected" for eight terms. He brought order to the countryside by establishing the rural police *(guardia rurales),* into which he incorporated former bandit leaders. He crushed uprisings, jailed and executed opponents, reorganized the Liberals into a centralized party, and completely dominated the congress and the courts. He controlled the military by establishing a system of rewards for generals and by frequent transfers of generals to prevent the growth of loyalty of troops to them. The *científicos*, social scientists of the Positivist school, were brought into government. They modernized the system and promoted honest administration, but their economic policies were unpopular. Díaz kept both church and anti-church forces at bay by alternating anticlerical with proclerical policies. Foreign investment was encouraged, and railroads, mining, petroleum production, and public utilities expanded rapidly. Agrarian policies favored the large landowners, so the latifundia system and haciendas increased in size and influence. The period ended when opposition from intellectuals, workers, and the great mass of Indian peasants finally exploded, resulting in the Mexican Revolution. Díaz fled Mexico in 1911. *See also* CIENTÍFICOS (26).

Significance

The *porfiriato* was a period of political stability and economic growth previously unmatched in the history of Mexico since its independence. Political control depended on a system of *pan o palo* ("bread or the club") in which patronage and favors were granted to supporters, and opponents were treated harshly. The political stability of the government and its economic policies produced a large foreign investment from the United States, Britain, Spain, France, and Germany. Much of the profits from these enterprises left the country, but enough remained so the national budget was balanced. Little was achieved in primary and secondary education, although the national university was established on a firm footing. Economic modernization produced by the system benefited the upper classes and foreign investors. The hacienda system grew immensely and, on the eve of the Mexican Revolution, almost 90 percent of the rural population subsisted under some form of debt peonage. Foreigners owned over 95 percent of the railroad, petroleum, and mining industries. Opposition to Díaz grew over the issues of his practice of continuing in office for successive terms, the domination of the Mexican economy and national resources by foreign investors, the transfer of much of the land to the great landlords, and the impoverishment of the industrial working class and peasants.

Reconquest ⟨40⟩

The long, religious-political struggle by which Christian forces regained control of the Iberian peninsula from Moslem rulers. The Reconquest (*Reconquista*) was fought sporadically for eight centuries from 717, when Moors invaded Iberia, until 1492, when the last Moorish stronghold of Granada fell. This long struggle had important consequences for the political, social, and economic institutions of Spain. Some of the more important consequences of the Reconquest were: (1) creating a strong aristocracy; (2) developing semifeudalism rather than a true feudal system; (3) increasing the importance of the knight and glorifying the warrior class; (4) strengthening the Catholic church in the religious, political, and economic life of the nation; (5) associating the land tenure system to military conquests; (6) promoting rural anarchy; and (7) consolidating and centralizing power in the monarchy after the marriage of Isabella of Castile to Ferdinand of Aragon in 1469. *See also* CONQUEST (28).

Significance
The Reconquest ended in the same year that Columbus discovered America, when its impact on Spanish national character and Spanish political and social institutions was at its peak. These traits and institutions were well suited to exploit the new opportunities that opened up in the Americas. The monarchy, the nobility, the knight and soldier, the risk-taking adventurer and entrepreneur, and the church responded enthusiastically and transplanted their characteristic traits in the New World. Thus the political, social, and economic systems of Reconquest Spain were in large measure carried over and structured the Latin American colonial institutions and political culture. These included the spirit of conquest, the granting of land to conquerors, the disdain for manual labor, the centralization of authority, the glorification of the strongman, the intolerance of other races and religions, xenophobia, and the dominance of the church, the military, and the landed oligarchy in the life of the country. Nourished in the colonial period, these features survived the break from Spain and have continued to exist in large measure during the period of independence.

Reforma, La ⟨41⟩

The period from 1855 to 1876 during which a major liberal, social, and political revolution occurred in Mexico. *La Reforma* or the Liberal Reformation of Mexico was a movement of middle-class *mestizos* who wanted to end the domination of independent Mexico by conservative, clerical, military, and royalist forces. Their objectives were to establish a liberal republic based on the principles of federalism, constitutionalism, separation of church and state, and democracy. Liberals drove the dictator, General Antonio López de Santa Anna, from power in 1855, enacted a number of anticlerical and antimilitary measures, and adopted the Constitution of 1857. They were strongly opposed by conservative and clerical forces, and a fierce civil war, the War of the Reform, devastated the country from

1858 to 1860. Conservative forces drove the liberals from the capital, and two rival governments were established. The liberals, led by President Benito Juárez, who was supported by the United States, retook Mexico City in December 1860. Opposition to Juárez's government continued, and conservatives and clericals sought support in Europe. The liberal government, in great financial difficulty, suspended payments of its foreign debts, whereupon France, Spain, and England occupied Veracruz. Spain and England soon departed, but France expanded its intervention in 1862, and the liberals were once again driven from power. With conservative and clerical support, the French Emperor, Napoleon III, installed Austrian Archduke Maximilian as Emperor of Mexico. Because of pressures from the United States and the need for troops in Europe, Napoleon withdrew most French troops from Mexico in 1866. Maximilian declined to flee, was defeated in the field by liberal forces, and was executed in 1867. Juárez was reinstalled as president and reelected in 1871, but he died in 1872. The liberal period was brought to a close in 1876 when General Porfirio Díaz, a former supporter of liberal causes, overthrew the liberal government and established a dictatorship. *See also* ANTICLERICALISM (50); MAXIMILAN AFFAIR (36); PORFIRIATO (39).

Significance
La Reforma is more noteworthy for the impact of its political ideals and achievements than for its economic and social accomplishments. By means of their policies and the wars they fought, liberals helped to establish a clear Mexican nationality and to integrate the people into one nation. They upgraded the *mestizo* and the Indian in Mexican political life; Benito Juárez, a full-blooded Zapotec Indian, became the national hero of Mexico. Royalist ambitions were ended, and groups that relied on European support were discredited. The liberal Constitution of 1857, with some changes, served the nation until 1917. Liberals introduced more political liberties to the country, but this often worked to their disadvantage by encouraging factional strife. They introduced separation of church and state, but failed to end the clerical-conservative domination of the country. Education and social welfare objectives were not achieved, and economic development lagged. Agrarian reform was a failure, and the peasant was worse off because of liberal policies. The latifundia system increased under liberal legislation because large landowners were able to buy church estates and communal Indian lands. The goal of establishing a system of free, middle-class farmers was lost completely as many Indian peasants were driven into debt peonage. Many lives were lost and atrocities committed in the civil wars during the reform period. Conservatives returned to power at the end of the period, but the Mexican people continued the process of nation-building initiated by the liberals during the reform era.

Ten Years War ⎡42⎤
An abortive struggle for Cuban independence from Spain fought from 1868 to 1878. The Ten Years War began when a group of Cuban nationalists, led by Carlos Manuel de Céspedes, took advantage of a revolution and civil war in Spain by proclaiming independence on 10 October 1868, a move that has since been called the *grito de Yara*. The rebels established a provisional government and at one point were able to control most of the eastern half of the island. Not all Cubans, however, were united on the goals of the revolution. Disagreement focused especially on the question of the abolition

of slavery and on the issue of whether to seek autonomy or independence. Wealthy Western planters and slaves did not support the revolt. Spanish forces retained control of Havana and other key points, but a guerrilla war dragged on for years, with bloodshed and many atrocities by both sides. When the political situation in Spain became stabilized, major troop reinforcements were sent to Cuba, at which point the nationalist leaders stopped fighting. A number of nationalists went into exile rather than accept the provisions of the Pact of Zanjón, under which Spain promised widespread political and economic reforms. These provisions were observed only in part, and Cuban discontent continued. *See also* SPANISH-AMERICAN WAR (281); WAR FOR CUBAN INDEPENDENCE (46).

Significance
The Ten Years War was the longest and bloodiest of the various nineteenth-century rebellions against Spanish authority in Cuba. An estimated 200,000 deaths occurred, and much property was destroyed. The fighting ended in Spain's favor, but stories of Spanish atrocities circulated by Cuban nationalists and the U.S. "yellow press" increased public sympathy and support for Cuban independence in the United States. Cuban grievances continued after the war, and Cuban nationalists in the United States prepared to renew the struggle for independence. Another revolt was put down in 1880, and sporadic revolutionary acts occurred throughout the next decade. The final abolition of slavery in 1886 removed a divisive factor among Cubans, and a major economic depression gave added support for the independence movement. The War for Cuban Independence broke out in 1895 and was successfully concluded when the United States entered the war against Spain in 1898. The Ten Years War thus set the stage for these later developments.

Thousand Day War | 43 |

A major civil war in Colombia in which Liberals fought Conservatives from 1899 to 1903. The Thousand Day War was the most serious of the many civil wars that have rocked Colombia since the 1830s. Nearly all parts of the country were affected, and an estimated 100,000 deaths resulted. The forces of the Conservative government won the struggle and began a lengthy period of uninterrupted Conservative rule. *See also* VIOLENCIA, LA (105).

Significance
The Thousand Day War brought to a close a turbulent era in Colombian politics. Numerous revolts and civil wars, in which Liberals were pitted against Conservatives, occurred throughout the nineteenth century. Major issues divided the two parties, and Colombia became a rare Latin American example of a country in which issues overshadowed personalities in political conflicts. Conservatives wanted a centralized government, and they defended the entrenched position of the upper classes and the continuation of church privileges. Liberals fought for a federal form of government, a secular state, religious toleration, and increased suffrage. As power changed hands in the nineteenth century, neither side was willing to accept the constitutional systems promulgated by the other. The victory of the Conservatives in 1903 ushered in a period of peace, but the economy was ruined and the people were demoralized. The Colombian civil wars and the Liberal-Conservative rivalry created a tradition of political violence in the national character that has been hard to erase. Families, villages, and regions became identified as Liberal or Conservative, and these partisans often would fight to the death to defend their position. This violent tradition

exploded again in 1948 in the rural civil war known as La Violencia.

Treaty of Tordesillas | 44 |

A pact between Spain and Portugal concluded in 1494 that established a north-south line of demarcation in the mid-Atlantic, reserving lands west of the line for Spain and lands east of the line for Portugal. The Treaty of Tordesillas modified a decision of Pope Alexander VI in 1493, which had awarded Spain lands west and south of a line passing 100 leagues (about 300 miles) west of the Azores and the Cape Verde Islands. The papal line of demarcation would have denied to Portugal any lands in the Western Hemisphere. The Tordesillas line, 370 leagues (about 1,100 miles) west of the Cape Verde Islands, ran through the eastern third of Brazil, and had the effect of reserving Brazil for Portugal. Despite the small area reserved for Portugal, Spanish preoccupation with the wealth of Peru permitted the Portuguese to expand the territory of Brazil much farther to the west and south. The expanded boundaries of the colony of Brazil were recognized by Spain in the Treaty of Madrid of 1750 and the Treaty of San Ildefonso of 1777.

Significance
The Treaty of Tordesillas created Portuguese territory in South America apparently before Brazil was discovered and claimed by Portuguese explorers. The treaty was negotiated at the insistence of Portugal, ostensibly for the purpose of safeguarding its rights of passage to the Indies around Africa and possibly westward, south of the discoveries of Columbus. Some historians believe that Portugal had already known of the existence of Brazil (the "Portuguese secret") well before Pedro Álvares Cabral's "accidental" discovery and claim of it while en route to the Indies around Africa in 1500. The thin slice of South America granted to Portugal by the Tordesillas line served as the opening wedge for Portuguese expansion in that continent. From this core, Portuguese America grew and ultimately resulted in the giant state of Brazil, which constitutes almost one-half of South America.

Walker Filibuster | 45 |

An expedition of soldiers of fortune led by William Walker, a U.S. citizen, who succeeded in establishing control over Nicaragua from 1855 to 1857. Walker had previously tried to establish a separate republic in the Mexican territory of Lower California and Sonora in 1853, but failed. Invited in 1855 by Nicaraguan Liberals from Léon to assist them in their civil war against Conservatives, Walker left California with a force of 58 men. Leading the Liberals and others who joined him, he captured the Conservative stronghold of Granada. He was made commander of the Nicaraguan army, outwitted both Liberals and Conservatives, and had himself "elected" president in 1856. He recruited "colonists" from the United States and was supported by U.S. capitalists who were competing against Cornelius Vanderbilt for economic opportunities in Nicaragua. Walker revoked Vanderbilt's transit concession across Nicaragua and took his ships. Other Central American republics joined in an alliance, and with the aid of Nicaraguan patriots, Vanderbilt's financial support, and British arms, fought and defeated Walker in the National War of Liberation. Walker launched another expedition, but was thwarted in Nicaraguan waters by U.S. naval forces, which were acting without orders. On a third expedition in 1860, he was captured by the British and turned over to Honduras, where he was executed. *See also* FILIBUSTER (32).

Significance
The Walker filibuster in Nicaragua was one of the most unusual episodes in Central American history. Walker's ultimate goal was to establish an empire in Central America, but, failing that, to have territory he controlled be annexed by the United States. He was strongly supported in southern U.S. slaveholding states and by advocates of Manifest Destiny. At one point he promised the readoption of slavery as an enticement for annexation. His government in Nicaragua was ultimately recognized by the United States when President Franklin Pierce acted to counter the rising British influence in Central America. The U.S. government usually did little to prevent filibusters from organizing, but Walker was prosecuted by President James Buchanan's government for violating U.S. neutrality laws. The jury acquitted him, however, and he was received in the American South as a returning hero. Alternately foolish and brilliant, Walker was able for a time to maneuver effectively in playing off one party against another in a number of conflicts. These included the partisan warfare in Nicaragua, the rivalry between Great Britain and the United States for influence in Central America, control over an interoceanic canal route, the slavery issue in the United States, and the competition among American capitalists for concessions in Nicaragua. He was ultimately defeated by a combination of Central American patriotism, great power interventionism, and capitalist expansionism. Because of their support for the discredited Walker, Nicaraguan Liberals lost popular support and did not return to power until 1893. Despite the fantastic aspects of his filibustering career, Walker is little known in the United States except by serious students of history. But the National War of Liberation that toppled him in Nicaragua is well remembered by Central Americans and is commemorated by many monuments.

War for Cuban Independence 46

The final and successful phase of the Cuban struggle for independence from Spain (1895–1898). After failing in the Ten Years War (1868–1878), Cuban nationalists, led by José Martí, renewed the struggle in the War for Cuban Independence. Factors contributing to the outbreak and increased support for the independence cause included a serious economic depression, the elimination of the divisive slavery issue (abolition came in 1886), the failure of Spain to live up to its promises for political and economic reforms as promised in the 1878 Pact of Zanjón, and the extreme brutality of Spanish forces in herding rural Cubans into protected towns as a strategic measure against guerrilla warfare. Cuban nationalists established a provisional government and expanded the war to the western side of the island, but Spanish reinforcements pushed the nationalists back. José Martí, killed in battle, later came to be considered Cuba's national hero. By late 1897 Spain was willing to grant autonomy, but the nationalists held out for independence and another long stalemated war seemed likely. The explosion and sinking of the U.S. battleship *Maine* in Havana harbor in January 1898, however, aroused U.S. opinion, and the United States and Spain went to war in April 1898. The Spanish-American War was brief but decisive, and in the Treaty of Paris of December 1898, Spain relinquished sovereignty over Cuba. *See also* SPANISH-AMERICAN WAR (281); TEN YEARS WAR (42).

Significance
The War for Cuban Independence did not bring immediate freedom for Cuba. U.S. military forces occupied the island until 1902, and the United States made a number of political,

economic, and public works improvements. Cuba was established as a sovereign republic when nationalist leaders reluctantly incorporated the provisions of the Platt Amendment into the new Cuban constitution. These provisions, imposed by the United States, placed limitations on Cuban treaty rights, gave the U.S. the right to establish military or naval bases in Cuba, and authorized the U.S. to intervene in Cuban affairs. Economic investment in Cuba rose dramatically after the war, and within a short time most productive property was owned by U.S. firms. Although the War for Cuban Independence eventually produced freedom from Spain, Cuba remained under the political tutelage of the United States for many years, and the domination of the Cuban economy by U.S. firms continued until Fidel Castro's government expropriated foreign-owned enterprises in the early 1960s.

War of the Pacific | 47

A conflict in which Chile fought Peru and Bolivia from 1879 to 1884 for control of the Atacama Desert. Also called the Nitrate War, the War of the Pacific broke out when Bolivia withdrew rights previously granted to Chilean nitrate extraction companies in Bolivian territory. The Atacama Desert, a barren coastal region 600 miles long, was originally shared and ignored by the three nations. It attracted much interest in the 1860s when business interests realized the great commercial value of its sodium nitrate deposits, which were used for the production of fertilizers and explosives. Various agreements had previously established the Chilean border south of the town of Antofagasta and had given Chilean companies concessions in Peruvian and Bolivian territory. In the early 1870s, Peru and Bolivia sought to limit Chilean expansion in the region, made a secret alliance, and attempted to take control of Chilean companies in their territories. When Bolivia increased the tax rate on a Chilean company, Chile occupied Antofagasta and quickly defeated Bolivian forces. Peru decided to support its ally, but Chile defeated the Peruvian fleet, captured the Peruvian towns of Arica and Tacna, and occupied Lima in 1881. Under the peace settlements, Chile annexed all the Bolivian coastal territory, took possession of the Peruvian province of Tarapaca, and occupied the Peruvian provinces of Tacna and Arica. A projected plebiscite to determine the future of these last two provinces was never held, and the Tacna-Arica controversy festered for years. In 1929, following a U.S. proposal, Tacna was returned to Peru and Arica was ceded to Chile.

Significance

The War of the Pacific had serious consequences for all three nations, and its territorial settlements remain a cause for controversy. Chile increased its national territory by a fourth, established political and military supremacy in the region, and entered into a period of economic prosperity, political modernization, and rapid economic growth. In Peru the national humiliation over lost territory was profound, and the economic effects of lost revenues and war costs were disastrous. The once magnificent colony and state was reduced to a minor power, a civil war broke out, government revenues fell by two-thirds, and the external debt increased dramatically; the disorganized economy was slow in recovering. Bolivia lost its coastal territory, its only seaport of Antofagasta, and nitrate revenues. It became a landlocked state, a condition that later gave impetus to the Chaco War when Bolivia sought access to the Atlantic Ocean through Paraguay. In the late 1970s, Peru, Bolivia, and Chile considered proposals by which Bolivia might regain a portion of its former Pacific coast, including Arica, but Chilean demands for reciprocal territorial compensation prevented a solution.

Wars of Independence (48)
The early nineteenth-century struggles through which most of the colonies in Latin America broke their political ties with Europe and achieved statehood. In Spanish America, the Wars of Independence began in 1810 and were concluded by 1826. In Brazil, no war occurred because the colonial government headed by Pedro I, crown prince of Portugal, declared independence from Portugal in 1822. In the French colony of Haiti, slave revolts against French settlers began in earnest in 1790, and by 1804 Haiti was the first colony in the region to achieve political freedom. Not all Spanish colonies were freed in the early part of the nineteenth century, for Cuba and Puerto Rico remained under Spanish rule until 1898. The Spanish section of the island of Hispaniola, calling itself the Dominican Republic, declared its independence in 1821, but it soon fell to the Haitians who controlled it from 1822 to 1844; the Dominicans date their independence from 1844. The causes of the Wars of Independence in Spanish America were: (1) the intellectual ferment in the colonies caused by the revolutions in North America and France and the spread of nationalism, republicanism, and the philosophy of natural rights; (2) the resentment among the creoles (whites born in the Americas) against the special privileges and powers that European-born Spaniards *(peninsulares)* had in the colonies; (3) the refusal of the colonists to accept Napoleon's placing his brother, Joseph Bonaparte, on the Spanish throne in 1808 and the restrictions that were reimposed by the Bourbon restoration in 1814; (4) the mercantile trade policy of Spain, which exploited the colonies and limited commercial development; and (5) the discontent resulting from the many political, social, and ecclesiastical restrictions levied by the colonial governments against the creoles. In Argentina and Paraguay, independence came early and rather easily, but in Mexico and northern and western South America the struggles were brutal and the tide of battle flowed back and forth. Mexican independence was achieved in 1821, and the last important battle in South America was fought at Ayacucho, Peru, on 9 December 1824, when a South American army defeated a Spanish royalist force nearly twice its size. *See also* GRITO (169); LIBERATORS (35).

Significance
The Wars of Independence in Spanish America are considered by many historians to be the most important colonial wars in modern history. A vast territory was freed, stretching from California and Florida in North America through Mexico and Central America to the southern tip of South America. Within a space of 15 years, two great colonial empires were eliminated in the Western Hemisphere. Latin American independence opened up the region to U.S., British, and French trade and investment, and the economic modernization of the region began. This in turn meant that although Latin America was politically independent of Spain and Portugal, it fell under the power of neocolonialism, for its economy came to be more and more controlled by foreign investors. The creoles took control of the governments of the Latin American republics, and the peninsulars who were not killed were sent packing. The Indians, however, did not benefit. Except in Haiti, where the slave revolt was successful, and in Mexico, where the first rebellion led by Father Hidalgo was of peasant

Indian origin, the Wars of Independence were waged by settlers and colonists, not by natives, serfs, or slaves. The Indians lost the protection of the Crown and came to be increasingly exploited by the creoles as their lands were taken away and they came under the system of debt peonage. The wars did not bring democratic government to the people, for the republics soon entered into a long period of civil war, rural anarchy, *caudillo* rule, government instability, and foreign intervention.

Political Culture and Ideology

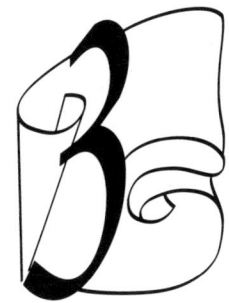

Americanismo (49)

The spirit of continental unity, especially among Spanish Americans, that has tended to encourage political, economic, and social movements aimed at achieving regional integration. *Americanismo* began to develop in the early part of the nineteenth century when a number of independent Latin American states emerged from colonialism. The leading spokesman for *Americanismo* was Simón Bolívar, who sought to bring Spanish Americans together politically through a triple federation consisting of: (1) Mexico and Central America; (2) the Spanish states of the northern portions of the continent; and (3) the nations of southern South America. Localism, a growing sense of nationalism, unique traditions, and numerous territorial disputes among the newly independent states, however, have tended to militate against the goals of *Americanismo*. *See also* INTER-AMERICAN SYSTEM (232).

Significance

Americanismo as a theory of political unity and solidarity among the nations of Latin America has proved stronger and more enduring than the institutions produced by the theory. Four Spanish American congresses were called between 1826 and 1865 to secure some measures of political integration, but none produced concrete results. The United States has adopted a dual approach toward *Americanismo*. Fear of U.S. expansionism, especially in the period following the Mexican War, gave support to those advocating closer ties among Latin states for security reasons. On the other hand, the United States, beginning in the latter part of the nineteenth century, encouraged a broader version of *Americanismo* in the form of hemispheric unity. In the post-World War II era, *Americanismo* as a political ideology waned, but it has reappeared as a pragmatic force encouraging a Latin movement toward economic integration.

Anticlericalism ⟨50⟩

A policy, an attitude, or a political movement that opposes the church's influence or power in political, economic, and social affairs. Anticlericalism primarily attacks the temporal power of the church, not its spiritual role. It is not necessarily antireligious or anti-Catholic, but its nineteenth- and early twentieth-century manifestations were vigorously restrictive. Political forces that hold anticlerical beliefs attempt to separate church and state, end special church privileges, and generally subordinate the church to the state. Typical policies enacted by anticlerical governments in Latin America have included establishing freedom of religion, requiring civil marriage and civil registration of births and deaths, confiscating church-owned estates and other property, closing of monasteries and convents, requiring secular education, taking control of church-run hospitals and welfare agencies, ending tithing, expelling foreign priests, and denying political rights to priests. *See also* CHURCH-STATE RELATIONS (109); CRISTERO REBELLION (30); FUERO (33); REFORMA, LA (41).

Significance
Anticlericalism was strong in Latin America in the nineteenth century when it was associated with nationalism, republicanism, and liberalism. Creole independence leaders and liberal political parties were especially anticlerical because the church was usually allied with their opponents—monarchists, the landed oligarchy, and the military. Anticlericalism has been present in most Spanish-speaking countries, and it has been especially strong in Mexico, Colombia, Chile, and Central America. In Mexico, anticlerical policies were pursued vigorously during the liberal reform period of 1858 to 1872 and following the 1910 revolution. By the 1950s, although anticlericalism was still present, some anticlerical provisions of the Constitution of 1917 were not enforced. In late December 1991, the Mexican Congress, reflecting changed practices and attitudes and the liberalization and modernization policies of President Carlos Salinas, enacted constitutional changes that formally ended 70 years of state hostility to the Catholic church and gave legal recognition to prevailing practices. Included among the changes were provisions for legalization of church schools, convents, and monasteries; permission of clergy to vote and to wear clerical garb in public; legalizing the presence of foreign clergy; and permitting churches to own property. The changes required the clergy to begin to pay income taxes as well. Despite many years of strong anticlerical policies, Mexico remained a strong Catholic country. The new laws end one of the most anticlerical constitutions in the world, but in many respects, given prevailing practices, they are symbolic of the general religious freedom found in Latin America. In Cuba, however, the Castro government has retained many antireligious and antichurch policies that went into effect under its rule.

Antiyankeeism (Antiyanquismo) ⟨51⟩

Widespread feeling among Latin Americans against the United States, its values, its presence in Latin countries, its policies, and its economic power. Historically, *antiyanquismo* began to emerge during the nineteenth century as the newly-independent countries of Latin America unsuccessfully looked to the United States as a leader that could help them move toward establishing democratic systems with economic independence. Soon many Latins were outraged by persistent political, economic, and military interventions, and their support and hope for an enlightened leadership from the "Colossus of the North" turned to disillusionment and frustration. Still, a love/hate relationship continued, with many Latin nations consciously trying to identify more closely with the United States and its system while at the same time being rebuffed or discouraged by actions taken by "Yankee" leaders. *See also* PLATT AMENDMENT (277); POINSETTISMO (278).

Significance
The evolution of antiyankeeism as a potent force in United States–Latin American relationships was the product of many factors. Growing nationalism, decreasing dependence upon the United States for security from European imperialism, the conflict engendered by the impact of different cultures, and a general xenophobic fear of outsiders in time became Yankeephobia. The demise of the ideology of *Americanismo* contributed to the growing suspicions and fears of their powerful northern neighbor by many Latins. In the modern era, beginning with the Clark Memorandum of 1928 and Franklin Roosevelt's Good Neighbor policy inaugurated during the 1930s, antiyankeeism was considerably reduced and a new understanding and cooperative working relationship began to emerge in the form of the Organization of American States and the Rio Treaty. After about 25 years of decreasing tension and growing understanding, U.S. interventions in Latin America after the 1950s—often based on a narrowly defined anticommunist policy—produced a gradually increasing rebirth of antiyankeeism. The important role of multinational corporations, most of which are home-based in the United States, and the large Latin public debts owed to U.S. banks contributed to a new emphasis on economic nationalism in Latin countries, which contains many of the seeds of the old Yankeephobia.

Batllismo ⎡52⎤
The political philosophy and social program of José Batlle y Ordóñez (1856–1929), the founder of modern Uruguay. Batlle served as president from 1903 to 1907 and from 1911 to 1915. As leader of the Colorado party, Batlle strove to reduce the venality in Uruguayan political life, democratize the political process, decentralize constitutional power, and improve the lot of women and the lower classes. He pushed for a plural or collegial executive *(colegiado)*, in which a national council would replace the single presidency. He helped to end the fighting between the Colorado and Blanco parties and brought political stability to the country. Batlle expanded the educational system, instituted major labor reforms, and adopted an extensive social welfare program. He also nationalized public utilities and created a state insurance bank. *See also* COLEGIADO (159); COLORADO PARTY (URUGUAY) (111).

Significance
The influence of *Batllismo* is still felt in Uruguay. Batlle's social and political reforms constitute the first modern social reformation in Latin America, especially significant in that it was achieved without violence. Although Batlle's proposal for a plural executive was not fully adopted until after he died, Uruguay became a model of a free, highly competitive democratic system and became known as the "Switzerland of South America." The plural executive was abolished in 1966 in a period when Uruguayan politics became unstable and unable to cope with economic problems. *Batllismo* was further diminished from 1973 to 1985 when the military ruled, but a legacy of political democracy and social reform remains.

Cartorial State 53

A term first used by Helio Jaguaribe, a Brazilian, that describes the political stage wherein the state functions as the guarantor of the status quo. In the cartorial state, the government tends to subsidize various middle-class interest groups in exchange for their political support. Most state revenues are provided through taxes on the middle class, which subsequently are returned to the middle class through favorable clientele policies.

Significance

The role of the cartorial state falls midway between the extremes of dictatorship or oligarchic rule by the upper class on the one hand and populist democracy on the other. Cartorial politics has typified the political systems of Brazil, Chile, and Uruguay. The basic model for the cartorial state is the United States, with its emphasis on the role of interest groups, its governmental policies that often exchange subsidy programs for electoral support, its rejection of left-wing and right-wing extremism in politics, and its strong emphasis on maintaining the status quo.

Castroism 54

The political, economic, and social ideology developed by Fidel Castro in Cuba beginning in the late 1950s. Castroism involves two basic ideas: how to seize power in a Latin American state from a corrupt but powerful dictator, and how to organize the state and its people so as to carry out a many-faceted economic and social revolution. The first, with its emphasis on initiating guerrilla warfare in rural areas, manifested itself in the development of *Fidelista* movements in many Latin countries. The second, drawing upon the basic ideas of Marxism-Leninism, provides for a uniquely Cuban road to socialism. Castroism domestically has involved such actions as expropriation of all foreign-owned properties, development of a powerful military force through Soviet support, large-scale collective farming to increase yields, stifling of dissent, eradication of illiteracy through mass educational programs, general health and welfare benefits, and forced savings to provide the means for economic growth. *See also* COMMUNIST PARTY OF CUBA (PCC) (114); FIDELISTA (89); REVOLUTION (100).

Significance

Castroism as a new adaptation of communist philosophy gained the support of many students, intellectuals, labor leaders, peasants, and urban proletariat throughout Latin America. The ideas of Castroism were more successfully transplanted than the means to power through guerrilla war found in *Fidelista* movements. Castroism as practiced in Cuba became increasingly nationalistic, with programs aimed at evoking a pride in the Cuban nation and defense of the revolution against U.S. intervention. In the foreign field, thousands of Cubans were sent to Africa to help communist revolutionary movements to win struggles for independence and the competition for power among rival indigenous groups. Whether or not Castroism will retain its ideological vigor after its charismatic leader dies is problematical.

Christian Democracy 55

A political movement based on a philosophy that combined Catholic social doctrine with the principles of political democracy. Christian democracy has progressive and conservative wings, both of which reject the atheistic materialism of Marxist socialism and the excesses of unregulated capitalism. Basing their ideas on the social encyclicals of Pope Leo XIII and Pope John XXIII, Christian democrats seek to improve the condition of the working class while also defending traditional institutions and values, such as the family, the community, Catholic schools, and religious education. Progressive Christian democrats, sometimes calling themselves Christian socialists, promote labor union activity, push for social welfare legislation, and call for the nationalization of large-scale enterprise. Conservative Christian democrats tend to support a sectarian version of traditional conservatism. They espouse church prerogatives, a hierarchical social system, and private property, and they call for a humane version of capitalism. *See also* SOCIAL CHRISTIAN PARTY (COPEI) (134).

Significance
Christian democratic parties were created in most Latin American nations after World War II. Unlike most European Christian democratic parties, which are often conservative, Latin parties tend to be progressive or moderate reformist parties. They differ from traditional Latin Catholic parties in that they typically are multiclass organizations that organize and defend the interests of urban workers, peasants, professional groups, university students, and some sectors of the middle class. Latin Christian democratic parties tend to be well-organized, attract good leadership, and seldom break up into splinter groups. Although they have been organized throughout the region, Christian democratic parties have been successful in winning power only in Chile, Venezuela, El Salvador, and Guatemala. Before the military coup of 1973, the Chilean Christian Democratic party was the largest and best organized Christian democratic party in the Americas, and its leader, Eduardo Frei, was elected president in 1964. The party returned to power in 1990 when Patricio Aylwin was elected president in late 1989. In Venezuela, the Social Christian party (COPEI) is the second largest party in that nation and has twice won the presidency—in 1969 and in 1979. In El Salvador, the Christian Democratic party was the largest party through most of the 1980s, and its leader, José Napoleón Duarte, was president from 1984 to 1989. In Guatemala, Marco Vinicio Cerezo of the Guatemalan Christian Democratic party (PDC) was president from 1986 to 1991, and the party was the largest congressional group for a time. Although Cerezo attempted to initiate some reforms in the context of a brutal civil war, his administration suffered from strong military influence, failed coups, economic decline, and many civilian deaths and human rights violations. The PDC presidential candidate fared poorly in the election of 1990, and the party's congressional delegation was reduced to a small size.

Clientelism (Clientelismo) | 56 |

Personal relationships that link patrons and clients together in a system in which jobs, favors, and protection are exchanged for labor, support, and loyalty. *Clientelismo* is typically found in agricultural regions where the landowner (*patrón*) supplies the peasant (*campesino*) with land, tools, and supplies in exchange for labor and a substantial portion of the harvest. Patron-client relationships are also found in urban areas, where employers, bosses, political leaders, and government figures provide opportunities for loyal and dependent employees and followers. The system of *clientelismo* is related to the cultural trait of personalism (*personalismo*), which stresses personal relationships rather than institutional ones, and to *compadrazgo*, a Catholic form of ritual kinship. In these mutually reinforcing systems, one seeks to expand one's network of well-placed friends, relatives, compadres, and patrons in order to maximize opportunities, maintain economic security, and defend personal interests. *See also* COMPADRAZGO (58); PERSONALISM (PERSONALISMO) (73).

Significance
Clientelismo pervades the world of government, politics, business, agriculture, and commerce in Latin America. The relationship between patron and client may appear to be an equally interdependent one, but in nations where wealth, power, or land ownership is concentrated in the hands of a few and a labor surplus exists, the patron plays a dominant role. Although advanced technology is widely disseminated in urban areas, social relationships in Latin America tend to follow traditional patterns. Face-to-face contacts, relationships based on ascriptive criteria, family connections, friends, and protectors are more important than individual merit or achievements. *Clientelismo* is rooted in the political culture, and because economic development and modernization require increasing levels of efficiency, its impact on those goals can be highly deleterious.

Communism 57

An ideology based largely on Marxist-Leninist concepts that seeks to establish a socialist society through the use of revolutionary methods. Communism holds that the ultimate goals of socialism are to create a society of pure communism that is classless, stateless, and propertyless. The doctrine asserts that the capitalist system must be overthrown by force and a socialist state established in which a single party exercises a party dictatorship during the transition to pure communism. In a socialist state operated by a communist party, property is nationalized, counterrevolutionary groups are suppressed, the masses are reeducated, the economic sector is modernized, and the social system is restructured in accordance with socialist egalitarian norms. A variety of communist approaches have competed with each other and with other socialist movements. Soviet or Leninist communism, long considered to be the orthodox model, followed the leadership of the Soviet Union. It advocated the use of political as well as forceful means to attain power, the need to organize the proletariat class, and the creation of revolutionary conditions before starting a violent revolution against capitalist governments. When in power, orthodox communism practices state socialism, centralizes economic planning, and retains wage differentials. Chinese or Maoist communism holds that less developed nations need to organize peasant-based revolutions, and that it is possible to move rapidly in eliminating capitalist economic and social structures. Yugoslav, Titoist, or national communism maintained its independence from Soviet dominance, adopted worker participation in management decisions, permitted internal freedoms, and used market mechanisms to regulate production. Trotskyite communism adhered to a radical vision of world revolution and criticized the bureaucratism of the Soviet system. Initially, Cuban or Castro communism relied on rural-based guerrilla forces to take power, advocated moral rather than material incentives to spur production, and fully collectivized the economy while promoting social egalitarianism, but later it adopted Soviet policies. Following the fall of communism and the disintegration of the Soviet Union in 1991, Cuban communism reaffirmed its adherence to Marxist-Leninist ideology and maintained its total control over Cuban society. *See also* CASTROISM (54); COMMUNIST PARTY OF CUBA (PCC) (114); ECONOMIC POLICY: MORAL INCENTIVES VS. MATERIAL INCENTIVES (207); SOCIALISM (78).

Significance

A few Latin American communist parties predated the Bolshevik Revolution of 1917 in Russia, but most were created in the 1920s. Orthodox Latin communist parties joined the Communist International (Comintern) and were much influenced by the doctrines and policies laid down by the Soviet Union. These policies varied from cooperating with socialist and reformist parties to rejecting them and pursuing an individual approach. In some Latin nations, communists operated openly, organized labor unions, united with socialists in popular fronts, and, in a few cases, supported reformist governments. In other periods, communist parties were banned and had to operate clandestinely. During the last part of World War II, Latin communists cooperated with other antifascist groups, received a measure of respectability, and were able to dominate the labor union movement. From 1940 to 1944, communists participated in the cabinet of Fulgencio Batista in Cuba. After the war, orthodox communist parties declined as they suffered from cold war anticommunist policies and from challenges from Chinese, Yugoslav, and Cuban-type communist movements. A measure of success was achieved in Chile, where communists helped elect the Marxist socialist, Salvador Allende, president in 1970 and participated in his government. In Cuba, Fidel Castro relied on his own guerrilla organization to take power rather than on the orthodox communist party, but he later amalgamated his "new" communists with the "old" communists into a united party. In the 1970s, a wave of neomilitarism in Latin America drove most communist parties underground, and they had little popular support in other nations. In the late 1980s, with the collapse of communist governments in Eastern Europe and later in Russia, orthodox communist parties had little relevance in Latin America. However, Maoist insurgents in Peru, Castro communists, and communist members of Central American revolutionary movements, especially in El Salvador and Guatemala, still maintain their separate vision of a communist society.

Compadrazgo | 58 |

The Spanish term for co-parenthood, a form of Catholic godparenthood or ritual kinship. The system of *compadrazgo* stems from the Catholic practice of requiring sponsors, or godparents, for a child's baptism. The godfather is called *padrino* and the godmother is called *madrino* by the godchild. The parents and godparents call each other *compadre* (co-father) and *comadre* (co-mother). Godparents undertake special spiritual and material obligations to the godchild, but the ties between *compadres* often have greater social, economic, and political significance. Ritual sponsorship is also required at other religious ceremonies, such as confirmation and marriage, and *compadres* are also used for special secular events. *Compadres* are drawn from friends, relatives, and especially from persons who might be in a position to do one favors. The comparable terms in Portuguese are *compadresco, padrinho,* and *madrinha.* **See also** CLIENTELISM (CLIENTELISMO) (56); PERSONALISM (PERSONALISMO) (73).

Significance

The *compadrazgo* system serves to increase the number of kinship ties and personal contacts among Latins. *Compadres* benefit from the system of mutual aid, as lower-status persons make links with influential persons and patrons increase the number of clients who are obliged to them. The *compadrazgo* system is widely used in rural areas and also in secular urban communities where family connections, friendship, and personal contacts are still important in the modern world of business, government, and politics.

Conservatism [59]

A political ideology that defends traditional institutions and practices in the political, social, and economic sectors. Conservatism places high value on the principles of hierarchy, community, and continuity. It prefers a society in which law and order are obeyed, the status quo is maintained or change occurs slowly and constitutionally, and privileged classes rule. In Latin America, conservatism has been supported by the landed oligarchy, urban social elites, industrial and commercial economic interests, the church, the military, and foreign interests. In the nineteenth century, conservative political forces favored a centralized state over federalism, monarchy over republicanism, church privileges over anticlericalism, and protectionist economic policies over free trade ideas. In the twentieth century, conservatism has been especially concerned with defending the interests of propertied classes against egalitarian and collectivistic political movements. It opposes state regulation of the economy, land reform, social welfarism, and nationalization of private enterprise. *See also* POLITICAL PARTY (131).

Significance
Conservative political forces were strong throughout Latin America in the nineteenth and early twentieth centuries before suffrage was universalized and lower-class parties were organized. During this time, conservative parties vied with traditional liberal parties for control of the government, and they dominated the political scene in a number of countries. Like traditional liberal parties, however, they generally could not compete against the newer, mass-based parties that drew their support from professional groups, the working class, and peasants. In a number of countries, conservative parties were captured and used by dictators or suppressed by military regimes. In the contemporary era, conservative political parties still exist in those Latin nations where full political competition is permitted, but they are usually small and unimportant. These conservative parties are generally weak, but conservative principles and ideas are also advocated by traditional oligarchic interest groups and right-wing parties, and they are applied by authoritarian regimes. Modern conservative parties that are more concerned with promoting free market economic policies than with maintaining traditional values and institutions are in certain nations, such as Colombia, main contenders for power in democratic systems.

Constitutionalism [60]

The principle of limited government. Constitutionalism requires that effective limitations be placed on the powers of government to protect the people from arbitrary rule. The principle is closely associated with the rule of law, which holds that the law is supreme and that the discretionary authority of government officials is limited. These limitations on government may be found in a written constitution (as in the United States) or in the customs, practices, and laws of the nation (as in the Great Britain). A written constitution limits the government by specific delegations of authority, guarantees of individual rights, and controls over the military and the police. In the absence of a popularly supported written constitution, a national consensus of attitudes and values that opposes arbitrary rule may be more effective. *See also* CONSTITUTION (160); DEMOCRACY (63); REPUBLICANISM (77).

Significance
Latin American states have written constitutions, but for the most part they have not practiced constitutionalism in the sense of limited government. Constitutionalism was an underlying principle of the liberal democratic political systems of Europe and North America that influenced the development of the Latin American constitutions of the nineteenth and first part of the twentieth centuries. These written constitutions, however, have not been effective in restricting governmental power. Throughout Latin American history, constitutions have been violated, suspended, or rewritten when they did not serve the will of the dominant political group. All Latin states practice a type of legalism that places a heavy emphasis on law and government regulation, but the purpose is to control the people, not to limit the government. The prospects for constitutionalism gaining widespread support throughout the region are problematical because the Hispanic tradition of centralized government remains strong. In addition, the more dynamic political movements and contemporary constitutions emphasize economic nationalism and social reform, which in turn tend to expand the powers of government and subordinate the rights of the individual to the interests of the nation. The contemporary move to free market economies in many Latin nations is more a reflection of the poor economic performance of state socialism and command economies than a complete acceptance of the principles of limited government.

Corporatism | 61 |
A political system in which economic interests are organized into hierarchical functional categories that are controlled by the state. The concept of corporatism is used both as an ideology and as an analytical tool by scholars to understand the Latin American experience. The ideology of corporatism calls for the elimination of the class struggle by uniting capital and labor in particular industries into single associations that are centrally managed by state authority. The society is organized into vertical units, and governmental elites make decisions for the common good. A corporativist society consequently is elitist, patrimonialist, authoritarian, and statist. Private property is usually retained, but there may be a significant sector of public enterprise. Corporatism differs from Marxist socialism in that it rejects the class interpretation of history and the Marxist goal of a stateless and classless society. Corporatism also rejects the individualism and political democracy of liberalism. Corporatism differs from other functionalist-oriented ideologies, such as syndicalism, because the latter doctrine would remove the managerial class, decentralize authority, eliminate the state, and establish a worker's society based on federations of trade unions. Corporatism in turn places high value on state direction of the economy and authoritative leadership. *See also* FASCISM (64); FUNCTIONAL REPRESENTATION (168).

Significance
Corporatism has become an increasingly used model for the analysis of Latin American political systems. A number of social science theorists have pointed out that corporatism, which has its roots in Catholic social theory, is a fundamental part of the Hispanic tradition. They argue that this unique feature of the Latin political tradition was reasserted in the militaristic authoritarianism that broke out in the 1960s and 1970s. The policies pursued by the regimes in Brazil, Peru, Chile, and Argentina were nationalistic, statist, paternalistic, and

corporatist. Although these nations returned to democratically elected governments in the late 1980s, corporatist policies and socioeconomic institutions still existed. It is further argued that this unique corporatist feature of the Latin culture helps to explain why previous theories concerning Latin American development were unsatisfactory. Other social science theorists, however, deny that Latin America has a unique form of development. They argue that corporatism is but one of the many historic cultural influences in the region and that the theoretical model of corporatism cannot account for the facts of social change in the region.

Créole [62]

The hybrid language spoken by the masses in Haiti. *Créole* is an amalgam, according to some linguists, of simplified French maritime trade dialects and West African grammar and syntax. *Créole* is understood by all Haitians and is the only language of about 90 percent of the people. The official language of Haiti is French, which is spoken by only 7 percent of the population. Upper- and middle-class Haitians speak French on formal occasions and tend to use *Créole* in informal settings. *Créole* traditionally was an unwritten language, and, because it was the language of the illiterate peasant masses, it had no prestige. In the twentieth century, some newspapers and social protest literature have been written in *Créole*. Black intellectuals have produced important literature and folklore scholarship in *Créole*, and black nationalists have promoted the use of *Créole*. In 1969, the government recognized *Créole* as an official language for certain purposes, but French remains the language of instruction in schools. *See also* CREOLE (CRIOLLO) (1); ÉLITE (4).

Significance
The two languages of Haiti, *Créole* and French, have served to separate the social and political *élite*, who are mostly mulattoes and a few wealthy blacks, from the black masses. Most Haitian peasants can neither read nor understand the language of the government. The literacy rate in Haiti is not much over 10 percent, and adult literacy programs in *Créole* have not been successful. In 1957, with the coming into power of François Duvalier, a middle-class intellectual who drew his power from the black masses, *Créole* slowly received some recognition, but black literary nationalism was suppressed under his oppressive dictatorship. *Créole* is growing as a recognized language, but it has various dialects, lacks a standardized form and method of instruction, and suffers from its traditional low prestige.

Democracy [63]

A system of government in which the people are the ultimate authority and rule primarily through their elected representatives. The theory of democracy argues that a governmental system ought to be based on certain ideals that in turn are protected or achieved by means of institutional arrangements. The substantive principles include freedom, equality, individualism, and human dignity, and the procedural principles include free elections, majority rule, and constitutional protections of personal rights. In a liberal democracy, the principle of liberty is stressed, and the system emphasizes freedom of speech and other civil liberties, competitive elections, political equality, and limited government. A social democracy stresses the principle of equality, and while not ignoring the requirements of political freedom, the system tends to emphasize positive government programs that promote economic and social equality for the people. The single-party communist states of the post-World War II period, which often called themselves "popular socialist democracies," were not democratic in the traditional sense. They were authoritarian dictatorships that prohibited political competition and denied fundamental liberties to citizens as the method for fully achieving the professed goals of economic and social equality. *See also* CONSTITUTIONALISM (60); REPUBLICANISM (77).

Significance
Neither liberal democracy nor social democracy has been firmly established in Latin America. The political history of the region is replete with dictatorships, military interventions, denials of human rights, brutal civil wars, and gross inequalities in political, economic, and social life. Following the Wars of Independence, Latin American constitutions were based on the ideals and institutions of liberal democracy. The governments of the new republics were ineffectual, however, and changes soon occurred that moved them toward elitism, dictatorships, militarism, revolutions, and foreign interventions. Among some Latin intellectuals, disillusionment with liberal democracy soon set in. This disillusionment was combined with resentment against the United States for its interventions in Latin affairs and its apparent success with liberal democracy. A number of important Latin thinkers consequently concluded that liberal democracy was not suited to Hispanic culture. They argued that Hispanic culture stressed strong leadership, centralized government, and an organic, hierarchical view of society, rather than political equality, limited government, and individualism. In the late nineteenth and early twentieth centuries, working-class, peasant, and populist forces were organized into various social democratic political movements. Their demands for social and economic egalitarian programs, however, were raised in societies that had yet to achieve the goals of liberal democracy. In addition, both liberal and social democratic political parties are challenged by movements of the extreme right and extreme left. Because of these political circumstances, many observers have concluded that the prospects for the establishment of stable, Western-style democracies throughout all of Latin America are not good.

Fascism 64

The doctrine of the extreme right that seeks to establish a totalitarian state. Fascism is based on the principles of aggressive nationalism, statism, one-man leadership, and racism. Fascist movements are headed by a single leader with charismatic qualities who uses demagogic appeals to build popular support for the party. Fascism attacks both Marxist communism and liberal democracy, promotes the concept of racial purity, and often adopts anti-Semitic policies. A fascist party typically has a symbol, uniforms, salutes, and a paramilitary organization. The movement tends to grow in times of economic and social crisis. Although fascism initially defends the nation, the family, and the church, after taking power it often attacks and seeks to control them. Fascism attempts to create a corporatist system in which the system of private property is retained, state enterprises are established, and the economy is directly managed by the state. Employers and employees are organized into associations that are controlled by the highly centralized single-party dictatorship. *See also* PERONISM (72).

Significance
Fascist political movements in Latin America arose in the 1930s and were closely modeled on European fascist parties. The most important Latin

fascist parties were organized in Brazil, Bolivia, Chile, and Mexico. The Brazilian Integralist party was organized in 1932 and was widely supported, but it was crushed by the dictator, Getúlio Vargas, when it attempted a coup in 1938. The Bolivian Socialist Falange was originally modeled on the Spanish Falange, but was untypically fascist regarding racial matters because it supported reforms to aid the Indians. The party became important after World War II, when, after the 1952 revolution of the National Revolutionary Movement (MNR), it attracted wide conservative support and discarded its fascist heritage. In Chile, the *Nacistas* (Nazis) appealed primarily to ethnic Germans. *Nacistas* attempted a coup in 1938 and failed, and they declined thereafter. The Mexican National Sinarchist Union organized militant Catholics, peasants, and workers in a fascist attack on Mexican liberalism and the Mexican Revolution. *Sinarquismo* ("with order") opposed the anarchism of the left, but the movement suffered from splits and government opposition, and it declined after the 1950s. Peronism in Argentina is sometimes classified as a type of fascist movement, but many scholars consider it to be a unique phenomenon. Fascism in Latin America declined with the defeat of the fascist powers in Europe. Contemporary right-wing extremist movements and repressive military dictatorships that are often called fascist by their opponents are not fascist in the traditional sense.

Freemasonry 65

The principles and practices of the secret fraternal society of Free and Accepted Masons. Freemasonry was established in Latin America by the end of the eighteenth century and became important in the political life of some countries. Masons were politically active in the independence movements of the early nineteenth century, and a significant number of government figures have been Masons. After Latin American countries achieved independence, Masons were in the forefront of various anticlerical movements. *See also* ANTICLERICALISM (50); POINSETTISMO (278).

Significance
Freemasonry has been politically important in Mexico, Brazil, Chile, Venezuela, Colombia, Ecuador, and Cuba. Masonic orders flourished in Brazil and were closely associated with the independence movement and the Brazilian monarchical government. Some clergy were active Masons, but when the papacy denounced Freemasonry, the society became an important issue in 1872 dividing the government and the church. Freemasonry has had its greatest impact on politics in Mexico, where rivalry between different Masonic branches was significant in the period after independence. York Rite Masons (*yorquinos*), who were liberal and federalist, competed with conservative and centralist Scottish Rite Masons (*escoceses*) for control of the Mexican government in the 1820s. The *yorquinos* were sponsored by U.S. minister Joel R. Poinsett against the *escoceses*, who were supported by the British envoy. Masonic rivalry in Latin America declined in later decades, but Masons have continued to play an important role in the Mexican government.

Legitimacy 66
The quality a political system has of being viewed by the people as just and proper, and which converts political power into rightful authority. The objects to which legitimacy is granted or withheld by the people include the constitutional order, government leaders, and the policies and procedures of the government. A political system is considered to be

legitimate when the constitutional system rests on a widespread popular consensus, and the people believe that government leaders achieved their positions properly, do not abuse their authority, and enact policies that do not go beyond acceptable bounds. Legitimacy is distinguished from legality because a regime may enact laws that are considered improper by the people. The legitimacy of a regime therefore depends not on the law, but on the attitudes, values, and beliefs of the people. *See also* LEGITIMACY VACUUM (67); POLITICAL CULTURE (75).

Significance
Latin American political regimes have often lacked legitimacy and are forced to rely on coercive power rather than popular support. These regimes are able to remain in office only so long as they can mobilize coercive power and defeat the opposition. The high degree of constitutional change, governmental instability, and social unrest typically found in Latin America are in large measure directly related to the absence of legitimacy. Some theorists argue that there exists a legitimacy vacuum in Latin America, that is, that the principles of the colonial system were never effectively replaced by the values of liberal democracy. Consequently, regimes must often resort to force to maintain control, and popular support for democratic governments is erratic.

Legitimacy Vacuum | 67 |

The theory that the high degree of political instability in Latin America is related to the failure of post-independence political institutions and democratic values to effectively replace the colonial system that was overthrown. The legitimacy vacuum thesis points out that legitimate authority in the colonial system came, under the philosophy of the divine right of kings, from the top, delegated from God through the Crown to colonial officials. Political authority in the Americas was exercised by Europeans *(peninsulares)* of high social status, who, like the king, were born to rule. The Wars of Independence swept away the colonial system, but the post-independence leaders were unable to base their authority on any lasting institutional consensus. The new constitutions were founded on the revolutionary notions of independence, republicanism, popular sovereignty, and democracy, but these ideals clashed with the prevailing political culture, which stressed personalism, manipulation of people, militarism, and the use of force to maintain control of government. The theory argues that Latin America is passing through a transition period, and democracy still has not taken hold. Until the legitimacy vacuum can be filled by effective political, economic, and social institutions that rest on a democratic political culture, the region will be generally marked by a high degree of political instability. *See also* LEGITIMACY (66); REVOLUTION (100).

Significance
The legitimacy vacuum thesis is useful in understanding some of the reasons for the high level of political instability that has retarded the development of many Latin American countries. So long as the theory remains at a high level of generality, its central thesis that a legitimacy vacuum exists is unassailable. This vacuum, however, may have existed before independence. For many years prior to the Wars of Independence, the colonial system of rule lacked legitimacy in the minds of the creoles (American-born whites), the mercantilist trade system that required the colonies to trade with Spain was violated, and bureaucratic officials generally ignored Spanish authority. Post-independence governments

also lacked legitimacy, but, more importantly, because of the unleashing of popular forces, they also lacked staying power. In a few countries, like Mexico, Costa Rica, and Uruguay, an apparently legitimate stability has been achieved, attributed by theorists to the progressive social and economic policies pursued by revolutionary or reformist governments. The legitimacy vacuum theory, however, does not explain why some countries that seem to have established legitimate systems by adopting political, economic, and social egalitarian policies sometimes revert to instability and militarism, as Chile and Uruguay did in 1973. Nor can it explain why some modernized countries, like Argentina, failed to develop a stable democratic system, or why the transition period is so lengthy in Latin America. Although most Latin states have been politically independent for over 150 years, their governments do not appear to be more stable than they were in the chaotic years following independence when *caudillos* vied for power. This transition period may only exist in the eyes of the beholder, for the concept reveals a bias in favor of political and social democracy. In 1991 almost all Latin American countries had democratically elected governments. But given the long history of dictatorships and military intervention in the region, some observers are reluctant to adopt the idea that political instability is no longer a permanent feature of Latin American politics.

Liberalism | 68 |

A political ideology that stresses the values of liberty, human dignity, individualism, and political democracy. Liberalism seeks to establish a constitutional order in which the civil liberties of the people are guaranteed, the powers of government are limited, political equality is granted to citizens, free political competition is practiced, and church and state are separated. In its classic or traditional form, liberalism opposed state intervention in the economy and emphasized free enterprise, individual initiative, and free trade. The modern or progressive liberalism of the mid- and late-twentieth century has retained the political and civil rights agenda of traditional liberalism, but it has abandoned the laissez-faire approach to economic and social questions. Modern liberalism encourages economic and social reforms through government regulation and promotion of the economy and positive social welfare programs. *See also* ANTICLERICALISM (50); DEMOCRACY (63); REFORMA, LA (41); POLITICAL PARTY (131).

Significance
Liberalism was strong among the makers of Latin American independence, and the first Latin constitutions were modeled on liberal ideals. In the nineteenth century, liberal parties and conservative parties contested each other in most Latin nations during a period of restricted suffrage, limited competition, and few issues. Near the end of the century, liberal parties lost popular support as suffrage was expanded and new middle-class, peasant, and working-class parties were organized. By the mid-twentieth century, most traditional liberal parties had died (as in Mexico), had become the vehicle for dictators (as in Nicaragua), or were amalgamated with conservative parties (as in Chile). The liberal parties that survived in an important way are those that adopted the program of progressive liberalism, as in the case of the Colorado party in Uruguay and the Liberal party in Colombia.

Liberation Theology | 69 |

An interpretation of the Bible and doctrine by certain clergy and laity within the Roman Catholic church that calls for major societal change. Liberation theology advocates revolutionary changes within the economic, social, and political system as the means to bring about a truly Christian society based on freedom and justice. Much influenced by Marxist ideas and the dependency theory of Latin American underdevelopment, liberation theology attempts to combine contemporary leftist social thought with traditional Christian values and a biblical-based theology. Liberation theology views the abject poverty and miserable conditions of peasants and the urban poor as an "institutional sin" that must be extirpated by direct action. Rejecting both capitalism and communism, its advocates seek to raise the awareness *(conscientización)* of Christians to the facts of oppression and the need for people to actively participate to win their freedom from poverty, which prevents one from having a spiritual relationship with God. *See also* CHURCH-STATE RELATIONS (109).

Significance
Liberation theology had a profound impact on some sectors of the Roman Catholic church in Latin America in the 1970s and 1980s. Some bishops were influenced by the reformist aspects of the interpretation, while other grass-roots clergy helped the poor organize Christian Base Communities, groups within parishes that studied and took on active political roles to bring about social change. At the 1979 conference in Puebla, Mexico, the Conference of Latin American Bishops condemned the excesses of capitalism and poverty and called for major structural reforms. These activities, and the more Marxist interpretations of some advocates, brought about condemnations from the church hierarchy. Political opponents of radical social change then targeted Catholic reformers. Hundreds of socially active priests were murdered, as was the archbishop of El Salvador, Oscar Romero, and nuns and Jesuit priests in El Salvador. Pope John Paul II visited Latin America and, while calling for social reform and criticizing uncontrolled capitalism, required priests not to directly participate in government and politics. In the 1990s, the doctrinaire Marxist version of liberation theology has declined, but the general themes of social and economic reform and the theological base that informs political activity continue to have an impact on clergy and laity alike.

Machismo | 70 |

A cultural trait that stresses male pride, virility, and aggressiveness in social and political relationships. The *macho* is an active man who displays strength, courage, self-confidence, daring, and sexual prowess. He is an extremely competitive man of action, proud of his manliness, and ready to exploit weaknesses in any social relationship. In his self-image he combines the roles of Don Juan, the *conquistador*, the solitary hero, the risk-taking adventurer, and the revolutionary fighter. The origins of *machismo* have been traced to both Spanish and Latin American sources. It is related to Spanish pride, to personal honor and dignity, to the Indian-*mestizo* fatalistic view of life, and to emotional self-expression encouraged in Latin culture. *See also* PERSONALISM (PERSONALISMO) (73).

Significance
Machismo serves as the basis for aggressive and uncooperative behavior in political life and as a typical backdrop for Latin American authority figures. The active, competitive, and political spheres of life are the province of males, but not all male roles, such as that of the priest and the intellectual, are *macho*, although some individuals in these fields

may display this characteristic. *Machismo* finds expression in feuds, violence, and political intransigence, with irregular, illegal, and unconstitutional modes of political change often resulting. Typical Latin American political features, such as lack of cooperation among political parties, personal dictatorships, aggressive student politics, militarism, political violence, and guerrilla warfare, are based in part on *machismo*. Some writers project that as social, economic, and political systems become more modern and as the movement for women's rights becomes more widespread, the influence of *machismo* will decline, but various government and feminist campaigns attacking *machismo* in some states have made little headway.

Negritude [71]
A concept that expresses the aspirations and glorifies the culture and achievements of the black race. The concept of negritude encompasses a bitter denunciation of white supremacy; a rejection of Western culture; a search for black identity; and praise for the values, culture, and achievements of black peoples. Originally a French word meaning "blackness," negritude was a major theme in black literary movements of the 1920s and 1930s in French Africa and the French Antilles. After World War II the concept was used by black writers in Africa, Europe, and the Americas—including English possessions in the Caribbean—and in the United States. Among the best-known writers who have used the concept are Aimé Césaire of Martinique, Léopold Senghor of Senegal, Léon Damas of French Guiana, Jean Price-Mars of Haiti, and Frantz Fanon of Martinique. *See also* CRÉOLE (62).

Significance
Negritude is a central concept of black nationalist and black consciousness movements in Latin America and the Caribbean. These movements developed a strong social protest literature and prompted the popular slogan, "Black is beautiful." Black intellectuals promoted the use of the *Créole* language in Haiti, made scholarly studies of black folklore and religion, documented the contributions of black culture in the Americas, and promoted the idea of universal brotherhood. Radical writers, who became the intellectual forebears of the Black Power movements of the 1960s and 1970s in the Caribbean and the United States, were less interested in proving that black culture was merely equivalent to white culture. They tended to reject all white culture, combined the concept of negritude with socialist and Marxist philosophy, and promoted the cause of revolution.

Peronism [72]
The political, economic, and social ideology developed by Juan Domingo Perón of Argentina. Peronism combined features of the political right, left, and center into a unique, individualized form of rule. Perón was greatly influenced during World War II by European fascist dictators, especially Francisco Franco of Spain, Adolf Hitler, and Benito Mussolini. His power base was the masses of poor people; he functioned early in his political career as spokesman for the poorly paid industrial workers and peasants working the huge estates. From his position as secretary of labor in 1943, Perón built a powerful political machine around the labor unions that enabled him to win power and be elected president in 1946. He was aided in developing his political support by Maria Eva Duarte (Evita), his mistress, later his wife, but always his shrewd political confidante and one who was able to use her own political base among the masses to cultivate

support for Perón. Peronism as a political doctrine, called *justicialismo* ("social justice"), emphasized *personalismo*, a macho image on the part of the leader, national socialism, industrialization, "economic emancipation" from foreign investors, and mutual support of the army and the Catholic church. Evita Perón controlled matters concerned with labor, health, and charity in the new regime, and she used this power with great effectiveness to support her husband in pursuit of his political goals. In international affairs, Perón tried to function as a mediator between capitalism and communism, offering *Peronismo* as a logical compromise. With the death of Evita in 1952, Perón's political base deteriorated as he progressively lost the support of the *descamisados* (the shirtless ones), the military, and the church. Finally, after much internal strife, an army coup forced Perón's resignation; he received asylum in several Latin states and, finally, in Spain. *See also* CAESARISM (138).

Significance
Peronism was a political movement particularly adaptable to the situational factors that existed in Argentina at the end of World War II. The traditionally conservative Argentine society came under great stresses in a new environment of unemployment, a mass movement from rural to urban areas, high expectations and mass frustrations, and powerful, fully politicized labor unions. Many of these same conditions had existed in Italy, Germany, and Spain, permitting dictators to exploit them to win power in much the same way that Perón achieved his victories. Following Perón's political demise, Peronism has continued for many years to function as an attractive and powerful political ideology, leading ultimately to Perón's return to Argentina in 1973. At that time, he again was elected president but died the following year. Peronism, unlike the typical *caudillismo*, involved more than a striving for personal political power; over the decade in which he wielded power in Argentina, he and Evita articulated basic political, economic, and social values that, as a body of ideas, served as the basis for an ideal social system or way of life. Like other ideologies, Peronism was concerned with the exercise of power, the role of the individual, the nature of the economic and social system, and the basic objectives of society. As a fundamental belief system, Peronism itself became a major value to be defended and exported to other societies. Its impact on Argentina continues in the form of various political movements, labor unions, and political parties.

Personalism (Personalismo) | 73 |

The dominance of the individual person, often a charismatic personality, in the political life of a nation. Where personalism is strong, political power is individualized rather than institutionalized. The people give their allegiance and loyalty to a political leader rather than to constitutional institutions, political organizations, or ideals. Traditional and contemporary *caudillos*, charismatic political leaders, and personalist political parties are political expressions of *personalismo*. Presidentialism, or the dominance of the chief executive in the governmental system, and clientelism in the bureaucracy are directly associated with this trait. Peronism and Castroism are two of many examples where the force of personality has dominated a popularly based political movement. *See also* PERSONALIST PARTY (130); PRESIDENTIALISM (177).

Significance
Personalism pervades many political institutions and political movements in Latin America. The power

of personalism has been an effective means for mobilizing mass political movements, centralizing the power of the state, and instituting innovative and revolutionary changes. Personalism has also, however, tended to retard the political development of nations in that the system it sustains is too dependent on the power and prestige of one man. The system tends to be a government of men, not a government of laws. In this case, political succession, institutional stability, and continuity of policy become major and persistent problems in the society.

Political Corruption 74

The practice of accepting or giving a valuable consideration for acting dishonestly in the performance of official duties. Political corruption, in the form of bribery, graft, and other types of venality, is commonplace in Latin America, and various words are used to describe the practice, such as *mordida* (bite), *miel* (honey), and *botella* (bottle). Typical forms of corruption include bribes to avoid or secure the enforcement of government regulations; bribes to influence the issuance of licenses; kickbacks and payoffs from private firms for government contracts; theft of government revenues or property; bribes of police and government officials by criminals in the narcotics, gambling, and prostitution rackets; and more subtle forms, such as consulting fees, jobs, or private business opportunities given to government officials. *See also* CLIENTELISM (CLIENTELISMO) (56).

Significance
The extent of political corruption in Latin America has never been fully documented, but there is widespread agreement that it involves vast sums of money in all Latin countries. The size of bribes ranges from small amounts to local policemen and government clerks to millions of dollars given by domestic firms, multinational corporations, and international traffickers in narcotics. Observers estimate that within a typically corrupt Mexican administration of six years, for example, the higher officials in government may receive the equivalent of up to $800 million. Attempts to curb the practice generally have not been successful in most countries, but some notorious presidents and high officials are occasionally removed from office or jailed. The "battle against corruption" is a constant theme of new administrations, reformist parties, and radical movements. Some theorists argue that the causes of the high levels of political corruption in Latin America are typical of less developed nations where traditional social structures and values promote private, personal, and family interests against those of the nation and the state. Despite the near-universal condemnation of the venal forms of political corruption, bribery of government officials has at times been able to achieve worthy ends by breaking logjams caused by inefficient and archaic bureaucracies. For the most part, however, the negative consequences of high levels of corruption are retrogressive in that they promote public cynicism regarding government and politics, the perpetuation of clientelism, the misdirection of large amounts of potential public resources into private hands, the inducement of criminal activity, and the retarding of socioeconomic development.

Political Culture 75

The system of attitudes, values, and beliefs by which people understand, evaluate, and respond to the institutions, policies, and leaders of their society. The political culture of a society includes: (1) empirical beliefs, or what people think the political world is really like based on their observation and experience; (2) value preferences, or what people think the government ought to do; and (3) emotional responses, or how people react to political phenomena. The content and stability of a nation's political culture depend on its system of political socialization, the process by which norms and behavior patterns are transmitted to each generation. Elements of a nation's political culture may be inconsistent with one another and not equally shared among all social groups. Also, important subcultures may exist within a society. Among the most important themes that distinguish political cultures are those relating to whether the people of a state (1) identify with the nation or with a region, locality, or social group; (2) believe that the political authority under which they live is legitimate or whether it is being exercised improperly; (3) trust or mistrust individuals and political institutions; (4) prefer a hierarchical system or an egalitarian one; (5) emphasize the benefits of liberty or stress the need for order; (6) feel an obligation to participate in political life or lack interest in it; (7) perceive that political activity is meaningless or personally rewarding and effective; and (8) are willing to sacrifice personal benefits for the good of the community or instead emphasize personal and family interests. *See also* LEGITIMACY (66).

Significance
The political culture of a nation is a powerful force in the actual operation of a political system. Such matters as national unity, government stability, the use of democratic means, honesty in government, the incidence of revolution and military coups, the degree of political violence, and economic and social policy—all of these and other characteristics are affected by the existing type of political culture. Many scholars believe that, although there are individual country differences in Latin America, a general political culture exists throughout the region. These features of the Latin political culture include, for example, personalism, clientelism, particularism, elitism, *machismo,* and the acceptance of militarism. They are not usually conducive to the successful operation of a constitutional order based on liberal democratic principles. Some of the more important exceptions to the general political culture of the region can be seen in Haiti, whose culture and politics more closely resemble those of black African republics; in Brazil, whose colonial history and Portuguese traditions affected the culture in many different ways, including a more tolerant acceptance of racial differences; and in the Andean Indian states of Ecuador, Bolivia, and Peru, where significant Indian subcultures exist.

Positivism [76]

The theory that empirical science is the basis of true knowledge and that social science can be used to cure social ills. In Latin America, positivism was largely based on the ideas of the French philosopher, Auguste Comte (1798–1867), which were highly influential in the nineteenth century. Positivism adopted the view that human nature is rational and social, and that society evolves through stages. The highest stage is that based on positivist concepts of rationality, science, and material progress. The theory rejected speculation and metaphysical inquiry as valid approaches to knowledge. Against traditional moral systems and revealed religions, positivism proposed an ethical system based on a type of humanism and a religion of humanity. It advocated the idea of "orderly progress," which was achievable by applying the principles and knowledge of the social sciences in government and public affairs. Some Latin positivists adopted ideas associated with Social Darwinism and utilitarianism. This group argued that social progress resulted from an evolutionary process akin to the survival of the fittest, that there were superior and inferior races, and that material progress could be hastened by empirically based social legislation. *See also* CIENTÍFICOS (26).

Significance
Positivism was adopted by many Latin American intellectuals in the late nineteenth and early twentieth centuries. Both liberal and conservative wings of positivism were formed, but generally positivists were nonrevolutionary. Although the doctrine was supported only by a small number of middle-class intellectuals, it was politically influential in a number of countries. In Chile, positivists promoted secular education, free inquiry, the scientific method, and social reform. Positivists in Brazil sided with republicans against the government of Pedro II and pushed for the abolition of slavery and the separation of church and state. In Mexico, liberal positivists were active in the Reform period when they promoted the liberal program of political freedom, social reform, public education, and anticlericalism. Following this period, conservative positivists, called *científicos* (scientists), were very influential in the government of Porfirio Díaz. They improved the system of public administration and promoted economic development, but their support of creole supremacy and of foreign investors made them very unpopular. Positivist ideas were also influential among some nationalist movements at the turn of the century and social democratic movements in the 1920s, but the doctrine ceased to be politically important in later decades.

Republicanism [77]

A political ideology or movement that advocates a state headed by a commoner, not a hereditary monarch. Republicanism also stresses the ideas that the people are the ultimate source of authority and that a representative form of government be established. As an ideal, republicanism is opposed to monarchy, whether it involves the exercise of absolute powers or takes the form of a constitutional monarchy. Republicanism is closely associated with democracy but not identical to it. Democracy is a more embracing concept that, in addition to representative government, stresses values and institutional arrangements associated with political, economic, and social egalitarianism. In practice, Latin American republics soon after independence came under the control of *caudillos* and other dictators who were as powerful as and often more despotic than the absolute monarchs of Europe. In the late eighteenth century, the notions of republicanism and independence were seen as twin ideals among many creoles in Spanish America. All the Spanish colonies became republics, although Mexico and Haiti were ruled for a brief time by self-styled emperors. In Brazil, the monarchical system was continued after independence until 1889, when a republic was established. *See also* DEMOCRACY (63); MONARCHY (174).

Significance
Republicanism is a fundamental part of Latin American ideology. All 20 Latin states are republics, but most of the former British colonies in the Caribbean have retained the British monarch as the formal head of state. Although republicanism is unchallenged in the Latin states, different kinds of political institutional arrangements vie for support. In contemporary times, the word "republicanism" has lost its rhetorical appeal

and partisan nature, and the debate turns on the meaning and practical application of the word "democracy." Under the umbrella of republicanism, Latin American political struggles concern constitutional structures; the distribution of governmental authority; the type of economic and social system; and issues concerned with political freedom, human rights, popular participation in decision making, and the distribution of the wealth of the country.

Socialism (78)

An ideology based on the principles of common ownership of the means of production and on seeking to achieve equality in the political, economic, and social spheres of life. Socialism aims to replace the capitalist system of free enterprise, private property, and production for profit with an economic system based on state or community ownership of productive property, production for use, and an equitable distribution of goods and services. Socialists believe that true freedom and true equality cannot be achieved until productive property is collectivized, the social structures of feudalism and capitalism are eliminated, and political institutions are brought under the control of the working classes. Various socialist political movements disagree over the philosophical bases, the organizational structures, and the methods to achieve the ultimate aims of socialism. Democratic socialism is often combined with liberal, humanist, or religious values and goals. It typically seeks to retain or implement the system of political democracy, establish equality of opportunity, implement a full program of social welfarism, and collectivize the means of production. Radical Marxist schools of socialism seek to establish a completely egalitarian, classless, and stateless society. They usually call for revolutionary means for achieving control of the state, and, once in power, engage in the rapid collectivization of property, suppress counterrevolutionary groups, and establish a single-party dictatorship. *See also* COMMUNISM (57); NATIONAL REVOLUTIONARY PARTIES (127).

Significance
Socialist political movements emerged in Latin America in the mid-nineteenth century, primarily in southern South America where European immigration was high. These groups were usually composed of middle-class intellectuals, had little success in winning broad working-class support, and were divided over Marxist, anarchist, syndicalist, and democratic approaches to socialism. In the twentieth century, socialist parties had been firmly established in some countries, like Argentina and Chile, but in many instances they were suppressed by dictatorial governments. Democratic socialist parties lost support to other leftist reform movements, such as multiclass national revolutionary parties (*Aprista*-type parties) that adopted part of the socialist program, including land reform, nationalization of foreign-owned enterprises, and social welfarism. The establishment of communist parties after World War I and radical "popular socialist" parties after World War II further divided the socialist movement. These parties were successful in attracting the support of workers and radical elements of the middle classes. In some places, socialist parties have attained power through constitutional means, as in Chile in 1970. In Cuba, they contributed to the establishment of a communist system in 1959, and in other countries they provided the base for guerrilla movements that were active in the 1960s, 1970s, and 1980s. Although democratic socialist parties are generally weak in Latin America, their

political theory remains influential, and many of their programs have been implemented by other parties.

Voodoo (Vodun) [79]

The folk religion of most of the people of Haiti. Voodoo is the popular word for *Vodun,* and the term literally means god or spirit. It is a mixture of traditional West African religious beliefs and Roman Catholic practices. The religion emerged in the eighteenth century among black slaves in Haiti who had been only nominally converted to Catholicism. Voodoo affirms the existence of a supreme god and hundreds of lesser spirits or deities, called *loa.* There is no formal theology or written scripture, and although there are priests *(houngans)* and priestesses *(mambos),* there is no hierarchical church. Priests resemble traditional medicine men and perform magic rites, engage in divination and prophecy, and effect cures. Believers worship their ancestors, invoke and propitiate the many gods, participate in ceremonial dances, and may be possessed by *loa* in a trance. Some rituals are based on those of the Catholic church and some *loa* resemble Catholic saints.

Significance
Voodoo is practiced by over 90 percent of the people in Haiti. As the religion of the peasant masses and the urban working classes, it has low prestige and is shunned by the traditional *élite,* who practice Catholicism. The Haitian government has at various times tried to suppress Voodoo or to officially ignore it, but neither approach has succeeded in reducing its hold on the people. A few presidents openly practiced Voodoo. As a family and community oriented religion, Voodoo contributes to social cohesion. Priests are important in the ritual and in the community life of villages, and they traditionally dominated rural areas. François Duvalier, who was president from 1957 to 1971, reduced the power of Voodoo priests in rural areas, but he cooperated with them and appointed some to high government positions. Although he professed Catholicism, at times he acted in the capacity of a Voodoo priest, and many peasants believed him to be the personification of the Voodoo god of death. Duvalier used his deep knowledge of Voodoo to maintain his popular base of support, to dominate the Voodoo priests, and to extend the power of the state in rural areas. Voodoo is also found to a much lesser extent in other Caribbean islands; in Cuba it is known as *santeria* and as *Shango* in Jamaica. In Brazil similar fetish cults are known as *macumba, candomblé,* and *xangô.*

Revolution and Political Change

Bogotazo [80]

The common name for the destructive riots that occurred in Bogotá, Colombia, following the assassination of the left-wing Liberal party leader, Jorge Eliécer Gaitán, on 9 April 1948. The riots continued for several days with mobs roaming the streets and much killing, looting, burning, and destruction of property. About 2,000 persons were killed, and the central city was severely damaged. Communists were accused of fomenting the riots, but this was not proved. *See also* VIOLENCIA, LA (105).

Significance The *bogotazo* occurred while the Ninth International Conference of American States was meeting in Bogotá to establish the Organization of American States. The uncontrolled mob actions caused the delegates to leave the central city and government officials to go into hiding. Gaitán would have been the Liberal candidate for president in 1950, and his murder intensified the partisan warfare between Liberals and Conservatives. Although order was restored within a few days in Bogotá and other cities, the incident unleashed the rural civil war known as *La Violencia*, which continued sporadically until 1958.

Contras [81]

Armed forces seeking to overturn the Sandinista government in Nicaragua, active from about 1981 to 1989. The term "contras," from the Spanish word for counterrevolutionaries, became the popular name for these forces, although they referred to themselves as the democratic resistance. An umbrella organization in later years was called the Nicaraguan Democratic Force (FDN). Contras were composed of a number of factions, including former National Guard members, peasants, former Sandinistas, democratic leaders, refugees, and exiles. Contras opposed the leftist thrust of the Sandinista government, its reliance on Cuban and Soviet aid, and the apparent establishment of a Cuban-style system in Nicaragua. Largely trained and supported by the United States with public, secret and private funds, the contras at one time reached a strength of about 17,000 men, but by 1987 they had basically retreated to bases in Honduras. Following various peace initiatives by Central American governments, a cease-fire in the civil war was announced in 1987 and the country prepared for free elections. A coalition of opposition parties defeated the Sandinistas in the election of 1990. A significant part of the peace plan of Esquipulas dealt with disarming the contras and reintegrating them into Nicaraguan society. Many contras were demobilized under international supervision, but few received land they had been promised, and others, not believing that the new democratic government would control the Sandinista army, refused to be absorbed into the Nicaraguan society. Those who retained their arms were called "recontras." *See also* IRAN-CONTRA AFFAIR (261); NICARAGUAN ELECTION OF 1990 (95).

Significance
Contras were effective in diverting Sandinista resources to military efforts and in highlighting the leftist thrust of the regime. So long as the United States was able to back the fighting groups secretly and fully, they achieved some of their aims but were unable to defeat the larger, better equipped Sandinista army. By 1987, however, political support in the United States had declined, and when the Iran-Contra affair broke, contra support in the U.S. was doomed. At that time, the efforts of the Central American governments in putting together a peace plan acceptable to all sides took root, and the civil war came to a close. Some contra leaders participated in the Nicaraguan elections of 1990, in which a wide coalition of parties helped elect Violeta Chamorro over the Sandinista president of the republic, Daniel Ortega. Supporters of the contra military effort and U.S. intervention claim that the Sandinista defeat in the democratic election of 1990 could not have come to pass without the contra resistance. Contra opponents condemn U.S. intervention in Nicaragua, point out that the contras were ineffective by 1987, and attribute the election to Sandinista acceptance of the Esquipulas plan as a way to end the fighting and continued U.S. intervention.

Death Squad | 82 |
The common name for an extreme right-wing terrorist group, often with links to state security agencies, which assassinates left-wing political leaders and other political opponents and their sympathizers. Death squads tend to flourish at times of political unrest when leftist or communist threats are perceived to be great and the state is under control of a repressive military government. Death squads operate as paramilitary groups with "cell" organizations. Their membership often includes persons in the secret police or security agencies from whom they receive secret intelligence on suspected subversives. Death squads use various techniques, such as publishing death lists (names of persons who are threatened with death unless they leave the country), kidnapping, "disappearing" persons, and outright murder. Their victims are usually the more vulnerable middle- and low-level members of political parties, labor unions, peasant leagues, and others who assist them, such as lawyers. *See also* POLITICAL VIOLENCE (97).

Significance
Death squads became quite active in southern South America in the 1960s and 1970s, particularly in Brazil and Argentina, and in Central America in the 1980s. They surfaced partly in

response to the growth of left-wing terrorist and guerrilla groups and supplemented the repression carried on by military governments and forces. From May 1973 to March 1976 in Argentina, for example, 1,358 persons were assassinated by left-wing and right-wing terrorists. The most prominent group in Argentina was the Argentine Anti-Communist Alliance (AAA). In Brazil, right-wing death squads are estimated to have killed as many as 3,000 persons. Death squads pose problems for military governments, which, although they may sympathize with the goal of eradicating opponents, try to demonstrate that they are capable of maintaining law and order. Death squad activity in southern South America declined in the late 1980s as democratic governments replaced military regimes. Death squads continued to be active in the 1980s and early 1990s in those countries where revolutionary movements were active, as in Peru, Colombia, El Salvador, and Guatemala. Especially in Colombia, death squad activities were carried out for nonideological purposes, such as extortions and narcotrafficking.

DINA 83

The National Intelligence Directorate, a Chilean state security agency in the military government of Augusto Pinochet that was active from 1973 to 1976. DINA was granted broad powers and a staff of about 4,000 persons, and it utilized a large network of informants. Following the overthrow of the Salvador Allende government in 1973, the agency arrested tens of thousands of people and executed and tortured thousands of prisoners. Its agents also assassinated prominent Chileans who were living in exile, including a former Socialist minister, Orlando Letelier, in Washington in 1976. The agency was abolished in the late 1970s. *See also* LETELIER AFFAIR (93).

Significance
DINA was the prime instrument by which the government of Augusto Pinochet established a brutal dictatorship in Chile. Under his administration, the repression in Chile reached massive proportions. Thousands were killed, about 1,500 disappeared without a trace, and about 40,000 Chileans went into exile. Violations of human rights were so extensive that Chile came under criticism from many national and international organizations. To prevent the isolation of Chile from the United States and to reduce pressures from the international community, Pinochet abolished DINA, released 300 political prisoners, and exchanged a Chilean communist leader for a Soviet dissident. He also permitted the extradition to the United States of an American citizen who was a DINA agent involved in the murder of Letelier, and he arrested the DINA officers who were implicated in that affair. When DINA was abolished, its functions were transferred to the National Center of Information (CNI).

Dirty War 84

Repression of the opposition to the Argentine military government in the period 1976 to 1982. Actions in the Dirty War consisted of arrests, kidnappings, tortures, killings, and disappearances of persons who were suspected of leftist leanings or subversive activities by government security agencies and allied death squads. Figures are unreliable, for they range from 10,000 to 20,000 persons, many of whom were killed or who disappeared without a trace. Mothers of the *desaparacidos* (the "disappeared" or "lost ones") have demonstrated weekly at the Plaza de Mayo in Buenos Aires since the military government was in office in order to get information on family members who disappeared. Following the loss to

Britain in the Falklands War, the military government was replaced by the civilian government of Raúl Alfonsín. Several former military dictators and police officers were convicted for murder and human rights abuses. Because of threats and attempted coups by the military, Alfonsín granted amnesties to lower-ranking officers. The next president, Carlos Menem, granted pardons to the military despite much opposition.

Significance
The Dirty War counted at least 10,000 persons among its victims, but it did not end opposition to the military regime. The repression divided the nation, brought disrepute to the military, and engendered international condemnation of a country that prided itself as one of the most advanced in Latin America. The issue of punishing the offenders greatly troubled the post-military governments of Alfonsín and Menem. Families of the victims continue to agitate for information about the *desaparacidos*, and over a million persons have signed petitions protesting the amnesties and pardons. Given the tendency of the Argentine military to intervene in government and the tenuous nature of civilian regimes, the matter of the Dirty War will continue to haunt Argentina for years to come.

Distensão and Apertura | 85 |
Portuguese words meaning "relaxation" and "opening" to democracy. The terms were used to describe the policies of political liberalization practiced sporadically by the military regime in Brazil from the mid-1970s to 1985. The policy of *distensão*, initiated by President Ernesto Geisel, included the reduction of press censorship, a decrease in the level of police repression, and permission for increased competition between the two approved political parties—the National Renovating Alliance (ARENA), the official government party, and the Brazilian Democratic Movement (MDB), the official opposition. When criticisms of the regime mounted and the opposition increased, Geisel reintroduced some repressive measures to no avail. General João Baptista Figueiredo won the presidential election of 1978, rescinded presidential powers to control congress and the courts, and resumed the policy of *distensão*. More openings to democracy followed when other parties were permitted to register and legislative elections were permitted in the states in the early 1980s. In 1985, Tancredo Neves, the candidate of the Brazilian Democratic Movement Party (PMDB—the former MDB), was chosen by the Electoral College to be president but was unable to take office because of a severe illness. Vice president elect José Sarney of the Liberal Front Party (PFL) became president in 1985, thus ending 21 years of military rule in Brazil. *See also* DEATH SQUAD (82); INSTITUTIONAL ACT (170).

Significance
The policy of *distensão* did not achieve Geisel's goal of moving Brazil safely towards the more liberal system that he called "relative democracy." Instead of maximizing the strength of the ARENA party, the relaxation of controls led to open criticism and opposition. President Figueiredo, who took office in 1979, indicated his desire to continue the *apertura* to democracy in a "slow and gradual" way, but he could not resist the mounting pressures for more democracy. In the end, the policies of *distensão* and *apertura* served well, although fitfully, to bring Brazil back to a democratic form of government.

Drug War | 86 |
Efforts to restrict the production, supply, and consumption of illegal narcotic drugs. The Drug War has

both domestic and international components. Domestically, in the United States and most affected Latin countries, programs are established to eradicate drug crops, interdict or control the shipment of drugs, enforce criminal laws against narcotraffickers, and provide for the treatment of drug addicts and for educational programs against drug abuse. International programs concentrate on crop eradication, crop substitution, the interdiction of drug shipments, the arrest and punishment of drug traffickers, and the control or elimination of drug money laundering practices. The United States has established a number of cooperative programs with Latin states by providing funds, equipment, training, and personnel to achieve these aims.

Significance
The Drug War has not been successful in eliminating trade in narcotic drugs for a number of fundamental reasons: (1) the high demand for drugs in the United States; (2) the corruption within Latin governments and links between government, military figures, and drug lords; (3) violence against law enforcement officers and judges; (4) control over localities and drug growing areas by drug lords or revolutionary groups, such as the *Sendero Luminoso;* and (5) the failure of crop eradication and substitution schemes to work on a large scale because of the reliance of hundreds of thousands of peasants who grow coca leaf for the drug trade. Drug lords in Colombia, as the Medellín and Cali cartels, have a vast network of suppliers, distributors, and protectors, and through violent means they have been able to force governments to withdraw plans to extradite drug traffickers (the "extraditables") to the United States for trial. Although the arrest of some notorious figures has taken place, and Panamanian dictator Manuel Noriega was brought back for trial in the U.S., by 1992 the Drug War had failed to stem the tide. For example, drug traffic through Panama doubled after Noriega's overthrow by U.S. forces in 1989.

Falklands War $\boxed{87}$
Armed hostilities between Argentina and Great Britain in 1982 over possession of the Falkland Islands, a British dependency in the south Atlantic Ocean. The Argentine military government of President Leopoldo Galtieri launched the invasion after sporadic negotiations with Britain failed to satisfy Argentina's claim of sovereignty. The islands were invaded on 2 April 1982 by a large Argentine force that overcame the small garrison; South Georgia Island, a dependency of the Falklands, was also taken. Meetings between Britain and Argentina, promoted by the United States, failed to resolve the matter, for Argentina refused to leave the islands as a precondition for negotiations. Britain, aided by the U.S. with military intelligence and equipment, mounted a naval task force that retook the islands in a series of very costly aeronaval strikes and land engagements. Argentine forces surrendered on 18 June 1982, having been defeated by a smaller British force. The 5,000 British troops captured 10,800 prisoners, who were later returned to Argentina. The Argentine air force performed well, but the navy was ineffective and quickly disposed of by the British. Over 700 Argentine and 550 British troops were killed; Argentina lost a cruiser, a submarine, and over 100 aircraft; Britain lost two destroyers, two frigates, two other ships, and 34 aircraft. *See also* DIRTY WAR (84).

Significance
Called the Malvinas by Argentina, the Falkland Islands are located 400 miles off the Argentine coast and

have been in the possession of Britain since 1833. Argentina's claim to sovereignty was based on successor rights to Spain and occasional occupation. The 1,800 residents of the islands, all British nationals, and the sheep-raising company that employed many of them, resisted any concessions to Argentina. The political consequences of the war in the two nations were quite different. The quick occupation of the islands was greatly celebrated in Argentina, which was apparently one of the goals of the military government—to divert attention from its repressive rule and economic failures. However, the poor showing of the navy and army, as well as the humiliating defeat, ended the military regime. Civilian government was restored in 1983, high-ranking military officers were purged, and Galtieri was court-martialed. Other military government officials were brought to trial for their activities in Argentina's Dirty War, the repression, torture, and killing of political opponents. In Britain, the government of Margaret Thatcher, which was on the brink of political defeat, won a big victory in the parliamentary elections of 1983. Following the conflict, Britain reinforced the permanent garrison and introduced some economic development schemes, but the hopes for offshore petroleum deposits have not yet materialized. In 1990 Britain and Argentina resumed diplomatic relations, and Britain permitted the families of Argentine soldiers who were buried in the Falklands to visit the military cemetery. The government of Carlos Menem continues to make a claim on the Falklands, but there seems to be little likelihood of a full transfer of sovereignty to Argentina in the near future.

Farabundo Martí Liberation Front (FMLN) | 88 |

Revolutionary movement in El Salvador that has been active since 1980. The Farabundo Martí Liberation Front (FMLN) is a coalition of leftist guerrilla groups that takes its name from Agustín de Farabundo Martí, a communist rebel who was active in the 1930s. The FMLN is the guerrilla arm of a broader coalition of revolutionary forces, the Democratic Revolutionary Front (FDR). The FDR includes a wide variety of popular organizations and parties, most of whom seek political and social change through peaceful means; it is legally recognized, although it has close links to the FMLN. In the civil war that has racked El Salvador for decades, a wide variety of groups have organized to oppose the government, with the FMLN-FDR being the leading opposition, combining democratic reformers and Marxist revolutionaries. Leaders of the FMLN include Joaquín Villalobos and Salvador Sánchez Cerén. The most important opponents of the FMLN-FDR include the military, various extremist groups, right-wing death squads, and the right-wing party—the National Republican Alliance (ARENA)—that was founded by Roberto d'Aubuisson. Leaders of the parties in the FDR include Rubén Zamora (Popular Social Christian Movement) and Guillermo Ungo (National Revolutionary Movement). *See also* JESUIT PRIEST MURDERS (92).

Significance
About 75,000 persons have been killed in the bloodiest and most brutal civil war in contemporary Latin America, in which the military, death squads, and guerrillas engage in assassinations, massacres, and terrorist operations, often leaving hundreds dead at brief encounters. The murders of Archbishop Oscar Arnulfo Romero in 1980 and six Jesuit priests in 1989 by death squads and military personnel are some of the most notorious cases. Peace talks began in 1984 under President José Napoleón Duarte (Christian Democratic party),

but his government was unable to control the military and the talks did not succeed. After Alfredo Christiani (ARENA) won the election of 1989, the FMLN launched a military offensive later in the year, which failed. Peace negotiations resumed in 1990, and an agreement was signed at the United Nations in January 1992. The plan provided for a cease-fire, the disbanding of guerrilla groups and government military and security units, the reduction of the size of the army, and economic and social reforms. Former members of the FMLN and the national police will be eligible to join a new national civil police force.

Fidelista 89

A Latin American insurgent or guerrilla who accepts and follows the model developed by Fidel Castro in his successful action in Cuba. *Fidelistas* regard revolution as the essential means for changing the political, economic, and social system according to Marxist-Leninist prescriptions. *Fidelista* movements, according to their supporters, must engage in guerrilla war and may use terror tactics against existing regimes if necessary to achieve their goals. Like their namesake, *Fidelista* movements appear to require dynamic and charismatic leadership to energize their members and supporters. *See also* CASTROISM (54); GUERRILLA WAR: FOCO THEORY (90); REVOLUTION (100).

Significance
Fidelista movements were organized in most Latin American countries following the success of the Castro revolution in Cuba. Leaders and members of such movements tended to look to Cuba for support in seeking to win power in the same manner that Castro and his guerrilla group successfully achieved that goal from 1956 to 1959. During the 1960s and 1970s *Fidelismo* proved to be a powerful motivating force in radicalizing the young and changing their value system from one supporting reformism to one that demanded revolutionary change. Shortly after Castro's success in Cuba, *Fidelista* groups began to emerge, first in Peru, then in Guatemala, Venezuela, Uruguay, Argentina, and Bolivia, and finally in most Latin countries. Despite some spectacular operations, movements claiming to be *Fidelista* failed to seize control of Latin governments. Improved counterinsurgency methods, ruthless military governments, poor guerrilla strategies, and lack of general popular support eliminated serious threats in most Latin states by the early 1980s. In some countries, guerrilla groups, such as the *Sendero Luminoso* in Peru, continue to plague or threaten democratic regimes, but these groups are not *Fidelista* in origin and are based on indigenous factors.

Guerrilla Warfare: Foco Theory 90

A strategy of rural guerrilla warfare that calls for the establishment of a focus of insurrectionary power in the countryside from which the revolution will spread. The main tenets of *foco* theory, or *foquismo*, include: (1) guerrilla war is necessary to make a revolution; (2) the conditions for successful revolution can be created by armed struggle; (3) remote rural areas are the best battlefield for guerrilla war in less developed countries; (4) guerrilla war ideally begins by the creation of a *foco* (focus or nucleus), a small band of guerrillas who operate in the countryside; and (5) through the process of armed struggle, the *foquistas*, who are primarily urban, middle-class revolutionaries, win over the peasantry to support the revolution. *Foquismo* rejects the orthodox communist approach to a revolution, which calls for the organization of the urban proletariat, the use of political measures, and the avoidance of insurrectionary activity until the "objective conditions" of a revolution exist. The *foco* doctrine also rejects the Chinese or Maoist approach to revolution, which calls for much prior political work among peasants and urban workers before launching the armed struggle, and for passing through the stages of terrorism, guerrilla war, and conventional war. Under the Chinese theory, rural territory would be seized and defended, land redistributions made, revolutionary institutions operated, and the peasantry won over by these revolutionary achievements. The *foco* doctrine downgrades the importance of urban activity and the necessity of establishing a strong political party before initiating armed struggle, and it argues that "revolutionary action creates revolutionary organization consciousness, and conditions." *See also* FIDELISTA (89); GUERRILLA WARFARE: URBAN WARFARE THEORY (91); REVOLUTION (100).

Significance
The *foco* theory of guerrilla warfare was derived from the experience of the Cuban revolution of Fidel Castro. The theory was set forth in the writings of the Argentine revolutionary, Ernesto "Che" Guevara (1928–1967), and reformulated and popularized by the French writer, Régis Debray. Because of the Cuban success, a large number of *focos* were initiated in South America by guerrilla bands in the 1960s and early 1970s, but none were successful. These failures have been attributed to: (1) the assistance by the United States concerning counterinsurgency methods offered to Latin American armies; (2) the poor security and recruitment methods of the *foquistas;* (3) the lack of support from urban communist parties; and (4) failure of the *foquistas* to appreciate the importance of revolutionary urban organization and activity. Che Guevara was killed in 1967 when he attempted to establish a *foco* in an isolated area of Bolivia where Indian peasants had already benefited from land reform and were unsympathetic to the aims of the foreign *foquistas.* Leftist critics of the *foco* theory assert that *foquistas* err by refusing to establish an urban revolutionary political structure. They argue that a "dual revolution" that combines urban revolutionary action with rural guerrilla operations is required under Latin American conditions.

Guerrilla Warfare: Urban Warfare Theory │91│
A strategy that advocates the use of urban terrorism as a preliminary stage in a radical socialist revolution. The doctrine of urban guerrilla warfare holds that the legitimacy of the government can be destroyed by using selective violence against its officers and against capitalist institutions, such as banks and foreign corporations. According to the theory, these violent acts build support for the revolution, reveal the government's inability to maintain order, and provoke the government to take excessive repressive measures that cost it popular support. Indiscriminate violence by urban guerrillas that harms ordinary citizens is avoided because the ultimate purpose is to secure popular support. Urban guerrillas use the high population density and material resources of the city as a source of supply, as a place to hide, and as a means of securing publicity. A typical guerrilla group is organized into small cells and functions independently under a general strategy determined by higher leadership. Typical guerrilla operations include assassinations, bank robberies, sabotage, and raids on police barracks for weapons. Another important technique involves the kidnapping of corporate executives, diplomats, and other high officials for ransom or the release of political prisoners. In all of these operations, securing favorable

publicity is an essential part of the strategy to win popular support. The doctrine does not hold that urban warfare alone will cause a successful revolution. For example, Brazilian revolutionary Carlos Marighela emphasized this point in his writings. For Marighela, urban warfare is the first stage, followed by rural guerrilla war, and, ultimately, a decisive victory in the countryside by a people's army. See also GUERRILLA WARFARE: FOCO THEORY (90); REVOLUTION (100).

Significance
Many urban guerrilla groups were organized in South America in the 1960s and early 1970s, particularly in Brazil, Uruguay, and Argentina. Among the more important groups were the Tupamaros (National Liberation Movement, MLN) in Uruguay; the National Liberation Action (ALM) of Carlos Marighela and the Popular Revolutionary Vanguard (VPR) of Carlos Lamarca in Brazil; and the People's Revolutionary Army (ERP) and the Montoneros in Argentina. Although many guerrilla operations were successful, urban warfare did not achieve its ultimate objectives in the 1970s. Most guerrillas had middle-class origins, and while some Robin Hood–style operations were popular with lower classes, the guerrillas were unable to generate sufficient popular support in Brazil and Argentina. In Uruguay, the Tupamaros had a large organization and a broader appeal. Their actions revealed the corruption within the administration of President Juan María Bordaberry, which led to military intervention in 1973. Urban guerrilla groups, including the Tupamaros, were overcome by a combination of strong repressive measures, such as extensive searches, massive arrests, officially sanctioned torture of prisoners, and assassinations of leftists by right-wing death squads. The killing of guerrilla leaders (including Marighela and Lamarca), lapses in guerrilla security, and a counterproductive use of terrorism also contributed to this decline. Some urban groups using nonselective terrorist methods continued to operate in the 1980s and 1990s, particularly in Peru.

Jesuit Priest Murders | 92 |

The assassination of six Jesuit priests, their housekeeper, and her daughter in El Salvador by persons dressed as Salvadoran military personnel in 1989. The priests, associated with a university, were killed because they had been constant critics of the government's support of violence, torture, and other human rights abuses and for their opposition to U.S. military assistance. The brutal murders and mutilation of the bodies resulted in a great deal of international condemnation, to which the government subsequently responded with an investigation and trials. In 1991, high ranking army officers were found guilty in a civilian trial for ordering the killings; two officers were given maximum 30 year prison terms and three others were also found guilty of conspiracy and given lighter sentences.

Significance
The Jesuit priests were killed at night and their bodies were dragged into the street and mutilated. This brazen public display of cruel savagery was intended to show the power of antirevolutionary forces and to intimidate critics of the political system. The action backfired and brought into vivid display the brutal nature of the civil war in El Salvador. Despite the great deal of influence the military had over the Salvadoran government on matters relating to the war, the international pressure to bring the responsible persons to justice could not be resisted.

Letelier Affair | 93 |

The assassination by agents of the Chilean secret police of Orlando

Letelier, a former cabinet minister and diplomat of Chile, in Washington, D.C., on 21 September 1976. Letelier was a Socialist and had served from 1970 to 1973 as foreign minister, defense minister, and ambassador to the United States in the government of the Marxist Socialist, Salvador Allende. Letelier and an assistant were killed when a bomb exploded in his automobile. U.S. citizen Michael V. Townley, an agent of DINA (the Chilean state security agency), confessed to the crime and implicated five Cubans and three Chilean intelligence officers, including the commander of DINA, General Manuel Contreras. Townley was extradited to the United States from Chile and gave information to U.S. authorities on the Letelier matter and other cases in which prominent opponents of the military government of Chile were assassinated or attacked. Townley was convicted and sentenced to a 10-year prison term. The Cubans implicated in the affair were members of a U.S.-based anti-Castro group known as the Cuban Nationalist Movement. The three Chilean intelligence officers were arrested, but in 1979 the Chilean Supreme Court refused to permit their extradition to the United States on the basis of plea-bargain evidence. In 1989, further evidence against Chilean officials was given by a retired Chilean diplomat in proceedings in Chile, and in 1992 the Supreme Court ruled that Contreras and others could be tried in civilian courts. *See also* DINA (83).

Significance
The Letelier Affair was the most notorious assassination directly associated with DINA, and it had important consequences for the government of General Augusto Pinochet. The brazen murders of a respected statesman in Washington and of other prominent Chileans abroad contributed substantially to the international criticism and isolation of the Pinochet government. In response, General Pinochet permitted Townley to be extradited to the United States, had the DINA officers implicated in the affair arrested, and dissolved DINA. Although DINA reported directly to the president, General Pinochet denied any knowledge of the affair and dissociated himself from General Contreras, DINA's commander, whom he accused of lying to him about the affair. After a 1988 plebiscite that in effect removed Pinochet from office, the subsequent civilian government pressed the case against the implicated military officers. In 1992 civilian authorities continued the investigation.

Machetismo 94
A crude and bloody form of political violence that is practiced mainly in rural and local areas. The term is derived from the Spanish word *machete*, the large, heavy-bladed knife used throughout Latin America for cutting sugar cane and vegetation, for construction purposes, and as a weapon. *Machetismo* implies excessive and sometimes uncontrolled violence, in which there is much killing, burning, looting, and destruction of property. The term primarily refers to rural violence in which peasants and common folk participate, but it is occasionally used for urban violence. *See also* POLITICAL VIOLENCE (97); VIOLENCIA, LA (105).

Significance
Machetismo has been used often throughout the post-independence period in all parts of Latin America. It has been used both for maintaining political control and for securing political change, but sometimes it is a violent frenzy accompanying political revenge and punishment. *Machetismo* was widespread in the nineteenth century, when it was the form of political violence on which *caudillos* rode to power. In rural localities, the

ability of leaders to mobilize the work force and exercise authority depended on their willingness to utilize this primitive form of political power. *Machetismo* has continued in the twentieth century and is still evident in peasant revolts, civil wars, and urban terrorism. It has been a typical feature of the revolutions in El Salvador, Guatemala, and Haiti. *La Violencia*, the rural violence that racked the countryside of Colombia from 1948 to 1953 and resulted in more than 160,000 deaths, is an extreme contemporary example. In the 1980s and early 1990s, *machetismo* is very evident in the brutal assassinations, murders, massacres, and extreme violence that characterize the actions of revolutionary and military forces, as well as death squads in El Salvador and Guatemala. Some writers contend that contemporary urban political violence is a form of *machetismo*, but in this case the terms "urban terrorism" and "urban guerrilla warfare" are more commonly used.

Nicaraguan Election of 1990 | 95

A watershed election in which the Nicaraguan Sandinista government was defeated by a coalition of opposition parties headed by conservative forces. The election of 9 February 1990 followed a cease-fire in the civil war between the Sandinista government and the armed resistance, commonly called the contras. Fourteen parties, some small, ranging from left to right, organized into the National Opposition Union (UNO) and supported the presidential candidacy of Violeta Barrios de Chamorro. President Daniel Ortega was the candidate of the Sandinist Front for National Liberation (FSLN), the group that had controlled Nicaragua since the overthrow of the Somoza regime in 1979. The election results were a dramatic reversal for the government: (1) in the presidential race, Chamorro defeated Ortega with 55 percent to 41 percent of the popular vote; (2) for the National Assembly, the UNO won 51 seats, FSLN 39, others 2; and (3) the UNO won control over 102 of 131 municipal councils. The stunning defeat of the government was attributed to the popular opposition to the war and the military draft; the very poor state of the economy and the expectation that the U.S. would give the country substantial aid; authoritarian actions and leftist policies of the Sandinistas that disaffected moderates, the church, coastal Indians, and others; and the government's links to Cuba and the Soviet Union. *See also* CONTRAS (81); SANDINIST FRONT FOR NATIONAL LIBERATION (FSLN) (133).

Significance
The Nicaraguan election was one of few instances when a revolutionary leftist government, permitting free, internationally supervised elections, was defeated in a popular vote. In Nicaragua, 1990 marked the first time since the 1920s that all parties participated in a national election. Violeta Chamorro is the widow of Pedro Juaquín Chamorro, the anti-Somoza newspaper publisher who was assassinated by supporters of the dictator, Anastasio Somoza, in 1978. She took office in April 1990, inheriting a host of problems, including the demobilization of the contras, the continued agitation of Sandinistas for retention of benefits they had gained, the need to restructure a badly torn economy, and the continued control over the military by the Sandinista defense minister, Humberto Ortega. Although the FSLN was defeated, it remained the largest single political party in the nation.

Nicaraguan Revolution | 96

Nicaraguan insurrection led by the Sandinistas, which overthrew the government of Anastasio Somoza Debayle in July 1979. The Sandinista guerrillas were members of the Sandinist National Liberation Front (FSLN), a coalition of several anti-Somoza groups. Sandinistas took their name from Augusto César Sandino, a guerrilla leader who fought the Nicaraguan government and U.S. Marines from 1927 to 1933. The FSLN was composed of only a few hundred men throughout the late 1960s and early 1970s, and its sporadic actions against the Somoza regime did not receive much popular support. In January 1978, the murder of Pedro Joaquín Chamorro, the editor of the conservative anti-Somoza newspaper, *La Prensa*, crystallized public opinion against Somoza. The Broad Front, composed of conservative, liberal, church, professional, and business leaders, called on Somoza to resign, but he refused. Sandinista forces grew, and guerrilla operations were escalated in 1978. A major Sandinista offensive was launched in June 1979, and the rebels, now grown to about 5,000 to 7,000 men, occupied a number of provincial towns and cities and the slums of Managua. Somoza, under pressure from the United States and with his armed forces disintegrating, resigned and fled the country in July 1979. A provisional government composed of Marxist radicals, democratic socialists, moderates, and pro-business leaders assumed power. Within a few years, moderates left the government, which came fully under the control of the Sandinistas, who moved the nation towards a Cuban-style socialistic system, while remaining nominally pluralistic. A civil war followed in which insurgents (the contras), aided by the U.S., fought the government to an apparent draw. A cease-fire and subsequent free election toppled the Sandinistas from the presidency in 1990. *See also* CONTRAS (81); NICARAGUAN ELECTION OF 1990 (95); SANDINIST FRONT FOR NATIONAL LIBERATION (FSLN) (133).

Significance
The Sandinista revolution in Nicaragua was the most successful guerrilla war in Latin America since the Castro revolution in Cuba. Opposition to Somoza was based on his harsh dictatorship and the Somoza family's domination of Nicaragua since 1933. Somoza's great wealth and his control over real estate, transportation, farmland, and construction materials, which he used in order to profit from the rebuilding of Managua after the 1972 earthquake, cost him the support of the middle classes. After the Human Rights Commission of the Organization of American States (OAS) published a report documenting the atrocities committed by the National Guard in the 1978 fighting, international opposition to Somoza grew stronger. In June 1979, the United States, which had supported his regime for many years, proposed that an Inter-American Peace Force be sent to Nicaragua. The Latin nations in the OAS rejected the proposal and instead called on Somoza to resign. By this time Somoza had lost the support of all popular and elite groups within Nicaragua, and he relied on the superior firepower of the National Guard to keep himself in office. As long as he retained the loyalty of the troops and international intervention was minimal, he was able to maintain himself in office. By mid-1979, however, the situation had changed. The Sandinistas were being supported and supplied by several Latin nations, such as Panama and Cuba, and opposition leaders were headquartered in Costa Rica. The United States finally pressured Somoza to resign and gave him asylum. The Nicaraguan revolution caused a great deal of destruction. Some cities and towns were leveled, about 600,000 persons were left homeless, and about 15,000 lives were lost. The nation could not hope to recover without massive amounts of foreign assistance. The Sandinista

government proclaimed democratic goals and adopted a socialist program in part, but its links to Cuba and reliance on Soviet assistance led many to believe that it betrayed the democratic goals of the revolution. The resultant civil war against the contras diverted many resources and caused more deaths and destruction, and the government lost popular support as the economy collapsed. Although the Sandinistas lost the election of 1990, they remain the largest single party in the nation and have been able to retain some of the revolutionary changes that were instituted.

Political Violence | 97 |

The use of measures involving injurious or destructive physical force for political purposes. Methods of political violence include assassination, massacre, execution, torture, rioting, destruction of property, terrorism, and civil war. Individuals and political movements have resorted to political violence to maintain control of government, to secure a political change, to mobilize political power, or to inflict punishment. Violence may be either limited or extensive, organized or spontaneous, rural or urban, involving few or many persons, and official or illegal. *Caudillos*, military regimes, dictators, and revolutionary regimes rely on violent methods to achieve their aims. Repressive dictatorships organize their use of violence under the aegis of the state. The military, secret police, state security agencies, and semisecret civilian gangs or vigilante groups associated with the government are used to flush out, imprison, torture, cause to "disappear," and kill suspected political opponents. Brutal civil wars are often fought with innumerable atrocities and massacres committed against people living in villages or districts suspected of harboring opponents. Popularly based democratic movements that want to install a constitutional system also resort to violence. Methods of securing political change in Latin America involving the use of political violence include *machetismo, golpe de estado* (coup d'etat), civil war, and revolution. These methods can be distinguished from "peaceful" but undemocratic methods of political control or change, such as *continuismo, imposición*, and bloodless coups. Narcoterrorism, or the killing of government officials, judges and others who attempt to control drug trafficking, is a form of political violence that pursues mercenary rather than revolutionary goals. *See also* POLITICAL VIOLENCE THEORY (98); VIOLENCIA, LA (105).

Significance
The tendency to rely on political violence to achieve political ends is a typical feature of Latin American politics. No Latin American country has escaped violence since independence, and violence still pervades the region today. It is the bulwark of dictatorial regimes and the method favored by revolutionary movements. Because violence has been so pervasive, it has been much studied, but it is not universally condemned as a moral evil. Revolutionaries of various kinds, including those with democratic goals, regularly write books and pamphlets that seek to justify the adoption, explain the techniques, and call for the use of violence. There is also a great amount of scholarly literature in which theorists attempt to explain the causes for the high incidence of violence throughout Latin American history. No completely satisfactory explanation exists, however, and political violence continues in both developed and less developed nations in the region.

Political Violence Theory | 98 |

A class of theories that seek to explain the high incidence of political violence in Latin American history. A host of factors have been cited in scholarly literature as causes or positive correlations of political violence in the region. In the nineteenth century, when the large extent of political violence became obvious, some Latin writers advanced rudimentary explanations that stressed a racial or ethnic factor, arguing that Indian, black, or mixed racial groups were more prone to violence than the white race. Others posited a type of geographical determinism and drew a close relationship between the tropical climate of Latin America and the inclination to violence. These two ideas have been discarded in recent times, and current theorists tend to stress cultural, political, economic, social, or psychological factors. Examples of these latter theories include those explanations that emphasize: (1) Latin cultural characteristics, such as the role of *machismo*, mistrust of others, admiration of the strong man, and the low status of democratic values; (2) political factors, such as the intensity of partisanship, the poor quality of leadership, and the ineffectiveness of political parties; (3) economic factors, such as the unequal distribution of wealth, the elite control of productive property, and the actual or perceived deprivation of material goods; (4) social aspects, such as the interclass struggle, the atomization and alienation of the individual, and the breakdown of traditional social restraints; and (5) psychological interpretations, such as the instinctive or learned aggressive behavior that is exacerbated by the violent traditions of the region or frustrated by unfulfilled social and economic expectations. *See also* POLITICAL VIOLENCE (97).

Significance
Because the phenomenon of political violence in Latin American history is so extensive and the intellectual challenge so inviting, many theories of political violence have been advanced. These explanations range from the simplistic to the complex, using both single and multifactor approaches. Recent explanations have moved from the more rudimentary racial, geographic, and institutional approaches to more complex social and psychological ones. Many contemporary studies, however, often lack a comparative focus and assume that all Latin American societies are alike and that Latin American history is much more violent than European history in its comparable periods of national development. Close comparisons show, however, that Latin American revolutions are no more violent than European or Asian ones, and that intraregional wars are indeed fewer and much less bloody than those of Europe, Asia, and the Middle East. In many of these explanations, Latin American political violence is viewed as a moral evil, a societal aberration, and a curable disease.

Redemocratization | 99 |
The process by which a nation under military rule or civilian dictatorship returns to a democratic form of government. Redemocratization takes place in those nations that had a working form of democracy before falling to military intervention, personal dictatorship, or a revolutionary movement that suspended democratic liberties and procedures. The process of redemocratization typically follows an erratic path of piecemeal changes that result in the reestablishment of political democracy. These changes include those in which political censorship of the media is eliminated, civil liberties are reintroduced, political exiles are permitted to return, political prisoners are freed, additional political parties are legalized, restrictions are lifted from the operations of interest groups, local or state elections are permitted, a new constitution is

drafted by a freely elected constituent assembly, and a government that is chosen by the people in competitive national elections takes office. Problems facing new democratic governments include matters such as maintaining the democratic coalition that may have overcome the previous regime, continuing or changing of former economic policies, integrating the society following years of social strife, deciding whether to bring to trial former leaders who may have committed criminal acts, and adopting policies that may have the effect of encouraging the military or undemocratic forces to overthrow the new government. *See also* DEMILITARIZATION (142).

Significance
Redemocratization should be distinguished from demilitarization, which may involve only the return of government to civilian rule in a society that may have little experience with democracy. Redemocratization typically involves the reinstitutionalization of political democracy, rather than a wholesale adoption of social democracy. The process may stop at the level of the politics and policies of the past. The fundamental goal that the forces for democracy agree on is to displace the dictatorial government in office. The coalition favoring democracy may include widely disparate groups as conservative business interests, traditional liberal democrats, socialists, and others who have a different vision of democracy. The parties believe that under a freely competitive system they may be able to lead the nation in establishing a form of democracy that reflects their vision. In the 1980s redemocratization occurred in a number of Latin nations that had fallen to military governments or restrictive revolutionary movements in the 1960s and 1970s. Brazil, Uruguay, and Chile are typical examples. Argentina and Peru also returned to a democratic form of government, but their record of political democracy in the twentieth century has been less consistent. Popularly elected governments were chosen in other nations, but they had little democratic tradition to rely on and their new governments stood on shaky grounds.

Revolution $\boxed{100}$

Fundamental transformation of the political, economic, and social systems in a state that results from the overthrowing of established power structures. In Latin America, revolution has been encouraged by a host of political, social, and economic factors, including the lack of political or social democracy, the concentration of wealth and poor distribution of national resources, extreme poverty, the population explosion, growing urbanization, concentration of land ownership, frustrations growing out of failures to achieve development goals, rigid class structures, and support for revolutionary movements by non-hemispheric powers. External factors include the success of the Cuban revolution and political and material support from Cuba, the Soviet Union, and other socialist states. Following Castro's successful overthrow of the dictatorship of Fulgencio Batista in 1959, *Fidelista* movements sprang up in most of the countries of Latin America. Such movements have typically engaged in insurgency against the governing elite, consisting in most states of dictatorships, oligarchies supported by the armed forces, or direct rule by military juntas. Tactics used include rural and urban guerrilla war, kidnappings and murders by terrorists, bank robberies, efforts to win the support of particular social groups such as peasants and the urban poor, political assassinations, and ideological penetration of the armed forces. Links with narcotraffickers and control of coca-growing areas by guerrilla forces became more evident in the late 1980s and early 1990s. After revolutionary forces win power, the new governments typically institute major political, economic, and social changes. Relations with foreign states may be seriously affected as a result of expropriation of foreign-owned property. *See also* DEVELOPMENT STRATEGY: REVOLUTIONARY APPROACH (185); FIDELISTA (89); GUERRILLA WARFARE: FOCO THEORY (90); GUERRILLA WARFARE: URBAN WARFARE THEORY (91).

Significance
After more than 34 years, the Cuban Revolution remains the only example of a full-scale revolution in Latin America. Castroism was the leading revolutionary ideology influencing insurgent movements, but it was influenced by and competed with other revolutionary dogmas and "calls to arms" proclaimed by such diverse revolutionary personalities as Vladimir Lenin, Mao Zedong, Leon Trotsky, and Ho Chi Minh. Support for revolutionary movements in Latin America has come mainly from the Soviet Union, China, and Cuba. For revolutionary socialists, one leading issue—whether or not Latin revolutions should be peaceful or violent—was answered definitively by the ill-fated experience of Salvador Allende's Marxist government in Chile in 1973. This effort to undertake a peaceful revolution was overthrown by the military, which was assisted by the U.S. Central Intelligence Agency (CIA) and large multinational corporations' efforts to destabilize the new government. Another issue—whether or not Latin revolutions should be guided by the Cuban, Russian, or Chinese approaches—has apparently been answered by the development of heterogeneous revolutionary movements in each country. A major tactical issue—whether revolution should operate mainly from a rural or urban base—seems to depend upon the nature of the agricultural system, the amount of discontent among the peons, and the level of urbanization in each country. The 1970s and 1980s saw significant revolutionary movements in Central America and some nations of South America; this period was also marked by military coups and repressive governments that quashed or limited revolutionary and reformist forces. As the 1990s unfolded, Central American revolutionary movements were being limited and controlled, and Cuba had lost its élan and influence in the face of the failure of communist systems in Europe. In South America, however, political violence, terrorism, and revolutionary activities were common in some nations, such as in Peru, where the Maoist Shining Path movement controlled parts of the countryside and threatened urban areas with its terrorist tactics. General experience since the end of World War II, however, tends to emphasize the conservative nature of the masses, the power of the military, and the tendency of terror tactics to evoke popular revulsion rather than encourage popular uprisings.

Shining Path (Sendero Luminoso) | 101 |

Maoist communist revolutionary movement in Peru that is the major threat to the existing political system. The Shining Path *(Sendero Luminoso*—SL) movement is an extremist terrorist group that is highly disciplined and uses all forms of violence against government officials, police, military, labor leaders, journalists, political opponents, other revolutionary groups, uncooperative peasants, the urban poor, and the public at large. Their general goal, based in part on the Cultural Revolution of Mao Zedong in China and the ideas of José Carlos Mariátegui of Peru, apparently is to create a primitive, agrarian society under totalitarian rule. Senderos number about 3,500 and also have about 2,000 others in local guerrilla groups. Their ruthless methods are condemned by other revolutionary groups, such as the Tupac Amarú Revolutionary Movement, which has more conventional Marxist revolutionary goals. The movement is headed by Abimael Guzmán.

Significance
Since 1980 the *Sendero Luminoso* has conducted a vicious terrorist guerrilla war that has claimed about 25,000 lives. The movement has spread from the southern highlands area near Ayacucho to Lima and other urban areas. Senderos control substantial portions of Huallaga Valley, the prime coca leaf–growing area of Peru, from which they derive much of their income. In early 1992 about 50 percent of the country was under emergency rule. Senderos have often carried out operations in Lima, disrupting public utilities such as electric power and water supplies. Many people living in urban shantytowns are intimidated or under their control. The Peruvian military's attempt to repress the SL with brutal tactics has not succeeded. In April 1992, President Alberto Fujimori, with support of the military, suspended the constitution, dismissed Congress, and assumed dictatorial powers in an attempt to turn the tide. Some observers have concluded, however, that this effort may backfire and give the Shining Path more opportunities for increasing its strength.

Tontons Macoutes | 102 |
The semisecret police force of Haiti that was established by President François Duvalier. Over the years *tontons macoutes* numbered from 2,000 to 5,000 men mostly drawn from the lower social classes. They were armed civilian thugs loosely organized into gangs that terrorized the people. They engaged in officially sanctioned spying, blackmail, extortion, torture, rape, and murder. A major instrument by which Duvalier maintained his police states, *tontons macoutes* reported directly to him. Members were used to crush opposition, eliminate Duvalier's enemies or drive them into exile, and strike fear in the hearts of the people. The term is also used in a wider sense in reference to the large national network of political activists, elite guards, regular secret police, and other persons placed in governmental and private enterprise positions who made up Duvalier's power base and who were also active in post-Duvalier years. *See also* POLITICAL VIOLENCE (97).

Significance
In *Créole,* the language used by the masses in Haiti, *tonton macoute* means "bagman" or "bogeyman," a dreaded mythological figure who kidnapped children. Under Duvalier's regime, *tontons macoutes* were an effective instrument in a political system that rested on coercion and fear. Because their many atrocities attracted international criticism in recent years, some leaders of the *tontons macoutes* were arrested and the groups' activities were restricted. After Duvalier's death in 1971, power was transferred to his son, Jean-Claude Duvalier, who restricted some of the activities of the *tontons macoutes* but fled in 1986 when officially sanctioned violence led to popular riots. In the chaotic years that followed, brutal violence by the *tontons macoutes*, the police, and the military have characterized Haitian politics and the daily life of the people.

Tupac Amarú Revolutionary Movement | 103 |
An urban-based revolutionary movement in Peru that became active in the mid-1980s. The Tupac

Amarú Revolutionary Movement (MRTA) has used political and military means to achieve its aim of establishing a revolutionary society along conventional Marxist lines in Peru. It has drawn its program primarily from José Carlos Mariátegui, a Marxist revolutionary intellectual who adapted the theory to Peruvian conditions. Primarily based in and near Lima, the MRTA has about 2,500 guerrillas who engage in terrorist acts, such as bombing electric power lines. The name is taken from Tupac Amarú, the last of the Inca line who fought Spain in the sixteenth century, and from an Indian who took this name in the 1780s and organized a large revolutionary force, but who was also crushed by the Spanish colonial government. The Tupac Amarú Revolutionary Movement in Peru should not be confused with the Tupamaros of Uruguay, an urban revolutionary movement with a similar name. That group was active in the late 1960s and 1970s, and it was brutally crushed by the Uruguayan military.

Significance
The Tupac Amarú Revolutionary Movement is smaller and less threatening to the Peruvian system than the Shining Path *(Sendero Luminoso)* revolutionary guerrillas. In the early 1980s the MRTA considered Senderos as fellow revolutionaries against the repressive Peruvian government, but this view ceased when MRTA militants were attacked by Senderos. The Shining Path is now viewed by the MRTA as uncontrolled terrorists whose vision of a Maoist, utopian, rural society is unrealistic, and who are contaminated by their collaboration with drug traffickers. In early 1992 the MRTA was moving towards abandoning the military approach to revolutionary change, but when President Alberto Fujimori instituted a coup d'etat, suspended the constitution, and dismissed Congress in April 1992, this transition to peaceful change was in doubt.

Twenty-Sixth of July Movement | 104 |
Fidel Castro's political organization of supporters and guerrilla fighters that helped to overthrow the Batista government in Cuba in 1959. The 26th of July Movement *(Movimiento 26 de Julio)* was named for 26 July 1953, the day Castro and a band of followers unsuccessfully attacked the Moncado army barracks in Santiago de Cuba. Following his imprisonment for this affair, Castro organized the movement in 1955 largely from urban middle class and student members of the *Ortodoxo* party, a reformist group. After Castro took power in January 1959, he permitted the 26th of July Movement to lapse, and he later amalgamated his followers with other radical organizations, including the old, orthodox Communist party, into a new Communist Party of Cuba (PCC). *See also* CASTROISM (54); COMMUNIST PARTY OF CUBA (PCC) (114).

Significance
The 26th of July Movement, and especially its guerrilla army, was a prime instrument that Castro used successfully to defeat Batista's forces. Although most of the fighting occurred in the rural areas of eastern Cuba, the members of the movement and guerrilla fighters were drawn primarily from urban areas and the middle class, and they included both radicals and reformists. By the end of 1959, however, most of the reformists had been purged from party and governmental posts, and some of the more noteworthy reformists, such as Hubert Matos, were imprisoned. The leadership of the Communist Party of Cuba is primarily made up of guerrilla fighters and "old" Communists, with the original Castro group predominating.

Violencia, La | 105 |
The common name for the virtual civil war that racked the rural areas

of Colombia, especially in the period from 1948 to 1953. *La Violencia* (The Violence) began on a small scale in 1946, was intensified by the April 1948 riots in Bogotá (the *bogotazo*), and continued sporadically until 1958 when the government ended the state of siege for most of the country. Primarily a rural partisan conflict between Conservatives and Liberals, the guerrilla war was also marked by banditry, criminal lawlessness, and personal feuds. The violent upheaval was also fed by the ultra-reactionary Conservative government of Laureano Gómez, which hunted down Liberals and purged them from the police force, local government, and the military. The destruction of lives and property was enormous, and thousands of rural residents fled to the cities. In some provinces, villages were destroyed and the residents slaughtered. Estimates of deaths range from 160,000 to 200,000, or almost 2 percent of the total population. After 1958 the political aspects of the rural violence subsided, although criminal banditry and personal vendettas continued in some localities. In the 1980s, however, the thousands of murders associated with drug trafficking and narcoterrorism became the new form of violence that continues to plague Colombia. *See also* BOGOTAZO (80); NATIONAL FRONT (COLOMBIA) (126); POLITICAL VIOLENCE (97).

Significance

La Violencia has had a profound impact on the political system of Colombia. Explanations for the ferocity and extent of this phenomenon have pointed to the tradition of political violence in Colombian history, the strong quasi-religious commitment to political parties, and a host of social, economic, and political factors. The violence occurred at a time when the smaller, reactionary Conservative party, which controlled the government, tried to limit the rising power of the larger Liberal party. The clerical-authoritarian Conservative government of Laureano Gómez (1950–1953) was replaced by the more brutal dictatorship of General Gustavo Rojas Pinilla (1953–1957). After Rojas fell, the Conservatives and Liberals, in order to establish a stable and peaceful democratic system, agreed to share government offices equally and to alternate the presidency between them.

Political Parties, Interest Groups, and Elections

American Popular Revolutionary Alliance (APRA) | 106 |

The largest political party in Peru and the prototype for democratic revolutionary parties in Latin America. APRA was organized in 1924 by Victor Raúl Haya de la Torre, a man who led the party for over 50 years. The party's original program, called *Aprismo* from its acronym, included the principles of land reform, nationalization of industry, solidarity of all oppressed classes, internationalization of the Panama Canal, opposition to Yankee imperialism, and political unity of Latin America. The party later adopted a full range of economic and social reforms, promoted the extension of political democracy, and opposed communism. APRA was organized as a multiclass mass party, and its program appealed to workers, peasants, students, professionals, intellectuals, and middle classes. It was later called the Peruvian Aprista Party *(Partido Aprista Peruano)*. *See also* NATIONAL REVOLUTIONARY PARTIES (127).

Significance
APRA became the largest political party in Peru, and its social reform program was very influential throughout Latin America. Other national revolutionary parties of the democratic left in the region came to be called *Aprista*-type parties. For much of the time in Peru, however, Haya de la Torre was in exile and APRA was banned. Because the military would not permit APRA to take control of the government despite its popular support, APRA was forced to play the role of loyal opposition or remain illegal. In the 1950s and early 1960s, APRA made alliances with conservative forces in an attempt to regain its legal status. This action split the party and caused it to lose popular support to Popular Action (AP), the centrist party of Fernando Belaúnde Terry. The military, led by General Juan Velasco Alvarado, overthrew Belaúnde's government in 1968 when it became dissatisfied with the slow pace of economic and social change and feared that APRA would win the presidential election

of 1969. Once in power, however, the military made a revolution of its own, initiating sweeping economic changes by collectivizing all large-scale productive property. This, in effect, put into practice many of the economic principles, but not the democratic ideals, of *Aprismo*. In 1978, President General Francisco Morales Bermudez permitted the election of a constituent assembly to draft a new constitution, and APRA, under Haya's leadership until his death in 1979, emerged again as the largest party. The presidential election of 1980 was won by Belaúnde Terry, but APRA won the subsequent election. The first APRA president of Peru was Alán García, who served from 1985 to 1990. His administration was an economic disaster, and the party fared poorly in the election of 1990.

Blanco Party (National Party) 107

The conservative party in Uruguay and traditional opponent of the Colorado party. The Blancos *(Partido Nacional)* trace their origins and common name to the 1830s, when conservative rural forces adopted the white *(blanco)* banner in their civil wars against the liberals, who adopted the red *(colorado)* banner. The civil wars between the Blancos and Colorados ended in 1904, but their political rivalry continued throughout the twentieth century. The predominant Blanco leader in the twentieth century was Luis Alberto de Herrera, a reactionary who controlled the party from 1920 until his death in 1959. After World War II, the Blanco party, always subject to more splits than the Colorados, had several important factions, including a progressive wing and the conservative Herreristas. Most Blanco support is drawn from rural areas, large landowners, and the urban upper classes. *See also* COLORADO PARTY (URUGUAY) (111); LEMA ELECTION SYSTEM (123).

Significance
For much of its history, the Blanco party has served as the main opposition party in the Uruguayan party system, which usually has been dominated by the Colorados. In the post–World War II period, however, Blancos controlled the presidency from 1958 to 1964. The late 1960s were a period of turmoil in Uruguay, and Colorado popular support suffered from major economic problems and from urban guerrilla operations undertaken by the Tupamaros. In the 1971 presidential election the progressive Blanco candidate, Wilson Ferreira Aldunate, received 50,000 more votes than the Colorado candidate, but he lost the election under the nation's complex *lema* election system. As Tupamaro violence mounted, parties were banned, and in 1976 the military removed the Colorado president, Juan María Bordaberry. When civilian government elections were restored in 1984, the Colorado candidate won the presidency and the Blancos resumed their position as the second party. The Blanco party received the most votes in the presidential election of 1989, and the leading Blanco candidate, Luis Alberto Lacalle, became president.

Candidato Único 108

An election in which there is only one candidate running for office. A *candidato único* election occurs: (1) following a military coup, when the dominant general wishes to legitimize his regime; (2) when traditional *caudillos* or modern dictators desire to stay in office and prefer not to use an alternate system known as *imposición*, in which other persons or groups may compete but only ineffectually; (3) when opposition political parties refuse to slate candidates or withdraw their candidates because they suspect that the election is rigged; and (4) in a modern one-party or dominant-party system when no opposition is permitted or none chooses to run. *Candidato único* differs from *imposición* in that, although both are used to ensure the continuation in power of the dominant person or group, in *imposición* voters are given a choice on the ballot even though it is usually meaningless. *See also* ALTERNATION AND PARITY (ALTERNACIÓN Y PARIDAD) (156); CONTINUISMO (161); IMPOSICIÓN (119).

Significance
The system of *candidato único* is little used today because, although rigged elections still occur, the system of *imposición* is a more respectable and "democratic" way to ensure results. Sometimes, however, an attempt at *imposición* will result in *candidato único* when an opposition group that is permitted to function withdraws or refuses to run candidates. Classic examples of *candidato único* include the 1948 election of General Manuel A. Odría in Peru and the 1954 and 1958 elections of General Alfredo Stroessner in Paraguay. A special form of *candidato único* based on the agreement of the two major parties was used in Colombia from 1958 to 1974. In order to put an end to the devastating partisan violence that rocked the country for years, the Liberals and Conservatives agreed to a constitutional change that ended partisan competition for 16 years. Only the two major parties were permitted to contest elections, the presidency was alternated between the two parties, and, regardless of party strength, legislative seats were equally divided between them. This system of alternation and parity, known as the National Front, eventually produced voter apathy, party factionalism, and the infiltration of the two major parties by opposition groups.

Church-State Relations 109

An issue in most Latin American states that refers to and often questions the role of the Roman Catholic church as an active force in political, economic, and social decision processes. The church, along with the military and the landed aristocracy, has been a powerful actor in the political systems of the region since the first Spanish and Portuguese colonies were established. By the beginning of the twentieth century, the Vatican carried on diplomatic relations with all of the nations of Latin America through papal nuncios (statesmen having rank equal to ambassadors), and church influence was transmitted through these as well as through church channels. Yet anticlericalism also developed as a powerful force, balancing the power and influence of the church. The church's power—and the counterforce of anticlericalism produced by that power—relates (1) to the fact that about 90 percent of the people of Latin America are Roman Catholic; (2) to the historical ownership of much property by the church, with many people directly or indirectly employed by the church; (3) to the role of clerical parties and the influence the church exerts over moderate and conservative parties; and (4) to the strong position taken by the church on social issues, which for many years was a major obstacle to social change and, in recent years, has been a strong support for moderate social and economic reform. During the 1960s and 1970s, some Catholic leaders in Latin America began to formulate a theology of liberation that supports left-wing causes and justifies revolution when necessary to change the established order to create a more equitable, just social system. In 1979, however, Pope John Paul II repudiated the idea of direct church involvement in Marxist or other causes calling for violent revolutionary change, but supported the need to achieve a just social order. These appeals for social reform and aid to the poor continued in the 1980s and 1990s, along with admonitions to priests to not participate directly in political life. *See also* ANTICLERICALISM (50); LIBERATION THEOLOGY (69).

Significance
The major goals of the Roman Catholic church as far as church-state relations in Latin America are concerned are to resist anticlericalism, influence state policies that relate to Catholic doctrine, encourage reform through moderate policies of economic and social change, and combat Marxism in all its Latin forms. Conservatives throughout Latin America continue to espouse tradition and authority as they emanate from church doctrine, whereas Catholic liberals want to use the church as a vehicle to establish democratic constitutional systems that undertake programs to combat poverty and underdevelopment. Key church-state issues in many countries have focused on population problems, with the church adamantly in opposition to birth control and abortion. To develop common church policy, the Conference of Latin American Bishops (CELAM) was established in 1953. In 1968, Pope Paul VI became the first pontiff to visit the region, and Pope John Paul II also demonstrated a growing concern with the church's position in Latin America with visits in 1979 and 1983. Both pontiffs addressed the CELAM, balancing their calls for social reform with theological conservatism. Since over half of the world's Catholics live in Latin America, and since that region is having the highest rate of population growth, its importance in church policies is likely to grow.

Colorado Party (Paraguay) | 110 |

The conservative party of Paraguay that has been one of the two major national parties since the nineteenth century. Officially called the National Republican Association (ANR), the Colorado party is composed of a moderate wing—supporting modest reform and a democratic opening—and a more militant wing that favors strong governmental control. General Alfredo Stroessner used the party as the vehicle for his elections and policies from 1954 to 1989. After his overthrow, General Andrés Rodríguez took control of the party and was elected president under its label in 1989 with over 70 percent of the popular vote. Under Paraguay's election system, which grants bonus seats to the largest party, the Colorados control two-thirds of the seats in the congress.

Significance
A traditional conservative party that typically contested the Liberal party for control of the nation for many years, the Colorado party was captured and used by Stroessner during his dictatorship. General Rodríguez, who overthrew the failing Stroessner in 1989, assumed control of the party. The Colorado's major opposition party, the Liberals, have only one-third of the legislative seats, but have been able to win local elections. The relative strength of the two major parties, and the policies that the Colorados will ultimately espouse, will not be fully determined until the nation adopts completely free national elections.

Colorado Party (Uruguay) | 111 |

The progressive liberal party in Uruguay. The origins of the Colorado Party *(Partido Colorado)* are those of a laissez-faire liberal party that traditionally contested the conservative Blanco party throughout much of the nineteenth century. The party was refashioned into a progressive social reform movement at the turn of the century by José Batlle y Odóñez. Deriving most of its support from urban middle and working classes, the Colorado party transformed Uruguay into a democratic, progressive society in the first half of the twentieth century. Uruguayan Colorados are quite unlike the Colorado party in Paraguay, which is a traditional, rural-based conservative party. *See also* BATLLISMO (52); BLANCO PARTY (NATIONAL PARTY) (107); LEMA ELECTION SYSTEM (123).

Significance
The Colorado party dominated Uruguayan politics for most of the time since the mid-nineteenth century. After the Batlle era, the party suffered from intense factionalism, which was encouraged by the nation's *lema* system for holding elections. Colorado presidents were in office when an urban guerrilla group, the Tupamaros, launched a daring series of attacks on the system in the 1960s and 1970s. In 1971, a conservative Colorado candidate, Juan María Bordaberry, won the presidency. Under the election system, he won with only a fourth of the popular vote, fewer than those of a leftist candidate, and substantially fewer than those of the Blanco party candidate. Tupamaros, who had infiltrated the government, revealed the corruption in Bordaberry's administration and the Colorado party's links to big business. The military intervened in 1973 and removed Bordaberry in 1976 when he tried to establish himself as a "constitutional dictator." After the military period, a Colorado candidate, Julio María Sanguinetti, won the 1984 presidential election with 39 percent of the vote. The Colorado candidate in the 1989 election, José Batlle Ibáñez, won only 30 percent of the vote, and the Blanco party won the presidency.

Command for No $\boxed{112}$
A coalition of 16 political parties that successfully won a plebiscite in 1988 rejecting General Augusto Pinochet's plan to continue as president of Chile for another eight-year term. The Command for No, which included parties of the left, center, and right, won by a vote of 54.7 percent to 43 percent. Pinochet honored the popular vote, and under existing rules continued as president for another year. A subsequent plebiscite in 1979 confirmed constitutional changes, and a general election was held in 1990. Most of the parties in the coalition supported the Christian Democrat, Patricio Aylwin, who defeated Hernán Buchi of the National Renovation party, which had supported Pinochet.

Significance
The Command for No, combining parties that opposed Pinochet's 15-year regime, organized an intensive campaign that resulted in a voter turnout of over 90 percent. The plebiscite was conducted under the terms of an authoritarian constitution that Pinochet had installed in 1980, and he expected to win. His strong showing of 43 percent did reveal that many Chileans preferred his government over the uncertainties of civilian rule. Chile's strong civilian, democratic tradition prevailed, however, as the coalition was led by the moderate Christian Democratic party. Bitter memories of the repression under Pinochet and the poor economic performance of the government in the preceding years contributed significantly to the opposition's victory. General Pinochet remained as commander of the armed forces after the new civilian government of Patricio Aylwin was installed in 1990.

Commercial and Industrial Associations $\boxed{113}$
Organizations of large-scale enterprise in the private sector. Private enterprise in Latin America is well organized into a number of national commercial and industrial associations. These include chambers of

commerce, chambers of industry, manufacturing associations, banking and financial associations, and trade associations. Except in Cuba, where private enterprise has been eliminated, these interest groups are closely linked to the government in many ways, such as through formal membership on regulatory and advisory agencies, informal consultation, and political pressure. Administrative and legislative lobbying is extensive, and close, personal relationships exist between businessmen and government officials. Commercial and industrial interests seek a wide variety of benefits from government, including tax exemptions, subsidies, reduction of export duties, favorable credit and monetary policies, and restrictions on labor unions. Commercial interests that are linked to foreign investors and foreign trade are at times in conflict with national businessmen. The former tend to favor free trade while the latter favor protectionism and import substitution. Latin businessmen are often limited in that they lack the superior technology, managerial skills, and investment capital of foreign corporations. *See also* CONSERVATISM (59); GUERRILLA WARFARE: URBAN WARFARE THEORY (91); LIBERALISM (68).

Significance
Commercial and industrial interests exercise great influence in many Latin nations, but in some places they have been under attack by radical and democratic socialist political movements that seek to nationalize natural resources, public utilities, and large-scale enterprises. Businessmen therefore have made links to the landed oligarchy, the military, and other conservative groups to defend the status quo. Where traditional conservative and liberal parties are weak, businessmen and industrialists connect with progressive liberal parties and national revolutionary parties and accept a modest amount of social reform. In Mexico, for example, the dominant Institutional Revolutionary party does not have a sector for large business organizations, but these groups have been able to advance their interests through pressure group activity. Outside of Cuba, commercial and industrial associations remain strong, and their influence increased in the late 1980s as the more developed nations eliminated a large number of state enterprises and adopted policies favoring a free market economy. This was especially the case in Mexico, Chile, Argentina, Brazil, and Venezuela.

Communist Party of Cuba (PCC) 114

The political party established by Fidel Castro in 1965. The Communist Party of Cuba (*Partido Comunista de Cuba*) was the last of three attempts by Castro to combine members of his former guerrilla organization, the 26th of July Movement, with the orthodox communist party in Cuba, the Popular Socialist Party (PSP). The first two attempts were the Integrated Revolutionary Organizations (ORI), created in 1961, and the United Party of the Socialist Revolution (PURS), organized in 1963. The current PCC is patterned on the organizational structure of the former Communist party of the Soviet Union. In the late 1980s, the PCC had about 500,000 members, a Central Committee of approximately 100 members, a 13-member Political Bureau (Politburo), and an 11-member Secretariat. From its inception, Fidel Castro has been the ranking member of the Politburo and the first secretary of the party; his brother, Raúl Castro, has been the second ranking member of the Politburo and the second secretary of the party. Although the PCC was organized in 1965, the first congress of the party (a convention of delegates) was not convened until 1975, when it approved the new constitution for Cuba. The PCC has mobilized most Cubans into its affiliated mass-membership organizations, such as the Committees for the Defense of the Revolution and worker, peasant, and youth groups. All important executive posts in the Cuban government are held by members of the PCC, and about 90 percent of the deputies in the National Assembly are members of the PCC or its affiliated mass organizations. *See also* CASTROISM (54); TWENTY-SIXTH OF JULY MOVEMENT (104).

Significance
The Communist Party of Cuba is the only political party permitted in Cuba. The party is dominated by the charismatic figure of Fidel Castro, and most of the party leaders were originally members of the 26th of July Movement rather than the old Communist party. Relations between Castro and the old Communists have not always been amicable. Castro disbanded the first attempt at unification, the Integrated Revolutionary Organizations, because the old-line Communist leader, Aníbal Escalante, was using his position in the ORI to supplant the Castro group with orthodox Communists. In 1968, Escalante and 34 other old-line Communists were arrested and given long prison sentences for establishing a pro-Soviet "microfaction" in the PCC. However, other orthodox Communists, such as Carlos Rafael Rodríguez and Blas Roca Calderío, hold high party and government posts. Some scholars have debated whether Castro captured control of the old Communists or whether the old Communist party took over his revolution. Such debate, however, seems meaningless, because by 1968 Castro had adopted not only the ideology but also the organizational structures, policies, and pro-Soviet allegiances of the old Communists. Despite the institutionalization that has characterized the Cuban revolution, Castro remains firmly in control, and observers debate whether the party can retain its control over Cuba once Castro leaves the scene, given the fall of communism in Russia.

Democratic Action (AD) | 115 |
The democratic, national revolutionary party of Venezuela, the largest party in the nation. Democratic Action (*Acción Democrática*) was reorganized in 1941 from a previous party that had opposed Venezuelan dictatorships. The newly organized party adopted the principles typical of a social democratic or national revolutionary party. In 1945, under the leadership of Rómulo Betancourt, AD participated with the military in a successful coup. For a three-year period (the *trienio*), Betancourt and Rómulo Gallegos, a constitutionally elected AD president, ruled Venezuela and instituted a number of significant reforms. In 1948, the Gallegos government was overthrown by a military junta that became increasingly harsh when Colonel Marcos Pérez Jiménez assumed the leadership role. Pérez Jiménez's brutal dictatorship was ended in 1958, when he was overthrown after attempting to continue himself in office for another term in violation of the nation's constitution. *Acción Democrática* emerged as the largest of the three mass parties in the democratic period that has existed since 1958. AD candidates have won five of the seven presidential elections in that period: Betancourt in 1958, Raúl Leoni in 1963, Carlos Andrés Pérez in 1973 and 1989, and Jaime Lusinchi in 1984. The elections of 1968 and 1978 were won by the Social Christian Party (COPEI). *See also* NATIONAL REVOLUTIONARY PARTIES (127); SOCIAL CHRISTIAN PARTY (COPEI) (134).

Significance
The Democratic Action party is the largest and best-organized party in Venezuela and is one of the most successful social democratic reformist parties in Latin America. It has functioned as a strong opponent of communism and as a bulwark of the democratic system in Venezuela. Drawing its support from a variety of rural and urban groups, AD has enacted a broad range of social reform measures, including those pertaining to social welfare, education, transportation, economic development, and land reform. In the first Andrés Pérez administration of 1974 to 1979, the party nationalized the petroleum industry and hastened the pace to industrialization. In 1978, however, the AD candidate, Luis Piñerúa Ordaz, lost the presidential election to the Social Christian candidate, Luis Herrera Campins. This defeat was attributed to splits in the party, charges of corruption, an inequitable distribution of the wealth that flowed to the country from petroleum exports, and the adoption of a similar center-left program of social reform by the Social Christian party. Subsequently, AD won two consecutive presidential elections, but the populist and progressive policies of earlier periods have been affected by economic decline, a drop in oil revenues, large foreign debt, inflation, and public disorders and food riots in 1989. In his second administration, Pérez adopted conservative economic policies, including price increases, wage cuts, subsidy and budget reductions, and privatization of some state firms.

Dominant Party System | 116

A semi-competitive political party system in which a single party wins a substantial majority of the popular vote and controls the political system. In a typical dominant party system, other parties compete in elections but win only a few seats in the congress. The dominant party system can be distinguished from the one-party system, in which a single party is authorized by law and noncompetitive elections are held for the purpose of legitimizing a dictatorial regime. The dominant party system often develops following a major political event, such as a war, revolution, or the gaining of independence, when a victorious nationalist party takes power and retains the loyalty of the masses. *See also* INSTITUTIONAL REVOLUTIONARY PARTY (PRI) (120); POLITICAL PARTY (131).

Significance
The dominant party system in Latin America is unlikely to arise under freely competitive conditions. Mexico comes closest to fitting the dominant party system model. There the Institutional Revolutionary Party (PRI) has for many years won about 85 to 90 percent of the popular vote in presidential elections, all Senate seats and governorships, and about 85 percent of seats in the Chamber of Deputies. Thus, some observers viewed most of the establishment minor parties in Mexico as collaborators of the PRI, asserting that these parties were permitted to win a few seats so long as they did not threaten the prestige and the dominant power position of the PRI. The dominant party system in Mexico, however, has been threatened by the rising power of the conservative National Action Party (PAN) and by a serious defection of the left wing in the elections of 1988. The PRI presidential candidate, Carlos Salinas, was declared the official winner with only 50.4 percent of the vote; the opposition won 48 percent of the Chamber of Deputies and four Senate seats. The PRI remained in firm control, however, as it recouped some losses in later elections.

Election System | 117

A method by which electors select government officials by casting votes. A wide variety of election systems are used in Latin America, including both direct, popular elections and indirect elections in which an electoral college or other body makes the choice. All lower chambers of the legislature, including the unicameral legislatures of Central America and Paraguay, are chosen directly by the people. Some of the election systems used to select legislators include: (1) single-member district elections, in which the candidate receiving the most votes wins the seat; (2) proportional representation (PR), which generally assigns seats to competing parties on the basis of the size of their popular vote; (3) bonus systems, in which the leading party receives a greater percentage of seats than its popular vote would indicate; (4) minority representation or limited voting, which produces seats for minority parties because the voter has fewer choices than the total number of seats to be filled in his district; (5) minimum percentage requirements, by which parties must win a certain percentage of the popular vote in order to win any seats; and (6) shared or parity systems, in which all seats are divided equally or disproportionately between the two leading parties, and other competing parties are denied any seats. Elections for chief executives are for the most part of the direct, popular, simple plurality or majority runoff type; however, some presidents are chosen by electoral colleges or by the legislature. *See also* LEMA ELECTION SYSTEM (123); SUFFRAGE (136).

Significance
A great variety of election systems are used in Latin America. The selection of a certain method by the ruling group usually serves some particular purposes, including efforts to: (1) maximize the choices available to the voter and represent all shades of opinions in the nation; (2) guarantee the representation of the largest political minority group while not permitting smaller groups to weaken either of the two larger parties; and (3) limit competition or eliminate it altogether, thus assuring unity and stability within the government. When full competition is permitted, most Latin American countries have chosen some kind of proportional representation system. These PR systems are usually associated with a large number of parties represented in the legislature and tend to result in unstable legislative majorities. Venezuela, Chile, and Uruguay are typical examples. Mexico, Brazil, the Dominican Republic, and Honduras at times have used the single-member district system. Ordinarily, this type of system reduces the number of parties that can compete effectively for power. Before and after the military period from 1964 to 1985, Brazil used proportional representation for assembly elections and direct popular elections for the presidency. Mexico introduced PR for 200 of 500 legislative seats in the 1960s, but when the opposition captured 48 percent of the seats in 1988, it provided that the leading party would be given over 50 percent of the seats. Before the 1973 military coup in Chile, the election system provided that the congress choose between the two leading presidential candidates when no absolute majority results from a popular election. This system was used in 1970 to elect the Marxist Socialist, Salvador Allende, as president of Chile, and it was readopted with the return of democracy in 1989. Uruguay uses an election system called the *lema* system, in which a primary and general election are combined on the same ballot. The Cuban Communist Constitution of 1976 provided for direct elections only to municipal councils, but direct elections for the National Assembly were introduced in 1992; the executive body, the Council of State, is chosen by the Na-

tional Assembly. Regardless of the formal election system used, free, fully competitive elections have been rare throughout the history of Latin America. Many elections have been fraudulent, competition has been restricted to acceptable groups, literacy or other requirements have limited participation, and elections have been suspended or the results set aside by unconstitutional assumptions of power.

Febrerista Movement $\boxed{118}$

A Paraguayan political movement that originated in the February 1936 coup of Colonel Rafael Franco. *Febrerismo* fed on the dissatisfactions that resulted from the peace settlements of the Chaco War. Patterned in part on European authoritarian movements of the 1930s, it called for a corporatist state that would integrate the social classes, practice economic nationalism, engage in state intervention into the economy, and institute agrarian and labor reforms. Originally a party of diverse social groups, it suffered from a number of splits. The core of the party moved to the left and adopted social democratic policies similar to those of a national revolutionary party of the *Aprista* type. In 1951 it was formally named *Partido Febrerista Revolucionario* or Revolutionary February Party (PRF). *See also* CHACO WAR (25); NATIONAL REVOLUTIONARY PARTIES (127).

Significance
Febreristas controlled the government of Paraguay for only a brief period from 1936 to 1937. Their influence on the national political system was important but not as lasting as that of the *Aprista* parties in Peru and Bolivia. The *Febrerista* party was banned from 1937 to 1964, and its leaders were jailed or exiled by military dictatorships. Having lost what popular base it once had, the party currently is composed of urban middle-class supporters, primarily intellectuals, professionals, and students. A small and divided party, it played only a minor role in the authoritarian system of General Alfredo Stroessner from 1954 to 1989. Following his overthrow, the PRF was unable to win any seats in the 1989 elections.

Imposición $\boxed{119}$

A method used for the peaceful transfer or maintenance of power by elections in which the dominant political group selects the candidate (or issue) and manipulates the electoral process to impose its will on the nation. *Imposición* is possible when the governing person or group: (1) is in control of the electoral machinery and the laws governing elections; (2) has so much prestige or power that opposition is meaningless; or (3) controls through a one-party or dominant-party system. Methods used to rig elections include: (1) banning opposition political parties from participating in the election; (2) jailing or exiling major opposition leaders; (3) eliminating the secret ballot and requiring oral voting; (4) pressuring voters by the threat of administrative or economic sanctions to vote for the government's choice; (5) censoring newspapers and prohibiting speeches or demonstrations; and (6) stuffing ballot boxes or counting ballots fraudulently. Unlike the single-candidate election *(candidato único)*, *imposición* implies that the voter is given a choice on the ballot, however meaningless this choice may be in practice. Consequently, because a choice is possible, the government is in the paradoxical position of constantly proclaiming that the elections are fair, while at the same time doing whatever is necessary to ensure its victory. Sometimes *imposición* is so blatant that opposition groups cast blank ballots, boycott the elections, or refuse to run candidates. An *imposición* that involves the president trying to continue himself in office beyond constitutional limits *(continuismo)* often invokes resentment and may lead to attempts to remove him by force. Consequently, the control or cooperation of the military is usually essential in a successful *imposición*. *See also* CANDIDATO ÚNICO (108); CONTINUISMO (161); ELECTION SYSTEM (117).

Significance
Imposición was used in the nineteenth century throughout Latin America. In the mid-twentieth century, the method was still utilized in both large and small as well as in less-developed and more-developed countries. More sophisticated methods are associated with the contemporary use of *imposición*, but cruder methods involving force and coercion are still used at times, particularly in rural areas. In Mexico, for example, the Institutional Revolutionary Party (PRI) has won all presidential elections, almost all senate seats and governorships, and most seats in the Chamber of Deputies. Some scholars believe that this dominant party system is a civilized form of *imposición*.

Institutional Revolutionary Party (PRI) | 120 |

The dominant political party in Mexico and heir to the leadership of the Mexican Revolution. The political party of the Mexican Revolution was first organized as the National Revolutionary Party (PNR) in 1929, renamed the Party of the Mexican Revolution (PRM) in 1937, and reorganized as the Institutional Revolutionary Party *(Partido Revolucionario Institucional,* PRI) in 1946. The PRI is composed of: (1) the agrarian sector, consisting primarily of *ejidatarios* (communal-farm peasants) in the National Peasants Confederation (CNC); (2) the labor sector, dominated by urban workers in the Confederation of Mexican Workers (CTM); and (3) the popular sector, which includes middle class organizations, such as teachers, small farmers, small businessmen, artisans, intellectuals, and youth groups. A military sector of the party was eliminated in 1940, and all presidents of Mexico since 1946 have been civilians. In theory, the principles of the PRI are identical with those of the Mexican Revolution and include land reform, economic nationalism, social welfarism, economic development, the non-reelection system, and an independent foreign policy. *See also* DOMINANT PARTY SYSTEM (116); EJIDO (3); MEXICAN CONSTITUTION OF 1917 (172); MEXICAN REVOLUTION (37).

Significance
The Institutional Revolutionary party has dominated Mexican politics since it was first organized in 1929. Until 1988 the PRI won presidential elections with about 80 to 90 percent of the popular vote, all senate seats, all governorships, and about 80 percent of the seats in the Chamber of Deputies. First organized as a coalition of parties and groups that supported the revolution, the party's prime function is to mobilize, aggregate, and represent these interests. Decisions are made within the party by a complex system of consultation and consensus, but power is held by the president and party oligarchs. Liberal and conservative wings exist within the party, and a practice has developed that alternates liberal presidents with conservatives ones. The PRI is identified with both the Mexican government and the revolution, and the achievements and failures of the government and the revolution reflect on the party. However, as a practical, governing party concerned with retaining power, meeting patronage demands, and serving sector interests, the PRI often fails to apply revolutionary principles.

Critics charge that the party, like the government, is the representative of the new middle class and not of the working class and peasants. Occasional revolts against PRI rule before 1988 were ineffectual because the dominant party system ensured PRI control, but in the watershed election of that year, the PRI won the presidency by only 50.4 percent and the Chamber of Deputies by 52 percent. Although the party retained control of the national government and all but a few states and municipalities in subsequent elections, observers concluded that Mexico had entered a new era of politics in which the PRI's dominant position may be seriously curtailed.

Interest Group | 121 |

A group of persons organized around economic system, occupation, region, ethnic group, race, gender, religion, or other major characteristic. An interest group is concerned with protecting and promoting the rights and goals of its members by attempting to influence public opinion and public policy. Activities include supporting particular political parties and candidates, legislative and administrative lobbying, participation in governmental councils and committees, public demonstrations, strikes, and the like. Typically, an interest group maintains an organizational structure separate from political parties, but there may be overlapping membership and leaders. In some cases, organized interest groups are direct members of a political party. Often called pressure groups, interest groups vary significantly in their ability to influence the outcome of governmental policy. Some societal interests are not organized and have no influence at all. *See also* CORPORATISM (61).

Significance
In Latin America, economic interest groups are well organized in many states and have had significant influence on the processes and policies of government. In nations where political parties are weak and governmental instability the norm, interest group organizations have provided the mechanisms for achieving the objectives of their members. Commercial, industrial, labor, peasant, professional, and military societies are integral features of Latin political systems. In many nations, the larger economic interests are linked to governmental agencies through corporatist institutions, in which consultation takes place. In Mexico, labor, peasant, and public service organizations are sector members of the dominant government party, the PRI.

Landed Oligarchy | 122 |

The small class of wealthy landlords who at times act as the ruling class. The landed oligarchy (*oligarchia*) is a small percentage of the rural population, but its members have great wealth, social prestige, and political influence. These characteristics derive from two fundamental features of agrarian life in Latin America—the large concentrations of land held by a few owners and the dependent relationships peasants have to landowners. The landed oligarchy has a traditional conservative approach to economic questions, taxation, land reform, and social change. They oppose peasant leagues, labor organizations, and populist parties and are allied with conservative political parties, the military, and the traditional church hierarchy. Landowners are well organized in some Latin nations, and their associations exercise a great degree of influence in the government. *See also* HACIENDA (8); LAND REFORM (10); LATIFUNDIA SYSTEM (LATIFUNDISMO) (11).

Significance
The landed oligarchy shared power with urban commercial and industrial elites in the nineteenth century

throughout Latin America. With the growth of populist rural forces and the organization of urban working classes, their power was effectively challenged in some nations. Where major land reform programs were undertaken, as in Mexico and Bolivia, the influence of the landed oligarchy has been curtailed. In socialist Cuba, the landed oligarchy has largely been eliminated as a social class. Large landowners are also under attack in most other Latin nations, and their long-range future is uncertain. Many individuals in the class, however, have diversified their interests and are allied with conservative urban industrial and commercial clites.

Lema Election System | 123 |

The election system used in Uruguay that combines a primary election and a general election on a single ballot. The *lema* ("motto") election system is also called the double simultaneous vote. It has been used for presidential and legislative elections, and for the previously used plural executive system *(colegiado)*. Under the *lema* system, candidates of a political party *(lema)* are listed on the ballot according to factions *(sublemas)* within that party. The voter casts a single vote for a *sublema* within a *lema*. The popular vote received by all *sublema* lists within a *lema* are cumulated to determine that party's total vote. The party with the highest total vote wins the presidency, and the candidate of that party whose *sublema* led others in his party is elected. For legislative elections, a proportional representation system is used to distribute seats to the *lemas* and *sublemas*. *See also* COLEGIADO (159); ELECTION SYSTEM (117).

Significance

When the *lema* system was introduced in 1910, it encouraged the growth of political parties and factions within parties. Only a few members are necessary for a party or a faction to receive official recognition as a *lema* or a *sublema*. The system is considered by Uruguayan politicians to be more democratic than other election systems, but on occasion the *lema* system produces results that are contrary to the majority will. In 1971, for example, Juan María Bordaberry was elected president because the total vote of his *lema*, the Colorado party, was greater than that of the Blanco party or that of a leftist coalition called the Broad Front *(Frente Amplio)*. The leading Blanco candidate and Broad Front candidate each won more personal votes than Bordaberry, with the Blanco candidate leading by 50,000 votes. Elections in Uruguay were suspended after the military assumed full authority in 1976, but the *lema* system was reinstituted when competitive elections were restored in 1984.

Multiparty System | 124 |

A competitive political party system in which popular support is spread over three or more parties and no single party is able to dominate the political scene. In a typical multiparty system, many parties compete for legislative seats, and the congress may have from 5 to 20 different parties. No single party typically is able to win a majority of the seats. Coalitions, therefore, are necessary to enact legislation, to sustain a prime minister in office, or to elect a president. Multiparty systems are usually associated with the proportional representation election system, coalition politics, and unstable cabinets if a parliamentary system is used. *See also* POLITICAL PARTY (131).

Significance

In Latin American countries, a freely competitive electoral system tends to result in the creation of a multiparty system. Multipartisanship was encouraged in the late nineteenth century by the failure of the traditional liberal and conservative parties to integrate lower classes into national politics. The adoption of proportional representation in many countries and the expansion of suffrage also encouraged this development. In nations that retained a type of two-party system in presidential elections, such as Colombia and Uruguay, important factions developed within the two main parties. Chile evolved a typical multiparty system that functions when the nation is not subject to military intervention.

National Action Party (PAN) — 125

A conservative party, which is the largest minor party in Mexico. The National Action Party *(Partido de Acción Nacional)* was organized in 1939 as a loyal opposition to the dominant Institutional Revolutionary Party (PRI). The National Action party supports conservative economic policies and opposes the anticlericalism of the Mexican state. It draws its support from northern states, big business, conservative Catholic forces, and urban upper-middle and professional classes. Since 1952, PAN has won from 8 to 18 percent of the popular vote in presidential elections, and before 1988 about 10 to 20 seats in the Chamber of Deputies and some seats in several state legislatures. In the watershed election of 1988, PAN did not improve much in the popular vote, for most opposition votes went to the PRI defector Cuauhtémoc Cárdenas, who won 31 percent of the vote but lost to the PRI candidate, Carlos Salinas. *See also* DOMINANT PARTY SYSTEM (116); INSTITUTIONAL REVOLUTIONARY PARTY (PRI) (120).

Significance
The National Action party is the principal opposition party in Mexico, but it has very little chance of taking control of the national government. It provides Mexicans with a limited opportunity to express displeasure with the policies of the Mexican government, to complain about official corruption, and to advance policy alternatives that might be acceptable to the government. The PRI tolerates the PAN more than leftist parties because PRI believes the PRI is the true leader of the Mexican Revolution, and because the conservative orientation of PAN tends to strengthen the popular appeal of the PRI. In recent elections PAN has won governorships and improved its position outside its typical northern base of support. Its limited appeal was evident in the 1988 election when a new coalition of opposition parties far surpassed its vote.

National Front (Colombia) — 126

The coalition of Liberal and Conservative parties that governed Colombia from 1958 to 1974. The National Front was instituted by a constitutional change that required the alternation of Conservative and Liberal presidents and parity (an equal sharing) of all legislative, executive, and judicial posts at all levels in the nation. Under the terms of the constitution, the alternation system ended in 1974, and the parity system ended in 1978. While the National Front system was in effect, two Liberals and two Conservatives served as president. *See also* ALTERNATION AND PARITY (ALTERNACIÓN Y PARIDAD) (156).

Significance
The National Front was a type of wartime bipartisan coalition created to help end the partisan civil war between Liberals and Conservatives and to replace the military dictatorship of General Gustavo Rojas Pinilla with a limited democracy. The larger Liberal party in effect sacrificed its majority position for the sake of national unity. The broad goals of the

National Front were generally achieved during the period of its existence, but it suffered from intense factionalism and infiltration from other groups. No legislative program could be agreed to, and the constitutional requirement of a two-thirds legislative majority prevented the passage of needed social reforms until 1968 when the constitution was changed. The National Front disbanded in 1974 at the close of its constitutionally mandated 16-year period.

National Revolutionary Parties | 127 |

A class of political parties, indigenous to Latin America, that advocates major political, economic, and social reforms to be achieved through the processes of political democracy. National revolutionary parties are multiclass organizations composed of peasants, workers, Indians, intellectuals, professionals, and small businessmen. Unlike traditional social democratic parties of Europe and Latin America, Latin national revolutionary parties are rarely based on a Marxist philosophy, although their platform in many ways is similar to that of a typical social democratic party. National revolutionary parties espouse the principles of political democracy, land reform, economic nationalism, and social welfarism. After it takes power, such a party typically would attempt to nationalize large-scale foreign-owned enterprises, break up the latifundia system and distribute the land to peasants, elevate the role of the Indian in national life, promote labor unions, expand educational opportunities, extend suffrage, protect civil liberties, and reduce the military's influence in public affairs. *See also* DEMOCRATIC ACTION (AD) (115); AMERICAN POPULAR REVOLUTIONARY ALLIANCE (APRA) (106).

Significance
National revolutionary parties have been organized in many Latin nations and have brought about major economic and social reforms in some of them. The first important party to be organized was the American Popular Revolutionary Alliance (APRA), a Peruvian party formed by Victor Raúl Haya de la Torre in 1924. For this reason, national revolutionary parties are often known as *Aprista* parties. Other important *Aprista* parties include Democratic Action (AD) in Venezuela, the National Liberation Party (PLN) in Costa Rica, the National Revolutionary Movement (MNR) in Bolivia, the Dominican Revolutionary Party (PRD), and, in the view of some observers, the Institutional Revolutionary Party (PRI) in Mexico. The parties in Bolivia, Costa Rica, Mexico, and Venezuela have made revolutionary changes, but in Peru, although APRA is the largest party, it was prevented from taking power by military intervention until 1985. When APRA came into power, large portions of its traditional program had been enacted—some of which were disastrous failures—and it inherited a nation beset with leftist revolutions, substantial foreign debt, and economic chaos. In Peru and other states, the principles of *Aprismo* (the party's philosophy and program) have been applied by groups whose origins are different and who are not typically labeled national revolutionary parties. *Aprista* parties are among the most important in Latin America, and in many states they will continue to be the main practical vehicle for socioeconomic change.

Organized Labor | 128 |

Industrial workers and other wage employees who are members of trade unions. Organizations of wage employees are also found in service, white-collar, and civil service occupations. Only a small percentage of Latin American employees are members of trade unions. Union membership ranges from less than 1 percent of the work force in some nations to about 35 percent in Argentina, the most unionized country. Other nations with at least 20 percent of the work force unionized include Chile, Colombia, Mexico, Peru, Uruguay, and Venezuela. A few unions, particularly in recent decades, have pursued economic unionism, the attempt to improve the wages, hours, and working conditions of its members. Most Latin American unions, however, have practiced political unionism, seeking political change as the method of improving the life of workers. Many unions have been created by political parties, demagogic political leaders, and governments primarily for political purposes, either to oppose or support the political system. Anarchist, syndicalist, radical socialist, and communist political movements view unions as a means to power, and democratic socialist and Christian democratic parties also practice political unionism. Political actions undertaken by unions include attempting to make a social revolution, overthrowing governments, striking and demonstrating for political purposes, electioneering, and lobbying. *See also* CHRISTIAN DEMOCRACY (55); COMMUNISM (57); NATIONAL REVOLUTIONARY PARTIES (127); SOCIALISM (78).

Significance
The organized labor movement in Latin America is generally weak in most nations. Unions lack a firm revenue base, depend on government for recognition and protection, suffer from the paternalism of employers, often have dishonest leaders, and exist in a political culture that encourages individualism rather than disciplined collective effort. Unions have often been outlawed, their leaders arrested or killed, collective bargaining rights withheld, and strikes prohibited. In a few instances, like Bolivia, unions helped bring down dictators and create a genuine social revolution. In Mexico, unionism was promoted by revolutionary governments. Mexican workers have benefited to some degree, but union leaders are part of the power structure that does not give high priority to labor interests. In Cuba, the socialist government forbids striking, and unions are used to indoctrinate workers and increase production. Factionalism and competition among unions weaken the potential power of the working class. In Argentina, the Latin nation with the greatest number and highest percentage of trade unions, at least four political currents vie for power. At the international level, communist unions are affiliated with the communist World Federation of Trade Unions (WFTU), democratic socialist unions are associated with the Inter-American Regional Organizations of Workers (ORIT) (an arm of the International Confederation of Free Trade Unions or ICFTU), and Catholic unions have joined the Latin American Confederation of Christian Trade Unions (CLASC) (an arm of the International Federation of Christian Trade Unions or IFCTU). The prospects for a free, organized labor movement in Latin America will depend in large measure on the establishment of political democracy, the depoliticization of unionism, and the steady increase in economic modernization. As Latin America entered the 1990s, it seemed unlikely that these conditions would all prevail.

Peasants | 129 |
The common name for small farmers and agricultural workers. The term "peasant" and its Spanish equivalent, *campesino,* are applied to different types of agricultural workers and small farmers, such as: (1) tenant sharecroppers and cash renters; (2) independent freeholders who own small plots; (3) communal farmers, some of whom may have small plots; (4) employees of a hacienda; (5) agricultural laborers who work for a wage on large plantations engaged in

export agriculture; (6) migratory farm laborers; and (7) any rural worker or countryman. The peasant population of Latin American nations ranges from 20 to 70 percent. Although the proportion of peasants in the total population has been reduced by migration, urbanization, and industrialization, in some nations the absolute number of peasants has increased because of the population explosion. Peasants typically live on small plots *(minifundios)*, and are illiterate, poor, undernourished, and indebted to landowners or rural patrons. The primary peasant demand has been for land reform. For many peasants, a revolution is complete when land has been redistributed, but a number of peasant organizations also seek technical and financial assistance as well as broad social reforms, such as education, medical care, and social services. *See also* EJIDO (3); GUERRILLA WARFARE: FOCO THEORY (90); LANDED OLIGARCHY (122); LAND REFORM (10).

Significance
Peasants constitute the largest potential revolutionary group in Latin America. The peasantry is therefore repressed by right-wing governments, recruited by national revolutionary parties, and used as a base by left-wing guerrilla movements. The effectiveness of peasant organizations varies with the country and type of government in office. After the military assumed power in 1968 in Brazil, the government crushed the peasant leagues that had been organized in some states. Attempts to organize agricultural workers on large plantations, such as those in Peru and Cuba, have been more successful than attempts aimed at hacienda peasants. Peasant organizations are an integral part of the political system where successful revolutions have been made in the name of land reform, such as in Mexico, Bolivia, and Cuba. These organizations, however, are usually dominated by party and government bureaucratic officials, and national agricultural policy is made without much peasant input. Generally, although the peasantry has been the largest social group in Latin America, it has been politically weak and is declining in size. The long-run trends in the region indicate the elimination of the peasantry as a social class in many nations. The liberal ideal of transforming peasants into independent farmers who own family-sized farms engaged in commercial agriculture, however, has not been generally successful. In the 1990s, it is not clear how long or what form the transformation of the peasantry will take.

Personalist Party | 130 |

A political party organized around a charismatic political leader. Personalist political parties are organized by political leaders to advance their personal careers rather than to represent the interests of an ideology or political program. Typical personalist parties include: the Dominican Party *(Partido Dominicano)* of Rafael Leónidas Trujillo, 1932–1961; Peru's Pradista Democratic Movement *(Movimiento Democrático Pradista,* MDP), 1956–1970; Peru's Odriista National Union *(Unión Nacional Odriista,* UNO), 1956–1971; and various organizational labels used by José María Velasco Ibarra, who was five times president of Ecuador over a 38-year period beginning in 1933. *See also* PERSONALISM (PERSONALISMO) (73); POLITICAL PARTY (131).

Significance
Personalist political parties and personalist factions within larger parties have played an important role at certain times in Latin America. These parties have been the typical vehicle by which dictators try to legitimize their rule and fallen dictators try to achieve political comebacks. Although a number have been successful while

the leader was politically strong, they seldom survive the leader's political demise. The Peronist party in Argentina is an exception to the latter case. Personalist parties tend to grow in a political environment where parties are weak, executive rule is the norm, charismatic strongmen capture public attention, and *personalismo* characterizes the political culture. Some theorists project that the number and importance of personalist parties will decline as political development progresses in Latin America.

Political Party 131

An organization that seeks to win elections, to take control of the machinery of government, and to determine public policy. Political parties can be distinguished from pressure groups, which instead seek to influence the policy of government through legislative and administrative lobbying, propaganda, and other means. Political parties in Latin America vary a great deal with respect to their structure, goals, and actual functions performed in the political system. Latin parties differ in political ideology, in adherence to democratic and constitutional methods, in their legislative programs, in the size of party membership, and in their socioeconomic bases of support. They operate in political environments with different traditions of partisanship, degrees of popular participation, and legal requirements regulating party competition. A typical spectrum of parties usually emerges in most Latin nations under conditions of free party competition. Since World War II, this spectrum has usually included communist, socialist, national revolutionary or social democratic, Christian democratic, liberal, and conservative parties. Populist parties, moderate catchall parties, parties formed around particular personalities, and regional and single-interest parties have also been active in the region with various degrees of success. *See also* DOMINANT PARTY SYSTEM (116); ELECTION SYSTEM (117); MULTIPARTY SYSTEM (124); PERSONALIST PARTY (130); TWO-PARTY SYSTEM (137).

Significance
Many hundreds of political parties have been organized in Latin America since independence, but most of them have been inconsequential and short-lived. A large number of parties have been captured by dictators, organized to promote the career of a particular personality, or artificially created by a political regime in order to give it legitimacy. In some Latin nations, political parties have effectively carried out typical democratic party functions, such as nominating candidates for office, recruiting membership, formulating policies, mobilizing popular support, creating interest in public affairs, influencing public opinion, criticizing the government, and participating in government. In the late 1970s, when many states were under military rule, these roles were performed by the larger parties in Colombia, Costa Rica, Cuba, the Dominican Republic, Mexico, and Venezuela. When civilian governments were restored in other nations in the late 1980s, parties resumed their typical roles in other states, particularly in Argentina, Brazil, Chile, Peru, and Uruguay. Generally, however, political parties have not played an important role in most Latin American political systems since independence. Strong executive government and the cultural traditions of personalism, dictatorship, and militarism have combined in various ways to retard the development of effective and lasting democratic party systems in the region.

Radical Parties 132

A class of political parties of the center-left that developed in the late nineteenth century as a representative of lower-middle-class interests. Unlike the more extremist parties of the socialist left, Radical parties were essentially progressive liberal parties that were dissatisfied with the domination of national life by the landed oligarchy and the military. They pushed for universal suffrage, fair elections, restrictions on the church, and the extension of education. Two important Radical parties were organized in South America: the Radical Civic Union *(Unión Cívica Radical)* in Argentina, and the Radical Party *(Partido Radical)* in Chile. In both instances, the original party split into other organizations that were also called Radical parties. *See also* LIBERALISM (68); PERONISM (72).

Significance
Radical parties were strong in the late nineteenth century and the first decades of the twentieth century. In Argentina, Radicals were the largest party in 1916. They controlled the government for a time, but they lost support with the coming of Peronism in 1945. The Intransigent Radical party under Arturo Frondizi and the Popular Radical party under Arturo Illia were able to win presidential elections in the 1950s and early 1960s. When Peronism was again permitted to participate in national presidential elections in the early 1970s, the Radical groups were reduced to minor parties. Following a disastrous military period, the Radical Civic Union was again in power from 1983 to 1989, with the election of Raúl Alfonsín, but it lost the next election to the Peronists. In Chile, Radicals were first organized in the 1860s, but did not become strong until the 1920s. Radicals dominated Chilean politics from 1938 to 1952. After that period, they lost support to the Christian Democrats, who controlled the center of the political spectrum, while Radicals split into left and right wings. In 1969, Marxist Radicals joined the coalition of Communists and Marxist Socialists in Popular Unity *(Unitad Popular)*. They helped elect the Marxist Socialist, Salvador Allende, as president in 1970 and participated in his government. When Allende was overthrown by the military in 1973, Radicals were purged along with other leftist parties. When democratic government was restored in 1989, the Radicals reemerged as a small group. Once strong in certain areas of Latin America, Radical parties have been bypassed by other parties of the democratic left, such as the national revolutionary parties and reformist Christian democratic parties.

Sandinist Front for National Liberation (FSLN) | 133 |

Revolutionary movement that overthrew the Nicaraguan dictator Anastasio Somoza in 1979 and ruled until 1990. Following the overthrow of Somoza, the FSLN dominated the provisional government coalition and put into effect revolutionary economic and social policies. It transformed itself from a guerrilla war organization into a ruling political party and provided officers and men for a new regular army that replaced Somoza's National Guard. FSLN commanders, such as Daniel Ortega and Humberto Ortega, assumed positions in the government and the military, but a few other commanders and anti-Somoza leaders joined the opposition and participated in the civil war that followed. The prime doctrinal emphasis in the party is Marxist revolutionary socialism, and its initial domestic and international policies convinced opponents that it was attempting to establish the Castro Cuban communist model in Nicaragua. The FSLN government did retain a pluralist economy, however, but it followed an erratic policy on tolerating opposition parties and groups, while devoting its attention to defending the revolution against the contras and U.S. intervention. In 1984 it won 67 percent of the popular vote in a multiparty election, which some opposition groups considered to be invalid. The FSLN government agreed to an internationally supervised election in 1990 as a condition to end the civil war. FSLN President Daniel Ortega was defeated by Violeta Chamorro, who led a coalition of parties, by a vote of 51 percent to 41 percent. *See also* CONTRAS (81); NICARAGUAN ELECTION OF 1990 (95); NICARAGUAN REVOLUTION (96).

Significance
The Sandinist Front for National Liberation is the largest single political party in Nicaragua. Although it lost the 1990 election to the National Opposition Union, a coalition of 14 parties, it has retained its organizational structure, popular support, and desire to return to office by democratic means. Daniel Ortega continued as head of the FSLN, and Humberto Ortega remained within the cabinet of the Chamorro government as defense minister. The FSLN has substantial support within labor unions and has been able, with demonstrations and strikes, to rescind policies that hurt workers and to retain property acquisitions that benefited party functionaries. Having shown that it can accept the results of a free election that removed it from office, it has acquired a new image at home and abroad. It retains substantial popular support and can exercise pressure to defend its supporters in a depressed economy, which the Chamorro government has not been able to turn around. Thus, the FSLN is in a good position to contest the next national election, providing that it makes further policy changes towards democratic social change in a period when Marxist socialism is in decline.

Social Christian Party (COPEI) | 134 |

The Christian democratic party in Venezuela, the second largest party in the nation. The Social Christian Party *(Partido Social Cristiano)* was first formed as the Committee Organized for Independent Elections (COPEI) in 1945, and it is still known by its original acronym. Originally a democratic Catholic party that attracted conservative support, COPEI soon adopted ideological positions of a center-left, Christian socialist party that advocates a strong social democratic program. Led for many years by Rafael Caldera, the party opposed the dictatorship of Colonel Marcos Pérez Jiménez in the 1950s and contributed to his overthrow in 1958. COPEI then grew from a moderate-sized regional group to become the second party in the nation that has shared the presidency with the larger Democratic Action party. In 1968 Caldera narrowly won the presidential election when Democratic Action (AD) was divided; in 1978 the COPEI candidate, Luis Herrera Campins, won the presidency with 46 percent of the popular vote. COPEI lost to AD in the elections of 1984 and 1989. *See also* CHRISTIAN DEMOCRACY (55); DEMOCRATIC ACTION (AD) (115).

Significance
The Social Christian party is one of the two most successful Christian democratic parties in Latin America, along with the Christian Democratic party in Chile. From 1958 to 1978, COPEI increased its popular vote for the presidency from about 20 percent to 46 percent. It has displayed effective leadership, party unity, and increased organizational strength. Within a period of 20 years, it grew from a regional party to a multiclass, well-organized national party with peasant, labor, student, and middle class support. It has played the roles of a coalition partner, of a loyal opposition, and of a presidential party.

Still taking second place to Democratic Action in the number of seats in the assembly, COPEI established itself as the second major party in Venezuela's two-party competition for the presidency, where it benefits from Democratic Action's lapses.

Student Activism | 135 |

Actions undertaken by university students for political purposes. Student activism in Latin America takes many forms, including electioneering, political organizing, demonstrations, strikes, marches, riots, sporadic violence, and urban guerrilla warfare. Few university students are politically active on a continuing basis, but on important occasions, thousands of students will participate in demonstrations and other direct actions. Although the proportion of students in the national population is relatively small, many students are enrolled in prestigious universities in national capitals where they have direct access to the institutions of government. University students in Latin America are drawn from the middle and upper social classes, but many of them are more radical than the established members of these classes. Student goals vary, but most political activism has been directed towards: (1) achieving university autonomy, or freedom from government interference in university affairs; (2) protecting student interests within the university on such matters as university governance, curriculum, and academic standards; (3) expressing student views on national political issues, including domestic and foreign policy matters; (4) removing authoritarian and dictatorial governments; and (5) promoting social reform and participating in social revolutions. National associations of students exist in every nation, and most national parties have affiliated student organizations. The spectrum of political opinion on university campuses is wide, and organizations often work at cross-purposes. *See also* GUERRILLA WARFARE: URBAN WARFARE THEORY (91).

Significance
Student activism in Latin America has achieved mixed results. Beginning in 1918, the University Reform Movement was instrumental in securing the Cordoba Reforms, changes aimed at university autonomy, social awareness, and student participation in university government. Students often use their power to lower academic standards and to purge unpopular professors and administrators. University autonomy has been used to protect the university from arbitrary government actions, but the campus has also been used as a base for urban guerrilla operations. Student activism helped to bring down some dictators, including Fulgencio Batista in Cuba and Marcos Pérez Jiménez in Venezuela. A large number of student activists have become important political leaders, including Víctor Raúl Haya de la Torre, Fidel Castro, Rómulo Betancourt, Raúl Leoni and other members of the "Generation of 1928" in Venezuela. Upon leaving the university, however, a large number of students enter the professional and industrial sectors and adopt the attitudes of the middle and upper classes. Left-wing students often see themselves as the revolutionary vanguard for less fortunate classes, but generally they have not been able to organize urban workers and rural peasants under their leadership. Student demonstrations and coercive public protests have changed government policies at times, but they have also provoked the closing of universities, arrests of students, and killings. In the 1968 "Battle of Tlatelolco," for example, following a demonstration of 150,000 Mexican students and other later protests, Mexican soldiers fired on an essentially peaceful demonstration

and killed up to 200 persons. Many students who were identified with leftist movements were killed or "disappeared" by the repressive military governments that were in place from the mid-1960s to the late 1980s. Student activism in Latin America has a long tradition and it is likely to continue, but it may play a less important role in the more developed states in the region.

Suffrage | 136 |

The right or privilege of voting in governmental elections. Universal manhood suffrage was provided throughout Latin America by the mid-1920s. In 1929, Ecuador was the first Latin state to grant suffrage to women, with most other states following its lead in the 1940s and 1950s. The practice became universal when Paraguay joined the others in 1963. The voting age usually ranges from 18 to 21, with some states using 18 for married persons. The Cuban Constitution of 1976 provides that persons aged 16 or older may vote for municipal councils. In 1988, Brazil lowered the voting age to 16. There are no poll taxes in Latin America, property qualifications are not significant, and gender qualifications have been abolished. Until very recent times, literacy requirements disfranchised many persons. Some Latin American nations deny the franchise to members of the armed forces, and other countries, usually not the same ones, prohibit clergy from voting. A few states have mandatory registration and several have mandatory voting, although the penalties for not voting are mild and are seldom enforced. *See also* CONTINUISMO (161); ELECTION SYSTEM (117).

Significance
Except for a few special cases, Latin American law typically provides for free, equal, direct, and universal suffrage. For many Latin Americans, however, these have been hollow guarantees because free elections and competitive political party systems have been rare. When cast, votes often meant nothing; many elections have been fraudulent and the results were often set aside. Secret voting was not practiced in some localities, various political parties were not permitted to participate, and many times there has been only a single candidate or voters are not given a real choice. A number of countries have followed the practice of *continuismo*, that is, of presidents maintaining themselves in office beyond legal or customary term restrictions. The motto of the Mexican Revolution—Effective suffrage; no reelection—is an apt reminder that universal suffrage and effective suffrage are not identical. In the period roughly from 1960 to 1990, for example, most states were under the control of: (1) traditional dictators who had manipulated the electoral process; (2) military governments that had suspended constitutional rights; (3) governments that had limited competition by barring parties; or (4) one-party states where no real choice was offered the voter. By the late 1980s, however, most states returned to democratic processes; in a number of countries, universal suffrage combined with free elections resulted in victories and the assumption of power by opposition parties.

Two-Party System | 137 |

A competitive political party system in which two major parties win the bulk of the popular vote and dominate the political scene. In a two-party system, the two main parties win all or most of the seats in congress, and one of the major parties usually wins a majority of the seats. Third parties may consistently win a few seats but not enough to prevent the largest party from winning a majority. Minor parties also compete in elections but rarely win seats. Over a long period of time, the two main parties tend to alternate in office. Two-party systems are usually associated with a single-member district system of elections, and they tend to result in stable government. *See also* POLITICAL PARTY (131).

Significance
Freely operating two-party systems at the legislative level are rare in Latin America. In the early and mid-nineteenth century, the two-party system was widespread as traditional liberal and conservative parties dominated politics in an era of greatly restricted suffrage. The system tended to disappear near the end of the nineteenth century as lower-middle-class and working-class parties began to appear, suffrage was increased, and proportional representation systems were adopted. In contemporary times, artificial two-party systems have been created by legally mandated, shared-vote systems—as in Colombia from 1958 to 1974—and by official two-party systems, such as that imposed by the military government in Brazil from 1964 to 1985. In Venezuela, a two-party system for presidential elections has emerged since 1958, with the Democratic Action and Social Christian parties sharing the presidency and dominating the congress. In Colombia, a modified form of the two-party presidential system exists, because although the Liberal party is dominant, the Conservatives are able to win when the Liberals are divided and run two candidates in presidential elections.

The Military

Caesarism   138
A form of dictatorship in which a particular individual, often a military officer, exercises absolute power in the state by virtue of his control over the armed forces. Caesarism can be distinguished from other forms of military rule in that a caesaristic dictator has a popular base of support, a modern political organization, and a dynamic personality with charismatic overtones. He typically pursues economic and social policies that transform the existing social system. In a praetorian state, on the other hand, no single individual dominates and the armed forces act as a corporate entity in ruling the state. The traditional military dictator, known as the *caudillo,* also exercises absolute power, but he lacks a modern political organization, is primarily interested in maintaining political power and maximizing personal gain, and does not disturb the existing social order. The caesaristic dictator, who may be a civilian or a civilianized military officer, uses his control over the army to defeat his political enemies. Although he creates or takes over an existing political ideology, he demands personal loyalty to himself, rather than to institutions or ideals. He adopts a modernizing socioeconomic program, centralizes power, tries to integrate the nation around his goals and programs, and adopts a nationalistic foreign policy. A caesaristic dictatorship may develop out of a praetorian state ruled by a military junta, or, less likely, from traditional *caudillismo.* A caesaristic dictator usually falls from office through a coup when he comes to rely more on his popular support than on his control over the armed forces and people. *See also* CAUDILLISMO (139); MILITARISM (145); PRAETORIANISM (154).

Significance
In Latin America, the traditional *caudillo* was a typical form of militarism in the nineteenth century, and although caesarism has been more in evidence in the twentieth century, praetorianism has been the more prevalent form. Two striking

examples of caesarism surfaced in South America in modern times—Getúlio Vargas in Brazil and Juan Perón in Argentina. Vargas (1883–1954), born into a military family, was unsuccessful in a military career, became active in politics, and led a successful revolt in 1930. He dominated the Brazilian political system as dictator from 1930 to 1945, using his power to put down rebellions, centralize the governmental system, reduce the power of the states, nationalize politics, modernize the economy, and enact much social legislation. In Argentina, Juan Perón (1895–1974), a professional military officer who had organized a political group in the officer corps, entered the cabinet when he and others overthrew the civilian government in 1943. He wrested control from the junta in 1946 and ruled until 1955. He enacted a broad program of social reform, created a lasting political movement, and pursued a nationalistic foreign policy. Both Vargas and Perón were removed from office by military coups, and both men later tried political comebacks as civilian politicians. Vargas became president again in 1951 by winning a free election, and he served until 1954 when he committed suicide following a military coup. Perón was permitted to return to Argentina from exile in 1973 and won the election of that year, but he died soon thereafter. Both men were ineffective in their second coming. The militarism that marked Latin American politics from the 1960s to the late 1980s was more of the praetorian state variety, but certain features of Latin political culture, especially *personalismo*, may once again give support to the rise of caesaristic dictators. The political career of Fidel Castro in Cuba comes close to fitting the caesaristic model.

Caudillismo |139|

The system of rule by a strong man who exercises dictatorial powers. *Caudillismo*—from the Spanish word *caudillo*, a leader or military chieftain—has taken various forms throughout its long history in Latin America. For the most part, *caudillos* have been military men interested in maintaining power, maximizing personal gain, and defeating rivals. The rule of a *caudillo* is usually extremely repressive, with political enemies imprisoned, killed, or exiled, and their property confiscated. The decades following the Wars of Independence in Spanish America are known as the Age of *Caudillos*. Military chieftains or provincial horsemen of the ranges organized private armies of *gauchos* or *llaneros* and vied for power. The period was chaotic and characterized by intermittent civil wars. A few countries were able to surmount this form of anarchy with a more stable system of constitutional rule, but in most countries national *caudillos* assumed power and tended to centralize authority. Some of the more notorious nineteenth-century *caudillos* were: in Venezuela, José Antonio Páez (1830–1836, 1861–1863) and Antonio Guzmán Blanco (1870–1888); in Argentina, Juan Manuel de Rosas (1829–1852); and in Mexico, Antonio López de Santa Anna (1829–1855). In the twentieth century, military men who have established extremely repressive *caudillo*-type personal dictatorships have been: Juan Vicente Gómez in Venezuela; Fulgencio Batista in Cuba; Rafael Leónidas Trujillo in the Dominican Republic; Anastasio Somoza and his son, Anastasio Somoza Debayle, in Nicaragua; and François Duvalier in Haiti. Recent examples of caesaristic *caudillos* who built a strong political base and adopted a number of economic and social reforms include Getúlio Vargas in Brazil (1930–1945) and Juan Perón in Argentina (1945–1955). *See also* CACIQUISMO (158); CAESARISM (138).

Significance

Caudillismo has been a fundamental feature of Latin American politics since independence. Its characteristic features—the personal rule of a dominant personality, a repressive dictatorship, the use of military force to gain and hold power, the centralization of authority—still prevailed in contemporary times. Some observers have argued that by creating stability and establishing order, national *caudillos* provided a service to the nation, and that *caudillismo* is a desirable part of the Latin American political tradition because it supplants the extremes of local boss rule and unstable national systems. Most writers, however, condemn *caudillos* for their despotism, brutality, cupidity, and antidemocracy. Explanations for the extent of *caudillismo* in Latin America have stressed the important role of the military strongman in the Christian Reconquest of Spain and the Spanish Conquest of America; the semi-feudal system of Spanish America that promoted regionalism and personalism; the post-independence disorders that called for strong, centralized authority; and cultural traits that support the personification of authority. *Caudillismo* is a legacy that Latin America thus far has been unable to outgrow. Some analysts consider Fidel Castro in Cuba to be another caesaristic *caudillo* who is not much different than the typical modern variety. For example, they cite his use of a private army to come into power, the force of his charismatic personality, his centralization of authority, and, especially, his personal rule over the island. Although his personal role continues, the transformation of the Cuban society and the institutionalization of the revolution would seem to have longer-lasting effects than those of an ordinary *caudillo*.

Coup d'Etat (Golpe de Estado) | 140

Seizure of government power with swift, decisive action by a military or political group from within the existing system. In Latin America, the coup d'etat, or *golpe de estado* as it is known in Spanish, is a frequently used means of gaining political power. A revolution differs from a coup in that it involves a mass uprising and a transformation in the established political, economic, and social institutions of society. Revolutionary changes, however, may be instituted following a coup by those who have seized power. To succeed, a coup requires strong leadership, direct or indirect support by key military leaders, swift and efficient action to seize the key loci of power, and, often, a measure of luck. Coup leaders typically seek to capture or kill opposition political and military leaders, to seize control of key government offices and the mass media, and to calm the people and gain their support for the new regime. *See also* CUARTELAZO (141); REVOLUTION (100).

Significance

The history of Latin America is punctuated by the coup d'etat. It has been used, for example, to overturn election results, to prevent revolution, to undertake a revolution, to protect conservative interests by counteracting a popular turn toward the political left, to bring the military to power, or to satisfy the power drive of individuals. Often, a countercoup, engineered by supporters of the ousted leadership or by bitter enemies of the new leaders, has followed the first coup. During the 1960s, coups in Brazil, Argentina, and Peru brought the military to power. The United States has often encouraged and supported Latin coups, as, for example, in Guatemala in the 1950s, in the Dominican Republic in the 1960s, and in Chile in the 1970s. As long as Latins refuse to play by the rules of the democratic game by using coups to change election results, democracy will remain an unstable and typically short-lived ideal in most of Latin America.

Cuartelazo 141

A barracks revolt, or, more generally, any military coup d'etat. The term, *cuartelazo*—from the Spanish word *cuartel,* meaning barracks—is sometimes used to refer to any attempted coup d'etat *(golpe de estado)* in which a portion of the armed forces participates. In its more technical usage, *cuartelazo* includes, among other things: (1) the undertaking of treasonable actions by a small unit or even by a single barracks; (2) issuing a *pronunciamiento* aimed at justifying the revolt and building support for it; (3) taking over communication centers and public utilities, the state's treasury, military supplies, government headquarters, and ultimately the capital and the entire nation; (4) informing the masses that the military group has taken over operations of the government; and (5) revealing the names of junta members. *Cuartelazo* differs from a *golpe de estado* in that a *cuartelazo* always involves a barracks revolt and a march on the capital, whereas a *golpe de estado* is a direct attack on the head of state by civilian, military, or guerrilla forces. A *golpe* usually involves a violent attack on the presidential palace, in which the purpose of the rebels is to secure an immediate change of government by assassinating, arresting, or sending into exile the head of state and loyal cabinet officers. *See also* COUP D'ETAT (GOLPE DE ESTADO) (140); PRONUNCIAMIENTO (155).

Significance
The *cuartelazo* had its origins in both Spain and Portugal and has been frequently attempted throughout the history of Latin America. When it succeeds, the *cuartelazo* is typically well organized and meticulously planned, and no blood is shed. It often begins at night and on holidays, and it usually involves one barracks or garrison, but may include several. Success of the maneuver depends on surprise, timing, the cooperation or acquiescence of other garrison commanders and regional *caudillos,* and the acceptance of the political change by the people. A successful *cuartelazo* is usually completed within a day or several at most. When a *cuartelazo* fails, it is usually because of poorly laid plans or bungled execution, misjudgments of the level of opposition to the government, failure to include key military officials in the operation, or the defeat of the rebel barracks by loyalist military forces. Examples of successful *cuartelazos* include those of General José Félix Uriburu in 1930 in Argentina; General Pedro P. Ramírez, General Arturo Rawson, and Colonel Juan D. Perón in 1953 in Argentina; General Fulgencio Batista in 1952 in Cuba; and General Manuel A. Odría in 1948 in Peru. With the rise of militarism in the 1960s, the *cuartelazo* was again extensively used throughout the region. Two significant examples are those of General Humberto Castelo Branco and others in 1964 in Brazil and of General Juan Velasco Alvarado and others in 1968 in Peru.

Demilitarization 142

The process by which the roles and influence exercised by the military in a society are reduced in favor of civilian control. In demilitarization, a series of actions and developments occur that typically include the turning over of the reins of government to civilians, a reduction of the influence the military has over the policy of government, a decrease in the size of the armed forces, cessation of a state of siege, elimination of restrictions on the civil liberties of citizens, redefinition of the mission of the military, and, on occasion, trials of military officers who committed criminal offenses during the military period. The process of demilitarization can occur suddenly or over an extended period, and with varied results. It often occurs when the leaders of a military government come to believe that they have removed a temporary threat to the political system, defeated or greatly reduced the power of insurrectionary or guerrilla forces, or failed to achieve the larger goals they may have had to renovate the society. Civilian forces, particularly in those nations that have strong democratic traditions, often hasten the process of demilitarization by opposition and demands that the military return to the barracks. Without civilian support, the military cannot administer the government, control economic development, or influence public opinion. *See also* MILITARISM (145).

Significance
Demilitarization took place in a large number of nations in Latin America in the 1980s. In the case of Argentina, it occurred quickly as a result of the loss of the Falklands War against the United Kingdom in 1982. In Chile the military government of Augusto Pinochet, which assumed power in 1973, was removed by the people in a plebiscite in 1988. The military government of Brazil that took power in 1964 slowly reduced tensions and opened the government to civilian control in a series of actions that culminated in a popularly elected government in 1985. Elections and the ending of civil wars in Central America by the early 1990s helped bring civilian governments into office in most of the states in the region. This demilitarization in turn has raised the issue of redefining the mission of the military in some of the states where insurrection and guerrilla wars have declined. It is suggested that the military be used against narcotrafficking, for building the infrastructure and public utilities in less developed areas, and to assist in handling natural disasters. Although the roles of some Latin military groups have declined, the broader and more significant issue for many states is how to integrate the military within a national democratic framework that is permanently under civilian control.

Golpismo 143
The practice of changing governments by *golpe de estado* (coup d'etat). The term *golpismo* may also refer to any irregular or unconstitutional change in government in which the armed forces participate. This includes the *cuartelazo*, or barracks revolt, and a *golpe* in which civilian groups cooperate with the military in overthrowing the government. *See also* COUP D'ETAT (GOLPE DE ESTADO) (141); CUARTELAZO (140); MILITARISM (145); MILITARISM: GUARDIAN THESIS (147).

Significance
Latin Americans have ambivalent feelings concerning *golpismo*. Military coups are universally condemned by those groups who have been removed from office, but they are often advocated by civilian groups who want change in government. Because *golpismo* has been practiced so frequently in Latin American history, it is considered to be an acceptable method of political change in the Latin political culture.

Junta 144
The Spanish word for any board or council, but in politics the term is more commonly used to describe a group of military officers who collectively exercise the powers of government. A military junta is typically established following a coup d'etat. Juntas are often headed by the three ranking officers of the army, navy, and air force, or the army chief of staff presides over a cabinet of officers drawn from the three military services. *See also* COUP D'ETAT (GOLPE DE ESTADO) (140); MILITARISM (145); PRAETORIANISM (154).

Significance
A junta of the three ranking service officers heading the government following a military coup symbolically represents the unity of the armed forces in the decision to overthrow the previous regime. The exclusion of civilians from the cabinet, often accompanied by a ban on all political parties, usually indicates the military's complete rejection of the previous system and the desire to make wholesale changes. The representation of all three services in the leadership or in the cabinet reflects the desire of each branch to protect its corporate interests, as well as the senior officers' need to establish safeguards against the emergence of a single military dictator.

Militarism 145
The influence or predominance of the armed forces in the political life of the nation. Forms and degrees of militarism range from situations in which the armed forces: (1) influence the policy of a civilian government; (2) hold a veto over the actions and personnel of government; (3) intervene in politics directly by temporarily removing a civilian government from office; and (4) establish a long-term military government, either under the control of a junta or a one-man dictatorship. Various theories have been advanced to explain the high incidence of military intervention in Latin American politics. Some explanations stress remote causes, such as the tradition of militarism that was created in Hispanic culture by the reconquest of Spain from the Moors, the military's role in the conquest of the New World, and the glorification of the military during and following the Wars of Independence. Other explanations emphasize the low level of political development in Latin America, the failure of democratic government to take root, and the political vacuum created by the absence of any effective legitimated institution that could challenge the military. Still other explanations stress the social class origins of the military and see militaristic intervention as a defense of allied groups, such as the church, the landed oligarchy, and the middle class. The immediate causes of a military coup are often traced to: (1) competition among various military officers for power; (2) the protection of the privileges and status of the military establishment; (3) the desire to remove corrupt, incompetent, or undemocratic politicians from office; (4) the need to reestablish law and order in a period of political and social unrest; (5) the removal of a leftist or otherwise radical regime from office; and (6) the desire to hasten the pace or direct the course of economic modernization. *See also* CAESARISM (138); PRAETORIANISM (154).

Significance
Militarism has been a salient feature of Latin American politics and endemic to the region. No other area of the world has shown a greater incidence of military rule over the past 150 years. In the nineteenth century, military rule was commonplace in Latin America, as professional military officers, regional *caudillos,* and leaders of irregular military forces vied for power. In the twentieth century, military governments were in office throughout the entire region for at least 40 percent of the time, and some states have been under the control of military governments for 60 to 70 percent of that period. Only Brazil, Chile, Costa Rica, Panama, and Uruguay have a long history of civilian governments. Cycles of military governments alternated with civilian rule in the twentieth century, and in the mid-1960s, militarism rose again, striking even those countries traditionally less subject to military rule. In 1978, of the 20 Latin republics only Mexico, Haiti, the Dominican Republic, Costa Rica, Colombia, and

Venezuela had civilian governments. This neomilitarism shattered the notion, advanced by some theorists, that the increased professionalization of the officer corps that has generally taken place in Latin America would lead to a decrease of military intervention. By 1980 a few military regimes had permitted civilian governments to be reestablished in Central and South America, and by the end of the decade most nations had returned to civilian rule. Some observers conclude that the current situation may be only another civilian period in recurring military-civilian cycles. They argue that the stability of civilian governments in the early 1990s is not assured, citing failed barracks revolts that occurred in Argentina, the military ousting the first democratically elected government of Haiti, guerrilla warfare that threatens the government of Peru, and the strong powers exercised by the Salvadoran military fighting revolutionary forces in that nation. However, for some states, such as Mexico, that had once been highly influenced and controlled by the military, military intervention does not appear to be a threat to civilian governments.

Militarism: Development Thesis 146

A class of theories that seek to explain the high incidence of militarism in Latin America by placing special emphasis on the political, economic, or social stage of development of the society. With regard to political modernization, the thesis argues that low levels of political development are related to high levels of military intervention. "Low political development" means little public participation in politics, lack of a widespread consensus on political institutions, absence of effective intermediate or broker groups such as political parties and pressure groups, and a low level of national integration. Similarly, low levels of economic modernization, industrialization, and social development are also directly linked to a high degree of militarism. The theories argue that as development proceeds, particularly political development, the incidence of military intervention in government will decline. *See also* MILITARISM (145).

Significance
As with other theories that try to explain long-standing and complex phenomena by stressing a single or closely related group of factors, the development thesis is open to criticism. The neomilitarism that burst on the Latin scene in the mid-1960s made a graveyard of much theoretical work that relied too heavily on drawing causal relationships between low levels of development and high levels of military intervention. In particular, the brutal military interventions in Argentina, Brazil, Chile, and Uruguay—countries with high stages of development and, except Argentina, low traditions of intervention—have required theorists to seek broader explanations. The history of Mexico is also seen as a case that challenges some development theories. Mexico has had a long history of rampant militarism, but it has been able to place clear limits on the political power of the military even though it is less modernized than Argentina. The last successful military coup in Mexico was in 1920, and since 1946 only civilians have been elected president. Because of Mexico and other cases, some theorists prefer to stress other factors, such as national culture, foreign influences, government policies, leadership roles, and government strategies for limiting militarism.

Militarism: Guardian Thesis 147

The theory that the proper political role of the armed forces is to defend the nation's constitutional system from violation by civilian governments or from usurpation by revolutionary groups. Under the guardian thesis, the military keeps a watchful eye on the government and applies pressure, issues warnings, and, if necessary, deposes the government and rules for a brief period when it believes that the constitution is being violated. According to the thesis, military rule would always be brief and the government would be returned to civilian authority whenever matters were set right and new elections were held. The purpose of the military intervention is to preserve the existing constitutional system, and, by implication, the existing socioeconomic order. *See also* MILITARISM (145); PRAETORIAN ARMY (153).

Significance
The guardian thesis has been widely believed and practiced by Latin American military establishments in the twentieth century. A number of Latin constitutions lend support to the theory because they recognize the armed forces as a fourth branch of government whose duty is to protect the existing constitutional order. Having few foreign wars to fight, the military has often viewed its role more as guardian of the constitutional system than as defender of the state. The guardian theory has been especially strong among the officers of the Brazilian armed forces. In order to maintain the appearance of loyalty to the government, Brazilian officers have historically placed pressure on civilian governments by making pronouncements from private military clubs rather than by official statements. In 1964, however, the guardian theory was abandoned as a justification for military intervention because, upon assuming power, the military proclaimed it was making a revolution. This statement implied that it would be necessary for the military to hold power for a substantial period of time. The Brazilian armed forces remained in control of the government at least until 1985, when a civilian government was elected. Under the 1988 constitution, however, the military retained its traditional right to defend the nation against foreign and domestic threats to the constitutional order.

**Militarism:
Middle Class Thesis** 148
The theory that seeks to explain the high degree of military intervention in Latin America by focusing on the coincidence of interests between the middle sectors of society and the military. The thesis also stresses the middle class origins of military personnel. It points out that the dominant political group in Latin America is the middle sector of society, not the landed oligarchy or urban working classes. It argues that the middle classes are essentially undemocratic and have elitist aspirations, but they are in competition with each other, lack firm policy goals, and are not united. Without military backing, they lack sufficient political resources to maintain control over the system. The middle class and upper middle class in particular are threatened by popularly based political movements or parties that, representing a more cohesive working class, might capture control of the government through elections or other means. Such lower-class-based governments would try to make changes in the socioeconomic system that would benefit the lower classes and harm the middle and upper middle classes. The military, whose origins, values, and interests overlap those of the middle classes, intervenes in government whenever this threat arises. Since many military coups occur just prior to or immediately after elections, this suggests that the apparent discrepancy between the popular choice for president and the military's preference is real. Thus the

primary result and usual purpose of the military coup is to protect middle-class interests and the socioeconomic status quo. Although increasing numbers of military officers are recruited from the lower middle class, these men have been politically socialized to accept and defend the value system, roles, and corporate interests of the military, thus perpetuating rather than changing the system. *See also* MILITARISM (145).

Significance
Although the middle class thesis is one of the better-known explanations for military intervention, it competes with a number of other equally well-known theories, some of which try to relate levels of socioeconomic or political development to the high incidence of militarism. Other theories place emphasis on the corporate interests of the military, the professionalization of the officer corps, or cultural and other factors. Because the number of military interventions in Latin America is so great, supporting or disproving evidence for any one explanation can be found. The fact that scholars disagree and often have mutually exclusive explanations seems to show that a satisfactory, comprehensive, multifactor theory has yet to be developed.

Militarism: Professionalization Thesis 149

The theory that seeks to explain the high level of military intervention in Latin America by focusing on the degree of professionalism in the armed forces. The professionalization thesis argues that, as the officer corps becomes more professional over time, military coups against the government will decline and the armed forces will tend thereafter to seek their goals as a pressure group. "Professionalization" means recruitment of officers on the basis of merit, advanced education in military science; promotion on the basis of merit rather than politics or family connections; advanced technical and administrative training for superior officers; modernization of weapons, organizations, strategies and tactics; and the establishment of disciplined relationships between officers and men. The theory argues that, as these factors develop, military officers will come to see their role as professionals whose purpose is the preservation of national security, which can be achieved by means other than direct military rule. *See also* MILITARISM (145).

Significance
The professionalization thesis has its supporters, but it is more often criticized then defended. A number of studies have shown that, despite the increased professionalization of Latin American armed forces, the degree of military intervention has not declined. The neomilitarism of the 1960s and 1970s appears to refute the thesis. In some countries where professionalization has been high and intervention traditionally low, such as Brazil, Chile, and Uruguay, the military nevertheless intervened in politics in a massive way in the 1960s and 1970s. The professionalism of many members of the officer corps, however, is a continuing force that impels them to "return to the barracks," especially when government policies fail, and to leave politics to the politicians. Where professionalism has been high, military governments are often short-lived.

Militarism: Renovation Thesis 150

The view, held by some military officials, that a proper mission of the military is to play a predominant role in renewing the social and political order and modernizing the economy. Under the renovation thesis, the military's mission is not only that of defending the nation against foreign or domestic threats to the public order or to national security, but also to make over the economic, social, and political system so that the nation can make full use of its national resources and take its rightful place in international affairs. This goal requires the military to intervene in government for a period long enough to eliminate misfunctioning institutions and ineffective policies. Military rule would necessarily be lengthy. The objectives would be to create a strong, centralized, efficient government, free of corruption; a political party system that was supportive; popular attitudes that supported national order and development; economic policies that contributed to growth and modernization; and a social system that was integrated and cohesive. The type of loyalty, patriotism, discipline, and dedication that characterize a society during major external wars would be the values that advocates of this view most prize. *See also* MILITARISM (145).

Significance
Advocates of national renovation through military leadership are distributed throughout the region, but they were especially strong in the period from the mid-1960s to the mid-1980s. During this time, military governments in Brazil, Chile, and Peru adopted policies that made fundamental changes in the economic system, political party politics, and the constitutional order. Some economic successes were achieved, but these regimes failed to create lasting popular support or to renovate the society. The social system and popular culture were barely affected, since the policies often continued past practices that reinforced the existing social order. Economic failures, increasing demands for democratic rule, and the growing view among many officers that they should return to the barracks helped bring this period to a close.

Military-Civilian Cycles | 151 |

Periods of time in which most Latin American nations were ruled by either military or civilian governments. Alternations of military and civilian governments have occurred on an irregular basis in the region and in individual nations. In the twentieth century, military governments have been in office throughout Latin America for over 40 percent of the time. The periods from 1901 to 1910, 1931 to 1940, 1951 to 1960, and 1980 to 1990 were especially marked with military intervention or military dictatorships. During the 1980s, most nations in Latin America were under some form of military rule, but by the end of the decade the region returned to civilian control. From the 1940s to the 1990s—except for Costa Rica, which has had stable civilian governments—Central America has had only brief interludes of civilian governments. *See also* NEOMILITARISM (152).

Significance
Cycles of military and civilian governments are often related to economic cycles and the rise of political movements or leaders that threaten the status quo. Given the high incidence of military intervention in the region, however, there are other factors that convince the military high command or individual commanders that the time is ripe to overturn the government. The values associated with civilian democratic rule are strong in Latin America, but military rule is also accepted and often demanded by large portions of Latin society in some circumstances. These conflicting aspects of Hispanic political culture, mixed with the rise and fall of economic and political factors, thus tend to produce periods in which particular nations or large parts of the area are dominated by one form or another. In the early 1990s, the region was under civilian rule, but events such as failed coups

in Argentina and Venezuela, a successful coup in Haiti, and continuing military influence and threats in other nations indicate that another round of militarism is not out of the question.

Neomilitarism — 152

The most recent period of military rule in Latin America from about the mid-1960s to the late 1980s, when military governments were established in most Latin American nations. Although military governments were often found in at least some Latin nations in the years after World War II, the period of neomilitarism was noted for the widespread adoption of military governments, even in nations typically less subject to military intervention, such as Brazil, Chile, and Uruguay. By the mid-1970s, all Latin governments in South America except Colombia and Venezuela were under military rule. The immediate causes that impelled the military to overthrow civilian regimes were basically three: (1) domestic insurgencies from leftist revolutionary groups; (2) threats that leftist parties and leaders who were pursuing a constitutional route to power would install a communist or revolutionary government; and (3) ineffective and corrupt civilian governments that could not maintain order, manage the economy, or pursue policies of national development that did not threaten the political and social status quo. Given the predisposition of military commanders to intervene and their assumed constitutional role to do so, these perceived threats and incidents were sufficient to bring about extensive intervention in the region. During this time, the military, state security agencies, and associated civilian death squads killed, tortured, and "disappeared" thousands of persons. By the late 1980s, military regimes were replaced by civilian governments in South America. In Central America, civilian governments were also established, but the military remained influential in light of the civil wars there. The period drew to a close in South America because of civilian opposition to military rule, especially over issues of failed economic policies, a disastrous foreign war (Argentina), gross violations of human rights by military regimes, and a feeling that most domestic threats from leftist forces had been brought under control. *See also* MILITARISM (145); MILITARY-CIVILIAN CYCLES (151).

Significance
The neomilitarism from the 1960s to the 1980s is the most recent of apparently recurring cycles of military and civilian governments in Latin America. The period was highlighted by the wide-scale adoption of militarism throughout the region, the lengthy term of regimes in nations where the military typically intervened for only a few years at a time, and the brutal nature of the repressive measures undertaken. These measures brought international criticism and foreign aid cutbacks, and contributed to strong feelings of antimilitarism among some groups that had initially supported the interventions. The civilian governments that were established in the late 1980s were left with major economic problems and with the challenge of reconciling popular demands for trying military leaders for atrocities and other crimes and implied and real threats of renewed intervention.

Praetorian Army — 153

A professional military force that intervenes in politics for the purpose of controlling the government. Praetorian armies can be distinguished from: (1) professional armies that are primarily concerned with national security and do not directly intervene in politics; (2) irregular armed forces under the control of regional strongmen or national *caudillos*; and (3) contemporary guerrilla armies that are primarily concerned with taking control of the government to effectuate revolutionary societal changes. Two types of modern praetorian armies have been identified by scholars. The arbitrator-type army accepts the existing social order and is primarily concerned with professional norms and career matters. Following a coup d'etat, it usually returns to the barracks soon after reestablishing order, settling political disputes among civilians, and installing an "acceptable" regime. Thereafter, the arbitrator-type army is less concerned with everyday politics and prefers to seek its political aims by acting as a pressure group. Examples of this in Latin America include the Argentine army following the fall of Juan Perón in 1955, the Chilean army from 1924 to 1933, and the Brazilian army before the coup of 1964. The second type of praetorian army recognized by scholars is the ruler type, which rejects the existing social order for one based on modernization, industrialization, and rapid economic growth. This type lacks confidence in civilian rule and has no expectation of returning soon to the barracks once it assumes power. The ruler-type praetorian army is committed to political action, operates in the open, and creates a political organization in order to legitimize its rule. It is ideologically more sophisticated and displays a strong commitment to nationalism. Examples of the ruler-type praetorian army in Latin America include the Brazilian army when it assumed power in 1964 and the Peruvian army following its assumption of power in 1968. *See also* MILITARISM (145); MILITARISM: GUARDIAN THESIS (147); MILITARISM: PROFESSIONALIZATION THESIS (149); PRAETORIANISM (154).

Significance
Most Latin America armies are either arbitrator-type or ruler-type praetorian armies. There are few instances of traditional *caudillo*-led armies and of armed forces that have ceased to intervene directly in government, as in Mexico. In Cuba, the irregular guerrilla army under Fidel Castro that took power in 1959 has been transformed into a professional revolutionary army. In that capacity, it has been a key instrument in the transformation of Cuba into a socialist society. Many Latin American armies have been modernized and their officer corps professionalized. These developments, however, did not lead to a decrease of military intervention in politics. The belief that the armed forces have the right and duty to change the government at will in order to protect their corporate existence, achieve their goals, or modernize the state continues to dominate the thinking of many Latin American officers. This is evident, for example, in Argentina and Chile after civilian rule returned in the late 1980s, and it is the case in most Central American nations.

Praetorianism | 154 |

A form of militarism in which the armed forces act as a corporate body to maintain control over government. The term "praetorianism" was originally coined in reference to the Roman Praetorian Guard, a specialized elite force that acted as the bodyguard of the Roman emperor. A primary function of the Praetorian Guard was to protect the imperial capital from rebellious army garrisons, but in time it came to control the selection of the emperor. In contemporary times, praetorianism is sometimes used to refer to any form of militarism, but, in more specialized usage, it refers to situations where the military, as a corporate institution, actively intervenes in politics to select or change the government. Praetorianism can be distinguished from: (1) *caudillismo*, the rule of traditional military chieftains; (2) caesarism, the dictatorship of a single, popularly supported charismatic personality who is usually a military officer; and (3) the garrison state, a nation that has transferred much power to the military because of a long-term national security crisis. Typical actions of a praetorian army include: (1) the deposition of a civilian president by a coup d'etat and the installation of another civilian who is controlled by the military; (2) the removal of a general-president who is threatening to establish or has established himself as a caesaristic dictator; (3) the conduct of elections in which the only candidates for the presidency are military officers; and (4) the creation of a military government for either a brief period to reestablish the existing social order or for a longer period to make fundamental societal changes. *See also* CAESARISM (138); CAUDILLISMO (139); JUNTA (144); MILITARISM (145); PRAETORIAN ARMY (153).

Significance
Of the various types of militarism, praetorianism is the most prevalent form in contemporary Latin America. Although caesaristic dictators, such as Getúlio Vargas of Brazil and Juan Perón of Argentina, are better known, and traditional *caudillos*, such as Alfredo Stroessner of Paraguay, survived in some of the less developed societies, the modern praetorian state is the norm for military governments. Praetorian armies characterize the military establishments not only in Latin America but also in Africa, the Middle East, and Southeast Asia. In contemporary times, praetorianism has tended to flourish in those states where political institutions lack legitimacy, the civilian government is ineffective or corrupt, political parties are weak, and social classes are polarized. Economic modernization has disrupted the traditional social order in many such states, but it has failed to establish a new societal consensus.

Pronunciamiento | 155 |

A public declaration or proclamation of a political nature. The term *pronunciamiento* is often used in a specialized way to refer to the public statement that a military commander issues during a *cuartelazo* or barracks revolt. Such an action informs the government and the people that the commander's forces are opposed to the government and are moving to overthrow it. The purpose of the *pronunciamiento* is to encourage other garrisons to join in the rebellion, force the hand of neutral or more cautious commanders, and bring about a quick resignation of the president. The term *pronunciamiento* is also used in reference to declarations of organized civilian forces, such as political parties or regional groups, that declare themselves in revolt against the government. The *pronunciamiento* is sometimes called a *manifiesto* or *grito*, although the term *grito* (literally, cry) is often reserved for more dramatic declarations of independence. *See also* CUARTELAZO (141); GRITO (169).

Significance
The *pronunciamiento* has been used extensively in Latin American history and is an essential feature of the *cuartelazo*. Although it seems that a public declaration would eliminate the element of surprise from a revolt, when it is uttered in conjunction with a *cuartelazo*, it is part of a well-planned maneuver. A *pronunciamiento* is usually made at the appropriate moment when it is expected to start a train of events that will result in the resignation of the government.

Governmental Institutions and Processes

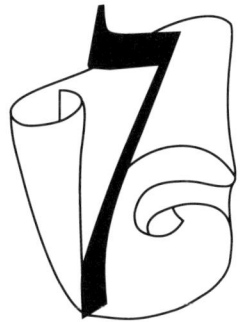

Alternation and Parity (Alternación y Paridad) | 156 |

An election and appointment system used in Colombia from 1958 to 1974 to end partisan violence. The alternation and parity system provided for the alternation of Conservatives and Liberals in the presidency; the equal sharing between Conservatives and Liberals of all legislative, executive, and judicial positions at the national, departmental, and municipal levels; and a ban on other parties. The coalition of Liberals and Conservatives, called the National Front, was authorized under the plan to govern for 16 years. The agreement also required a two-thirds majority in both houses of the legislature to pass legislation. The alternation and parity system was formulated by the Liberal party leader, Alberto Lleras Carmago, and the Conservative party leader, Laureano Gómez, in the Sitges Agreement of 1957, and it was adopted by a plebiscite in the same year. The two party leaders believed that this system would end the brutal partisan civil war *(La Violencia)* that had been ravaging Colombia since 1948. They also thought the new system would create a viable, limited democracy following the removal of General Gustavo Rojas Pinilla, the dictator who had ruled Colombia from 1953 to 1957. *See also* NATIONAL FRONT (COLOMBIA) (126); VIOLENCIA, LA (105).

Significance
The alternation and parity system helped to end Conservative-Liberal civil violence, but the granting of equal power to the minority party Conservatives retarded the adoption of needed socioeconomic reforms. The bipartisan agreement was difficult to initiate because the Conservatives, who were to nominate the first president, could not agree on a candidate, and the Liberal party leader, Lleras Carmago, was consequently selected. In addition, strong factions were formed within each party, and intense partisanship in the National Congress prevented the passage of legislation. Other parties, not permitted under law, organized groups that

infiltrated the two major parties, and other candidates competed in presidential elections against the official candidate of the National Front. The system also resulted in a high level of voter apathy, as the abstention rate reached 65 percent of potential voters in presidential elections and 70 percent in congressional elections. The formal requirement of alternation between Conservatives and Liberals was adhered to, however, and the agreement on parity of government posts was also implemented. In order to break the legislative stalemate, the Liberal president, Carlos Lleras Restrepo, introduced constitutional changes in 1967 that authorized socioeconomic reforms and removed the two-thirds majority requirement in the legislature. Other parties were permitted in 1968, and competitive elections were introduced at the departmental and municipal levels in 1970. The National Front was disbanded prior to the 1974 presidential election of the Liberal, Alfonso López Michelsen, but the parity system continued throughout his term. With the alternation system no longer in effect, the Liberal party continued in office with the election of Julio César Turbay as president in 1978.

Bicameralism 157

The constitutional principle of a two-chamber legislature. Bicameralism can be contrasted with unicameralism, which provides for a single-chamber legislature. Bicameralism is found in 12 of the 20 Latin American republics, including Mexico, Nicaragua, the Dominican Republic, and in all the states of South America except Paraguay. Where bicameralism exists in Latin America, the second chamber or upper house is called the Senate and the popular or lower house is called the Chamber of Deputies. Deputies are always directly elected (except under the 1976 communist constitution in Cuba), but in a few countries senators are indirectly elected, and some are appointed or receive their seats *ex officio*, such as former presidents. Senators usually have a longer term of office, a higher qualifying age, represent a larger geographical territory, and are fewer in number than deputies. *See also* UNICAMERALISM (179).

Significance
Bicameralism is found in the four federal states of Latin America, because it is linked to the representation of states in the national legislature. Except for Brazil, however, federalism is weak in Latin America. Senates have not proved to be effective in protecting states from central government encroachment on their constitutional rights, nor have they been able to limit presidential powers. Wherever they exist, senates are powerful only where the legislature as a whole is powerful. A good example of a strong bicameral legislature is that which existed in Chile before the military coup of 1973.

Caciquismo 158

The system of local rule by a strong political boss. *Caciquismo* is derived from the Indian word *cacique*, meaning an Indian chief of a village or tribe. During the colonial period in South America, Spaniards ruled through Indian *caciques*, who were given special privileges and were used as bosses in the *repartimiento* and other forced labor systems. After independence, the term *cacique* referred to any strong local leader, and *caciquismo* became a way of life in rural areas. A *cacique* who established his power beyond the locality and who exercised regional or national control is called a *caudillo*. In contemporary times, *caciquismo* is not only widespread in rural towns but also in urban slums where rural migrants have congregated. A *cacique* maintains himself in power by a complex system of nepotism, patronage for his clients, control over local government services, illegal activities, and the use of force. In Peru, *caciques* are known as *curacas*. In Brazil, local bosses are called *coroneis*, and a close equivalent of *caciquismo* is known as *coronelismo*. *See also* CAUDILLISMO (139); CORONELISMO (162).

Significance
Caciquismo is the local form of personal autocratic rule that characterizes much Latin American political life. It perpetuates at the local level a system of government based on face-to-face contact, friendship and family ties, and extralegal relationships. By providing benefits for its clients and power for its leaders, *caciquismo* has tended to retard the development of modern political systems in Latin America.

Colegiado — 159

A constitutional system having a collegial or plural executive, which has been used at various times in Uruguay. A modified form of the *colegiado* was put into effect by the Uruguayan Constitution of 1918. It provided for a popularly elected nine-member National Council of Administration that shared executive powers with a popularly elected president. This dual executive system was abolished following a coup in 1933. The *colegiado* was adopted in a pure form by the Uruguayan Constitution of 1951. The single presidency was eliminated and replaced by a popularly elected National Council of Government that possessed all executive powers. Six council seats were reserved for the largest party and three for the second party; the presidency of the council rotated annually among members of the largest party. In 1966, the people decided in a plebiscite to return to a single presidency. *See also* BATLLISMO (52); PRESIDENTIALISM (177).

Significance
The *colegiado* was proposed in 1913 by the Colorado party leader, José Batlle y Ordóñez, who wanted to pattern Uruguayan government on the Swiss model. Ideally, the *colegiado* would preserve democracy by eliminating one-man dictatorships and presidentialism and by guaranteeing representation in the executive branch to the minority party. The practical experience with the *colegiado*, however, was generally unsatisfactory. Competition between the Colorado and Blanco parties and personal rivalries among political leaders limited the ability of the *colegiado* to cope with major economic problems facing the country in the late 1950s and early 1960s. Popular dissatisfaction with the *colegiado* is seen in the sizeable 60 percent majority that rejected the system in 1966. Uruguay remains the only Latin American country to experiment with a collegial or plural executive form, and a strong, single presidency has been and remains the norm.

Constitution — 160

The fundamental law of a state that sets forth the principles of government. A typical constitution creates a legal order, establishes a framework of government, delegates authority, limits the exercise of power, and guarantees the rights of the people. Latin American constitutions in the nineteenth century were patterned after ideas found in the liberal Spanish Constitution of 1812, in French republican constitutions, and, to a limited extent, in the Constitution of the United States. Principles found in most Latin American constitutions include republicanism, centralization of governmental authority, presidential dominance, separation of powers, political democracy, protection of human rights, a code law system, and the non-reelection principle. Four Latin countries have adopted federalism, five have unicameral legislatures, several have experimented with a parliamentary form of government, one experimented with a plural executive, and others have affirmed the principle of judicial review. Being written documents rather than constitutions based on custom and usage, Latin American constitutions have been promulgated primarily by constitutional conventions or legislatures and in a few instances by executive decree. Most Latin American constitutions are quite lengthy, often containing such details as (1) the administrative organization and powers of governmental departments; (2) extensive statements setting forth the philosophy and principles governing economic and social legislation; and (3) less important matters of public policy ordinarily found in statutes. Over 200 constitutions have been in force in Latin America since independence. Venezuela and the Dominican Republic have had over 20, 12 nations have had over 10, and Panama and Paraguay have had fewer than 5 each. The average for all of Latin America is about ten for each country. No constitution now in force dates from independence. Although most have been in force for short periods, there are noteworthy examples of long-lived constitutions in Argentina, Chile, Costa Rica, Mexico, and Uruguay. About half of the constitutions now in force date from the 1960s. The most unusual contemporary one is the Cuban Constitution of 1976, the only communist constitution in the Western Hemisphere. *See also* CONSTITUTIONALISM (60); CUBAN CONSTITUTION OF 1976 (164); MEXICAN CONSTITUTION OF 1917 (172).

Significance
Although constitutional instability in Latin America is very high, the large number and short life of these documents may be misleading. Some Latin American governments preferred to revise rather than amend their fundamental law. Constitutions tend to multiply in an environment that is conducive to military interventionism and political instability. Revolutionary governments prefer to begin anew, and they often try to legitimize their regimes and achieve respectability by promulgating new constitutions. The average number of constitutions per country in Latin America, for example, is no greater than that of France since its revolution of 1789. Many nineteenth century Latin American constitutions were based on foreign models, and their liberal and democratic principles turned out to be inoperable in the Hispanic environment. A number of changes have been made in the twentieth century, and constitutions now are based more on local custom and national ideals, with the social democratic Mexican Constitution of 1917 serving as a model. Yet there is a great discrepancy between the guarantees and procedures proclaimed by Latin American constitutions and the reality of political life. This contrast is so great that some scholars prefer to distinguish between the "paper constitution" and the "real constitution." The reality of Latin American politics is that many constitutional provisions are either ignored, suspended, or rewritten at the will of the group in power. This was no less true for the liberal constitutions of the nineteenth century than it is for modern constitutions with their nationalistic and social reform overtones. Latin American constitutions do not serve the same functions in the political system as do constitutions in North America or Western Europe. In Latin states, constitutions act more as a set of ideals than as a check on government. They are often viewed as philosophical statements that prescribe a program for the future, and their role is primarily symbolic. Insofar as the prevailing

political culture (which is part of the "real constitution") is incorporated into the written document—as, for example, the non-reelection principle—any violation of the constitution may be a cause for rebellion.

Continuismo 161

The practice of maintaining the chief executive in office beyond constitutional limits. Because the laws and constitutional customs of Latin America usually prohibit consecutive terms for the president, dictators and popular leaders have clearly used the techniques of *continuismo* to retain power. Peaceful methods of continuing a president in office include: (1) amending the law of constitution to provide for consecutive terms; (2) adopting a new constitution under which the prohibition of consecutive terms begins anew and is not applied to the incumbent or is discarded; (3) securing a favorable constitutional interpretation by a court; or (4) justifying continuation in office by the use of a plebiscite. Attempts to prevent *continuismo* include the placing of strong provisions in constitutions that prohibit reelection or consecutive reelection, and legal provisions or theories that assert or imply the people's right of revolution whenever *continuismo* is practiced. Strong dictators often practice *continuismo*, but weaker ones who attempt it do not always succeed because their attempts invariably lead to increased opposition and, in some cases, coups d'etat. *See also* IMPOSICIÓN (119); NON-REELECTION PRINCIPLE (175).

Significance
Continuismo has been widely practiced in the nineteenth and twentieth centuries throughout Latin America, especially in Central America and the Caribbean. Modern examples include those of Jorge Ubico of Guatemala, who served from 1935 to 1941; and Anastasio Somoza of Nicaragua, who took power in 1937, extended his term to serve from 1939 to 1948, returned to office in 1950, and was assassinated in 1956 after another attempt at *continuismo*. In Brazil, Getúlio Vargas took power in 1930, changed the constitution, and served until 1945 when he was overthrown by a coup. In Argentina, Juan Perón eliminated a 100-year-old constitutional provision against reelection, was reelected in 1951, and was overthrown by a coup in 1955. President Marcos Pérez Jiménez of Venezuela ran a plebiscite in which voters could cast a yes or no vote on whether he might continue in office. The rigged "election" resulted in an 85 percent affirmative vote, but he was overthrown by a combined civilian and military coup a few weeks later. General Alfredo Stroessner of Paraguay took power in 1954, removed the constitutional restriction prohibiting reelection after two terms, and was elected in seven consecutive elections; he was overthrown by a military coup in 1989 after holding office for 35 years. The left-leaning President João Goulart of Brazil, whose constitutional power as president had been much reduced by a temporary move to a parliamentary system, argued that the prohibition against reelection did not apply to a president whose powers of office had been restricted. His stated desire to run again for office in October 1965 was one of the reasons for his overthrow by a military coup in 1964. In Haiti, a novel form of *continuismo* was practiced by President François Duvalier, who along with his successor-son, President Jean-Claude Duvalier, was named President-for-Life. "Papa Doc" Duvalier died in 1971 after 14 years in power, and his successor, "Baby Doc" Duvalier, fled the country during riots in 1986. In Cuba, Fidel Castro has established what is probably the longest record of a Latin leader exercising continuous

political and governmental power. In 1992 he had been in power since January 1959—33 years.

Coronelismo `162`

A system of local political control in Brazil by strong political bosses. The term *coronelismo* is derived from the Portuguese word *coronel* (plural, *coroneis)*, literally meaning a military "colonel," but especially referring to a civilian political boss of a rural municipality or region. A *coronel* was originally a large rural landowner who had received that title for membership in the National Guard. Under the system of *coronelismo*, a prestigious local political leader organized rural voters into a political machine that provided votes to state and federal officials in exchange for favors, patronage, and municipal control. The *coronel* dominated the local scene and distributed benefits to his dependents. *Coronelismo* is somewhat analogous to *caciquismo* in Spanish America, except that the *coronels* were usually prestigious local gentry and never Indians or *mestizos*, as has often been the case in Spanish America. *See also* CACIQUISMO (158).

Significance
Coronelismo was practiced in rural areas of Brazil in the nineteenth and early twentieth centuries, and it was still used in remote areas when a democratic republic was reestablished in 1946. *Coronelismo* functioned as a form of personal rule characteristic of semi-feudal societies dominated by the landed gentry. The *coronel* acted as a political broker or intermediary between the enfranchised but essentially powerless masses and state and national political leaders. In this fashion, local power was integrated into the national system, but the political system remained essentially personalistic, decentralized, and oligarchic.

Cuban Committees for the Defense of the Revolution (CDR) `163`

Mass mobilization organizations established in Cuba by Fidel Castro in 1960. Committees for the Defense of the Revolution were set up in neighborhoods throughout Cuba for the purpose of rooting out counter-revolutionary forces, educating the people about socialism, communicating government policy, and mobilizing "voluntary" work groups and attendance at rallies and parades. By the mid-1960s, the CDRs included over 2 million members. *See also* CASTROISM (54).

Significance
By serving as a national vigilance network, Committees for the Defense of the Revolution strengthened Castro's hand against opponents and factions within the revolution who were contesting him for power. The CDRs gave many people an opportunity to participate directly in the work of the revolution. Critics of the Castro regime consider members of the CDRs to be neighborhood spies who, along with the military and other mass mobilization organizations, helped organize Cuba into a highly regimented society.

Cuban Constitution of 1976 `164`

The fundamental law of Cuba, which is the only communist constitution in force in the Western Hemisphere. Following public discussions of a draft document, the Cuban Constitution of 1976 was approved by the first congress of the Cuban Communist party in December 1975. It was adopted by 98 percent of the voters and took effect in 1976. The constitution declares that Cuba is a "socialist state of workers, peasants, and other manual and intellectual workers." It provides that the national economy is based on socialist principles, but some private property is recognized in agriculture, and personal property acquired by working or through inheritance is protected. The constitution guarantees the freedom and inviolability of the individual, and it protects freedoms of speech, press, and religion so long as they conform to the goals of a socialist society and are not used to oppose the socialist revolution or the defense of the state. A new framework of government, called Organs of Popular Power, is created by the charter. These institutions include directly elected municipal assemblies, directly elected provincial assemblies (since 1992), and a directly elected and appointive national assembly. The National Assembly is the supreme organ of the state; it elects the Council of State, whose chairman is head of state, head of government, and commander-in-chief of the armed forces. The constitution recognizes the Communist party as the "highest leading force of the society and state," and acknowledges the "friendship, aid, and cooperation of the Soviet Union and other socialist countries." *See also* COMMUNIST PARTY OF CUBA (PCC) (114); CONSTITUTION (160); CUBAN ORGANS OF POPULAR POWER (165).

Significance
The Cuban Constitution of 1976 was adopted 16 years after the revolutionary forces of Fidel Castro succeeded in overthrowing the regime of Fulgencio Batista. From 1959 to 1976, Cuba had no constitution and Fidel Castro ruled by virtue of his revolutionary authority. The constitution was patterned on the communist constitution of the Soviet Union with respect to: (1) classification of the people into workers, peasants, and intellectual workers; (2) the nature of the socialist system; (3) the special place accorded to the Communist party; (4) the affirmation and limitations placed on personal rights and civil liberties; and (5) the structure of government. Unlike the Mexican Constitution of 1917, with its innovations that had a great impact in Latin America, the Cuban Communist Constitution has had little influence in the region. Within Cuba, however, the charter formally represents the institutionalization of the Castro revolution, and it proclaims the depersonalization of political power, the decentralization of governmental authority, and the broadening of popular participation in government. Inasmuch as political opposition is not permitted in Cuba and President Castro remains the dominant political figure, it is not yet clear whether the constitution or the 1992 amendments will be a permanent and effective instrument following his leaving government.

Cuban Organs of Popular Power | 165

The representative institutions of the Cuban governmental system established by the Constitution of 1976. The Organs of Popular Power (*Organos de Poder Popular*—OPP) include municipal assemblies, provincial assemblies, and the National Assembly. Delegates to municipal assemblies are directly elected for a two-and-one-half-year term by all citizens aged 16 or over. Municipal assemblies are responsible for regulating local services, such as restaurants, stores, hospitals, and local transportation. Constitutional changes in 1992 provided for direct elections of provincial and national assembly members. Provincial assemblies may control provincial matters such as intercity transportation and provincial commerce. The National Assembly is the "supreme organ of the state" and has a five-year term. Previously, municipal assemblies selected a majority of the National Assembly members and the remainder were appointed by the Communist party. The National Assembly selects the 31 members of its executive arm, the Council of State, and the Council of Ministers.

See also COMMUNIST PARTY OF CUBA (PCC) (114); CUBAN CONSTITUTION OF 1976 (164).

Significance
The Organs of Popular Power represent an attempt to legitimize and institutionalize the Castro revolution in Cuba. The functions of government were formally decentralized, and for the first time since Fidel Castro seized power in 1959, the people were able to participate in nationwide elections. The framework of government is based on that of the former Soviet Union. Members of the various assemblies are only part-time legislators who keep their regular jobs, and day-to-day functions of these bodies are carried out by their respective executive organs. Popular elections for delegates to the municipal assemblies have attracted high voter turnouts, competition among several candidates is common, and runoffs to produce a majority are sometimes required. Other parties are not permitted, however, and all candidates are nominated by the Communist party or its affiliated mass organizations. The former indirect election and the new direct election system in a one-party state assure that local Communist party activists will win and maintain the status quo in Cuba. Beginning in 1976, about 90 percent of the National Assembly deputies are members of the Communist party or its affiliated organizations. At the executive level, an interlocking directorate of government and party posts prevails. Following the 1976 elections, for example, 30 of the 31 members of the Council of State were members of the Central Committee of the party, and all members of the party's Politburo were members of the Council of State. The 1976 constitution envisaged a depersonalization of power, but by 1990 this had not yet manifested itself. Fidel Castro simultaneously holds the positions of president of the Council of State, chairman of the Council of Ministers, ranking member of the party Politburo, and first secretary of the party. His brother, Raúl Castro, holds the second highest position in all these agencies. Although the Organs of Popular Power are new representative institutions, traditional Latin America features of presidentialism and personalism still tend to prevail in Cuba.

Decree-law | 166 |
A law issued by a president rather than enacted by a legislature. The authority to promulgate a decree-law (decreto-ley) is authorized by the nation's constitution, delegated to the president by the congress, or assumed by the president as a matter of traditional practice. Decree-laws have the same legal standing as congressional laws and are generally recognized as valid by the courts. *See also* PRESIDENTIALISM (177).

Significance
The decree-law is a key power utilized in the system of presidentialism, which is characteristic of Latin America. Much law in the region has been issued through presidential decrees. This is common practice when the legislature is not in session, which is often the case during periods of emergency, a state of siege, or when a revolutionary government has taken power. Some Latin American countries have tried to limit the use of decree-law by constitutional restrictions, such as requiring subsequent congressional approval of decrees, limiting the issuance of decrees to periods when the legislature is not in session and during a state of emergency.

Federalism | 167 |
A political system that constitutionally divides the powers and functions of government between central

and regional governments. Federalism can be contrasted with the unitary form of government, in which all constitutional authority is concentrated in a central government that delegates certain functions to local units. Argentina, Brazil, Mexico, and Venezuela formally are federal unions, and the other 16 republics of Latin America are unitary states. In Brazil, Mexico, and Venezuela, the regional governments are called states, while in Argentina they are called provinces. All four federations have placed their national capital cities in Federal Districts, and all four have national territories that are not organized as states. The constitutional division of powers between the national and state governments generally follows the U.S. model, with the national (often called the federal) government having delegated or enumerated powers and the states having residual or reserved powers. The actual distribution of powers, however, very much favors the federal government, which has a long list of enumerated powers. Generally, states have a very small revenue base, do not collect taxes, and subsist on federal grants-in-aid. The federal government has much exclusive authority, enacts the civil and criminal codes of law, has the right to intervene in state affairs, and may set aside state authorities and laws. In Venezuela, the president appoints state governors. *See also* CENTRAL AMERICAN FEDERATION (24); UNITARY GOVERNMENT (180).

Significance
Federalism is weak in Spanish America. Following independence, the colonial tradition of centralized rule was attacked by liberals who believed that federalism was necessarily linked with republicanism, civil liberties, and separation of church and state. Conservatives wanted to establish a unitary state, tended to favor monarchical government and a state church, and preferred a restricted suffrage. A Central American Federation was established in 1824, but it broke up into its constituent units in 1831. Chile experimented with a federal form in 1826, and Honduras installed a federal system from 1824 to 1831. The federalist-centralist struggles in the nineteenth century were especially bitter and bloody in Argentina, Colombia, Mexico, and Venezuela. In Colombia, a partial form of federalism was adopted in various stages from 1853 to 1886, but the country suffered greatly from federalist-centralist wars from the 1830s to 1903. The federal systems that emerged in Mexico, Argentina, and Venezuela were dominated by strong nationalists, military governments, and dictators. Currently, Venezuela is only nominally federal, and in Argentina and Mexico the central government dominates the states. In Brazil, the colonial tradition was different because the Portuguese Crown permitted much decentralized authority to be exercised. This tradition continued past independence, and the Brazilian states became firmly entrenched and often acted independently of national authority. Getúlio Vargas, who ruled Brazil from 1930 to 1945, restricted the powers of the states and centralized national authority in his presidency. Brazil returned to true federalism in the democratic period following Vargas's rule, but the military regime of 1964 to 1985 centralized authority and weakened state governments again. Traditional Brazilian federalism was reinstituted under the constitution of 1988. Generally, the prospects for an expansion of federalism in Latin America are poor, not only because of a weak historical tradition but also because many modernizers believe that strong, centralized government is needed to cope with the problems of national development.

Functional Representation | 168 |

A system of representing people according to their occupational or social affiliations rather than according to their place of residence. Functional representation organizes people into categories, such as agriculture, industry, labor, and education, with representatives to the national legislature chosen by these groups. The concept has been advocated by both leftist and rightist political movements as a more meaningful form of representation than the near-universal system of geographic or territorial representation. Functional representation is especially associated with syndicalism, a radical leftist movement that would transfer power from the territorial congress to federated bodies of industrial workers. Corporatism is an example of a right-wing adaptation of the principle of functional organization. *See also* CORPORATISM (61).

Significance
A few Latin American countries have experimented briefly with functional representation, but only Ecuador has used the system regularly since 1929. In the Ecuadorian Senate, 12 functional senators, equally divided between the highlands and coastal regions, supplement the larger group of territorial senators. Functional senators represent agricultural, commercial, industrial, and labor groups. Four additional functional senators represent private education, public education, the armed forces, and journalistic, scientific, and literary societies. In Ecuador, as in other societies, the interests of occupational and social groups are represented mainly by pressure groups and class-based political parties that operate within the system of territorial representation.

Grito | 169 |

A dramatic declaration of independence or revolution. The Spanish word *grito* literally means "cry," and it is used to describe dramatic statements by political figures who proclaim a revolution against established authority. Included among the major historical *gritos* in Latin America are: the *grito de Dolores* of Father Miguel Hidalgo y Costilla in Dolores, Mexico, on 16 September 1810, which was a declaration of independence from Spain; the *grito de Ypiranga* of the Portuguese crown prince, Pedro I, the regent of Brazil, who declared the independence of Brazil on the banks of the Ypiranga River in the province of São Paulo on 7 September 1822; and the *grito de Yara* by a group of Cuban patriots whose call for the independence of Cuba from Spain began the Ten Years War in October 1868. *See also* PRONUNCIAMIENTO (155).

Significance
As in other declarations of independence, the purpose of the *grito* is to rally support for the revolution. The proclamation often outlines the major evils of the established authority, sets forth the goals of the revolution, and calls for support by other patriots. In the case of declarations of independence against the colonial authority, the day of the *grito* is usually celebrated as independence day.

Institutional Act | 170 |

An organic law that suspends or replaces provisions of the constitution or legal system. Institutional acts are means by which new revolutionary governments change the legal order and legalize their actions. These fundamental laws make changes in the framework of government, suspend constitutional guarantees, delegate additional powers to the president, and remove or reduce the constitutional powers of other branches and levels of government. The acts are decreed by the revolutionary authority or by the new head of state, and they are identified by number. *See also* CONSTITUTION (160).

Significance
Institutional acts were used by the military government of Brazil from 1964 to 1985 and by the military government of Uruguay from 1973 to 1985. The acts were the principal legal means by which these governments carried out their renovating tasks, operating, in effect, under broad grants of authority they delegated to themselves. In Brazil, institutional acts empowered the president to suspend the civil and political liberties of persons; remove civil servants from office; cancel the mandates of elected national, state, and local officials; authorize arrests; declare a state of siege; and make law without congressional consent. Other acts dissolved political parties, changed the election system for national and state offices, eliminated direct elections for mayors of capital cities, imposed censorship on the press and the arts, and permitted arbitrary arrest and imprisonment. The most notorious of Brazil's laws, Institutional Act 5, granted the president great powers over the structure and authority of congress and the courts. In Uruguay, the military government that assumed direction of the country in 1973 patterned a number of its institutional acts on Brazilian models.

Judicial Review │171│

The constitutional principle that courts have the final authority to decide the constitutionality of statutory laws and executive actions. In a constitutional system incorporating the principle of judicial review, the written constitution is the supreme law of the land, other laws and governmental actions must be authorized by the constitution, and a court is the final judge of the permissibility of these laws and actions. Judicial review is provided in one form or another in most Latin American constitutions. In some countries, the judicial review power of the courts is shared with the congress, is denied altogether, or the power to interpret the constitution is given only to the congress. Mexico, for example, has a limited form of judicial review that is frequently invoked. Under the writ of *amparo*, a citizen may seek judicial relief from the denial of personal rights that are guaranteed by the constitution. If granted, the writ suspends the application of the law in the case under consideration. Because the law is not declared invalid, a separate decision is required in each case, and the courts have been overburdened with many appeals. *See also* CONSTITUTION (160); MILITARISM: GUARDIAN THESIS (147).

Significance
Although the principle of judicial review in Latin American constitutions was patterned after the U.S. experience, it has not functioned in the same way. It is rare that a court will declare a law or an executive action to be unconstitutional. Judicial review in Latin America has consequently been confined to cases involving the administrative application of the law. Judicial review cannot function in a political system where governments are unstable and constitutions are often overturned, suspended, or rewritten at the will of the dominant political group. Where governments are stable, they are dominated by the executive branch, and judicial review is also insignificant. The task of defending the constitution, therefore, has fallen to political groups and popular action or to the military, which acts as guardian of the constitution.

Mexican Constitution of 1917 │172│

The fundamental law of Mexico, which has served as a model for other Latin American constitutions. The Mexican Constitution of 1917 was adopted in the closing period of the civil war that followed the Mexican Revolution of 1910. It was written at a constitutional convention called by President Venustiano Carranza. He preferred a traditional liberal democratic constitution, but more revolutionary leaders took control and produced a completely new charter. The constitution reaffirmed the principles of political democracy, but individual rights were limited by the superior rights of the group or the nation. The constitution is noteworthy because it proclaimed a wide-ranging series of labor, social, and agrarian reforms, the two most copied sections being Articles 27 and 123. Article 27, which was based on a collective theory of productive property, provided that subsoil minerals belonged to the nation and could not be alienated; all land was vested in the nation, which in turn could transmit it to private persons; ownership of property by foreigners was limited, and foreigners were excluded from owning certain land and water rights; and Indian communal lands were protected. Article 123, which proclaimed an extensive program of labor legislation, established maximum hour and minimum wage limits, protections for women and child labor, social insurance programs that provided for unemployment and workman's compensation and old-age benefits, profit sharing, and the right to unionize and strike. The constitution also provided for free public education, strengthened the office of president against congress, reaffirmed the non-reelection principle, and continued anticlerical laws. *See also* CONSTITUTION (160); MEXICAN REVOLUTION (37).

Significance
The Mexican Constitution of 1917 was the first modern charter to proclaim a social revolution. It made a sharp break with other Latin American constitutions, which still were much influenced by European or North American liberal democratic ideas. Instead of stressing the principles of individualism, limited government, political equality, and traditional civil liberties, the Mexican Constitution emphasized the rights of the nation in the field of natural resources and the power of the state to regulate and expropriate property and to encourage economic and social egalitarianism. The constitution was very influential throughout Latin America, especially Articles 27 and 123, which found their way into numerous constitutions, including those of Cuba (1940), Brazil (1946), and Venezuela (1961). The 1917 constitution provided the legal authority for sweeping reforms in Mexico, including massive land reforms, nationalization of the petroleum industry in 1938, the placing of limits on foreign investment, and the organization of powerful labor unions. In other Latin countries, constitutional provisions have also resulted in the nationalization of petroleum and other mineral wealth, and in the regulation or expropriation of industrial, commercial, financial, and agricultural property. Although many objectives of the social revolution have not been achieved in Mexico or in most other countries, the principles of economic nationalism, state socialism, centralized economic planning, and social egalitarianism are enshrined in many Latin American constitutions. In late 1991, the Mexican Congress rescinded the anticlerical provisions of the 1917 constitution.

Ministry of Gobernación | 173 |

The Ministry of Government, a cabinet-level department, often translated as Ministry of Interior. The typical functions of the Ministry of *Gobernación* include supervision of provincial and municipal government, administration of the electoral process, and control of the national police.

Significance
The Minister of *Gobernación* is often the most important cabinet minister and second-ranking person in the government after the president. The importance of the position derives from the centralization of governmental authority that is typical in Latin America, from the national control of the electoral process, and from national police powers. The political importance of the office is enhanced in those nations where illegal political opposition to the government is strong, fraudulent elections are commonplace, and patronage in local government is controlled by a national party. In Mexico, for example, the Minister of *Gobernación* was often tapped to be the next president. In recent years under new democratic governments (including Mexico's), the election-supervising functions of the Ministry of Government have been transferred to independent electoral commissions. There is no direct counterpart to this cabinet department in the U.S. government.

Monarchy | 174 |

A state headed by a king, queen, or emperor. Monarchies existed in pre-Colombian America among the Aztec, Inca, and other tribes. The European states that colonized Latin America had hereditary, absolute monarchs who jealously guarded their powers and installed a centralized form of government in the colonies. This was not true of Portuguese rule in Brazil, however, which was highly decentralized. Generally, the Indian tribes of the highlands that had monarchies were better able to adapt to colonial rule than the decentralized, less-developed tribes of the lowlands. At the time of the Wars of Independence in the first decades of the nineteenth century, republicanism was strong and many patriots rejected both the rule of Spain and the monarchical principle. Some military and conservative leaders, however, wanted to retain the institution of monarchy because they believed that Latins needed to be ruled by a strong personal authority. In Mexico, in the Plan of Iguala, monarchists proposed an independent Mexican state under the rule of a European prince. When this plan was rejected by Spain, Agustín de Iturbide (1783–1824) seized power and reigned as emperor from May 1822 to February 1823, when he was overthrown by republican forces. In 1864 the French, who had been occupying Mexico, installed the Austrian archduke Maximilian, who reigned until he was defeated by the forces of Benito Juárez in 1867. For brief periods after independence in Haiti, parts of the country were ruled by Jean Jacques Dessalines and Henri Christophe, who styled themselves emperors. The monarchical system was of a more substantial nature in Brazil. Instead of gaining independence by a war against Portugal, sovereignty came by virtue of a declaration in 1822 by the crown prince and regent of Brazil, Pedro I, who refused to obey his father's order to return to Portugal. The Brazilian monarchy continued until 1889 when Pedro II, who had ruled for 48 years in an enlightened manner, was overthrown by the military who declared Brazil to be a republic. *See also* DEMOCRACY (63); REPUBLICANISM (77).

Significance
Today, monarchy no longer exists in the Latin states of the Western Hemisphere. Monarchical rule in the colonial period contributed much to the establishment and retention of centralization of authority, executive dominance, and statism in Spanish America. In the republican period, surrogates for the king can be seen in

the *caudillo*, the caesaristic dictator, and the strong president. Most of the former British colonies in the Caribbean area have retained the monarchical system, with the British Crown as the formal head of state. Other former British colonies—Guyana and Trinidad and Tobago—along with the former Dutch colony of Suriname, have adopted the republican form of government.

Non-Reelection Principle | 175 |

A constitutional provision that prohibits successive terms for the chief executive and, in some cases, for other elective officials. The non-reelection principle has been used by all Latin American nations at one time or another, and it is especially applied to the office of president. Most countries prohibit immediate reelection of the president, but a few, Mexico being the foremost, prohibit any reelection of presidents. Mexico also forbids the reelection of state governors. Some countries, such as Guatemala, prohibit the election of a person who originally took power by a military coup d'etat. The non-reelection principle in Latin America is often violated by the practice of *continuismo*, under which a president maintains himself in office beyond his first term by changing the constitution to permit reelection. *See also* CONTINUISMO (161); PRESIDENTIALISM (177).

Significance
The non-reelection principle is a fundamental part of Latin American political culture. Although the principle is violated almost as often as it is honored, it is typically reaffirmed after each violation. Attempts at *continuismo* by dictators and populist leaders have often been successful, but just as often these attempts have tended to rally the opposition and have resulted in some type of overthrow. The motto of the Mexican Revolution—Effective suffrage; no reelection—displays this deeply held belief, which in Mexico has been faithfully observed since the revolution was consolidated in 1920.

Parliamentary System | 176 |

A form of government in which there is a fusion of the executive and legislative branches, and the head of government and cabinet are responsible to the parliament. In a parliamentary system, the head of government (called the prime minister or premier) and the cabinet are drawn from the leadership of the majority party or coalition in parliament. The prime minister and cabinet may stay in office only so long as they are able to maintain majority support in parliament. Failure to do this results in either a change of the prime minister and cabinet or a parliamentary election. The head of state in a parliamentary system (either a president or monarch) is usually a ceremonial officer. *See also* COLEGIADO (159); PRESIDENTIALISM (177).

Significance
The parliamentary system is little used in Latin America, and most governments are based on an undiluted presidential model. Brazil formally used the parliamentary system in the nineteenth century during the empire period, but the Brazilian republics have been presidential with one brief exception. In 1961, the military forced the adoption of a parliamentary system as a way to prevent the leftist, João Goulart, from exercising full presidential powers. The system was ineffective and was rejected by the people in a plebiscite in 1963. In Chile, a parliamentary form was used from 1891 to 1925, but it suffered from cabinet instability, with over 100 cabinets and 500 ministers holding office during that period. Some countries, such as Peru, Bolivia, Cuba, and Honduras, have

experimented with a semi-parliamentary system in which a cabinet minister may be questioned by the congress and forced to resign by a censure vote. When Fidel Castro took power in Cuba in 1959, he maintained the distinction between the head of state and head of government and took the latter position as prime minister. Elections were never held, however, and no legislative assembly was called into session for 17 years. This situation continued until 1976, when a new constitution based on the Soviet model was adopted. Under the new constitution, Castro is the president of the State Council and chairman of the Council of Ministers, thus functioning as both head of state and head of government. Latin American experiments with parliamentary or semi-parliamentary forms have not succeeded in diminishing the predominant position of the president.

Presidentialism | 177 |

A governmental system in which the president dominates all institutions of government and is the major locus of political power in the country. Presidentialism, or *presidentialismo,* is based in part on the great authority granted to the office of the president by a typical Latin American constitution. In many cases, the president exercises a broad collection of executive, legislative, administrative, and judicial powers. Included among his many powers is the authority to issue decrees; make cabinet, administrative, and judicial appointments; declare a state of siege; suspend the constitution; command the military; control the state budget and public revenues; grant pardons; and, in federal states, intervene in state matters. In addition to his constitutional powers, the president is often the strongest political leader in the country, and he uses this political power to supplement his constitutional authority to dominate the legislative, military, and judicial branches of government. In many instances, his power is absolute, and among the masses he is often viewed as a semidivine father figure. *See also* CONSTITUTION (160); PARLIAMENTARY SYSTEM (176); PERSONALISM (PERSONALISMO) (73).

Significance
Presidentialism became the norm in Latin America even though many Latin constitutional systems were patterned on the U.S. model, with its separation of powers and three equal branches of government. In Costa Rica, and before 1973 in Chile and Uruguay, the constitutional and political powers of presidents were limited by strong legislatures. The more typical situation of presidentialism, however, is reinforced in many countries by the large number of military or civilian dictators. Yet there is no better example of presidentialism than in Mexico, where stable, civilian governments have been the norm since the 1940s. Presidentialism in Latin America can be traced to the strong tradition of authoritarianism in the colonial period, the inability of constitutional government to take root, Latin cultural traits that emphasize personalism and power, centralized government, and weak political parties. During the twentieth century, the increased functions assumed by government in economic and social fields have also served to strengthen the supremacy of the president in the governmental system.

State of Siege | 178 |

A situation in which constitutional guarantees have been suspended and emergency powers are exercised by the president. Provisions for a state of siege *(estado de sitio)* are included in all constitutions in Latin America, although some countries place restrictions on its use. A state of siege is intended to meet an emergency created by an invasion or a major domestic disturbance by granting dictatorial powers to the president. It is usually declared by the legislature or by the president when the legislature is not in session. In the latter case, the president must usually recall the legislature and secure authorization for continuing the emergency. Under the authority of a state of siege, the president may exercise all executive and legislative powers and suspend court prerogatives. Unlike martial law provisions used in the United States, the police, civil government, and civil courts continue to function and are not replaced by military authority. Most Latin countries use the term "state of siege," but it is also referred to as suspension of guarantees, grant of extraordinary powers, state of national emergency, or measures of security. *See also* PRESIDENTIALISM (177).

Significance
A state of siege has been declared at least occasionally in every Latin American nation. Some countries use the procedure infrequently, whereas in others a state of siege is a normal occurrence. In most cases, the state of siege is declared for domestic emergencies rather than to meet the threat of invasion. Abuse of the power is widespread, for it is often used by dictators and military governments as the legal pretext for the exercise of extraordinary powers against their political enemies. Democratic governments have also used the provision to handle the problem of internal disturbances. In many cases, the state of siege is continued long after the immediate problem is controlled. Some states have been ruled by emergency powers for years. This was true, for example, in Argentina under Juan Perón from 1945 to 1955 and in Colombia during much of the violent period from 1948 to 1958. Some states have attempted to limit the powers or restrict the time period of a state of siege. This approach seems to be effective only where the legislature has retained some of its power or a measure of political stability has been achieved, such as in Costa Rica and Mexico.

Unicameralism [179]
The constitutional principle of a single-chamber legislature. Unicameralism can be contrasted with bicameralism, or a legislature having two chambers. Unicameral national assemblies are used in Costa Rica, Cuba, El Salvador, Guatemala, Haiti, Honduras, Panama, and Paraguay. From 1857 to 1874, Mexico also experimented with unicameralism. In 1961, Haiti dropped bicameralism when President François Duvalier instituted unicameralism and uncontested elections as a way to control the legislature. In Cuba, after 17 years of power, Fidel Castro's government adopted a constitution that provided for the single-chamber, indirectly elected National Assembly. *See also* BICAMERALISM (157).

Significance
Unicameralism is used in most of the smaller countries of Latin America, particularly in Central America where there is greater cultural homogeneity. Although many arguments have been advanced in favor of unicameralism or for bicameralism, neither form has been able to produce strong legislatures in Latin America. Both types of legislatures are weak and both tend to be dominated by the executive branch. One of the few effective and independent national legislatures, however, is found in the single-chamber Legislative Assembly of Costa Rica.

Unitary Government [180]
A political system in which all constitutional authority resides in the central government. In a unitary form of government, there is no constitutional grant of local autonomy to

provincial governments, and all lower levels of government are creations of the central government and subject to it. Unitary government is contrasted with federalism, in which state or provincial governments are independent of the central government and receive their powers from the nation's constitution. Of the 20 Latin American republics, 16 have the unitary form, and Argentina, Brazil, Mexico, and Venezuela constitutionally have the federal form. *See also* FEDERALISM (167).

Significance
The system of unitary government was typical during the colonial period and was carried over into the period of independence. The tradition of the "free city" with its council (*cabildo*) had been strong in Spain and the institutional form was used in Spanish America, but after the centralization of the Spanish kingdom, little real authority was exercised by the *cabildos*. Following the Wars of Independence in Latin America, bitter struggles took place between federalists and unitarians, and for the most part the supporters of unitary government prevailed. True federalism took hold only in Brazil, where decentralized government was the norm. Some unitary states, however, such as Uruguay, Costa Rica, and Chile, have usually practiced a form of local self-government in which provincial or local authorities have exercised more autonomy than comparable levels in some federal states.

Economic Modernization and Political Development

Development Strategy: Conservative Modernization | 181

A view that economic development and modernization in Latin America can best be achieved by following the developmental examples of the United States and Western European capitalist states. Supporters of the strategy of conservative modernization reject both the emphasis on retaining the economic status quo of the traditionalist approach and the reformism and interventionist governmental role advocated by the progressives. The conservative approach focuses mainly on capitalism and the role of entrepreneurs to expand the nation's economy. Government should refrain from major campaigns to promote rapid social change and to ensure social justice. Conservatives hold that political, economic, and social stability are the key elements in successful development because the environment must be conducive to encouraging local investors and to attracting substantial inflows of foreign capital. While conservatives favor industrialization and rural modernization, they believe that only the private sector can provide the means and the initiative essential to achieving those goals. *See also* DEVELOPMENT STRATEGY: MACRO APPROACH (182); DEVELOPMENT STRATEGY: MICRO APPROACH (183); DEVELOPMENT STRATEGY: PROGRESSIVE MODERNIZATION (184); DEVELOPMENT STRATEGY: REVOLUTIONARY APPROACH (185); DEVELOPMENT STRATEGY: TRADITIONAL APPROACH (186).

Significance
The conservative approach as a development strategy dates back to the writings of classical economists, such as Adam Smith and David Ricardo, and to the policies and programs of active leaders, such as Alexander Hamilton. Are such policies applicable to the countries of Latin America with their unique historical backgrounds and indigenous social conditions? Conservatives reply in the affirmative, holding that capitalism unfettered by government policies that discourage private initiatives

can provide the moving force needed to develop and modernize. The export strategy of the traditionalists is also rejected by the conservatives, who tend to agree with the main goals of the progressives to build a strong industrial economy with an efficient agricultural base. For the conservatives, this means that emphasis should be placed on the workings of the market economy, on encouraging savings and their transfer into investments, and on production rather than consumption. Monetary stability is a *sine qua non* for the conservatives, and inflation that has reached epidemic proportions in some Latin countries is the major enemy of successful development programs. Few Latin governments have been able or willing to pursue the conservative approach despite its attractions to the upper and middle classes. Typical conservative policies, such as the requirement of a united role for government, improvement for the masses only as benefits tend to trickle down from the wealthy, and the lack of an organized campaign to combat social injustices, placed conservatism out of step with the masses, but the failures of socialist and state interventionist policies have led many governments in the late 1980s to privatize state enterprises and adopt free market policies.

Development Strategy: Macro Approach 182

Economic advancement sought through national or regional programs based on a single plan or on a related series of plans. The macro approach differs from the micro approach in that the latter sees development occurring as a result of numerous, often autonomous projects that contribute to the growth of the national product as they are brought to fruition. The macro approach places emphasis on government planning and government contributions to development through the building of socialized industries or the subsidization of private companies. The macro approach may proceed from a national or regional master plan, from a coordinated series of plans, or, less formally, from a grand strategy. *See also* DEVELOPMENT STRATEGY: MICRO APPROACH (183).

Significance
Many countries of Latin America have developed national plans to provide a macro approach to guide their societies through a series of stages of development that culminate eventually in modernization. In addition, Latin development has also been greatly affected by macro programs developed through the Inter-American system and through the United Nations. The United States began to encourage a macro approach to Latin development in the late 1930s through a program of technical assistance, followed in 1949 by the Point Four Program and the Alliance for Progress in the early 1960s. The United States continues to provide annual aid to most Latin countries through the Agency for International Development (AID). The United Nations has provided much developmental help of a macro nature through the United Nations Development Program (UNDP), the Economic Commission for Latin America (ECLA), the World Bank Group and International Monetary Fund (IMF), and through special programs and agencies, such as the United Nations Conference on Trade and Development (UNCTAD) and the United Nations Industrial Development Organization (UNIDO). The main arguments favoring the macro approach to development are that it encourages an infusion of external aid and it views the problem of development from a broad, overview perspective. The main arguments against it are, as suggested by empirical evidence, that it often does not speed up the development process,

that too much decision-making power is centralized in the hands of national or regional planning personnel, and that most of the planned projects do not provide substantial help for those most in need of it.

Development Strategy: Micro Approach |183|

Economic progress sought through a series of decentralized projects that are largely unplanned and uncoordinated. The micro approach differs from the macro approach in that the latter tends to foster developmental progress through large-scale national or regional plans. The micro approach conversely envisions large-scale development occurring as a result of the impact of many local projects that together contribute to general progress of the nation or region. *See also* DEVELOPMENT STRATEGY: MACRO APPROACH (182).

Significance

The micro approach to development in Latin America has been fostered by private foundations and by various private, national, and international lending institutions that do not require the projects they support to be part of a master plan for development. Micro projects receiving external assistance have tended to focus on specific areas, such as certain health problems or educational needs. Most emphasis in the micro approach, however, is placed on the role of private capital and individual entrepreneurs who undertake their projects in anticipation of personal gain. The main argument favoring the micro approach to development is that it does not entail the risk inherent in a linear-styled development strategy, which, if poorly organized or implemented, tends to produce a general failure. Its strength lies in its variety and decentralized decision making. The main argument against it is that the micro approach fails to recognize that most developmental problems are closely interrelated and, therefore, a common approach can be used most effectively to cope with common problems. The micro approach lends itself more to free enterprise capitalism and tends to shun massive planning schemes of the type utilized for many years in the Soviet Union (the Five-Year Plans).

Development Strategy: Progressive Modernization |184|

A view that economic development and modernization in Latin America can best be achieved by positive governmental programs aimed at dismantling cumbersome, unproductive structures and replacing them with efficient and equitable ones. Supporters of the strategy of progressive modernization advocate middle-ground approaches between the extremes of traditionalism and revolution. Progressives have received their ideological inspirations from such diverse sources as Keynesian economic theories, Roman Catholic social doctrines, the New Deal of President Franklin Roosevelt, and "democratic Marxism," such as that attempted by Salvador Allende in Chile during the early 1970s. Encouragement for applying the ideas of progressive modernization in Latin America has come from the United Nations Economic Commission for Latin America (ECLA), which for three decades has fostered a structuralist approach to development that posits the need for drastic political, economic, and social changes within nations and a major overhauling of the international economic system. Major goals for progressives include: (1) rural changes, such as land reform, social justice, and diversification of agriculture; (2) industrialization that reduces dependence on imports and increases the value of exports; and (3) a reordering of the world market system so as to stabilize commodity prices and improve the terms of trade of Latin countries vis-à-vis the industrialized world. All changes must be carefully orchestrated by planners and carried out either directly by government or under its watchful eye. In the economic area, emphasis is given to maintaining consumption as well as production, with an expanding equilibrium maintained between the two. *See also* DEVELOPMENT STRATEGY: CONSERVATIVE MODERNIZATION (181); DEVELOPMENT STRATEGY: MACRO APPROACH (182); DEVELOPMENT STRATEGY: MICRO APPROACH (183); DEVELOPMENT STRATEGY: REVOLUTIONARY APPROACH (185); DEVELOPMENT STRATEGY: TRADITIONAL APPROACH (186).

Significance
The theory of progressive modernization is pursued as a development strategy throughout most of Latin America. It holds that, once under way, the system will engender support for continued change. In practice, however, most of the nations of Latin America have seen the theory and its goals weakened or smashed by failures to achieve rural reform, substantial industrialization, or changes in the world economic system favorable to developing countries. Supporters of progressive modernization, however, have not conceded defeat since they believe the alternative would be either stagnation or revolution. Increasingly, Latin countries have joined with others of the Third World to utilize the United Nations system for issuing demands and applying pressures on the industrialized bloc for changes in the form of a New International Economic Order (NIEO). In order to progress according to plan, many countries have borrowed heavily from the World Bank Group, the International Monetary Fund, the U.S. Export-Import Bank, the Inter-American Development Bank, and various other public and private banks. This heavy foreign debt burden weakened development programs because much of the developing nations' annual income must be devoted to amortizing debts rather than applied to expanding, self-supporting growth. In some countries, political reforms essential to providing social justice and gaining the support of the masses have failed either because the governing elite has been able to resist popular pressures or because the democratically governed systems have been unable to gain enough popular support to implement necessary changes. Other factors in Latin America that have contributed to the slow pace of modernization include rapid population growth, competitive arms races, depressed prices for primary commodities in the world market, heavy inflation in both developed and developing states, and reduced programs of foreign aid. The future of progressive modernization as a development strategy depends on many factors. Perhaps the key issue concerns the degree of political unity among Latin countries and the extent to which they demonstrate their willingness to undertake a harmonization of their policies in seeking common objectives. The main obstacle to progressive modernization in the 1990s is the huge debt and interest payments acquired by most Latin states during the 1970s and 1980s.

Development Strategy: Revolutionary Approach | 185 |

The position that economic development and modernization in Latin America cannot be achieved until a revolution occurs that mixes or replaces capitalism with socialism. In the revolutionary approach, laissez-faire capitalism is regarded as the main obstacle to successful development. Without revolution, the country seeking development exists in a dependency status, exploited both by powerful external and internal capitalists. According to most revolutionaries, social changes that could stimulate development and produce social justice are blocked by an establishment or power elite that defines its self-interest in narrow terms. To win power, revolution needs the dedicated support of the masses for the cause, a weak disoriented government, and the right conditions, such as support from the military or from an external source of power. Once entrenched, the implementation of revolutionary objectives requires a rallying and unifying ideology, a mass political movement, an external or internal enemy or scapegoat, and a large, efficient, thoroughly politicized bureaucracy. A spirit of nationalism tends to pervade revolutionary movements, inculcating the masses with a collective sense of mission and serving as the means for achieving legitimacy for the regime and unleashing the spirit and energy of the people. Typically, a charismatic leader or father figure becomes the central focus of authority and serves as the means for mobilizing support for the movement and for the nation. In the revolutionary approach, the means utilized in seeking to achieve the goals of the movement include: (1) instituting broad social changes to bring all the people of the nation into the movement; (2) ending illiteracy and teaching ideological "truths" and the skills needed for a modernized society; (3) ending or reducing dependence on foreign capital and markets; (4) reorganizing economic and social institutions to expand economic growth and increase productivity; (5) undertaking land reform and other rural changes; and (6) ending unemployment by creating a program of mass participation in infrastructure development and other social projects. *See also* REVOLUTION (100); DEVELOPMENT STRATEGY: CONSERVATIVE MODERNIZATION (181); DEVELOPMENT STRATEGY: MACRO APPROACH (182); DEVELOPMENT STRATEGY: MICRO APPROACH (183); DEVELOPMENT STRATEGY: PROGRESSIVE MODERNIZATION (184); DEVELOPMENT STRATEGY: TRADITIONAL APPROACH (186).

Significance
In Latin America, three revolutionary models stand out: Mexico, Chile, and Cuba. In coming to power, the Mexican revolutionaries endured a long civil war and many struggles for power among the movement's generals and their factions before the revolution was won and consolidated. In Chile, the Marxist regime of Salvador Allende won power through democratic constitutional procedures. In Cuba, Fidel Castro and his revolutionary movement won power after carrying on a limited guerrilla war and as a result of the opposition of the masses to the Fulgencio Batista dictatorship. In terms of means and objectives, the three models again reflect major differences. The Mexican Revolution sought to reduce dependence on foreign investors while maintaining a mixed capitalist/socialist economy. Rural reform (including ending the *latifundio* system) and industrialization based on domestic capital accumulation constituted the two main revolutionary objectives. The Chilean Revolution sought to institute a democratic socialist state based on Marxist principles. The basic strategy for Allende's Popular Unity government involved the progressive socialization of the economy and rural development based on an agrarian reform program. In addition, Allende sought to achieve a redistribution of income favoring the lower classes so as to increase demand to encourage production and to gain the mass support needed to usher in the revolutionary program. The Cuban Revolution, conversely, is based on the pre-Gorbachev Soviet and Eastern European model that involves the establishment of autocratic power and heavy emphasis on

state planning, forced savings, the building of new social and economic institutions, expropriation of foreign-owned properties, and industrialization. In evaluating the three models, the Mexican Revolution appears to have consolidated its many gains and is moving the society rapidly toward full modernization. The Cuban Revolution has gone through several phases, and, while much has been accomplished, the society remains essentially non-industrial with a relatively low standard of living and a heavy foreign debt. With the collapse of the Soviet model in the USSR and Eastern Europe in 1990, the Castro model appears to be doomed, since critical Soviet aid is ended. Finally, the Chilean Revolution appears to have provided a negative answer to the long-standing question of whether Marxist socialism can be instituted in a nation through democratic procedures. The overthrow of the Salvador Allende regime, its replacement by a military autocracy, and the role played by the intervention of the United States all tend to support that negative assumption. The three revolutions and their outcomes are destined to influence Latin American political and economic development strategies for many years.

Development Strategy: Traditional Approach | 186 |

A view that economic development and modernization in Latin America can best be achieved by following time-tested strategies and techniques. The traditionalist approach to development dates back to the days following the winning of independence in the nineteenth century. Emphasis is placed on the classical economic theory of comparative advantage, which holds that each society should specialize in the production of those goods that can be produced most efficiently, and the rest of the nation's needs should be supplied through trade. For Latin America, the traditional way means that, for the most part, each nation should concentrate on utilizing its natural endowments most effectively in supplying raw materials and primary commodities to the industrialized countries. Foreign exchange earned through these activities can then be used to raise living standards and support reasonable measures of investment and growth that encourage a slow but steady development of the nation's economy. In short, traditionalists place primary emphasis on private property, a market economy, entrepreneurship, and the encouragement of inflows of foreign capital. The traditional approach differs from the conservative in that the former views modernization as a consequence of specialization in the supplying of primary commodities, whereas the latter stresses industrialization based on private capital and entrepreneurship. It differs from dependency theory in that traditionalists regard underdevelopment as a result of internal failures of the nation's economy, whereas dependency theorists view it as a process inherent in the unequal nature of the world economic system, as described by Karl Marx.

Significance
The traditional approach as a development strategy has largely been discarded as unsuitable for the contemporary world of Latin America. The emergence of many new factors and the growing complexity of long-standing problems—the population explosion, mass poverty, urbanization, political instability, the power of multinational corporations, and others—demand more rapid action and tangible progress. Also, a "revolution of rising expectations" has swept over the masses of Latin America as it has in other areas of the Third World. Societies are no longer

willing to accept a traditionalist approach if it tends to caution moderation and opposes change. Only a few Latin American countries openly place strong emphasis on the traditionalist approach today, although its basic emphasis on expanding commodity sales continues to influence policymakers in Latin societies.

Development Theory: Cultural Approach   187

An explanation of Latin American underdevelopment that emphasizes the role of Hispanic political culture as the primary causative factor. The cultural interpretation of underdevelopment argues that typical Hispanic values and attitudes concerning social status, wealth, work, personal relations, power, authority, and government retard economic and political development in the region. The Hispanic culture has economic and political consequences, including support for centralized government, militarism, authoritarianism, clientelism, patrimonialism, and corporatism. The economic system is consequently inefficient and exploitative, management is corrupt, and landowners and industrialists are more interested in protecting, with violence if necessary, their status and wealth, rather than promoting growth through entrepreneurship and risk-taking investment. *See also* CORPORATISM (61); DEVELOPMENT THEORY: DEPENDENCY (188); POLITICAL CULTURE (75).

Significance
The cultural approach to understanding the causes of underdevelopment, which has both Latin and North American proponents, evolved as a reaction to economic dependency theory, which has been the predominant theoretical approach among Latin American academic theorists. Cultural theorists criticize dependency theory for its overemphasis on structural features of the international economic system, its anti-capitalism, its uncritical acceptance of Marxist categories of thought, and its unwillingness to acknowledge the developmental benefits that accrue from foreign investment in Latin America. While acknowledging that there are many factors that impact development, they attempt to show how culture, religion, myth, and tradition negatively affect entrepreneurship.

Development Theory: Dependency   188

A class of theories that draws a dependent economic relationship between the most developed nations and less developed nations. Dependency theory has been applied to explain the continuing problems in Latin America of underdevelopment and political conflict. Dependency theory is based on the continued existence of an imperialistic relationship between the industrialized countries of Western Europe, the United States, and Japan on the one hand and the developing nations of Latin America and the Third World on the other. Although many versions of the dependency theory have been put forth by analysts, ranging from moderate to radical Marxist revolutionary types, they are all built around the theme that Latin America's economic life is characterized by exploitation by powerful capitalist states from outside the region. *See also* DEVELOPMENT THEORY: CULTURAL APPROACH (187); DEVELOPMENT THEORY: DESTABILIZATION (189); DEVELOPMENT THEORY: DIFFUSION (190); DEVELOPMENT THEORY: DUAL SOCIETY (191); DEVELOPMENT THEORY: IMPOVERISHMENT (192); DEVELOPMENT THEORY: INTERNAL COLONIALISM (193); DEVELOPMENT THEORY: MARGINALITY (194); DEVELOPMENT THEORY: POLITICAL DEVELOPMENT (195).

Significance
The dependency theory has had the support of a number of contemporary scholars in Latin America and the United States who believe it to be the main explanation for developmental failures. Many Latins blame the imperialistic relationship for determining the nature of their region's development, which has its main focus on resource extraction and a world market system that keeps them in economic bondage. Multinational corporations also intervene to support the power of local elites and to perpetuate rigid class structures. Industrialization is limited to enclaves that are the overseas extensions of the corporations' domestic operations, with the remainder of the country continuing to live in dire poverty. For radical dependency theorists, this neo-imperialist relationship must be destroyed by revolution, and a new international economic order attuned to the needs and realities of development must be created. The collapse of communism in the Soviet Union and in Eastern Europe has strengthened the view of some dependency theorists that the world economy involves a continuing struggle between the rich capitalist states and those societies in the Third World that remain impoverished and fully dependent on the most highly developed states. Other observers see the collapse of Marxist socialist systems as proof that the dependency theory—and the Marxist ideas that inform it—is incapable of providing either a satisfactory explanation of underdevelopment or a successful solution to it.

Development Theory: Destabilization 189

A theory that seeks to explain why neo-Keynesian capitalist development approaches have generally failed to produce either substantial economic advances or social and political stability. According to the theory, destabilization in Latin America appears to be a natural product of the process of industrialization, in which rapid socioeconomic change tends to result in increased frustrations among the masses as their expectations rise faster than their standard of living, resulting in a veritable "frustration gap" between expectations and reality. Progress, because it can never be rapid enough to satisfy the demands for change in the status quo, tends to increase rather than diminish the level of frustration in the society. Consequently, these conditions often result in the development of authoritarian systems rather than accelerating movement toward democracy. *See also* DEVELOPMENT THEORY: CULTURAL APPROACH (187); DEVELOPMENT THEORY: DEPENDENCY (188); DEVELOPMENT THEORY: DIFFUSION (190); DEVELOPMENT THEORY: DUAL SOCIETY (191); DEVELOPMENT THEORY: IMPOVERISHMENT (192); DEVELOPMENT THEORY: INTERNAL COLONIALISM (193); DEVELOPMENT THEORY: MARGINALITY (194); DEVELOPMENT THEORY: POLITICAL DEVELOPMENT (195).

Significance
Although some development strategies postulate the development of democratic systems of government as economic modernization occurs, empirical evidence in Latin America suggests that the opposite or destabilization is more likely to occur. During the 1980s and early 1990s, many Latin countries have moved toward freedom and democracy and away from autocratic control systems that were in the past a result of reactionary movements or military coups. Some observers posit the hypothesis that, because most growth occurs as a result of infusions of foreign capital, if democracy becomes a victim of integral nationalism used by the military or oligarchic groups in the society to justify their seizure of power, development progress may be a victim for lack of capital infusions.

Development Theory: Diffusion | 190

A class of theories concerning socioeconomic development that focuses on the transmission of material goods and cultural patterns from the modernized to the traditional sectors of society. The main points of diffusion theory with respect to Latin America are (1) national and subnational regions advance through various stages of development; (2) less developed nations are composed of two societies, one modernized, capitalistic, and advanced, and the other traditional, feudalistic, and backward; (3) a conflict exists between methods and values of the industrial bourgeoisie of the modernized sector and the traditional landed oligarchy; (4) less developed nations and the underdeveloped hinterlands of transitional nations require the infusion of outside capital and technology and the adoption of modern social relations and values to become fully developed; (5) certain political and economic conditions, such as political stability and incentive-producing taxation systems, need to be established in less-developed nations to attract foreign investment; and (6) the United States can help Latin America develop by political and military intervention, cultural penetration, and economic investment and foreign aid. *See also* DEVELOPMENT THEORY: CULTURAL APPROACH (187); DEVELOPMENT THEORY: DEPENDENCY (188); DEVELOPMENT THEORY: DESTABILIZATION (189); DEVELOPMENT THEORY: DUAL SOCIETY (191); DEVELOPMENT THEORY: IMPOVERISHMENT (192); DEVELOPMENT THEORY: INTERNAL COLONIALISM (193); DEVELOPMENT THEORY: MARGINALITY (194); DEVELOPMENT THEORY: POLITICAL DEVELOPMENT (195).

Significance
Diffusion theory and dependency theory are two broad schools of thought that seek to explain the causes of Latin American underdevelopment. The main ideas of diffusion theory are much criticized by dependency theorists, the more radical of whom reject the premises, values, and conclusions of diffusionists. Generally, dependency theory traces the causes of retarded development to the dependent relationship that exists between the exploited, resource-bearing nations and subnational rural regions on the one hand, and the capitalist, technologically advanced foreign powers and subnational urban areas on the other. Not all diffusion theorists, however, are supporters of a capitalist or pluralist approach to development. All diffusion theorists and most dependency theorists assume that development—defined as industrialization, the adoption of modern technology, and the spread of consumer goods among the masses—is the goal that all less-developed societies ought to pursue.

Development Theory: Dual Society | 191

The theory that Latin American countries are composed of two separate social systems. According to the dual society thesis, each country has an urban, developed, modernized capitalistic sector and a rural, agrarian, and traditional feudalistic sector. People who live in the modernized society have advanced technological skills and progressive, utilitarian, and meritocratic attitudes and values. The "archaic" or traditional society is composed of conservative social groups who are primarily engaged in feudalistic agriculture and who retain traditional social relationships based on ascriptive and personalistic criteria. According to some versions of the dual society theory, progress and socioeconomic development occur insofar as the attitudes, values, economic processes, and industrial products of the modernized sector spread to the traditional sector. *See also* DEVELOPMENT THEORY: CULTURAL APPROACH (187); DEVELOP-

MENT THEORY: DEPENDENCY (188); DEVELOPMENT THEORY: DESTABILIZATION (189); DEVELOPMENT THEORY: DIFFUSION (190); DEVELOPMENT THEORY: IMPOVERISHMENT (192); DEVELOPMENT THEORY: INTERNAL COLONIALISM (193); DEVELOPMENT THEORY: MARGINALITY (194); DEVELOPMENT THEORY: POLITICAL DEVELOPMENT (195).

Significance
The dual society thesis must be distinguished from the descriptions of writers who simply note the great contrasts that exist between the urban and rural, modernized and less developed, and Indian and non-Indian facets of Latin American life. The dual society thesis is held by a number of theorists who go beyond these contrasts and seek to explain the process of development and the causes of underdevelopment. The thesis is attacked by those dependency theorists who advocate the internal colonialism thesis, which holds that despite the surface differences that exist between modernized and traditional regions, Latin American countries are single, integrated societies in which the modernized sector exploits the traditional sector. Dual society theorists defend progressive capitalism and the national bourgeoisie, and attack the feudalistic, landowning oligarchy for retarding the spread of industrialism. The dual society thesis is a variation of the diffusion theory, which argues that the underdevelopment of Latin America can be eliminated by placing major emphasis on the spread of capital, technology, and industrial products to backward areas.

Development Theory: Impoverishment 192

A theory that seeks to explain the failure of Latin American states to develop and modernize because indigenous economic conditions have made it impossible for them to become highly productive, mass-consuming societies. The impoverishment theory holds that mass poverty is a natural condition in most Latin states despite major industrialization programs and other policies aimed at alleviating poverty and ushering in an era of plenty. *See also* DEVELOPMENT THEORY: CULTURAL APPROACH (187); DEVELOPMENT THEORY: DEPENDENCY (188); DEVELOPMENT THEORY: DESTABILIZATION (189); DEVELOPMENT THEORY: DIFFUSION (190); DEVELOPMENT THEORY: DUAL SOCIETY (191); DEVELOPMENT THEORY: INTERNAL COLONIALISM (193); DEVELOPMENT THEORY: MARGINALITY (194); DEVELOPMENT THEORY: POLITICAL DEVELOPMENT (195).

Significance
The impoverishment or scarcity theory has become prophetic and self-fulfilling in many Latin countries where mass poverty is increasingly accepted as a condition determined by historical, geographical, cultural, and other largely unchanging factors. Moreover, because development progress can more easily occur in one or several urban centers than having it spread evenly throughout the country, enclave modernization has resulted. Such developments produce relatively high living standards for the people living in a small geographical area, while the major portion of the population continues to endure grinding poverty. The result is that some planners have begun to reject industrialization as the major goal and have instead begun to focus on rural reform and development in order to have a bigger impact on coping with poverty. According to the impoverishment theory, populations that double within 20 to 30 years—adding to increasing competition within and between Latin American countries—are inescapable products of the unrelenting conditions of poverty. Poverty, under these conditions, is both cause and effect.

Development Theory: Internal Colonialism — 193

The theory that Latin American countries are single, unified societies in which the urban, modernized sector exploits the rural, underdeveloped sector. The internal colonialism thesis rejects the dual society theory, which asserts that two separate social systems exist in Latin America—one based on progressive capitalism and the other on traditional feudalism. Advocates of the internal colonialism thesis argue that the Latin American economy has always been exploitative and that the dominant urban sector has extracted the agricultural and mineral wealth of the hinterlands and exploited its labor. Moreover, the less developed regions of Latin America have always been internal colonies of the developed urban areas. The theory rejects the ideas that national capitalists desire the economic development of the hinterlands, that the urban entrepreneurs have a conflict of interest with the landed oligarchy, and that the middle class is progressive, enlightened, and hostile to the ruling class. *See also* DEVELOPMENT THEORY: CULTURAL APPROACH (187); DEVELOPMENT THEORY: DEPENDENCY (188); DEVELOPMENT THEORY: DESTABILIZATION (189); DEVELOPMENT THEORY: DIFFUSION (190); DEVELOPMENT THEORY: DUAL SOCIETY (191); DEVELOPMENT THEORY: IMPOVERISHMENT (192); DEVELOPMENT THEORY: MARGINALITY (194); DEVELOPMENT THEORY: POLITICAL DEVELOPMENT (195).

Significance
A variation of dependency theory, the internal colonialism thesis has been formulated to specifically reject the dual society thesis and the related diffusionist theory. The latter holds that less developed regions within a country can be developed by the spread of modern capital and technology. The internal colonialism theorists sharpen the broader concepts of dependency and imperialism to show the parallel relationships that exist between the exploitation of the economies of Latin America by external powers and the internal exploitation of rural areas by urban forces.

Development Theory: Marginality — 194

A concept used by different schools of thought to explain the poor political, economic, and social conditions of either individuals within a society, social classes with the nation, or nations within the larger world community. The concept of marginality emphasizes the lack of political power, poor economic condition, and low social status of individuals, groups, or nations. In modernization theory, an underdeveloped nation is composed of two parts: an advanced, modern sector and a backward, underdeveloped sector. As nations industrialize and modernize, some groups, characterized by poverty or remoteness from national life, are left behind; their relative poverty increases, and they are not integrated into the socioeconomic system. This understanding of marginality is sometimes referred to as dualism or the dual society thesis. In this view, modernization proceeds by the spread of goods and values to backward areas (the diffusion thesis), and the urban poor are assisted by social reformist programs of an ameliorative nature. In Marxist dependency theory, emphasis is placed on a nation's marginality within the global capitalist system. This condition is the consequence of the exploitation of the physical resources and labor of less developed states by monopoly capitalist enterprises and the developed nations. The poor nations themselves are not composed of dual societies but are single societies in which the more developed sectors exploit the backward sectors. These ideas are often referred to as the single society thesis and internal colonialism.

See also DEVELOPMENT THEORY: CULTURAL APPROACH (187); DEVELOPMENT THEORY: DEPENDENCY (188); DEVELOPMENT THEORY: DESTABILIZATION (189); DEVELOPMENT THEORY: DIFFUSION (190); DEVELOPMENT THEORY: DUAL SOCIETY (191); DEVELOPMENT THEORY: IMPOVERISHMENT (192); DEVELOPMENT THEORY: INTERNAL COLONIALISM (193); DEVELOPMENT THEORY: POLITICAL DEVELOPMENT (195).

Significance
As it was redefined over decades of debate, the concept of marginality passed through several definitions and emphases. Marxist dependency theorists criticized the modernization notion of marginality by pointing out its inadequate explanation of the causes of poverty and underdevelopment, and for its stressing cultural differences instead of social class differences. They also disparaged the idea that reformist policies, such as education and social welfare, could create just, equitable societies or transform weak, exploited nations into highly developed and powerful ones in the world community. Critics of the Marxist dependency notion of marginality point out that internal economic factors are more causative of marginality than external ones, and that marginal groups have a more productive role than that which dependency theory ascribes to them. The debate over the meaning and role of marginality between modernization and dependency theorists enabled them to sharpen their understanding about the phenomenon. Much of the debate has been ideological, but it serves to reinforce the broader notion that the nature and causes of so-called marginal individuals, groups, or nations are complex and cannot be ascribed to one factor.

Development Theory: Political Development | 195 |

The process by which a political system increases its capacity to govern, attain legitimacy, and solve economic, social, and political problems. Political development is distinguished from economic development, which stresses the transition from subsistence agriculture, rudimentary transportation and communication systems, export of raw materials, and low level of manufacturing to an economic system characterized by industrialization, rise in the gross national product, high standard of living, and self-sustaining economic growth. Political development is also distinguished from social development, which stresses the increases in social and occupational differentiation and social mobility, improvements in literacy and education, population stabilization, migration of labor to industrial centers, urbanization, and an increase in the number and types of social and community organizations. Political development is primarily concerned with nation building and state building. In nation building, there is an increasing identification of the masses with the institutions, symbols, and values of the nation. The state has a central government that is capable of exercising its authority throughout the land. Governments are stable, political leaders are changed orderly and peacefully, and the military does not regularly intervene in politics. There is a general popular consensus on the constitutional system, governmental institutions, and national goals, and the political system is accepted as legitimate by the people. Representative institutions are effective and political parties reflect the will of the people. Governmental institutions are able to cope with the complex economic and social problems that confront the nation, and the administrative institutions of the state help solve public policy matters in an efficient and acceptable fashion. In a nation that is politically developed, there is widespread public participation in leader selection and determination of public policy. Some authorities argue that, although political democracy as practiced in North America and Europe is not necessary for a nation to be politically developed, certain international standards of moral behavior by governments and dominant political movements and parties are essential, along with widespread public participation in national decision making. *See also* LEGITIMACY (66); LEGITIMACY VACUUM (67).

Significance
Latin American nations are in different stages of political development, and some have yet to meet the challenges that face both developed and less developed nations. Localism, paternalism, militarism, clientelism, governmental instability, revolution, executive dominance, ineffective and corrupt administration, fraudulent elections, constitutional dissensus, and extremes of political violence have long characterized the region. In addition, there are important anomalies, such as Argentina, that have a modernized economic system and advanced society, yet exhibit political behaviors that include unstable governments, military intervention, ineffective political parties, and social conflict. Explanations for these contradictions and differences in development concentrate on the different stages of economic and social development a nation may be in, the dependent nature of the economies of Latin American states, and the inherited Latin political culture, which gives prominence to the role of privileged groups.

Economic Factors: Commodity Agreement | 196 |

An international contractual arrangement through which signatory states seek to establish a favorable world marketing and pricing system for a primary commodity. Commodity agreements are typically aimed at ending destructive competition among suppliers that results from large-scale overproduction and creates a world buyers' market. Commodity producers that are parties to the agreement try to maximize world export prices by establishing production controls, by regulating exports, by establishing either a single world price or maximum and minimum price levels, and by providing for surpluses to go into a national or an international reserve. Some commodity agreements provide for membership by consumer as well as producer nations. *See also* INTERNATIONAL COFFEE AGREEMENT (224).

Significance
Commodity agreements have increasingly involved the membership and active support of many Latin American states. In 1960, for example, Venezuela was a leading organizer and charter member of the most effective worldwide commodity agreement, the Organization of Petroleum Exporting Countries (OPEC). Ecuador joined in 1973, bringing the membership of OPEC to 13. During the next year, oil prices quadrupled, testifying to the effectiveness of the cartel approach fostered through commodity agreements. Although the United States has opposed cartel arrangements when consumer nations are not represented, Latin American states have followed the OPEC example by joining tin, copper, iron ore, bauxite, banana, coffee, and other marketing arrangements. Other commodity agreements, however, have not worked as well as OPEC. Difficulties in agreeing upon production and marketing quotas, as well as competition from commodities produced in the advanced as well as in developing states, have limited their effectiveness. A successful commodity agreement needs a base of political unity, a common definition of self-interest, and a world consumer demand

that remains fairly stable despite higher prices. Even OPEC has had its good periods, when oil prices soared, and its fair or bad periods, when prices dropped precipitously and its members failed to live up to its production quotas and pricing agreements.

Economic Factors: Foreign Debt Crisis │ 197 │

Dangers facing the international economy as a result of the inability of many Third World states to make regular interest and amortization payments on their foreign debt. The debt—now well over $1 trillion, with Latin American states owing almost one-half of this amount—began its meteoric rise during the 1970s and continued to increase during the 1980s and 1990s. The debt crisis stems from overextended loans made by private and public capital-supplying institutions, including many private American banks and multilateral agencies, such as the International Monetary Fund, the World Bank, and the Inter-American Development Bank. Defaults on debt payments have increased even though many Latin countries have received additional loans to help them make their debt payments. Currently, Brazil owes about $120 billion, Mexico about $100 billion, Argentina over $70 billion, and Venezuela $50 billion. On a per capita basis, Costa Rica is the region's heaviest debtor. *See also* INTERNATIONAL MONETARY FUND (IMF) (225); WORLD BANK GROUP (231).

Significance
Latin America's foreign debt of nearly one-half trillion dollars is an awesome sum most of which will probably never be repaid. The problem is particularly difficult because the loans must be repaid in hard currency, a scarce commodity for many defaulting countries. The debt is largely a product of hyperinflation in many debtor countries, world oil crises, high interest rates on the loans, and an overwhelming urge to secure the capital needed to develop and modernize the economy. The massive debt has created serious national and international crises for lenders and borrowers alike. Defaults and threats of defaults have resulted in rescheduling of debts (typically, extending the payment period and perhaps changing interest rates) and new loans, especially from the IMF and the World Bank. In receiving such loans, debtor countries must agree to make changes in their national economies, reduce government spending, and institute austerity programs for their societies. Austerity programs, in particular, have tended to create bad feelings and, in some countries, rioting and rebellion. One worst-case scenario might occur if a serious economic recession results in the stopping of payments in debtor countries and the collapse of many Western banks, leading to a worldwide depression. Dangers such as this have led the Ronald Reagan and George Bush administrations to take action to ameliorate the debt crisis. In 1985, U.S. Treasury Secretary James Baker III proposed a plan that promised "growth-oriented adjustment." It introduced a "menu of options" that provided alternative ways of seeking growth and paying debts. None of the options, however, provided relief for either banks or debtors during the remaining years of the Reagan administration. In 1989, the Brady Plan (formulated by U.S. Treasury Secretary Nicholas Brady) was developed as a response to the crisis. It provides for reduction in the size of the debt through forgiveness of some debt and reduced interest rates for both public and private banks. The objective is to get debtor countries growing again through investment and trade. Critics claim that the Brady Plan would benefit the banks more

than the debtors. In 1990, President George Bush unveiled a new proposal for Latin debtors, known as the Enterprise for the Americas Initiative, which will emphasize debt forgiveness and increased trade, with the ultimate objective of a Western Hemisphere common market with debt-free members. A few Latin countries have been able to emerge in the early 1990s from the debt-induced depression of the 1980s, but the region as a whole shows little indication of returning to high-level economic growth as experienced from 1945 to 1980.

Economic Factors: Green Revolution | 198 |

A dramatic change in Third World agricultural production resulting from the development of new, high-yielding hybrid grain seeds along with greatly increased applications of water and fertilizer. The Green Revolution was led by Nobel Prize-winning geneticist, Norman E. Borlaug, who with his associates experimentally developed new hybrid wheat and rice seeds that have been used since the 1960s to increase production. *See also* RAINFOREST DILEMMA (19).

Significance
The Green Revolution, by providing increased supplies of food and improved ways of growing it, has helped to break the famine cycles that have plagued some Third World countries for centuries. For the first time, some developing societies have achieved self-sufficiency, and a few have become major exporters of food grains. Latin American states, like those in Asia and Africa, have benefited from the Green Revolution. The World Bank and the regional development banks have aided states in their efforts to become self-sufficient in food by financing the building of new research centers and to grow large amounts of food in semiarid conditions. Despite the high cost of pumping water and using large amounts of fertilizer, great increases in production occurred during the 1970s and 1980s. By the 1990s, however, severe drought conditions in some states and massive floods in others, the inability of many states to acquire the skills needed to grow the grain crops heralded by the Green Revolution, and the high cost of energy needed to make fertilizer and pump water combined to limit the impact of the Green Revolution. Scientists around the world have now embarked on an effort to launch a second Green Revolution that would be more environmentally aware and more compatible with a world energy shortage. War, insurgencies, bad weather, political conflicts, huge debts, hyperinflation, population explosions, and the failure of many development programs have reduced or eliminated the beneficial impact of the Green Revolution in Latin America. Clearing the vast rainforests of the Amazon Basin for agricultural purposes has not proved to be an effective means of coping with the food needs of burgeoning populations in that region.

Economic Factors: Hyperinflation | 199 |

A vast deterioration in the value of a nation's currency in which the value of money, in terms of its purchasing power and its exchange rate with other world currencies, is substantially reduced. Hyperinflation may be the result of such factors as war, political instability, or a deteriorating economy. During economic boom years, virtually all states have at least a moderate inflation of their currencies, ranging for most at an annual rate from 3 percent to 10 percent. Although there is no specific figure that indicates a change from moderate inflation to hyperinflation, the latter usually becomes obvious because of the speed with which the nation's currency loses its value.

Theories that seek to explain the nature and causes of inflation and hyperinflation include: (1) "demand-pull" inflation, whereby a shortage of consumer goods and/or an increase in the amount of money and credit available encourages consumers to bid up prices; (2) "cost-push" inflation, stemming from rapidly increasing costs of production resulting from higher prices for raw materials, energy supplies (especially oil), and wages; and (3) "profit-pull" inflation, whereby huge multinational corporations with little or no competition maintain or increase prices at a time when their costs are being reduced. Reasonable inflation rates can quickly be turned into hyperinflation if mass psychological factors keep reinforcing the depreciation in the value of a nation's currency through fear, producing a tendency for the inflationary movement to feed on itself. *See also* ECONOMIC POLICY: MONETARISTS VS. STRUCTURALISTS (206).

Significance
Latin America, more so than any other region of the world, has suffered from hyperinflation in recent years. Inflation rates in countries like Argentina, Chile, Brazil, Nicaragua, and Mexico have ranged annually from percentage changes in the hundreds to over 3,000 percent. Bolivia held the world inflation record in 1985 when it reached more than 11,000 percent, but in 1990 Nicaragua surpassed the Bolivian record. The vast debt accumulated from public and private national and international banks during the 1970s and 1980s has been a leading contributor to hyperinflation, with interest rates for some states claiming as much as 6 percent of the gross national product. Political upheavals involving revolutionary movements in a number of Latin states have resulted in "flight capital" with a vast output of "printing press currency" to take its place, resulting in a deterioration in currency values. Hyperinflation typically causes black-marketeering to flourish. One of the alleged advantages of hyperinflation—the paying off of all debts with almost worthless currency—has not had the salutary effect in Latin America that it had in other regions, such as in several countries of Europe after both world wars, largely because the loans must be paid to foreigners in hard currency. Because of the deterioration of the currency of many Latin countries, new loans are hard to come by from private sources, and the International Monetary Fund and World Bank require conservative monetary policies and general austerity for the nation's economy as conditions for new loans. The resulting high unemployment has helped stabilize currency values but has added to political instability in the region.

Economic Factors: Monoculture 200
A national economic system based primarily on a single export product. A nation that has a monoculture economy typically is a supplier of raw materials or agricultural products to the more developed world. It produces one or two agricultural commodities (such as sugar or coffee) or minerals (such as oil or copper) for export. This major export earns the great bulk of the nation's foreign exchange. Monoculture economies are subject to great fluctuations in the economic cycle. A fall of prices on the world market, the introduction of a substitute, a loss of markets, a decline in demand, and competition with other nations exporting the same product can cause an economic crisis in the monoculture state. Such nations often attempt to avoid the disadvantages of monoculture by diversifying the economy or by creating commodity agreements that control the production and price of primary products.

See also ECONOMIC FACTORS: COMMODITY AGREEMENT (196); ECONOMIC FACTORS: NEOCOLONIALISM (202).

Significance

Many Latin states have traditionally had monoculture economies. In recent years, for example, Venezuela received 90 percent of its foreign earnings from the export of petroleum. In other states, similar conditions have prevailed: Cuba, sugar, 80 percent; El Salvador, coffee, 80 percent; Bolivia, tin, 70 to 80 percent; Colombia, coffee, 70 percent; Chile, copper, 60 percent; Costa Rica, coffee, 65 percent; and Honduras, bananas, 55 percent. Various Latin attempts to diversify the economy or establish commodity agreements have not always been successful. In 1975, the percentages of export value for Venezuela, Cuba, and Chile were not much different than in 1960. In the other cases, the exports of a second primary product were increased, but the nation still showed the features of a monoculture economy. Monoculture in Latin America often results from special historic circumstances rather than from the advantages of specialization or from the presence in national territory of only a single mineral. Critics of neocolonialism often point out that foreign investors are less affected by the disadvantages of monoculture than the government of the monoculture state. These governments derive most of their revenue from indirect taxation on exports or royalties on the extraction of minerals. Foreign investors, being primarily interested in a high return, benefit from the advantages of monoculture, which include specialization that reduces unit costs, manipulation of prices by controlling production, and the domination of the local economy. Investors are also able to diversify their holdings across national and sector lines.

Economic Factors: Multinational Corporation (MNC) | 201 |

A large business organization that has its ownership and management based mainly in one country but carries on much of its operations in foreign countries. Multinational corporations (often called transnational corporations) are active throughout Latin America with the exception of Cuba. Much of the capital that contributes to development programs and many of the technology transfers to Latin countries are the result of MNC operations. U.S.-based MNCs, such as International Telephone and Telegraph and General Motors, carry on the major portion of business activity by foreign corporations in Latin America, although European and Japanese MNCs have been expanding their operations in the region in recent years. MNCs function as system actors in the Latin political environment by affecting many political, economic, and social outcomes. That role dates back to the chartered trading companies of colonial times, but it has changed greatly over the past several decades as the number and power of MNCs have increased. The political clout of the more than 4,000 MNCs that operate in Latin America relates mainly to their economic role, since much international trade, both export and import, as well as investments in Latin countries, is carried on by these huge organizations. MNCs are particularly powerful in determining market conditions for primary commodities—the main foreign exchange earners for Latin countries—and for manufacturing, energy, and electronics, which include those products most needed by developing countries. MNCs have also been significant owners of public utilities, transportation, banks, and export-import firms. *See also* ECONOMIC FACTORS: NEOCOLONIALISM (202).

Significance
The countries and peoples of Latin America appear to be ambivalent about the role of multinational corporations and the impact they have on national economies. Liberals tend to oppose their economic operations and to charge them with support for autocratic regimes in the hemisphere. Many leftists, especially Marxists, regard MNCs as the contemporary form of imperialist and interventionist foreign policy operations. They charge that MNCs are largely responsible for lagging developmental programs because their failure to plow back profits in the form of new investments has kept the gap between the rich and poor nations—the industrialized and the developing—growing wider rather than narrowing. Proposals for the creation of a New International Economic Order (NIEO), for example, emphasize that the power and influence of such a concentration of economic wealth and its ability to affect world market conditions to the detriment of developing countries must be brought under international control. In the United Nations, efforts to institute an international control system over MNCs are focused in its Commission on Transnational Corporations (CTC) and its related Center on Transnational Corporations (CTNC), which have given top priority to formulating a code of conduct for MNCs. The code would provide guidelines for MNCs in their dealing with countries and for the host country in its treatment of MNCs. It would establish standards of fair competition, fair pricing, and honesty in cross-boundary business operations. Although the United States was the first to propose standards for MNC operations, the Ronald Reagan and George Bush administrations have not given their support to the code, and it appears that controversy over the code will continue throughout the 1990s. There have, however, been fundamental differences between developed and developing states over the code's substance. Direct intervention in the political affairs of Latin American states, such as that of ITT in helping to bring about the downfall of Chile's Marxist president, Salvador Allende, in 1973, has been documented in investigations by the U.S. Congress. Conservative parties and groups conversely tend to support MNCs in their economic role and to reject allegations of their interventions in political affairs. To their defenders, MNCs stimulate economic activity in developing countries by providing investment capital and needed technologies. Moreover, they make capitalism work on a global basis because they help to rationalize the world market system and maximize production and consumption in those countries in which they carry on their operations. The fact that various Latin countries have successfully expropriated local MNC operations demonstrates that, according to their supporters, MNCs are not so powerful as claimed and they can be brought under control if that proves necessary. Nevertheless, MNCs remain a controversial issue in Latin America, and governments are concerned both with attracting them as investors and with controlling them as potential or actual actors that can affect political and economic outcomes.

Economic Factors: Neocolonialism [202]

A dependent relationship in which the economy of a politically independent state is controlled by foreign investors or international market forces. In neocolonialism, a colony has gained political independence and statehood, but a large part of its productive capacity, resources, economic infrastructure, and financial institutions are owned by foreign corporations. The neocolonial state typically has a large external debt.

Failure of the neocolonial state to meet its obligations to foreign investors, to maintain order for the effective operation of business and industrial enterprise, and to provide opportunities for investors may lead to various degrees of political intervention by the governments of the investors' states. *See also* DEVELOPMENT THEORY: DEPENDENCY (188); DOLLAR DIPLOMACY (253); ECONOMIC FACTORS: MONOCULTURE (200); ECONOMIC FACTORS: MULTINATIONAL CORPORATION (MNC) (201); LEGAL POLICIES: EXPROPRIATION (245).

Significance
Neocolonialism arose in Latin America soon after the Wars of Independence were concluded in the early nineteenth century. The removal of Spanish authority in the Americas opened the region to a massive influx of British, German, and U.S. capital. The new Latin states also borrowed heavily from foreign banks to pay their war debts or for reconstruction. Frequently unable to repay these loans, they suffered from political and military intervention by foreign governments. By 1900, foreigners owned all or most of the transportation facilities, communication systems, mines and mineral deposits, plantations and ranches, manufacturing and processing plants, and banks and trading companies in the region. Although the Spanish monopoly of the colonial period was finally ended by these wars, Latin states remained primarily suppliers of raw materials and food products for foreign nations and receivers of capital, technology, business management, and manufactured goods. Foreign investment contributed to a rapid development of the infrastructure and the industrial capacity in Latin America, but it also resulted in the transfer of wealth to foreign investors and to Latin agricultural and commercial elites. Reaction to these features of neocolonialism contributed to the rise of Latin political movements and attitudes that attacked all forms of colonialism, advocated economic nationalism and expropriation of foreign-owned enterprises in the twentieth century, and rejected foreign interventionism.

Economic Policy: Dirigismo | 203

A "directed economy" approach to the problem of securing economic development and modernization in Latin American countries. *Dirigismo* rejects dependence on foreign investment capital, free enterprise as the basic approach to economic growth, free markets, and other components of laissez-faire. The most effective approach for developing states in the contemporary world, according to advocates of *dirigismo,* is a Latin American brand of state socialism. Thus *dirigismo* focuses on generation of local capital, a major effort by government toward developing the nation's infrastructure, central planning, and government ownership and operation of all basic industries. Some advocates of *dirigismo* regard it as a system that offers a compromise between laissez-faire capitalism and Chinese-style communism.

Significance
The acceptance of *dirigismo* by Latin countries as the best if not the only road to successful development and modernization stemmed from the frustrations and disillusionments over the failure of imported foreign capital and local free enterprise to achieve good results after World War II. With problems of exploding populations and increasing poverty, and with masses of unemployed people in the larger cities of the region constituting a dangerously explosive social force, economists and political leaders accepted *dirigismo* as a desirable alternative to the status quo. The failure of the Latin

American Free Trade Association (LAFTA) and the Central American Common Market (CACM) to spur their members' economies to the desired level of growth also contributed to the search for an alternative road. In the late 1980s and the early 1990s, however, *dirigismo* was in retreat as strong practitioners like Mexico, Venezuela, Brazil, Argentina, and Chile moved to free market policies and sold off many state-owned firms.

Economic Policy: Import Substitution | 204 |

An economic policy to foster industrialization by promoting the expansion of domestic industries through restricting the importation of specific manufactured goods. Import substitution is a form of protectionism undertaken to create development capital by manufacturing goods at home that were previously imported. A nation practicing import-substituting industrialization would spend less of its foreign exchange earnings from the export of its primary goods for the purchase of goods manufactured abroad. According to the strategy, capital would thus be generated through these savings for additional industrialization, the economy would be diversified, and the exploitation by foreign investors would be significantly reduced. As applied to Latin America, the theory had some weaknesses. The domestic market in most Latin states was too small, the domestically produced manufactured goods were too costly and could not compete on the international market, and most states had an insufficient variety of resources for building a domestic industry. There was also a large labor force, which was increasingly supplied by migration from rural areas. This apparent advantage kept the price of labor low, but low labor costs limited worker income, thus keeping the masses out of the durable consumer goods market. Also, little savings of foreign exchange could be made because the new industries were built by the purchase of machinery and spare parts from developed states.

Significance
The strategy of import substitution was put into force in small industries by some Latin nations before World War II with partial success in Argentina, Mexico, Brazil, Chile, and Colombia. After World War II, import-substituting industrialization was promoted by the United Nations Economic Commission for Latin America (ECLA), but the policy was unable to generate sufficient development capital. Latin states were too dependent on foreign technology, they were unable to apply the strategy to large-scale industry, and protectionism proved too costly. A number of Latin states then shifted to other strategies, such as attempting to broaden regional markets, pushing for unencumbered capital from international agencies, accepting foreign capital, nationalizing foreign-owned industries, and promoting the use of commodity agreements or cartels to stabilize production and increase income from the export of primary goods. None of these strategies has proved successful and durable, although in the 1970s and 1980s many Latin states were able to borrow huge amounts of capital. This massive foreign debt makes import substitution increasingly appealing to some planners since huge amounts must be diverted from paying for imports to making interest and amortization payments on the debt. But past import substitution failures and current emphasis on increasing trade mitigate against large-scale adoption of the policy.

Economic Policy: Maquiladoras | 205 |

Mexican assembly or production plants near the U.S. border. *Maquiladoras* are mostly foreign-owned plants that export finished products to the United States. There are about 2,000 plants employing about 500,000 persons at wages far below those prevailing in the United States. *Maquiladoras* benefit from Mexican law that permits the importation of materials that would in turn be assembled for export, as well as the U.S. tariff law that taxes only the value added to a product from processing abroad. Components are shipped to Mexico for assembly and are exported back to the United States. Assembled items include garments, textiles, automobiles, and electric and electronics goods, with the high-technology manufactures making up the largest portion.

Significance
Maquiladoras account for about 25 percent of Mexican manufactured exports. They were first established in the 1960s and expanded greatly in the 1980s. About 20 percent are now located in other parts of Mexico. Originally created to tap the vast U.S. market, Mexican law now provides that a percentage of the assembled goods may be sold within Mexico. About 75 percent of the plants are controlled by foreign companies, and many Mexican firms act as subcontractors to the foreign-owned companies. Japanese electronic firms have significantly expanded their *maquiladora* operations in recent years to tap the U.S. market, but also for global exports. These and other plants have helped create a strong high-technology industry in Mexico, but the cheap labor and poorly regulated environmental conditions have created other problems of job-related illnesses and environmental degradation. U.S. labor unions have objected to the transfer of many assembly jobs to Mexico, but they have been unable to stem the tide. They oppose the proposal for the North American Free Trade Area that would create a free trade zone that would include the U.S., Mexico, and Canada.

Economic Policy: Monetarists vs. Structuralists 206

Alternative approaches to achieving economic growth and modernization in Latin American countries. Monetarists offer a generally conservative economic growth strategy, focusing mainly on policies that will keep inflation under control and maintain a sound national currency. Structuralists, on the other hand, advocate Keynesian and neo-Keynesian policies of governmental stimulative actions accompanied by basic institutional changes that will encourage economic development and modernization. Monetarists believe that by controlling inflation, conservative, sound-money policies will increase export earnings and encourage foreign and domestic investments. Social and political stability will emerge out of this kind of control over the value of the nation's currency. Structuralists reject monetarist policies, charging that they retard growth and support the status quo. Structural reform is aimed at preparing the base for a strong surge of self-sustaining economic growth leading to a modernized economy. *See also* DEVELOPMENT STRATEGY: MACRO APPROACH (182).

Significance
The debate in Latin America over the issue of whether a monetarist or structuralist approach is needed to achieve economic goals is similar to policy conflicts that exist in other Third World countries as well as in the industrialized states of the First World. The issue came to the fore in most Latin states in the decade following World War II, when dictatorships were overthrown and new approaches became the subjects for political controversy. The debate

continues today. Leading monetarist thinkers include Brazilian Roberto Campos and the leading world spokesman for monetarist policies, economist Milton Friedman. The intellectual and ideological leaders of the structuralist school include Argentine economist Raúl Prebisch and Brazil's Celso Furtado. Monetarists have generally sought support for their policies from the International Monetary Fund (IMF), the World Bank Group, and from private enterprise, especially multinational corporations. Structuralists worked mainly through the United Nations Commission for Latin America (ECLA) in seeking to bring about reforms they regarded as the essential prelude to successful developmental programs. They also strongly supported Third World policies and objectives aimed at changing their weak posture in world trade and finance by advocating, through the United Nations system, the creation of a New International Economic Order (NIEO). Noting the failures of some developmentalist policies to create stable economies, some structuralists and others renounced a reformist approach in favor of a socialist revolution that would place national economies under the control and direction of governments that would attack underdevelopment by instituting fundamental social and economic changes. Alternately, monetarists claim to have helped rescue the economies of a number of nations in the late 1980s and early 1990s that had gone bankrupt or were overcome by hyperinflation and stagnant growth. The failure of socialist policies in Europe and Latin America has given more credence and brought more political support for free market policies as the mechanism for growth and development.

Economic Policy: Moral Incentives vs. Material Incentives   207

A debate among socialists and communists, particularly relevant to Cuba, concerning the basis of motivation for workers in a socialist society. Those who argued for moral incentives believed that it was possible to create a "new socialist man" who, once his social consciousness was raised, would be completely selfless and freely give his labor for the good of the collectivity. Material incentivists believed that concrete material rewards and differential wage structures were still necessary to motivate workers in a socialist society. This debate was very pronounced in Cuba in the 1960s. Ernesto "Che" Guevara, the prime exponent of moral incentives, believed that material incentives were leftovers from capitalism that were incompatible with socialism, and he argued for their progressive elimination. The material incentive line was advocated by defenders of Soviet economic practices, particularly by former members of the Popular Socialist party, the "old" orthodox communist party in Cuba. In the early 1960s, Fidel Castro moved back and forth between these positions, but by 1966 he adopted the moral incentive approach as the basis for generating capital accumulation and for mobilizing the great amount of voluntary labor needed to achieve the production goals established for the late 1960s. These goals were not achieved, and the Cuban economy was set back by the dislocations caused by the attempt to vastly increase the production of sugar. Castro was forced to rely on the Soviet Union for an increased amount of economic assistance, and in 1980 he permitted free peasant markets, street vendors, and cottage industries that operated for profit and production bonuses. These led to corruption, profiteering, and dislocations, and in 1986 he adopted a policy of "rectification" that reemphasized moral incentives and sacrifice. The 1990s look bleak for Cuba as a result of the substantial cuts in foreign aid once supplied by the Soviet Union and the difficulty in imparting moral incentives when material ones are failing to produce the new society. *See also* CASTROISM (54); ECONOMIC POLICY: RECTIFICATION CAMPAIGN (210); ECONOMIC POLICY: REVOLUTIONARY OFFENSIVE OF 1968 (CUBA) (211).

Significance
The debate over moral incentives versus material incentives continues to divide leftist intellectuals outside Cuba. The more radical thinkers, who saw Castro's Cuba as a model for a true socialist society, felt betrayed when Castro abandoned the moral incentives program. They believe that moral incentives, which they prefer to call collective incentives, can succeed, and that a true socialist society can never exist under capitalist norms, such as differential wage rates, the continued reliance on a money economy, and the use of cost-accounting procedures to evaluate labor efficiency. Leftist critics of the moral incentive experiment in Cuba point out that the program of moral incentives was counterproductive, and that instead of producing more labor for economic development, labor was directed into personally rewarding enterprises, such as the black market in food. They note that absenteeism and low labor productivity also resulted, and that the application of a moral incentive program under conditions of austerity could only be achieved through coercion. When Cuba returned to material incentives in the 1970s, wage differentials remained much more narrow than in most socialist countries. Fidel Castro's switch between the two approaches was brief and pragmatic, for his fundamental belief is in the doctrine of moral incentives. With the demise or major alteration of socialism in the Soviet Union and East European countries, Castro's Cuba has become the main locale for socialist experimentation and policy development of a collective nature in the Western world.

Economic Policy: Privatization 208
The sale of publicly owned enterprises to the private sector. In privatization, the government sells selected state enterprises to private companies in order to reduce the high cost of state subsidies to inefficient firms, reduce the size of the public debt, increase productivity, promote private sector investment, and increase exports. The policy of privatizing state enterprises is typically adopted by governments that believe an economic turnaround will occur by reducing the large public sector—often amounting to 40 to 60 percent of the gross national product. Concurrent with privatization are other policies of economic liberalism, such as reducing the size of government, curtailing social programs, and promoting free enterprise and a free market economy.

Significance
Privatization became widespread in Latin America in the late 1980s with the coming into power of new governments that adopted conservative economic policies. In Argentina, Brazil, Chile, Mexico, and Venezuela, substantial properties were sold to private firms. These included telephone, railways, hotels, banks, steel mills, petrochemical plants, copper mines, and other industries. In some instances the sale brought opposition from labor unions that expected a resulting loss of jobs or from political forces that decried the transfer of national property to foreign-owned firms. Although many industries have been targeted for sale, those linked to strong national feelings and historical struggles, such as petroleum industry in Mexico, cannot for political reasons be put up for sale.

Economic Policy: Pronasol (209)

Acronym for National Solidarity Program, a Mexican economic program that transfers development and social welfare funds directly to local communities for particular projects. Pronasol was established by President Carlos Salinas in 1989 as a more efficient method of development than using existing state and local bureaucratic agencies. Committees, often using self-help labor, administer the funds for infrastructure and social service projects. Projects that have benefited include health clinics, hospitals, schools, water projects, electricity and housing projects, university scholarships, and food distribution programs. A substantial number of projects have been aided in the over 28,000 communities that have participated in the program. In 1990 over $1 billion was spent, with most of the funds coming from the sale of public enterprises to the private sector.

Significance
Pronasol was created to get more practical results from development funds by channeling them through local community organizations. The program has been used by the president to increase his political support by bringing projects to localities where the political opposition was strong in the 1988 elections. Pronasol benefits the urban poor, but it also creates new loyalties for the dominant Institutional Revolutionary party among community leaders.

Economic Policy: Rectification Campaign (210)

An economic policy adopted by Fidel Castro in Cuba in 1986 to move Cuba back to a pure socialist model of development. Known officially as the campaign for "rectification of errors and negative tendencies," the program closed private peasant markets, street vendors, and cottage industries that operated for a profit. Production bonuses and overtime pay in state firms were curtailed as well. An attack was also launched against absenteeism, indolence, administrative corruption, and bureaucratism. Castro condemned the loss of revolutionary consciousness and once again attempted to move the nation back to a system of moral incentives and self-sacrifice as opposed to using material incentives to build socialism. *See also* ECONOMIC POLICY: MORAL INCENTIVES VS. MATERIAL INCENTIVES (207).

Significance
The rectification campaign was adopted as a way to stem the increasing economic problems the nation faced: decline of economic growth, a large trade deficit, and increasing debt to the Soviet Union. Many of these ills Castro attributed to the corruption, private enrichment and profit-making, and diversion of public goods for private purposes that occurred from 1980 to 1986, when small private enterprises were permitted. Economic problems of the nation mounted in the closing years of the decade, however, for the former Soviet Union, beset with substantial economic problems, withdrew much of its economic support for Cuba. By 1992, the rectification campaign had not succeeded in reversing the economic collapse as the nation suffered from food shortages, rationing, and scarcity of consumer goods.

Economic Policy: Revolutionary Offensive of 1968 (Cuba) (211)

An economic program of the Cuban government that included the confiscation of small business enterprises, the mobilization of labor for increased agricultural production, and a greater stress on moral incentives for workers. The revolutionary offensive was undertaken to promote rapid economic development, to achieve capital accumulation by restricting consumption, and to generate foreign earnings by a large increase in sugar production. The Fidel Castro government confiscated over 55,000 small retail, service, and handicraft shops, one-half of which had no employees; attacked "parasitism" by securing a "volunteer" labor force through coercion; attacked the black market in food; and tried to raise the revolutionary consciousness of workers by stressing moral incentives, such as patriotism and the spirit of selflessness. A political offensive was also launched against all dissidents, including a pro-Soviet microfaction in the Communist Party of Cuba and critics of the government in the union of writers and artists. *See also* ECONOMIC POLICY: MORAL INCENTIVES VS. MATERIAL INCENTIVES (207).

Significance
The Revolutionary Offensive of 1968 resulted in the total socialization of the Cuban economy except for the agricultural sector, but the objectives concerning labor efficiency and capital accumulation were not achieved. The plan to produce a 10-million-ton sugar harvest in 1970 fell short of the goal, and the increased production did not generate more foreign exchange earnings because the price of sugar fell on the world market. The Cuban economy was seriously disrupted by the transfer of labor into sugar production. The moral incentive program did not work because labor productivity fell and absenteeism was high. Many of the confiscated retail shops closed because the new managers, housewives in the Committees for the Defense of the Revolution, did not have the necessary skills to run them efficiently. The Cuban society became more regimented and militarized as labor had to be coerced. In the early 1970s, Fidel Castro publicly admitted his economic ignorance and mistakes and pointed out that Cubans had to continue to sacrifice and suffer shortages for the sake of the revolution. Castro turned more to the Soviet Union for economic assistance and accepted Soviet advice to reinstitute material incentives for labor, reduce sugar production, promote the efficient use of labor and resources by requiring accounting procedures, and diversify the economy. By 1990, Cubans, including Castro, became aware that Soviet advice was useless since the Soviet economy was near collapse, and Soviet assistance increasingly took the form of military objects, such as tanks, that the Soviets no longer wanted or needed.

Economic Integration

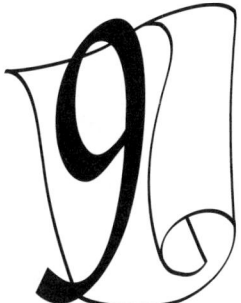

Amazon Pact (AP) | 212

A treaty that seeks to coordinate the development of the Amazon Basin to protect the region's ecology and ensure the rational utilization of its resources. Eight nations—Bolivia, Brazil, Colombia, Ecuador, Guyana, Peru, Suriname, and Venezuela–are signatories to the Amazon Pact, which was signed by the foreign ministers of the member countries on 3 July 1978. The treaty, which is composed of 28 articles, provides for (1) free navigation of all rivers in the Amazon region; (2) the rational use of the region's water resources; (3) the right of each member to develop its Amazon territory so long as it does not produce any harmful impact on other members' territories; (4) the development of a common research effort and the exchange of research that relates to the region; (5) the improvement of health and the building of a transportation and communication infrastructure; and (6) the promotion of tourism in the Amazon region. The foreign ministers of member countries meet every two years to develop common policies and programs, and each member has established a national commission to implement joint decisions. In addition, an Amazon Cooperation Council composed of diplomatic representatives of all member countries meets annually to oversee the implementation of the policies and programs adopted by the foreign ministers. *See also* RAINFOREST DILEMMA (9).

Significance

The Amazon Pact is not an example of a strong, vibrant integration movement building a supranational decision-making structure with a complex institutional base. Rather it focuses on encouraging some measure of regional cooperation among member countries, each of which is engaged in carrying out its own development projects in the Amazon region. The main objective, in a sense, is to try to use the organization to stop a competitive, ecologically disastrous plundering of the resources of the Amazon Basin. The pact has also reduced the possibility of political and military hostilities growing out of national competition in opening the vast area to exploitation. For example, relations between Brazil and Venezuela, strained for many years, were improved by their joint adherence to the pact. The Amazon Pact, however, is only a means for influencing national actions. It has symbolic as well as practical value that together contribute favorably to the ecological protection and rationalization of the resources of the region.

Andean Common Market (ACM)   213

An economic group originally created in 1969 as a subregional market to improve its members' bargaining power within the Latin American Free Trade Association (LAFTA) and to encourage increased trade and more rapid development. Officially known as the Cartagena Agreement, it is also known as the Andean Group and the Andean Pact. Its members include Bolivia, Colombia, Ecuador, Peru, and Venezuela; Chile withdrew from the group in 1976. Andean Common Market states joined together because they were concerned about the slow pace of economic integration in LAFTA, but they remained members of the latter organization in the hope that the new arrangements would revitalize it. Main objectives sought under the Andean Group include: (1) establishment of a common market and a common external tariff for members; (2) encouragement of industrialization by specialization through assignment of industry rights among members; (3) extension of control over multinational corporations operating within the Andean Common Market; and (4) special concessions for the poorer members to encourage their progress. The Commission functions as the supreme organ of the Andean Group at its headquarters in Lima, aided by the Andean Council and the Junta, a technical body. In addition, the Andean Group has established an Andean Development Corporation to help finance development projects. *See also* LATIN AMERICAN FREE TRADE ASSOCIATION (LAFTA) (227).

Significance
The Andean Common Market emerged largely as a product of the ineffectiveness and lack of movement within LAFTA. Unlike LAFTA and the Central American Common Market (CACM), the Andean Group originally rejected the free trade, laissez-faire, competitive model for achieving economic integration. As a common market, the Andean Group was unusual in its original policies of establishing controls over foreign private investments and the operations of multinational corporations (MNCs). These controls, however, served to weaken the organization in many cases because of conflicts over waivers and exceptions. In 1987, its members signed the Quito Protocol, which modified the Cartágena Agreement of 1969 by relaxing controls on foreign investors and permitting member states to determine their own rules on foreign investment. Although some tariffs have been reduced, the organization has limited success because trade among members accounts for a small portion of total foreign trade and worldwide recessions have hurt intra-regional trade as well.

Caribbean Basin Initiative (CBI)   214

A program of the United States aimed at promoting economic development in Central America and the Caribbean area. The Caribbean Basin Initiative (CBI) involves U.S. policies to provide economic stimulation in the region through an increased ability for these countries to raise their foreign exchange earnings, diversify their economies, and increase employment opportunities for their people. Duty-free treatment is accorded by the United States for most products important to the region. The CBI was announced by President Ronald Reagan in 1982 at a meeting of the Organization of American States (OAS), and it took effect in 1984 for a 12-year period. CBI participation includes 22 states and territories. *See also* CARIBBEAN COMMUNITY AND COMMON MARKET (CARICOM) (215).

Significance
The Caribbean Basin Initiative was an effort by the Reagan administration to encourage free enterprise and increased trade in the region. It was designed to help promote economic development throughout Latin America by giving special treatment to the countries of Central America and the Caribbean. The CBI seeks to provide incentives for such growth but does not attempt to improve conditions through large increases in direct aid. Objectives sought by the United States in promoting the program include increased trade and investment opportunities in the region, development of democratic and capitalistic values by the people of the CBI states, and neutralization of revolutionary left-wing threats, as in Cuba, Nicaragua, and El Salvador. Although some CBI states have benefited extensively from the program, such as Jamaica, Costa Rica, and the Dominican Republic, reduced sugar quotas and lower oil prices (until 1990) lowered total exports of the region by 30 percent since the CBI began in 1984.

Caribbean Community and Common Market (CARICOM) | 215 |

A customs union created by the Treaty of Chaguaramas of 1973 that provides for elimination of trade barriers among members, a common external tariff, and the harmonization of certain domestic economic policies. CARICOM was a direct outgrowth of the Caribbean Free Trade Association (CARIFTA), established in 1968, an organization that moved the independent and nonsovereign entities of the region toward the elimination of trade barriers and established institutions for various kinds of economic cooperation. CARICOM's members include 12 former British colonies and one nonsovereign colony. Its main objectives, as provided in the charter, are to achieve the highest level of economic integration compatible with the interests of members, more rapid and balanced development, a more effective economic bargaining posture toward other regional groups, and a Common Protective Policy aimed at encouraging the development of local agriculture and industry by offering import protection. The Heads of Government Conference (HGC) is the central governing body for CARICOM, and the Common Market Council (CMC), composed of a minister from each member, makes policy recommendations to the HGC. The Caribbean Community Secretariat, located at headquarters in Georgetown, Guyana, functions as the chief administrative organ for both CARIFTA and CARICOM. Numerous subsidiary agencies operate in specialized areas to help carry out CARICOM's mandate to secure mutual economic benefits for all members. *See also* CARIBBEAN FREE TRADE ASSOCIATION (CARIFTA) (217).

Significance
The Caribbean Community and Common Market provides an excellent example of how a diverse group of developing states can, through regional economic integration, achieve mutual economic benefits that move them toward their basic objective of modernization. Thus, CARICOM

may provide a working model for other Third World states of Asia, Africa, and Latin America. Unlike the Latin American Free Trade Association (LAFTA) and the Central American Common Market (CACM), CARICOM continues to make slow but steady progress toward a higher level of economic and political integration based on the European Community model. As was the case with CARIFTA, CARICOM's initial problems stemmed from conflict within the organization between the perspectives and demands of less developed nations (LDCs) versus those of more developed nations (MDCs). Elimination of local protection for industry and agriculture can and often does lead to conflict within economic groups, with the economically stronger members tending to reap most of the benefits from the freer trade climate. By the late 1970s, the split between MDCs and LDCs assumed crisis proportions, raising questions about the feasibility of achieving higher levels of integration in the region. Intra-regional trade fell in the 1980s, but by the end of the decade members agreed to push forward on establishing a common external tariff, creating a single Caribbean market and adopting measures to promote development and self-sufficiency. Despite its problems, CARICOM remains a leading actor in the developing world, demonstrating that, by concerting economic and political policies, weak Third World states can overcome problems and become a more decisive force in the contemporary international economic order.

Caribbean Development Bank (Caribank) | 216 |

A regional financial agency established in 1969 that seeks to help developing member countries in their economic growth and modernization programs. Members of Caribank include Anguilla, the British Virgin Islands, the Cayman Islands, and the Turks and Caicos Islands (developing members), plus Britain, Canada, Colombia, France, Mexico, and Venezuela (developed members). Funds for its lending operations are provided by the developed members, by international institutions like the World Bank and the Inter-American Development Bank, and by other donor states, such as the United States, Germany, Sweden, and New Zealand. Specialized funds have been created to provide help for such projects as small-scale farming, housing, livestock production, and various forms of technical assistance. Loan funds are available for both small and large projects that can be either public or private ventures. *See also* INTER-AMERICAN DEVELOPMENT BANK (IDB) (223).

Significance
The Caribbean Development Bank has provided many helpful loans to its less-developed members, but it suffers from low levels of funding. Inflation, oil crises, the debt crisis, and economic recessions in the developed states have all weakened its operations, as have low prices for the developing members' products and high prices in hard currency for imports. Its close working relationship with the Caribbean Community and Common Market (CARICOM) has helped it to concert its economic policies and broaden its vision concerning the development process.

Caribbean Free Trade Association (CARIFTA) | 217 |

A regional organization established in 1968 to foster economic cooperation and free trade among its members. CARIFTA membership originally included five independent states, six semi-independent "States in

Association with Great Britain," and one British colony. CARIFTA was replaced by the Caribbean Community and Common Market (CARICOM). *See also* CARIBBEAN COMMUNITY AND COMMON MARKET (CARICOM) (215).

Significance
The founders of the Caribbean Free Trade Association regarded it as the first step in a continuing process of economic and political integration for the diverse entities of the region. This goal was partially achieved with the signing of the Treaty of Chaguaramas in 1973, which created the Caribbean Community and Common Market (CARICOM), with all CARIFTA members adhering to the new charter. This integration was the first example in the Third World of a free trade area evolving into a customs union. Based on the European Economic Community model, the Caribbean group realized a significant increase in trade among its members. Economic benefits, however, were not great enough to promote a movement toward political integration and economic union. Like all free trade systems, most of the benefits tended to accrue to the stronger (MDC) members, especially in the field of agricultural policies, at the expense of the weaker (LDC) members, or so the latter believed. Members tended to produce many competing rather than complementary products. One main objective—to reduce the heavy external trade dependence of members, especially with Britain and the United States—was not achieved. Inflation in the industrial countries also served to worsen the terms of trade of members with the outside world. The successor organization, CARICOM, inherited some of these problems, which delayed progress, but by the early 1990s, CARICOM was moving forward toward the goal of economic integration.

Central American Common Market (CACM) | 218 |

A regional organization founded in 1960 to promote economic development in member states through a customs union and industrial integration. CACM membership includes Costa Rica, El Salvador, Guatemala, Honduras, and Nicaragua, with Panama and the Dominican Republic having indicated an interest in joining. The organizations' operations are based mainly on two instruments: the General Treaty of Central American Economic Integration and the Convention Chartering the Central Bank for Economic Integration. These treaties, plus several protocols and supplementary agreements, provide for continuing progress toward integration of the economies of member states. CACM decisions are made by (1) the Economic Council, composed of members' economic ministers and charged with developing policies to further integrate members' economies; (2) an Executive Council that implements decisions made by the Economic Council; and (3) a Permanent Secretariat, located at CACM headquarters in Guatemala City, which provides administrative and technical assistance. Other agencies—such as the Central American Bank for Economic Integration and the Central American Clearing House—carry on functions that are related and often coordinated through CACM. *See also* LATIN AMERICAN FREE TRADE ASSOCIATION (LAFTA) (227); INTER-AMERICAN SYSTEM: ORGANIZATION OF CENTRAL AMERICAN STATES (ODECA) (236).

Significance
Based on the European Common Market model, the Central American Common Market aims at fostering industrialization and specialization by attracting foreign capital to the broader market and free trade arrangement.

Some progress has been made since 1960 toward achieving CACM's basic goals of creating a free trade area and adopting common tariffs on imports from other countries. Many articles of trade are duty-free within the market, and trade among the five members has been stimulated. CACM's successes, however, have been challenged by a 1969 war between Honduras and El Salvador and growing political disagreements that for a time brought CACM to the brink of dissolution. Intra-regional trade increased in the 1970s but declined until the late 1980s. Progress toward creation of a hemispheric common market has lagged, however, and CACM continues to function as a regional group.

Central American Parliament (Parlecen) | 219 |

An organization composed of Central American republics devoted to the goal of regional economic and political integration. The Central American Parliament (Parlecen) was inaugurated in late 1991 in Esquipulas, Guatemala, under the authority of the Constituent Treaty of the Central American Parliament, which was signed by five Central American republics in 1987. Initial member states include El Salvador, Guatemala, and Honduras, with Nicaragua intending to fully participate. Costa Rica signed but did not ratify the treaty. Deputies to the parliament are elected directly by popular vote; each member state has 20 deputies, and former presidents and vice presidents of member states are deputies for five years after their terms of office. The powers of the body are limited in that its decisions are not binding on members. The organization is expected to act as a political forum with the hope that its decisions will be enacted by the parliaments of member states. *See also* INTER-AMERICAN SYSTEM: ORGANIZATION OF CENTRAL AMERICAN STATES (ODECA) (236).

Significance
The Central American Parliament was first proposed in 1986 as a mechanism to surmount the national interests of regional states that promoted harmful competition. Its founders recognized that previous regional organizations, such as the Organization of Central American States (ODECA), were unsuccessful in bringing about regional economic and political integration. By having deputies chosen directly by the people, they hoped that cross-national political and economic interests would prevail in the body's deliberations and decisions. The initial meeting was inauspicious, however, because it was attended by deputies from only El Salvador, Guatemala, and Honduras. As the organization began its work in 1991, it was faced with the realization that civil wars have greatly harmed national economies, and that political integration is a distant goal in light of historical traditions for separation and the continuing struggles for national integration.

Economic Commission for Latin America and the Caribbean (ECLAC) | 220 |

A United Nations regional economic commission established in 1948 as the Economic Commission for Latin America (ECLA), which in 1984 was expanded in its operations and title to include the Caribbean. ECLAC's main functions are to initiate and coordinate policies aimed at promoting the economic development of Latin American and Caribbean states and territories. In addition to the countries and territories of Latin America and the Caribbean, ECLAC's membership includes Britain, Canada, France, the Netherlands, Portugal, Spain, and the United States. It is one of five regional commissions established by the United Nations, with the other four being the Economic

Commission for Africa, the Economic Commission for Europe, the Economic and Social Commission for Asia and the Pacific, and the Economic and Social Commission for Western Asia. Headquarters for ECLAC are located in Santiago, Chile. *See also* DEVELOPMENT STRATEGY: PROGRESSIVE MODERNIZATION (184); ECONOMIC POLICY: IMPORT SUBSTITUTION (204).

Significance
ECLAC seeks to help its members to develop and modernize by conducting research on regional economic and social problems, by giving advice to the United Nations Economic and Social Council (ECOSOC) and other UN bodies and specialized agencies, and by making recommendations to member governments. ECLA, under the leadership of Raúl Prebisch from 1950 to 1963, placed emphasis on economic integration of countries into regional groups to foster a common attack on economic and social problems. ECLA's studies, conferences, and recommendations led to the creation of the Central American Common Market (CACM) in 1959, the Latin American Free Trade Association (LAFTA) in 1960, and the Inter-American Development Bank (IDB) in 1959. Emphasis has shifted from simple development initiatives to broad-scale planning for the entire region, the training of officials, and the management of forest, water, and environmental resources. Despite ECLAC's efforts, economic growth has proceeded unevenly and often competitively rather than cooperatively. Exploding populations, stagnant social systems, local arms races, insurgencies, terrorism, drug trafficking, environmental problems, and the massive hard currency debt constitute some of the major problems confronting many Latin American and Caribbean countries. Some of ECLAC's recommendations, such as import substitution as a means of fostering development, have received little economic or political support in the region. Yet ECLAC's initiatives have helped spur interest in and support for policies of change in a region that needs dramatic change to meet its growing problems.

Fourth World 221
Developing countries of Latin America, Africa, Asia, and the Middle East that have extremely low annual per capita incomes. The United Nations has designated 28 of its members as least developed countries or LDCs, which are also referred to as the Fourth World. Fourth World countries not only suffer from low per capita incomes but also enjoy little in the way of financial reserves, have small capacities for and little expectation of economic growth and modernization, have exploding populations, have life-styles conditioned by poverty, and have little in the way of energy and raw materials to support development efforts. *See also* DEVELOPMENT THEORY: IMPOVERISHMENT (192); THIRD WORLD (229).

Significance
One-half of the world's population lives in 62 countries, each of which has an annual per capita gross national product under $500. Almost half of these—the Fourth World countries—have incomes of only $200 or less per capita, thus constituting the poorest of the poor or, as they are sometimes called, the economic basket cases of the world. Although most Fourth World countries are in Africa and a few are in Asia, in the Western Hemisphere only Haiti has been so designated by the United Nations. Several others—Guyana, Honduras, El Salvador, and Nicaragua—belong to the larger category of poor states with under $500 per capita incomes and are often included in the Fourth World category. Some special programs provided by the United Nations and regional groups have been aimed at helping Fourth

World states to escape from their economic hopelessness and begin the process of growth and development. In most cases, little progress has resulted because key ingredients of the development process, both human and material, are lacking.

General Agreement on Tariffs and Trade (GATT) — 222

An international organization that promotes trade among its members by negotiating agreements to reduce tariffs and other impediments to the flow of commerce. Negotiations are conducted by GATT's Trade Negotiations Committee, and its decisions take the form of trade agreements. In each agreement concluded between members of GATT, the most-favored-nation clause must be inserted, thus providing for equal, nondiscriminatory trade among all GATT members, whether or not they are parties to that agreement. GATT became the world's leading trade organization in the late 1940s when the U.S. Senate refused to accept the treaty that would have created the International Trade Organization (ITO) for that role. Since GATT is based on executive agreements rather than treaties, it does not need U.S. Senate consent for ratification of decisions reached to lower barriers to trade. In 1990, GATT sought to conclude negotiations in what was called the Uruguay Round, the eighth series of talks in GATT's history. The Uruguay Round, so called because it was launched by a 1986 meeting in that country, was aimed at removing taxes and trade restrictions on exports and imports—especially nontariff barriers, such as quotas, customs, and export subsidies—by all GATT countries. *See also* LATIN AMERICAN FREE TRADE ASSOCIATION (LAFTA) (227); UNITED NATIONS CONFERENCE ON TRADE AND DEVELOPMENT (UNCTAD) (230).

Significance

Latin American countries played a major role in creating GATT in 1947 and in its subsequent 45 years of negotiations. GATT agreements have helped to open U.S. and European markets to Latin American exports of foods, fibers, oil, raw materials, and some manufactures. As the membership of Third World countries in GATT increased over the years, so, too, has their influence in the decision processes of the organization. For some years, Third World nations regarded GATT as "the rich man's club," but in the 1980s and 1990s this view gave way to the universal desire to develop and modernize their economies, which for many of them has meant joining and actively participating in GATT. As well, East European countries that had long held GATT to be the epitome of capitalism and imperialism now seek membership. The main problem in GATT that has adversely affected Latin America has been the inability to reach agreement on eliminating all barriers to trade in agricultural products, which are both heavily protected and extensively subsidized in many member countries, especially in the European Community. Also, trade in textiles and clothing, vital to many Latin American and Caribbean countries, has been removed from GATT's jurisdiction so that protective tariff rates can be applied.

Inter-American Development Bank (IDB) — 223

A regional lending agency established to promote the achievement of the economic and social goals of its Latin American members. IDB membership of 44 nations includes most Latin American states, the United States, Canada, and a number of West European and other non-regional countries (Austria, Belgium, Britain, Denmark, France, Israel, Japan, the Netherlands, Spain, Switzerland,

Germany, and Yugoslavia). The agreement creating the IDB was drawn up by a special committee of the Organization of American States (OAS) signed in 1959, and the IDB began its operations in Washington in 1960. It was authorized a capital of $1 billion initially, with 55 percent provided by the Latin American members. Most of IDB's loanable funds are borrowed from the capital markets of Europe, Japan, Latin America, the Caribbean, and the United States. Although normally its loans are "hard," a Fund for Special Operations (FSO) finances "soft" loans repayable in local currencies for projects that are not self-liquidating. Its guaranteed loan fund is financed by contributions of members, especially the United States, and by the sale of bank bonds, with voting power in the IDB weighted according to the size of a member's contributions. The IDB's highest authority is its Board of Governors, on which each member country is represented. Its headquarters are in Washington, but it operates field offices throughout Latin America and the Caribbean. *See also* WORLD BANK GROUP (231); INTER-AMERICAN SYSTEM (232).

Significance
The Inter-American Development Bank provided a model for financing regional development that led to the creation of the Asian and African Development Banks. Non-regional members have added substantially to the Bank's lending capabilities while securing opportunities to share in the export market to Latin America growing out of development projects underwritten by the IDB. Latin American states, uneasy about the dominant role of the United States in the IDB for many years, have welcomed the new European members and the infusion of new capital. IDB resources total almost $15 billion, with a cumulative lending total of about $10 billion for over 1,000 development projects. IDB efforts to finance development in Latin America are supplemented by World Bank Group loans, by Export-Import Bank loans, and by grants and loans from member countries and private banks, all of which cooperate in making consortium (joint) loans for major projects. The Third World debt crisis, which has hit Latin America very hard, has increased the value of development loans from the IDB as a means of meeting this crisis.

International Coffee Agreement | 224

An international commodity agreement aimed at maintaining stable market conditions for exporters and importers of coffee. To implement the agreement, members created the International Coffee organization in 1963, with its headquarters in London. The organization includes in its membership 51 coffee-exporting and 24 coffee-importing countries, with most of Latin America and some of the Caribbean countries included. It makes decisions concerning coffee production and pricing through an International Council, consisting of representatives from all member countries with an executive board of eight exporting and eight importing nations. *See also* ECONOMIC FACTORS: COMMODITY AGREEMENT (196).

Significance
The International Coffee Agreement and its International Coffee Organization seek to avoid ruinous competition among producers and exporters while maintaining a steady supply of coffee beans to market countries at a reasonable price. Prior to the adoption of commodity agreements like that for coffee, the world market was highly volatile and unpredictable for both sellers and buyers. Since 1963, a reasonable balance has been maintained through the organization's efforts, with adequate supplies available at fair prices.

Almost all world production of coffee is covered by the agreement and its operational organization. When the Organization of Oil Producing Countries (OPEC) succeeded in raising prices of oil on several occasions, coffee-producing states pressured the organization for coffee-price increases. International commodity agreements, like those for oil, tin, rubber, and coffee, seek to maintain a free market for their commodities while maintaining a semblance of production and sales orderliness.

International Monetary Fund (IMF) | 225 |

A specialized agency of the United Nations created by the Bretton Woods Monetary and Financial Conference of 1944 to promote international monetary and financial cooperation. The major objectives of the IMF are exchange stability, maintenance of a worldwide multilateral payments system, providing monetary reserves to help members overcome disequilibria in their balances of payments, and the operation of a forum to develop specific monetary and financial policies through mutual agreement. In 1990, over 150 nations were members of the IMF. Most nonmembers are communist or former communist states that for many years remained aloof, believing the IMF represented capitalism and imperialism in its operations. Since the late 1980s, however, most of these nations have indicated an interest in becoming members. *See also* INTER-AMERICAN DEVELOPMENT BANK (IDB) (223); WORLD BANK GROUP (231).

Significance
Latin American states played a major role in creating the IMF at the Bretton Woods Conference, and they have since been major users of IMF services. In recent years, Latin countries have become the largest debtor states involved in the Third World debt crisis. This has meant that countries like Brazil, Mexico, Argentina, Chile, and Venezuela have become increasingly dependent on IMF loans for making interest and loan amortization payments and avoiding national bankruptcy. The IMF typically has attached conditions to these loans, with the main one a requirement that the state receiving the loan pursue an austerity program. The result of such austerity programs has produced, in many Latin states, high unemployment, an end to economic growth, and unstable political conditions, including some rioting. Providing new loans with the proviso that they be used to make payments on old loans has failed both as an economic and political approach. Neither the Baker Plan (proposed by U.S. Secretary of State James Baker in 1985) nor the Brady Plan (formulated by U.S. Secretary of State Nicholas Brady in 1989) have succeeded in their objective of reducing Third World (and especially Latin American) debt through rescheduling and by such maneuvers as "debt-equity swaps," while at the same time trying to restore economic growth to increasingly stagnant Latin American economies. The IMF has been meeting annually with the World Bank in an effort to deal with the world debt crisis, recognizing that the lending nations of the First World are threatened also by Third World failure to repay loans. In 1990, the IMF sought to discourage member nations from taking advantage of the debt crisis as an excuse for not making repayments on schedule by deciding that members who were "persistently not cooperating" could have their voting rights suspended.

Latin American Economic System (SELA) | 226 |

An organization that was created in 1975 to function as a permanent consultative and coordination arrangement to enable the countries of Latin America to adopt common policies to promote economic and social well-being. Most Latin American nations are members of SELA or have indicated they will join. SELA (from *Sistema Económica Latinoamericana*) was established largely as a result of the initiatives undertaken by Mexican President Luis Echeverría, who regarded joint policies and actions as indispensable to the economic growth of Latin countries. SELA's operational goal is to establish a system for pooling resources and creating multilateral, government-owned agencies to develop and sell primary commodities on the world market, such as chrome, bauxite, nickel, sugar, and coffee. SELA also seeks to gain a more advantageous bargaining position toward other countries and regional groups by cultivating close political ties. SELA decisions are made in its principal organ, the Latin American Council, which meets annually and is composed of ministers from all member states. SELA members also caucus before participating in meetings of the Group of Seventy-Seven, a caucusing group composed of more than 115 Third World countries that meet to concert their policies prior to meetings of the United Nations General Assembly and other major agencies and conferences. They were also particularly active at the sessions of the United Nations Conference on Trade and Development in Nairobi in 1976 (UNCTAD IV). A Permanent Secretariat for SELA, headed by a secretary general, is located in Caracas. *See also* UNITED NATIONS CONFERENCE ON TRADE AND DEVELOPMENT (UNCTAD) (230).

Significance
The Latin American Economic System (SELA) in many ways tends to resemble the highly successful Organization of Petroleum Exporting Countries (OPEC) in its tactics, purposes, goals, and mode of operations. It recognizes that if the countries of Latin America tend to produce the same commodities and to compete with each other in the world market, all will suffer from the consequences of overproduction, unrestrained competition, market gluts, and depressed prices. The answer is to join together in organizations such as SELA to limit production, reduce harmful competition, control supplies placed on the world market, and fix prices. Thus, SELA is an effort on the part of many Latin American countries to improve their future economic outlook through joint cooperative actions. Its success or failure will depend on whether member countries are truly willing to engage in common enterprises, whether countries from outside the hemisphere can substantially affect prices and market conditions for SELA members, and whether a system of common pricing can endure.

Latin American Integration Association (LAIA) | 227

A regional group founded by the Montevideo Treaty of 1980 to increase trade and foster economic and social development and promote regional integration. LAIA replaced the Latin American Free Trade Association (LAFTA), which was created in 1960. LAIA's membership includes 11 Latin American states (Argentina, Bolivia, Brazil, Chile, Colombia, Ecuador, Mexico, Paraguay, Peru, Uruguay, and Venezuela), which represent three-fourths of the population south of the U.S. border. The Council of Ministers establishes LAIA's policies; a secretariat is located in Montevideo. *See also* ANDEAN COMMON MARKET (ACM) (213); CENTRAL AMERICAN COMMON MARKET (CACM) (218).

Significance
The Latin American Integration Association was created because of the

failure of LAFTA to reduce tariffs and trade barriers in sufficient numbers to produce a common market in the region. From its beginning in 1961, LAFTA was beset with difficulties stemming from: (1) differences in the stages of development among member states; (2) disagreements between the Big Three industrial states (Argentina, Brazil, and Mexico) and the smaller, less developed members; and (3) failure of member states to implement the goal of national specialization by refusing to honor the principle of complementarity, which required that they not manufacture products assigned to other states. Failure of LAFTA to make meaningful progress in liberalizing trade among its members or to move toward more extensive integration led to the creation of LAIA. The new organization moved from a system of across-the-board tariff cuts to a system of regional preferential trade agreements, which are based on a member's stage of development. Members are classified as most developed (Argentina, Brazil, Mexico), intermediate (Chile, Colombia, Peru, Uruguay, Venezuela), and least developed (Bolivia, Ecuador, Paraguay). LAIA retained some LAFTA agreements and renegotiated many new regional agreements. By the late 1980s, LAIA's approach to promoting regional trade and integration had achieved some successes and the organization developed programs for promoting trade, expanding areas of cooperation, and supporting the least developed members.

Special Latin American Coordinating Committee (CECLA) 228

A caucusing group established in 1964 to encourage regional harmony in developing economic bargaining power with non-regional states and international organizations. CECLA's Charter of Alta Gracia describes its role as that of a "permanent agency to serve as a Latin forum in which to discuss specific questions arising in UNCTAD and to deal with any other matters associated with international trade and economic development." The charter emphasized the prevailing inequality in world trade between the industrially developed countries of the First World and the developing nations of Latin America, Africa, Asia, Europe, and Oceania. To overcome this problem, CECLA called for, among other things, making foreign trade an effective instrument supporting economic development, solidarity among all developing states, and a restructuring of the world trade system by the industrial countries through adoption of a "preferential, generalized, non-reciprocal, and non-discriminatory treatment, beneficial to all developing countries." *See also* UNITED NATIONS CONFERENCE ON TRADE AND DEVELOPMENT (UNCTAD) (230).

Significance
The Special Latin American Coordinating Committee has been mainly concerned with lobbying efforts carried on at meetings of UNCTAD, GATT, IMF, World Bank Group, and other organizations concerned with aid, trade, and development. It functions as a "continuing conference" rather than as an institutionalized system, meeting whenever its members believe a session would serve a useful purpose. CECLA's objectives as set forth in its plan of action greatly influenced the architects of the proposed New International Economic Order (NIEO) more than a decade after CECLA's birth. CECLA has also functioned as a special caucusing group in the Organization of American States (OAS), serving as a counterforce to the political power of the United States in that organization. While CECLA's performance has been mixed over the years, its inability to function more effectively relates partly to conflicting interests on

many issues between the larger and economically more advanced countries, such as Argentina, Mexico, and Brazil, and the weaker, less developed countries that make up the majority of members.

Third World — 229

A development that began in 1947 in which nations not committed to either the East or the West in the cold war professed policies of neutralism and nonalignment. Third World countries developed a sense of solidarity and adopted various policies to avoid entanglements with the United States or Soviet Union. Although Latin American states have been allied militarily and politically with the United States, during the 1960s many began to move ideologically and politically into the Third World camp as their economic and political interests became more congruent with those of the new nations of Asia and Africa. By the 1970s, Third World nations constituted a large majority of the states in the international political system, and about 25 of them are Western Hemisphere countries. Third World states generally can be described as poor, underdeveloped, debtors, have nots, and southern. Some analysts recognize that Third World nations vary greatly in their resources, per capita income, and development progress. They prefer, therefore, to use the term "Fourth World" to describe the poorer members of the Third World group. Although most Fourth World countries are in Africa, several Western Hemisphere countries, such as Haiti, Honduras, Guyana, and El Salvador, are usually placed in this category. Third World unity has developed through a series of international conferences that focused on economic and political issues. *See also* FOURTH WORLD (221); SPECIAL LATIN AMERICAN COORDINATING COMMITTEE (CECLA) (228).

Significance
Latin American states over the past two decades have moved increasingly from a position of political and economic alignment with the United States to one of sympathy with the Third World and toward neutralism, noncommitment, and the role of a third force. In the United Nations, this has meant that the Latin American voting bloc has merged with the African and Asian groups to produce a two-thirds majority vote on most issues taken up by the General Assembly in its regular and special sessions and in UN-sponsored major international conferences in critical issue areas. East/West cold war issues have been generally kept off the agendas and have been replaced with North/South issues. The latter place emphasis in three critical areas: (1) fostering the process of modernization and development, (2) ending all forms of colonialism, and (3) protecting human rights. Latin American states have increasingly taken leadership roles in trying to cope with those issues that directly affect the developing world. They have participated in the Caucus of the Seventy-Seven (an informal meeting of developing countries to determine common policy positions) at all UNCTAD meetings and United Nations and special conference meetings. In 1974 at the Sixth Special Session of the General Assembly, for example, they joined other Third World states in adopting the Declaration on the Establishment of a New International Economic Order (NIEO). This declaration was a demand to change the international economic system from one dominated by the rich and powerful to one that would offer benefits to all and contribute effectively to the development and modernization of the developing states. The Conference of Non-Aligned Nations, another manifestation of Third World unity and neutrality, was created at the Bandung

Conference in 1955 and continues to meet every three or four years with more than 100 nations participating.

United Nations Conference on Trade and Development 230

An agency established by the United Nations General Assembly to develop trade policies that will foster economic development. UNCTAD began as an ad hoc conference in 1964, called at the insistence of Third World developing states. Its initial success led the General Assembly to convert it into a permanent body. UNCTAD has been convened in plenary session every three or four years, typically in the capitals of Third World countries, such as New Delhi, Santiago, Nairobi and Manila. A 55-member Trade and Development Board develops policy proposals between sessions, and a secretariat is located at UNCTAD's Geneva headquarters. *See also* SPECIAL LATIN AMERICAN COORDINATING COMMITTEE (CECLA) (228); THIRD WORLD (229).

Significance
The United Nations Conference on Trade and Development, with a total membership including around 160 First, Second, Third, and Fourth World nations, reflects the strongly held view of the Third World that the global economic system favors the rich countries and needs some fundamental change through which the interests of developing states will be more effectively recognized and accommodated. UNCTAD was originally created through the developing bloc's efforts to establish a balance to the General Agreement on Tariffs and Trade (GATT), which Third World countries generally regarded as "the rich man's club" and not particularly interested in their trade and development problems. Regional caucusing groups, such as the Special Latin American Coordinating Committee (CECLA) and a Third World Caucus of the Seventy-Seven (since grown to include 120 developing states) have met prior to each UNCTAD session to develop and coordinate their policies. Latin American influence led to the appointment of Raúl Prebisch as first secretary-general of UNCTAD and to the selection of Manuel Pérez-Guerrero of Venezuela as his successor. UNCTAD has placed major emphasis on changes that will improve the terms of trade for developing countries to provide additional capital needed to foster economic growth. Although a political success, UNCTAD has produced few economic victories for the Third World despite its continuing demand for the creation of the New International Economic Order (NIEO). Issues that have particularly concerned Latin Americans have been those relating to reducing trade barriers in the developed countries without reciprocation, stabilizing commodity prices, and controlling the operations of multinational corporations in developing states. The pace of change has been slow, however, producing much frustration in Latin American and other developing states and leading them to place increasing emphasis on commodity agreements and cartel operations as means for improving their international economic position. A major concrete accomplishment of UNCTAD, however, has been the adoption of a General System of Preferences (GSP) by which the industrialized countries of the First World (Western Europe, United States, and Japan) have unilaterally reduced their tariffs on many hundreds of articles of commerce exported to them by developing countries.

World Bank Group 231

The four institutions—International Bank for Reconstruction and Development (IBRD), the International Finance Corporation (IFC), the International

Development Association (IDA), and the Multilateral Investment Guarantee Agency (MIGA)—which function collectively as the world's major lending group. The IBRD early in its history made loans mainly to Western European countries following World War II to help them rebuild their war-shattered economies. Then began the process that continues today of financing economic development programs of Third World countries, especially those of Latin America, which in the post-war period had the largest number of independent countries struggling to develop and modernize. The IBRD, like the International Monetary Fund (IMF), was created by the Bretton Woods Agreement of 1944, with each ordained to cooperate with the other in the promotion of world trade, higher standards of living for all peoples, and economic development of underdeveloped and developing states. The bank's main sources of funds are capital subscriptions from member states (over 150 members) and, to carry on its operations, sales of World Bank bonds to private subscribers. Voting in the bank's decision-making process is based on the amount of subscribed capital provided by each member to underwrite the bank's operations. The United States, which provides about 20 percent of the subscribed capital, has the largest bloc of votes. The former communist states of Eastern Europe long avoided membership in what they charged was an "instrument of capitalist imperialism," but they have begun to apply for membership following the revolutionary changes that have occurred in that area. The International Finance Corporation since its creation in 1956 has helped to promote capitalism and free enterprise by making loans to and providing risk capital for private companies and joint ventures in Third and Fourth World countries. In 1960, to meet the criticism that IBRD's lending policies were too strict, the International Development Association was created as an affiliate of the bank to offer 50-year, zero-interest loans to qualifying states. The Multilateral Investment Guarantee Agency was established in 1988 to encourage direct equity investment in developing countries by investors in industrialized nations. Since many loans were used to make interest and amortization payments, MIGA's purpose is to promote development by guaranteeing private investment. *See also* INTER-AMERICAN DEVELOPMENT BANK (223); INTERNATIONAL MONETARY FUND (IMF) (225).

Significance
By the early 1990s, the World Bank Group had collectively made over 4,000 loans valued at around $150 billion. The Latin American and Caribbean region has received more loan aid through the World Bank Group than any other region in the world. Most loans are made only after a careful screening process gives some assurance that loan repayment will occur. Increasingly, however, IBRD loans are made in conjunction with IMF loans aimed at staving off national bankruptcy and seeking to avoid debt default by many countries. Since the Third World debt crisis focuses mainly on Latin America and the Caribbean, the countries of this region have been the main recipients of World Bank loans in the past decade. Because many of these countries have overextended their repayment capacities, the Western world's private banking system—which accounts for most of the loan defaults—is threatened with severe problems or even collapse. That is why loans made to countries with debt-ridden economies are earmarked by the bank not only for helping to make repayments on schedule but also to provide additional capital so that many debtor states will be able to grow their way out of debt. Latin countries that receive most of these kinds of loans because they are leading debtor states include Brazil, Mexico, Argentina, Venezuela, and Chile.

International Law and Organization

Inter-American System 232
The institutional structure created by the Pan-American movement as it developed during the nineteenth and twentieth centuries. Although unilateral action by the United States under the Monroe Doctrine typified most of the nineteenth century, the First International Conference of American States was held in Washington (1889–1890). At that Conference, the rudimentary framework of the inter-American regional system was created in the form of an International Union of American States and a Commercial Bureau of the American Republics. Agreement was reached on fostering closer economic relationships, although the U.S. proposal for Pan-American customs union was rejected by the Latin American states. Over the first half of the twentieth century, eight more International Conferences of American States were held in major Latin American cities (Mexico City, 1901–1902; Rio de Janeiro, 1906; Buenos Aires, 1910; Santiago, 1923; Havana, 1928; Montevideo, 1933; Lima, 1938; and Bogotá, 1948). At the last of these conferences, the Charter of Bogotá was proclaimed, establishing the Organization of American States (OAS) and changing the title of the major meetings from International Conference of American States to the Inter-American Conference. In addition to the basic political structure, special conferences have created additional security, economic, and social institutional arrangements. These include: (1) the Act of Chapultepec (1945), adopted at a special conference held in Mexico City to provide for collective hemispheric security until a formal treaty could be concluded; (2) the Inter-American Treaty of Reciprocal Assistance (Rio Treaty), which provides for a mutual security system to counter acts of aggression committed in the Western Hemisphere, as defined in the treaty; and (3) the Inter-American Treaty on Pacific Settlement (Pact of Bogotá), which was aimed at settling all American disputes peacefully and was concluded at the same conference that established

the OAS. *See also* INTER-AMERICAN DEVELOPMENT BANK (IDB) (223); INTER-AMERICAN SYSTEM: ACT OF CHAPULTEPEC (233); INTER-AMERICAN SYSTEM: ORGANIZATION OF AMERICAN STATES (OAS) (235); SECURITY ARRANGEMENTS: PACT OF BOGOTA (247); SECURITY ARRANGEMENTS: RIO TREATY (INTER-AMERICAN TREATY OF RECIPROCAL ASSISTANCE) (248).

Significance
The development and expansion of the inter-American system reflect the growing understandings and solidarity developed among the nations of the Western Hemisphere during the past century. These closer relationships—as represented by the building of numerous institutional structures—have not been based on a steady, progressive integration, but rather have in their growth tended to reflect the volatile nature of the associations developed between the United States and the countries of Latin America, and among the latter as well. With the advent of the Good Neighbor policy in the 1930s, however, the base was established on which a variegated institutional structure could be built and continue to rest. With the breakup of the bipolar world in the 1960s, hemispheric policies also began to change. Increasingly, Latin American states have identified with the Third World and its emphasis on economic and social matters, while placing less emphasis on political and security problems given priority by the United States. Issues such as those involving direct or indirect interventions by the United States in Cuba, Guatemala, the Dominican Republic, Chile, and Nicaragua have rekindled long-standing suspicions of U.S. policies and actions. Nonetheless, the inter-American system remains today an excellent example of regional cooperation and integration through institution building.

**Inter-American System:
Act of Chapultepec** 233
A declaration made by the 21 American republics at the Chapultepec Conference held in Mexico City in 1945, providing for common action against an aggressor from outside or inside the region. The Act of Chapultepec declared that an attack against any American state would be considered an act of aggression against all, thus calling for collective action against the aggressor. *See also* INTER-AMERICAN SYSTEM: ORGANIZATION OF AMERICAN STATES (OAS) (235); SECURITY ARRANGEMENTS: RIO TREATY (INTER-AMERICAN TREATY OF RECIPROCAL ASSISTANCE) (248).

Significance
The Act of Chapultepec was a milestone in the development of inter-American relations in that it expanded the Monroe Doctrine's unilateral guarantee against intervention in the hemisphere into a mutual security system. In addition, for the first time it included provisions that would outlaw aggression by one American state against another. Because Latin Americans feared that the emphasis placed on the United Nations by the United States would erode the progressive development of inter-American institutions, the Chapultepec Conference called for the negotiation of a treaty of reciprocal assistance, the creation of a basic constitution and political organization, and a general agreement on peaceful settlement of disputes. Thus the conference foreshadowed the development of the Rio Treaty in 1947, the creation of the Organization of American States (OAS) in 1948, and the Pact of Bogotá of 1948, providing for peaceful resolution of inter-American disputes. U.S. support for the Act of Chapultepec was based on the desirability of improved relations with Latin states in the post-war period and a policy of ensuring that the

proposed Security Council of the United Nations would not prohibit American states from undertaking common action to safeguard security in the hemisphere.

Inter-American System: Commission on Human Rights 234

An organization created in 1959 that establishes and promotes human rights observance in the hemisphere and investigates complaints about violations. It consists of seven individuals nominated by member governments and elected by the Council of the Organization of American States (OAS). The commission functions as a collateral body to the General Assembly of the Organization of American States in support of OAS objectives. In this capacity, it studies, investigates, and makes recommendations concerning allegations of human rights violations by OAS members. Members are required under OAS and commission rules to provide information on their human rights activities or lack of them. The commission also implements provisions of the American Convention on Human Rights adopted by most American states in 1969. This document guarantees basic political and civil rights, such as the right to life, humane treatment, personal freedom, privacy, fair trial, equal protection of the laws, freedom from slavery, and fair compensation for property taken by government under eminent domain. A court that resembles the European Court of Human Rights has been set up in Costa Rica to interpret and apply provisions of the American Convention. *See also* RACIAL GROUP (18).

Significance
The Inter-American Commission on Human Rights was the first step undertaken in the Western Hemisphere toward building an effective system for protecting the individual's rights in all countries functioning in the inter-American system. Although effective enforcement machinery is lacking, the commission functions as a mediatory body. It also issues reports that can serve as a form of sanction against a government that violates rights. When right-wing military groups seized control of the government of Chile, for example, the commission was unable to stop gross violations of human rights that resulted in the disappearance and death of thousands of innocent civilians in the 1970s. Criticism of General Augusto Pinochet's Chilean government for its gross violations of human rights led in time to almost universal condemnation and post hoc efforts to right many wrongs. In Argentina, human rights violations led to jail sentences for military officers, and before relinquishing their power in Brazil, El Salvador, Guatemala, and Uruguay, military officers demanded pledges that they would not be subjected to Argentine-style trials for human rights violations. The massive wave of support by OAS members for human rights protection led eventually to a democratization movement throughout the hemisphere. The Inter-American Commission continues to receive hundreds of complaints of alleged violations each year, but very few cases result in public debate since the commission prefers quiet persuasion.

Inter-American System: Organization of American States (OAS) 235

A major regional organization composed of the United States and most Latin American states that determines common political, defense, economic, and social policies and provides for coordination of various inter-American agencies. The OAS was established by the Ninth International Conference of American States held in Bogotá in 1948, but it was substantially changed by charter amendments contained in the 1967 Protocol of Buenos Aires. Twenty-one American republics initially ratified the OAS charter, but the Castro government of Cuba was expelled in 1962 although Cuba as a state remained a member. Several newly independent states in the region have joined in recent years. A primary responsibility of the OAS is to implement the Inter-American Treaty of Reciprocal Assistance (Rio Treaty) when any threat to the security of the region arises. Many OAS meetings are concerned with consideration of political issues, developing economic programs, and cultivating social understanding. Major organs of the OAS include: (1) the General Assembly, the supreme organ that is assigned responsibility to develop broad policy guidelines; (2) the Meeting of Consultation of Ministers of Foreign Affairs, which considers specific security issues, dispute settlement, and political/economic problems when called into session by a majority of OAS members; (3) the Permanent Council of the OAS (PCOAS), composed of an ambassador from each member state, which serves as peacekeeping mediator and takes up matters assigned to it by the foreign ministers at its headquarters in Washington, D.C.; (4) the Inter-American Economic and Social Council, which is charged with coordinating all OAS economic and social development programs and promotes economic integration; (5) the Inter-American Council for Education, Science, and Culture, which promotes these fields through cooperation and exchanges; (6) the General Secretariat, also called the Pan American Union, which functions as a secretariat for the OAS and coordinates economic and social programs carried on by various agencies; (7) the Specialized Conferences, consisting of agencies, institutes, committees, boards, and commissions that deal with technical or specialized matters in the region; and (8) the Specialized Organizations, which are intergovernmental agencies that carry on cooperative programs in fields such as health, education, child welfare, and agriculture. Two bodies that function in a capacity subordinate to the General Assembly are the Inter-American Juridical Committee, whose 11 jurists are elected by the General Assembly to advise the OAS on juridical matters and promote the development of international law, and the Inter-American Commission on Human Rights, which promotes human rights observance in the hemisphere and investigates complaints about violations. Vital issues facing the OAS and its member states in the 1990s include developing and managing resources, having secure energy sources, protecting the environment, combating terrorism, coping with the AIDS disease, and preventing nuclear weapons proliferation. *See also* SECURITY ARRANGEMENTS: RIO TREATY (INTER-AMERICAN TREATY OF RECIPROCAL ASSISTANCE) (248).

Significance
Sovereignty, state equality, and nonintervention are the three fundamental principles on which the Organization of American States is based. The OAS is a regional organization that can function within the framework provided by the Charter of the United Nations in helping to settle disputes and maintain peace and security in the world. The major controversies to come before the OAS since 1948 have mainly been those associated with efforts—led by the United States—to keep communism out of the hemisphere, whether the threat emanates from outside the region or from within. Leading issues taken up by the OAS have included U.S. efforts to secure multilateral support for policies aimed at preventing or removing communism from Nicaragua, El Salvador, Guatemala, Cuba, the Dominican Republic, and Chile. U.S. calls for joint military operations have been re-

jected by OAS members. By 1991, however, only El Salvador and Cuba remained as "communist problems." Fostering economic development and promoting integration have also frequently been on the OAS agenda, and social programs have received some consideration as well. Conflicts between the United Nations Security Council and the OAS over jurisdiction of Latin American disputes have usually been won by the latter, with the United States playing a major role in demanding that regional problems be settled within the region. The United States continues to play a major role in the OAS decision processes dealing with threats of aggression and in financing collective efforts to develop Latin economies. Canada, which has Permanent Observer status with the OAS, is the only major hemispheric state that has chosen not to join the organization, perhaps because of its perception of the dominant role of the United States in the system. The major challenge facing the OAS today involves the problem of dealing with subversion and indirect aggression in the region without stifling the peaceful economic and social revolutions needed to produce progress.

Inter-American System: Organization of Central American States (ODECA) 236

A regional organization created to foster political, economic, and social cooperation. Established by the 1951 Charter of San Salvador, ODECA's members are Costa Rica, El Salvador, Guatemala, Honduras, and Nicaragua. A revised charter was agreed to in Panama City in 1962, and Panama was invited to join. ODECA's principal organs include: (1) the Meeting of Heads of State, which constitutes the "supreme organ"; (2) the Conference of Ministers of Foreign Affairs, the "principal organ" charged with initiating proposals and serving as the major decision-making body, with unanimity needed for all substantive decisions; (3) the Executive Council, designated the "permanent organ," which meets regularly and serves as a communication link between the organization and its member states; (4) the Legislative Council, composed of three legislators from each of the five state assemblies, which offers advice on such matters as uniform legislation; (5) the Court of Justice, composed of the presidents of the supreme courts of the members, which decides legal issues submitted to it; (6) the Economic Council, which is responsible for developing and implementing economic integration; (7) the Cultural and Educational Council, which is charged with promoting cultural exchanges and fostering educational development in the region; and (8) the Defense Council, which members consult concerning security matters in the region. In addition, the Central American Bureau, headed by a secretary-general, functions as a secretariat for the organization. *See also* CENTRAL AMERICAN COMMON MARKET (CACM) (218).

Significance
The Organization of Central American States reflects the historical impetus toward political unity in the region. Following independence in the 1820s, five provinces joined together into the single nation known as the Federation of Central America, but political conflict led to the dissolving of the federation and the emergence of five sovereign states in 1838. The contemporary effort to move toward political integration through ODECA has also suffered from a variety of disputes and, occasionally, open conflict. ODECA's main accomplishments have been in the field of economic integration, where the adoption of common programs and agencies ultimately led to the creation of the Central American Common Market (CACM). Whether closer political ties are possible in the

future depends on the performance of CACM and how each state views its national interest.

Inter-American System: Treaty for the Prohibition of Nuclear Weapons in Latin America | 237 |

A treaty aimed at preventing the introduction of nuclear weapons into the region and safeguarding the use of nuclear materials and facilities for peaceful purposes. Also known as the Treaty of Tlatelolco (named for the international section of Mexico City where it was signed in 1967), the treaty entered into force in 1968. It forbids "testing, use, manufacture, production, or acquisition ... [and the] receipt, storage, installation, deployment, and any form of possession of any nuclear weapons, directly or indirectly." Two protocols supplement the treaty in attempting to apply its provisions to states outside the region. Protocol I—ratified by Britain and the Netherlands, but not by France and the United States—requires colonial states to place their dependent territories in Latin America under treaty restrictions. Protocol II—ratified by Britain, China, France, and the United States, but not by the former Soviet Union—binds nuclear weapons states to respect the main treaty provision to keep nuclear weapons out of the region.

Significance
The Treaty for the Prohibition of Nuclear Weapons in Latin America was an outgrowth of the activity of Third World states in the United Nations. During the 1960s, resolutions were adopted by the General Assembly declaring Africa, Asia, and Latin America to be nuclear-free zones. Leadership in developing the treaty in Latin America came mainly from Brazil and Mexico, two potential nuclear weapons states. The 1962 Cuban missile crisis provided much of the incentive to conclude the treaty. The United States gave little support to the treaty's objectives, refusing to declare Puerto Rico and the Guantanamo Bay naval station in Cuba nuclear-free territories. In 1969, the treaty was supplemented by the establishment of the Organization for the Prohibition of Nuclear Weapons in Latin America (OPANAL). The treaty plowed new ground in that it provided the first legal commitment by states within a region to renounce the acquisition of nuclear weapons, and because it was the first nuclear arms control agreement of any kind entered into by France and the People's Republic of China. Treaty objectives were supplemented in 1970 by the Nonproliferation of Nuclear Weapons Treaty (NPT), open to ratification by all states. By 1991, no violations of treaty provisions had occurred.

Intervention | 238 |

Coercive action undertaken by one state or group of states against another state or group of states. Intervention may constitute interference in either a state's internal or external affairs, and it may take the form of military, political, or economic coercion. International law recognizes intervention as a legal action: (1) if requested by the government of the state; (2) if the intervening state is exercising a right guaranteed by treaty; (3) if it is a reprisal for an illegal act; (4) when such an action is necessary to protect citizens of the intervening state; and (5) when the United Nations or a regional organization intervenes to settle a dispute or stop an aggression and acts within its delegated powers. *See also* CIA OPERATIONS (251).

Significance
Since gaining their independence, many Latin American states have been prime targets of interventions, especially by the United States and Europe's great powers. Latin states particularly susceptible to intervention have included Cuba, the Dominican Republic, Haiti, Mexico,

Nicaragua, and the countries of Central America. In the Monroe Doctrine of 1823 the United States declared that European states no longer had the right to intervene in the Western Hemisphere. The United States, however, enunciated a new interpretation of the doctrine in the form of the Roosevelt Corollary of 1904, establishing the "right" of the United States to intervene in Latin American countries when required by flagrant wrongdoing. The Clark Memorandum of 1928, the Good Neighbor policy of the 1930s, and the establishment of the Organization of American States (OAS) in 1948 were aimed at reducing or eliminating the threat of U.S. interventions or "multilateralizing" them when they were considered essential. Nevertheless, U.S. unilateral interventions have continued in an effort to keep communism out of the hemisphere, with the most obvious cases involving Guatemala, Cuba, the Dominican Republic, Grenada, Panama, El Salvador, Nicaragua, and Chile. Policymakers in the United States have tended to regard incursions of communist doctrine and influence into the hemisphere as illegal interventions in violation of the Monroe Doctrine. On the other hand, Latin Americans have often criticized the United States for its "nonintervention" that lends support to right-wing dictators, and many Latins advocate an active policy of intervention for democracy rather than simply against communism or socialism. A recent U.S. intervention of a political, economic, and diplomatic nature is its opposition to the military takeover in Haiti against the democratically elected government of Jean-Bertrand Aristide in 1991.

Legal Institutions: Central American Court of International Justice | 239 |

A regional court through which the Central American states sought to resolve their disputes and avoid war. Established under the terms of the Central American Peace Conference of 1907 (also known as the Washington Conference of 1907), members of the Central American Court included Guatemala, El Salvador, Honduras, Nicaragua, and Costa Rica. Each state appointed one judge to the five-member court, and the judges were expected to render decisions objectively without national or personal bias. The signatory states agreed to submit all disputes to the court that could not be resolved through other peaceful settlement procedures. The court functioned for the 10 years provided by its charter, but controversial decisions made it impossible to extend its life.

Significance
The Central American Court of International Justice was the first regional experiment in the settlement of disputes through adjudication. It heard and rendered decisions on 10 cases before it went out of existence in 1918. The final case was also its most controversial. Three members—Costa Rica, El Salvador, and Honduras—contested Nicaragua's right to grant concessions unilaterally to the United States to build a canal and establish naval bases, claiming that these actions infringed upon their sovereignty. The court held against Nicaragua, but neither Nicaragua nor the United States accepted the decision. In 1923, the same states sought to establish a second court, but the attempt failed. The importance of the court was not in its performance in cases but rather in its role of emphasizing the need for a judicial body as a substitute for the anarchy that typically has prevailed in the relationships of Central American nations.

Legal Institutions: Inter-American Council of Jurists | 240 |

A specialized agency that functions as an advisory body to the Council of the Organization of American States

(OAS) concerning juridical matters. The Inter-American Council of Jurists is composed of legal experts from all member states. Among its responsibilities are those of promoting the development and codification of public and private international law. The charter of the OAS also assigns it the responsibility of "making uniform the laws of the various American countries insofar as it appears desirable." Meetings of the Council of Jurists are convened by the OAS Council periodically, typically every two years. Between sessions, an Inter-American Juridical Committee, elected by the Council of Jurists and headquartered in Rio de Janeiro, functions as a staff or secretariat, doing legal research and preparing materials for consideration at meetings of the Council of Jurists. All major organs of the OAS system may assign or suggest matters for consideration by the Juridical Committee. *See also* INTER-AMERICAN SYSTEM: ORGANIZATION OF AMERICAN STATES (OAS) (235).

Significance
Both the Inter-American Council of Jurists and the Inter-American Juridical Committee have been called upon from time to time to issue legal opinions concerning interpretations and applications of the OAS charter. Both are also available to render legal opinions on matters of dispute between American states when called upon by the organ having jurisdiction over the dispute. The Council of Jurists has also prepared a draft for an Inter-American Convention on Human Rights based on the European Convention on Human Rights that entered into force in 1953. The draft has not as yet, however, been submitted to an Inter-American Conference for approval, and its status appears uncertain. Despite the efforts of both the Council of Jurists and the Juridical Committee, the emphasis in the inter-American system remains on political and diplomatic approaches to resolving issues, but with much lip service paid to legal approaches.

Legal Institutions: International Court of Justice (ICJ) | 241

The major legal organ of the United Nations, established in 1945. The International Court of Justice, also known as the World Court, is one of the six major organs of the United Nations system. It adjudicates justiciable disputes between nations and renders decisions on such cases. It also hears and renders advisory opinions to organs of the United Nations. Headquartered at the Hague, the World Court has 15 judges elected by the General Assembly and the Security Council (with the veto applicable). No two judges can be nationals of the same state. Decisions of the court are final, and, if any nation fails to accept a decision, the other party may bring the case before the Security Council and request enforcement action. *See also* LEGAL INSTITUTIONS: INTER-AMERICAN COUNCIL OF JURISTS (240).

Significance
The effectiveness of the World Court has been impaired because its power to decide cases extends only to cases in which the states concerned have accepted its jurisdiction. No national court system could function under such a limitation. Efforts to correct this weakness have taken the form of seeking to get states to accept the "optional clause" by which they would voluntarily agree to the jurisdiction of the court. The United States in its acceptance, however, attached the reservation (known as the Connally Amendment) by which the United States retained the right to decide whether the issue was justiciable. In nearly 50 years of operation, the court has decided only 40-some cases and rendered about 20 advisory opinions. One of the more notable cases in recent years has been

Nicaragua v. The United States, a case brought to the ICJ by the government of Nicaragua and charging that U.S.-assisted mining of Nicaraguan harbors and U.S. support for the contra insurgents were both violations of international law. In bringing the case, Nicaragua claimed an infringement of its sovereignty and pointed out that the United States carried on its efforts to topple the Nicaraguan regime despite its continued recognition of the Sandinista government and formal exchange of diplomatic personnel. The United States denied the jurisdiction of the ICJ in this case, but in every issue raised by the case, the court rendered nearly unanimous condemnations of U.S. actions and called for reparations. In 1990, however, the Sandinistas were voted out of power and interest in pursuing the matter lapsed. The United States, however, continues to be criticized by many states for its refusal to accept the jurisdiction of the court.

Legal Policies: Calvo Clause | 242

A section often inserted by Latin American governments in public contracts concluded with citizens of other states and aimed at avoiding intervention by foreign governments in cases of default or controversy. The Calvo Clause provision was strongly advocated as a means to protect a state's sovereign rights by the famous Argentine jurist, Carlos Calvo, in a book published in 1868. According to the Calvo doctrine, if controversies arise under a contractual arrangement, the alien party agrees in the contract to rely solely on local remedies and not request diplomatic or other forms of support from his government. Disagreements have existed among international arbitral tribunals and jurists as to whether, under international law, such clauses are binding and can prevent foreign governments from intervening in such disputes. *See also* LEGAL POLICIES: DRAGO DOCTRINE (243).

Significance
The Calvo Clause is one of many efforts by Latin American states to reduce or eliminate the threat of intervention in their domestic affairs by great power states. It served for many years as a rallying point for Latin Americans who wished to maintain full sovereignty and territorial inviolability for weak as well as powerful states. The Calvo Clause challenged the doctrine espoused by European states that their citizens had a right to just treatment with regard to claims growing out of wars, revolutions, breaches of contract, and the like, regardless of the treatment accorded by Latin states to their own citizens. European leaders insisted that when individuals signed such contractual arrangements they were not binding upon their governments, which always have responsibility to protect their citizens and ensure justice for them. In 1902, an intervention in Venezuela by three European states in violation of the Calvo Clause led to its restatement as the Drago Doctrine, barring military interventions for debt-collection purposes.

Legal Policies: Drago Doctrine | 243

A policy opposing the use of military intervention in Latin American states as a means for collecting a public debt. The Drago Doctrine was enunciated in 1902 by Venezuelan Foreign Minister Luis María Drago in the form of a communication sent to the Argentine Minister in Washington. In that note, Drago states: "There can be no territorial expansion in America on the part of Europe.... The public debt cannot occasion armed intervention, nor even the actual occupation of the territory of American nations by a European power." The Drago Doctrine was a direct result of a 1902 naval blockade of Venezuela carried out by Britain, Germany, and Italy. That action resulted when Venezuela defaulted on its public debt and other claims held by citizens of the intervening countries. *See also* LEGAL POLICIES: CALVO CLAUSE (242).

Significance
The Drago Doctrine was a restatement of the Calvo Clause of 1868, stressing sovereignty and territorial inviolability, which the three European states intervening in Venezuela had rejected by their actions. The Drago Doctrine contributed during an era of great power imperialism to the growing emphasis placed on the Monroe Doctrine's proscription against European intervention in the Western Hemisphere. The United States at first warmly supported the Drago Doctrine. In 1907, however, the United States under treaty provisions took over the customs houses of the Dominican Republic to ensure payment of foreign debts so as to avoid European intervention. In the contemporary world, forcible intervention by one state to collect debts owed to its citizens by another state is inadmissible under international law. Diplomatic intervention by a state on behalf of its citizens, however, is still an acceptable practice, although it is not often successful.

Legal Policies: Estrada Doctrine | 244 |

A policy advocated by Mexican Foreign Minister Genaro Estrada in 1930, which rejects the granting or withholding of diplomatic recognition to a state or a government for political reasons. According to the Estrada Doctrine, governments should refrain completely from undertaking a formal act of recognition so as to avoid judging the political acceptability of a new regime. Thus recognition should be automatic and not bestow approval on a new government or state, but merely acknowledge its existence and its effective control over its people and territory. The Estrada Doctrine was aimed particularly at providing legitimacy for the Mexican and other governments that may come into power through revolution. The Estrada Doctrine challenged the Tobar Doctrine enunciated in 1907, which held that governments and states that come into existence by other than constitutional and democratic processes should be denied legitimacy by a collective refusal to recognize them. *See also* LEGAL POLICIES: TOBAR DOCTRINE (246).

Significance
The Estrada Doctrine and its supporters sought to remove the act of recognition from the political arena so that states could engage in continuous diplomacy in their relations with each other. The issue of whether recognition theory and practice should be declarative (i.e., based on the de facto existence of a new regime and its control over territory and people, regardless of how it came to power) or constitutive (i.e., based only on democratic, constitutional change) has been a matter of dispute in the entire state system as well as in Latin America. The Estrada Doctrine in effect states that the formal recognition process as used in the traditional way should be abandoned because it is too rigid. Some states, however, reject both the Estrada and Tobar doctrines and base their recognition and nonrecognition decisions strictly on national interest considerations. Since the administration of President Woodrow Wilson, for example, this kind of politicization of recognition policy has been followed by the United States.

Legal Policies: Expropriation | 245 |

Seizure by a government of privately owned property and assumption of ownership by the state. In Latin American states, expropriation has often involved seizure of properties owned by foreign nations and corporations, especially those owned by U.S. and European companies. Expropriation involves (1) the issue of whether the process is legally permissible under international law; (2) the procedures utilized to carry out the policy; and (3) the issue of what constitutes "just compensation" for the seized properties. International law recognizes expropriation as a proper exercise of sovereign power but requires that it be exercised for neither discriminatory nor retaliatory purposes and that the action be conditional on the payment of fair and just compensation to the former owners. Major expropriations of foreign-owned properties typically occur following revolutionary changes of governments. *See also* REVOLUTION (100).

Significance
Expropriation of enemy-owned properties always occurs during times of war, but in Latin America most nationalizations have involved economic or political motivations. In some cases, expropriations have resulted in major confrontations between the expropriating state and foreign governments. In defending the property interests of their nations, foreign governments have challenged the basic doctrine of nonintervention historically enunciated by Latin states. Major expropriation cases involving seizure of properties owned by United States–based companies include the Bolivian government's seizure of Standard Oil Company holdings in 1937, Mexican nationalization of oil and agricultural lands, and Peru's seizure of agricultural, mineral, and utility properties in the 1960s. Seizures by the Castro regime in Cuba of about $1.8 billion of properties owned by U.S. citizens have served to strain relations between the two countries for many years. Although the U.S. government has generally recognized the right of sovereign states to expropriate private properties, it typically has brought diplomatic and economic pressure to bear on expropriating states. In recent years, Latin states have expropriated many foreign-owned properties in their drive to develop and modernize, particularly major export industries or public utilities. Most of these cases have been settled as a result of prolonged negotiations between the governments and private companies involved.

Legal Policies: Tobar Doctrine 246

A policy of collective nonrecognition proposed in 1907 by an Ecuadorian diplomat, Carlos R. Tobar, that was aimed at denying legitimacy to governments that come to power by nondemocratic means. The Tobar Doctrine sought to reduce the threat of revolution, civil war, and coup d'etat as means for assuming power in Latin states. Tobar's position was that it is in the interest of all existing governments to collectively seek to establish constitutionalism and the democratic process as the means for effecting political change in the hemisphere. The Tobar Doctrine was challenged by the Estrada Doctrine (proposed in 1930 by the Mexican foreign minister), which holds that a new government should be automatically recognized when it is in political control of the state. *See also* LEGAL POLICIES: ESTRADA DOCTRINE (244).

Significance
The Tobar Doctrine and its supporters sought to use collective nonrecognition as a means for fostering stability and legitimacy in the political arenas of Latin America. Declarative recognition is based on the de facto existence of a new regime and its control over territory and people, regardless of how it secured power; constitutive recognition accepts only democratic, constitutional change. In effect, the Tobar Doctrine holds that, as far as the international community is concerned, a new state or government can be created only through its

recognition by other members of the state system. The Tobar Doctrine has increasingly given way to the application of the Estrada Doctrine or the politicization of the recognition process during an era in which traditional colonialism has ended and many new states and governments have emerged through a variety of means other than democratic and constitutional.

Security Arrangements: Pact of Bogotá (247)

The international instrument, formally known as the Inter-American Treaty on Pacific Settlement, that establishes an obligation for all signatory states to settle their disputes peacefully. The Pact of Bogotá calls for the use of traditional settlement procedures, including diplomacy, good offices, mediation, investigation, conciliation, arbitration, and adjudication, including, in the last case, the use of the World Court. The pact applies only to states that ratify it, and all existing peaceful settlement agreements in force for those states are superseded by the pact when ratified. The pact was negotiated at the Bogotá Conference of 1948, which also wrote the basic constitution for the OAS known as the Charter of Bogotá. *See also* INTER-AMERICAN SYSTEM: ORGANIZATION OF AMERICAN STATES (OAS) (235).

Significance
The Pact of Bogotá has been ratified and put into force by only 13 Latin states: Brazil, Colombia, Costa Rica, Dominican Republic, El Salvador, Haiti, Honduras, Mexico, Nicaragua, Panama, Paraguay, Peru, and Uruguay. States that have refused to ratify the pact oppose the provisions for third party settlement procedures and reject compulsory submission of disputes in favor of voluntarism. Conflicts over boundary lines, territorial sovereignty, fishing rights, trade policies, law of the sea jurisdiction, and related issues have increased tensions among Latin states, but many prefer not to be bound by stipulated settlement procedures. An arms race among some neighboring states threatens to increase such tensions in the future. The United States encouraged but did not participate in the framing of the Pact of Bogotá.

Security Arrangements: Rio Treaty (Inter-American Treaty of Reciprocal Assistance) (248)

A regional alliance, signed in Rio de Janeiro in 1947, that established a mutual security system to safeguard the Western Hemisphere from aggression. Signatories to the Rio Treaty include the United States and 20 Latin American republics. The treaty established a zone from the North Pole to the South Pole and provides for assistance in the case of an armed attack within the zone, for mutual consultation if some other form of aggression occurs within the zone, or for any form of aggression against a signatory state occurring outside the zone. Decisions are made by the Meeting of Consultation of Ministers of Foreign Affairs, or, provisionally, by the Organization of American States (OAS) Council. A two-thirds vote of alliance states may invoke compulsory sanctions that range from diplomatic and economic to military actions. The heart of the treaty is found in the commitment that "an armed attack by any State against an American State shall be considered as an attack against all." *See also* INTER-AMERICAN SYSTEM: ORGANIZATION OF AMERICAN STATES (OAS) (235).

Significance
The Rio Treaty constituted the first permanent alliance treaty entered into by the United States. The treaty served as a model for the North Atlantic Treaty and other cold war alliances. It culminated half a century of efforts to establish machinery for

hemispheric security, thereby converting the Monroe Doctrine's opposition to foreign intervention in the hemisphere from a unilateral proclamation into a multilateral commitment. The treaty has been applied since 1947 to more than 20 situations threatening peace, most of which have been in the Caribbean area, with none originating outside the hemisphere. Most controversies taken up under the Rio Treaty have involved revolutions, civil wars, subversion, and terrorism. These have often tended to reopen old questions about U.S. interventions and may have contributed to stifling social revolutions essential for economic progress. In 1975, a special conference approved, over U.S. objections, a Protocol of Amendment to the Rio Treaty that, when ratified, would establish the principle of "ideological pluralism" and would simplify the rescinding of sanctions. In the cases of many hemispheric controversies or insurgencies—such as in the cases of Cuba, Chile, El Salvador, and Nicaragua—jurisdictional conflicts have arisen between the OAS invoking the Rio Treaty and the United Nations Security Council invoking the U.N. Charter. The United States has generally led in efforts to keep hemispheric disputes within OAS jurisdiction, where it can exercise its power and influence most effectively and where a great power veto of its actions does not exist.

United States–Latin American Relations

Alliance for Progress | 249 |

A long-range program to help develop and modernize Latin American states, established in 1961 at Punta del Este, Uruguay, under the leadership of President John F. Kennedy. The Alliance for Progress was created as a common program involving various forms of foreign aid from the United States to all Latin states except Castro's Cuba. Alliance agreements established the objective of an inflow of $20 billion from external sources over the first 10-year period. Most of this assistance would come from public sources, and the United States was committed to providing a major portion of it. One of the main instruments to foster modernization was development loans offered at very low or zero interest rates to provide the capital needed to fuel the engine of economic growth. The long-range program cost was estimated at $100 billion, with $80 billion of that amount to be generated through private investment. The program in effect called for a peaceful revolution throughout Latin America with reform of tax laws, economic integration, new monetary and fiscal policies, housing development, agrarian reform, improved wages and working conditions, encouragement of private enterprise, control over world market price fluctuations for primary commodities, and the building of democratic institutions. Special emphasis was also placed on improving health and education. *See also* DEVELOPMENT STRATEGY: MACRO APPROACH (182).

Significance

The Alliance for Progress program was launched dramatically and much effort and money were poured into it for several years. The two major variables involved were, first, the willingness of Latin states to undertake the drastic economic and social changes needed, and second, the determination of the United States to remain steadfast in its pursuit of Alliance objectives over a period of years. An evaluation of the Alliance for Progress indicates that conservative forces in most Latin countries have blocked many of the needed reforms, and the United States, as a result of the Vietnam War and various economic problems, has lost interest. Alliance failures can be explained partly by the magnitude of the problems involved in fostering a controlled socioeconomic revolution of continental proportions. Additional factors include a population explosion, weak market conditions for primary commodities, inflation in the industrialized countries, high energy costs, and a general lack of local capital for investment purposes. The Alliance for Progress continues to languish amidst hemispheric bickering and recrimination, and because of failure to implement its most basic principle—that political change must precede social and economic reform. In addition, the huge debt Latin states acquired during the 1970s and 1980s has limited their ability to pursue Alliance policies and objectives.

Bay of Pigs Invasion | 250 |

An abortive invasion of Cuba attempted in April 1961 by a force of 1,500 Cuban exiles seeking to overthrow the Fidel Castro regime. The U.S. Central Intelligence Agency (CIA) recruited, armed, and trained the Bay of Pigs invasion force and orchestrated its attack. The objective of the attack was to touch off a general revolt of the Cuban people against the Castro government. Originally planned and organized under the administration of President Dwight D. Eisenhower, the final decision to launch the attack was made by President John F. Kennedy. The Bay of Pigs invasion was a complete failure. No uprising occurred, and most of the invasion force was either killed or captured by Cuban military forces. Prisoners captured during the invasion were later exchanged for medical and other supplies financed by private groups in the United States. *See also* CUBAN MISSILE CRISIS (252).

Significance
The failure of the Bay of Pigs invasion was largely the result of faulty CIA intelligence estimates, which had predicted that the attack would serve as a catalyst to produce a mass uprising against the Castro regime. The abortive invasion had many repercussions. The Soviet Union, for example, began to send nuclear missiles to Cuba ostensibly to deter another attack, resulting in the 1962 Cuban Missile Crisis. In settling that crisis, the Soviets agreed to remove all their missiles and nuclear warheads from Cuba in exchange for a promise by President Kennedy that no further invasions would be supported or attempted by the United States. Following the Bay of Pigs, the CIA undertook a strategy of attempting to assassinate Fidel Castro, and, according to congressional investigation evidence, at least eight assassination attempts were made, all unsuccessful. At one point, the CIA enlisted the services of organized crime in their efforts to kill Castro. The failure of the invasion also led to stepped-up efforts by the United States to topple the Castro regime through diplomatic and economic isolation. Cuba, in response, began a calculated campaign to spread Castroism throughout Latin America as a new adaptation of Marxism-Leninism. The Soviet Union supported Cuba by greatly expanding its economic and military aid. The Bay of Pigs awakened U.S. policymakers to the reality that many Cubans supported Castroism against the United States, that CIA intelligence estimates may be faulty and lead to poorly considered policies, and that Latin Americans for the most part continue to oppose interventions regardless of their intent.

CIA Operations | 251 |

The role of the U.S. Central Intelligence Agency in affecting political outcomes in Latin America. Created by the National Security Act of 1947, the CIA is responsible to the National Security Council and to the president. In Latin America, as in much of the world, the CIA has participated extensively in anti-communist activities, in gathering intelligence data, and in carrying on covert operations. The latter have become particularly controversial because of revelations by congressional investigating committees and exposés by former CIA agents. Wherever leftist governments have come to power or have threatened to win power, the CIA has intervened covertly in both the public and private sectors to destabilize such regimes or destroy their effectiveness. These efforts have included such activities as attempted assassinations of political leaders, fomenting of strikes and political disorders, the training of private armies, the widespread use of bribery, financial support for conservative and moderate groups, the rigging of elections, the promotion of civil strife, and other techniques. *See also* BAY OF PIGS INVASION (250); INTERVENTION (238).

Significance
Congressional investigations have revealed the extent to which the CIA has been willing to go in its efforts to avoid communist or pro-communist penetrations in Latin America. Included as primary subjects for CIA interventionary tactics have been Guatemala in the 1950s, Cuba and the Dominican Republic in the 1960s, Chile in the 1970s, and Grenada and Panama in the 1980s. American policymakers utilizing the CIA were successful in helping to determine the political outcomes in all these cases except Cuba. On balance, the clandestine operations carried on by the CIA in Latin America have probably weakened rather than strengthened U.S. policies and have caused an erosion of public support as a result of many unfavorable revelations. The CIA has come to be identified, especially in Latin American and the Caribbean, as a secret force manipulating people and events so that outcomes, both political and military, are in the interest of the U.S. government as interpreted by the CIA.

Cuban Missile Crisis 252
A major confrontation in 1962 between the United States and the Soviet Union over the attempted emplacement in Cuba of Soviet missiles with nuclear warheads. During the crisis, Soviet decisions were made by Premier Nikita Khrushchev. He held that the missiles were defensive in nature, aimed at deterring the United States from attempting or supporting another invasion like the CIA-supported Bay of Pigs invasion the previous year. President John Kennedy and his advisers viewed the Soviet move as a challenge aimed at altering the strategic military balance not only in the Western Hemisphere but in the entire world as well. His advisers, however, disagreed over how the threat should be met, and offered Kennedy these basic options: (1) that the United States need undertake no action because Soviet missiles in Cuba did not affect the global power balance; (2) that the missiles constituted a major threat to U.S. security, and drastic military measures should be used, including bombing missile bases to eliminate that threat; and (3) that a naval "quarantine" or blockade of Cuba should be undertaken and Soviet ships intercepted and prevented from delivering their missiles and nuclear warheads to Cuban ports. President Kennedy rejected the first option as too weak and the second as too dangerous and likely to provoke Soviet retaliation in Europe or, conceivably, a nuclear war. In adopting the blockade approach, he reasoned that the threat was great enough to warrant the unusual action of stopping Soviet ships on the high

seas and forcing them to turn away from Cuba. In announcing his quarantine policy, President Kennedy also stated that, if any missiles were launched against the United States from Cuba, swift retaliation would be undertaken not only against Cuba but against the Soviet Union as well. Ultimately, the Soviets publicly agreed to withdraw all of their missiles from Cuba in return for a personal guarantee by President Kennedy that no more military efforts would be undertaken or supported by the United States to end Fidel Castro's role in Cuba. Both sides consequently claimed a victory. Documents published in 1990, however, show that the United States also secretly agreed to remove its medium-range missiles from Turkey, a concession that was publicly denied by President Kennedy at the time. *See also* BAY OF PIGS INVASION (250).

Significance
The Cuban Missile Crisis was one of the most dangerous confrontations between the two superpowers since the end of World War II. Both parties were put to a major test. For the United States, it was a test of will over whether the nation would risk the danger of nuclear war to prevent the emplacement of Soviet missiles in the Western Hemisphere. For the Soviets, themselves surrounded by U.S. missile bases in Turkey and Western Europe, it was a test over whether they were willing to risk a major war in seeking to achieve a less unfavorable position in the balance of power. The quid pro quo that apparently resolved the crisis—that is, the Soviets agreeing not to establish missile bases in the Western Hemisphere in return for a U.S. promise not to invade Cuba—mitigated a situation fraught with danger for the world. The U.S. pullout of obsolete missiles from Turkey also helped improve relations with the Soviets concerning Cuba. That public understanding, initially agreed to by Premier Nikita Khrushchev and President John Kennedy, was reaffirmed by President Lyndon Johnson following Kennedy's assassination and by President Richard Nixon and Soviet leader Leonid Brezhnev in 1970. The great power interactions during the crisis took place largely without consulting Cuba's Fidel Castro, lending some credence to charges that Cuba was a Soviet pawn in the cold war and Fidel Castro was a Soviet puppet. President Kennedy and his advisers likewise were concerned mainly with the global consequences and did not consult other Latin American countries. Following the crisis, the Soviets shifted their emphasis to building a major nuclear submarine base at Cienfuegos in Cuba, and during the 1960s and 1970s, they built up a sizeable submarine and surface fleet that periodically became operational in the Caribbean area. In addition to the impact of the crisis in the Latin American region, it also contributed to the conclusion of a United States–Soviet agreement to establish a communications link (hot line) between Washington and Moscow, to the signing of a Partial Nuclear Test-Ban Treaty (Moscow Treaty of 1963), and to a period of detente during which relations between the two superpowers were improved. By 1991, Soviet efforts to establish socialist systems in the Western Hemisphere had ended, and economic and military aid to Cuba by Russia was being phased out.

Dollar Diplomacy [253]
The use of U.S. foreign policy to promote and protect private American interests and foreign investments. Historically, the term "dollar diplomacy" has been used by Latin Americans to show their disapproval of the role that U.S. government and large American corporations have played in using economic, diplomatic, and military power to open up and to

protect investment and market opportunities. Many Latin Americans equate dollar diplomacy with exploitation of the peoples of their region. They also emphasize that economic penetration has often led to political domination and colonialism. *See also* INTERVENTION (238).

Significance
Money and power have always been closely linked, and dollar diplomacy as state policy reflects this relationship. Although dollar diplomacy can be traced back to the earliest days of the United States, it flowered as state policy under the administrations of Presidents Theodore Roosevelt and William Howard Taft. President Woodrow Wilson repudiated dollar diplomacy and stated that his administration was not interested in promoting or protecting any "special group or interests." American relations with Latin America improved with the Clark Memorandum of 1928 and the inauguration of the Good Neighbor policy during the 1930s. Yet much ill will and suspicion remain and are exploited by political leaders in Latin America. In the contemporary world, the operations of giant multinational corporations wielding immense economic and political power—often with the direct or indirect support of the U.S. government—help many Latin Americans recall those earlier days of dollar diplomacy.

Dominican Republic Intervention | 254 |

Actions undertaken in 1965 by President Lyndon B. Johnson involving the use of U.S. military forces to end a civil war and restore stability in the Dominican Republic. Beginning with the assassination of Rafael Trujillo, which ended a 30-year dictatorship, the civil war was followed by contested elections and several coups d'etat. The civil war pitted the army and other right-wing elements known as the "loyalists" against a military faction and civilian centrist and left-wing groups known as the "constitutionalists." The latter group was headed by reform leader Juan Bosch, who had won the presidential election in 1963 only to be overthrown by a military coup. In 1965, the Bosch-led group attempted a countercoup, leading to the U.S. intervention. *See also* INTERVENTION (238).

Significance
The Dominican intervention was the first military intervention undertaken by U.S. forces since the 1920s (prior to the adoption of the Good Neighbor policy). Although President Johnson justified the intervention initially on the ground that U.S. citizens needed protection, he later indicated that he had been influenced by Castroism in Cuba and was determined to prevent "another communist state in this hemisphere." Although the U.S. forces committed to the action numbered more than 30,000, President Johnson took the matter to the Organization of American States (OAS), which created a multilateral force and legitimized the intervention as a necessary peacekeeping venture. Within a year, the two warring factions reached a settlement and all foreign military forces were withdrawn. The Dominican intervention emphasized the problem facing U.S. presidents when Latin revolutions and civil wars pit revolutionary forces against those defending the established order, which has often been some form of elite rule.

Gadsden Purchase | 255 |

A strip of land located in southern Arizona and southern New Mexico that was purchased for $10 million by the United States from Mexico in 1853. The purchase was negotiated by James Gadsden, the U.S. minister to Mexico, who was a railroad promoter and an advocate of a southern railroad route to California. *See also* MEXICAN WAR (264).

Significance
The United States made the Gadsden Purchase because it wanted clear title to land in the Mesilla Valley south of the Gila River, an area that could serve as a good southern railroad route to California. Mexican president, General Antonio López de Santa Anna, sold the territory because he needed money to perpetuate his wasteful and opulent regime. The sale of national territory, added to the losses suffered as a result of the Mexican War, piled another humiliation on the Mexican people. Many protests were made by Santa Anna's opponents, but they were strongly repressed. The proceeds from the sale of Mexican territory bought a brief reprieve for the Mexican dictator, but opposition to his harsh regime mounted and he fled the country in 1855.

Good Neighbor Policy 256
A U.S. policy initiated during the 1930s aimed at reestablishing good relations with Latin American countries. President Herbert Hoover adopted the good neighbor theme and began the espousal of the Clark Memorandum of 1928 that repudiated interventionism. The policy flowered during the administration of President Franklin Roosevelt. In his inaugural address in March 1933, President Roosevelt set the tone for subsequent policy changes in proclaiming his dedication to "the policy of the good neighbor—the neighbor who resolutely respects himself and because he does so, respects the rights of others." Although the policy was at first directed toward the entire world, it soon became descriptive of a new approach of treating Latin American nations as friends and equals. *See also* INTERVENTION (238); MONROE DOCTRINE: CLARK MEMORANDUM OF 1928 (266); PLATT AMENDMENT (277).

Significance
The Good Neighbor policy sought to overcome a half-century of ill will created in response to U.S. imperialism, interventionism, commercial domination, and military occupation. The policy initiated a trend toward "multilateralizing" the Monroe Doctrine rather than using it as an instrument to justify interventionist policies. Since its inception, the policy has resulted in such concrete actions as (1) repudiating the Platt Amendment, which had limited Cuban sovereignty; (2) strengthening the Inter-American Conference machinery; (3) establishing the Reciprocal Trade Agreements program to encourage an increase in imports from Latin America; and (4) establishing the Export-Import Bank to extend credits to Latin states. Although generally successful, the Good Neighbor policy occasionally comes under strain as a result of unilateral actions by the United States, such as the CIA-supported invasion of Cuba in 1961 and U.S. military intervention in the Dominican Republic in 1965.

Grenada Intervention 257
The military action begun on 25 October 1983 and aimed at ending rule on the island by a Marxist military government. President Ronald Reagan, acting on the claimed request of six members of the Organization of Eastern Caribbean States (OECS) and two nonmembers, Barbados and Jamaica, ordered 1,900 U.S. Marines and Army Rangers to invade the island. This force was supported by 400 troops from the six members of OECS. *See also* INTERVENTION (238).

Significance
The Grenada intervention occurred following the assassination of Prime

Minister Maurice Bishop and some of his supporters by Marxist extremists. Although Bishop claimed to be a communist, the coup perpetrators alleged that he lacked revolutionary zeal. President Reagan justified the U.S. action as a means of protecting American lives in Grenada—mostly students attending St. George's University School of Medicine. He also claimed that Grenada was "a Soviet-Cuban colony being readied as a major military bastion." Criticism of the invasion came from throughout the world, including Britain and France and most of the 29 states that, along with the United States, comprise the membership of the Organization of American States (OAS). The United States used its veto power to block a United Nations Security Council resolution condemning the action. Following the holding of free elections, much of the criticism was muted. In 1987, 14 people who had participated in the slaying of Prime Minister Maurice Bishop were sentenced to be hanged, but because of appeals the sentences were not yet carried out by early 1992.

Guadalupe Hidalgo Treaty — 258

The treaty, signed on 2 February 1848, that terminated the war between Mexico and the United States. Under the main provisions of the Treaty of Guadalupe Hidalgo, (1) Mexico ceded almost half of its total territory to the United States; (2) Mexico gave up its claims to Texas; (3) the United States paid Mexico $15 million and accepted the unpaid claims amounting to $3.25 million made by U.S. citizens against Mexico; (4) the Rio Grande was established as the United States–Mexico boundary; and (5) the United States withdrew its troops from Mexican soil. The vast territory gained by the United States as a result of the terms of the treaty is known as the Mexican Cession. *See also* MEXICAN WAR (264).

Significance
The Treaty of Guadalupe Hidalgo climaxed a series of events that began in 1836 when Texas declared its independence from Mexico. Subsequently, Texas defeated Mexican armies sent to restore Texas to Mexican sovereignty. Although the admission of Texas into the United States was delayed because of British and French opposition and conflict over the slavery issue, Congress annexed Texas in 1845 as a new state. Continuing controversies over the annexation and boundary issues led to war between the United States and Mexico from 1846 to 1848. The Guadalupe Hidalgo Treaty did not end all border issues, and those relating to the Rio Grande and Colorado rivers continued until the 1960s and 1970s, when they were settled through joint agreement.

Guatemalan Intervention — 259

Actions undertaken by the United States in the early 1950s aimed at overthrowing the leftist government of Guatemala headed by Jacobo Arbenz Guzmán. American actions that led to the Guatemalan intervention were undertaken by the Eisenhower administration's Central Intelligence Agency (CIA), based on the fear that the Arbenz regime's radical policies and actions might lead to a domino effect throughout Central America. These actions included the expropriation of idle lands owned by the United Fruit Company, the implementation of various social reforms, permitting political freedom and civil rights in the country, and the importation of weapons from East Germany. The CIA engineered the intervention by organizing an opposition of Arbenz's political enemies, by providing them with arms and a sanctuary in Honduras, and by providing them with a clandestine radio station to be used solely for overthrowing the Arbenz regime. The American ambassador to Guatemala was able to persuade Guatemalan military leaders not to support the government when the exile army marched across the border into Guatemala. Inspired and directed by the U.S., this subversion succeeded and the Arbenz regime collapsed. *See also* INTERVENTION (238).

Significance
The Guatemalan intervention by the United States, although opposed politically by some Latin American regimes and many political leaders, was nevertheless considered a success by the American people. The Eisenhower administration regarded the Arbenz regime, although duly elected, as communist oriented and a threat to the hemisphere. The Guatemalan government appealed to the United Nations Security Council to declare the U.S. actions to be aggression and requested action to halt attacks launched against it from Honduras and Nicaragua. Although the Soviet Union vetoed a U.S. effort to remove the case from Security Council jurisdiction and transfer it to the jurisdiction of the Organization of American States (OAS), the United States rejected the Soviet action, and the OAS assumed jurisdiction. The new Guatemalan government, under the leadership of Colonel Carlos Castillo Armas, informed the Security Council that the case was closed. The Guatemalan intervention demonstrated the long-continuing ability of the United States to intervene successfully in Latin America when it considers some vital interest is at stake. In addition, the case demonstrated that the United Nations can do little to prevent a transfer of jurisdiction of a dispute when a great power prefers that the matter be handled regionally.

Immigration Reform and Control Act of 1986 260

A major U.S. immigration law aimed at controlling the flood of illegal immigrants and providing amnesty for illegal immigrants already in the United States. Main contents of the law provide that (1) aliens who entered the United States illegally prior to 1 January 1982 are eligible for amnesty, residential status, and, eventually, American citizenship; (2) employers violate the law if they hire illegal immigrants, and all employers are responsible for verifying the legal status of their employees; (3) seasonal migrant agricultural workers may be granted residential status under special arrangements; and (4) an Office of Special Counsel be created in the Justice Department to protect migrants from employer discrimination. *See also* MIGRATION (13); POPULATION (17).

Significance
The Simpson-Mazzoli bill was bitterly debated in several sessions of Congress, but eventually it was passed and became the Immigration Reform and Control Act of 1986. It was feared by employers, who shunned the responsibility of ensuring that their employees were not illegals. Farmers and fruit growers feared that the law would deprive them of desperately needed laborers, since most Americans refuse this type of work. Illegal residential aliens feared having to prove their residency before 1982 when they led a shadowy existence, always fearful of deportation. Nevertheless, passage of the law was an attempt to humanize a process that had been a festering problem for many years. While it has not solved the problem of illegals, it has improved and clarified it; however, the exploding birthrate in countries south of the border, especially in Mexico, ensures that the problem will remain for the foreseeable future. In the late 1980s and early 1990s, smuggling of aliens into the United States became big business involving an estimated $1 billion annually. As many as one-half of the illegals entering the

United States currently are assisted by smugglers. The law has never worked as expected because of the failure of Congress to provide the funds for personnel needed to make it function effectively. Techniques used to frustrate the law and its enforcers include bribery, the use of fake documents, and what are known as "safe houses" where illegals can find refuge.

Iran-Contra Affair 261

The secret sale of American arms to Iran and the diversion of profits from the sale to the armed resistance against the Nicaraguan Sandinista government in the mid-1980s. Beginning in 1985, the United States shipped arms to Iran in order to get the release of American hostages held by pro-Iranian forces in Lebanon. In 1984, U.S. officials, blocked by Congress from aiding the anti-Sandinista forces (contras) militarily, established a number of secret operations, financed by private and public funds, to buy and ship arms to the contra forces. Staff officials of the U.S. National Security Council diverted some proceeds from the "arms-for-hostages" operations to the armed resistance to the Nicaraguan government. Lt. Col. Oliver North, Admiral John Poindexter, and Robert C. McFarlane were the key figures in the Iran-Contra Affair, along with William Casey, the director of the Central Intelligence Agency (CIA). President Ronald Reagan, who had authorized the sale of arms to Iran and the solicitation of private funds for the contras, denied any knowledge of the diversion of public funds to the Nicaraguan resistance. Following public disclosures and a congressional investigation, North, Poindexter, and other private citizens were tried and convicted for diverting public funds; North later won an appeal when information that was gained during congressional testimony could not be used against him in a retrial. *See also* CONTRAS (81).

Significance

The Iran-Contra Affair was the most notorious scandal within the American government since the Watergate affair that toppled Richard Nixon from office in 1974. Although President Reagan escaped serious political harm, he was accused of not supervising his closest White House staff, of deceiving the public on his opposition to Iran, and of skirting congressional opposition to continued American aid to the contras. Public opinion was divided on the issue, and patriotic groups sympathetically rallied around North. The episode did reveal the secretiveness, elitism, and the ineptitude of White House staff, and at least the inattentiveness of the president. When the story broke, it ended any possibility that the United States could further support the contras in any significant manner.

Manifest Destiny 262

A mass psychological movement in the United States during the nineteenth century that impacted directly and substantially on several, and indirectly on many, Latin American states. The spirit of Manifest Destiny was based on the belief that the United States had created a new and near-perfect economic, political, and social system, and that it was its destiny as a nation to spread the benefits of this system to other societies and peoples. This belief supported continental expansionist policies during the early part of the nineteenth century, culminating in the war with Mexico and the annexation by the U.S. of its vast Upper California territory. In the latter part of that century, the spirit of Manifest Destiny was reborn and used to justify overseas expansionist policies that, inter alia, resulted in the annexation of Samoa, the Hawaiian Islands, the

Philippines, Puerto Rico, and the Panama Canal Zone, as well as the establishment of a protectorate over Cuba. *See also* MEXICAN WAR (264); SPANISH-AMERICAN WAR (281).

Significance
Manifest Destiny provided an ideological base and a rallying spirit that justified and fostered aggressive U.S. policies during the nineteenth century. President John Quincy Adams, in concluding treaties with Britain and Spain in 1818 and 1819, initially expounded the idea of Manifest Destiny in calling for continental expansion, the eventual absorption of all of North America, and the elimination of European colonies that limited the realization of the territorial objectives of "a great, powerful, and rapidly-growing nation." The proclamation of the Monroe Doctrine in 1823 contributed to this emerging belief in the nation's ultimate destiny, and the Mexican War (1846–1848) bolstered support for it. Overseas expansion during the latter part of the nineteenth century resulted in a number of interventions, annexations, and protectorates in Latin America. This latter phase was supported by nationalist interpretations of the ideas of Charles Darwin—a strong nation has a "right to expand in order to survive"—and the geopolitical theories of Admiral Alfred T. Mahan—seapower is the key to the realization of the ultimate destiny of the United States as a nation. Latin American states generally viewed the aspirations and policies engendered by the spirit of Manifest Destiny as incompatible with their independence, security, and well-being.

Mariel Boatlift   263
The exodus of 125,000 Cubans to the United States from the Cuban port of Mariel in 1980. The Mariel boatlift resulted after Fidel Castro permitted Cubans to leave the island when a number of them began seeking asylum in Latin embassies in Havana. For weeks, many small private boats from Florida, chartered by families, made frequent trips to Mariel to bring relatives and others to the United States. When it became obvious that thousands wanted to leave Cuba, Castro forced the boats to take others he considered socially undesirable, such as criminals, the mentally insane, and homosexuals. With apparently many more Cubans willing to leave the island, Castro then ended the exodus and rallied his supporters to demonstrate in favor of the Cuban revolution. Most of the *Marielitos* were absorbed into the Cuban-American community, but about 3,000 were arrested and tried for criminal activities in the United States. U.S. attempts to repatriate these persons in 1985 failed when Cuba objected to U.S. radio broadcasts beamed to Cuba over Radio Martí, and again in 1987 when Cuban inmates rioted in U.S. prisons.

Significance
The Mariel boatlift showed that many Cubans preferred to leave their homeland rather than live under communist rule. *Marielitos* were assimilated with the 500,000 Cubans who left Cuba in the 1960s. This increased the number of Cuban-Americans in southern Florida and elsewhere, swelling the ethnic character of particular localities and imposing additional costs on local governments. The criminals, who often continued their violent behavior in the U.S., gave other *Marielitos* a bad reputation for a time. The failure of the United States to return the criminals to Cuba despite Castro's willingness to accept them resulted primarily from ineptness in the U.S. administration and the prisoners' preference for American jails. The refugees and the larger Cuban-American community, who are fiercely anti-Castro, continue to hope and work for Castro's downfall.

Mexican War   264

A conflict between Mexico and the United States from 1846 to 1848 that resulted in Mexico losing almost half of its national territory. The causes of the Mexican War were (1) Mexican embitterment over the secession of Texas in 1836 and its desire to regain that territory; (2) the annexation of Texas by the United States in 1845; (3) a dispute over the southwestern boundary of Texas; (4) Mexico's default of payment of claims of U.S. citizens; (5) the Manifest Destiny sentiment in the United States; and (6) Mexico's refusal to consider President James K. Polk's proposal to purchase its California and other western territories. The war began when U.S. troops, led by General Zachary Taylor, entered into disputed territory north of the Rio Grande. Taylor later invaded northern Mexico and engaged a larger force of Mexicans under General Antonio López de Santa Anna at Buena Vista in February 1847. Both sides suffered heavy losses in the Battle of Buena Vista, but because Santa Anna withdrew first, the United States claimed victory. Other U.S. forces took Santa Fe and marched on to California, parts of which had already been taken by U.S. naval forces. General Winfield Scott invaded Mexico at Veracruz and captured Mexico City in September 1847. Under the Guadalupe Hidalgo Treaty of 1848, Mexico recognized the loss of Texas to the United States; the Rio Grande was established as the international boundary; Mexico ceded the western territories, which became the states of California, Arizona, New Mexico, Nevada, Utah, and parts of Colorado and Wyoming; the United States agreed to pay Mexico $15 million for the western territories; and the United States assumed the claims ($3.25 million) of its citizens against Mexico. *See also* GUADALUPE HIDALGO TREATY (258).

Significance
Mexico lost about half of its national territory as a result of the Mexican War. The war occurred at a time when U.S. citizens were pushing westward and Manifest Destiny ambitions were encouraged with the election of President James K. Polk in 1844. Mexican politics were in turmoil, and the country could not establish a stable or effective government. Both sides were eager to fight, and, although Mexican forces were larger, they were not as well organized and commanded. The loss brought a deep sense of humiliation and moral defeat to Mexicans, and it encouraged Indian uprisings and separatist movements in several Mexican states. Some Mexicans were so demoralized by the defeat that they called for the annexation of their entire country by the United States. The war, however, left some U.S. citizens with a sense of guilt. The Mexican cession was essentially what President Polk had wanted to purchase before the war began, and although victorious, the United States imposed no additional territorial demands on Mexico.

Monroe Doctrine   265

Basic principles guiding U.S. foreign policy that oppose foreign intervention in the Western Hemisphere and reject American intervention in the affairs of Europe. The Monroe Doctrine was enunciated as a unilateral policy statement by President James Monroe in his State of the Union message to Congress on 2 December 1823. The basic principle of "hands off!"—that the lands of the Western Hemisphere would "henceforth not be considered as subjects for future colonization by any European power"—was a direct rebuttal to the announced objectives of the Holy Alliance of Prussia, Austria, France, and Russia to help Spain regain her Latin American colonies that had won their independence following the Napoleonic wars. If any European powers did intervene in the Western Hemisphere, President Monroe stated, the United States would "consider any attempt on their part to extend their system to any portion of this hemisphere as dangerous to our peace and safety." At the same time, President Monroe disclaimed any intention of interfering with the existing colonies or dependencies of any European power located in the Western Hemisphere. *See also* MONROE DOCTRINE: LODGE COROLLARY (267); MONROE DOCTRINE: OLNEY COROLLARY (268); MONROE DOCTRINE: POLK RESTATEMENT (269); MONROE DOCTRINE: ROOSEVELT COROLLARY (270).

Significance
The Monroe Doctrine has provided basic guidelines for U.S. foreign policy in the Western Hemisphere for over a century and a half. Before being proclaimed, George Canning, the British foreign secretary, tried to convince President Monroe that a joint Anglo-American declaration should be issued against intervention in Latin America, but growing nationalism and suspicions of British intentions resulted in the unilateral statement. Nevertheless, because of the military weakness of the United States, the immediate success of the nonintervention policy depended on British policy and the power of the British navy. For many years, the *Pax Britannica*, based on British seapower, served to support the Monroe Doctrine because of parallel British and American interests in the Western Hemisphere. U.S. policymakers, however, increasingly thought of it as based strictly on American power and responsibility, and by the end of the nineteenth century the United States had become militarily capable of implementing the Monroe Doctrine. Much to the distaste of Latin Americans, the United States expanded the doctrine through the Polk Restatement and the Olney, Roosevelt, and Lodge corollaries. Interventions and other unilateral actions and the assumption of a general "Big Brother" attitude by the United States increased the hostility of Latins toward the Monroe Doctrine. Beginning with the Clark Memorandum of 1928 and the Good Neighbor policy of the Franklin Roosevelt administration in 1933, the United States began to change its basic approach by "multilateralizing" the policy. Under this new approach, the United States joined with the countries of Latin America to create the Organization of American States (OAS) to foster common action on political issues, and to create the Rio Treaty to provide for a mutual security system to protect the hemisphere from external forces. In the United States today, policymakers and the public continue to regard the Monroe Doctrine as one of the major bulwarks of the nation's foreign policy, and Latin Americans remain suspicious and fearful of possible future interventions justified by how it is interpreted and applied by North Americans.

Monroe Doctrine: Clark Memorandum of 1928 | 266 |

A Memorandum on the Monroe Doctrine—issued by the United States and circulated among Latin American governments—that was aimed at improving relations between the United States and Latin America. The Clark Memorandum repudiated the Roosevelt Corollary as an invalid interpretation of the Monroe Doctrine, and sought to restate the doctrine in its original form and meaning. The Clark Memorandum, developed by Under Secretary of State J. Reuben Clark, Jr., in 1928 and published in 1930, reflected the position of the administration of President Herbert Hoover. *See also* GOOD NEIGHBOR POLICY (256); MONROE DOCTRINE (265).

Significance
The Clark Memorandum gained a place in history because it signified an abrupt shift in U.S. foreign policy. Out of it emerged the Good Neighbor policy of the 1930s, fostered by the administrations of both Herbert Hoover and Franklin Roosevelt. Although the Clark Memorandum rejected Theodore Roosevelt's corollary that assigned the United States the role of hemispheric policeman, it did not flatly reject intervention as a policy instrument. The Clark Memorandum initiative ultimately led to the "multilateralization" of the Monroe Doctrine through the establishment of the Organization of American States (OAS) and the conclusion of the Rio Treaty. Interventions—direct, indirect, and covert—have continued in the post–World War II period, including those involving Cuba, the Dominican Republic, Guatemala, Chile, and Nicaragua.

Monroe Doctrine: Lodge Corollary | 267 |

A U.S. Senate resolution, authored by Senator Henry Cabot Lodge, which proclaimed that the United States would be willing to undertake action to prevent a non-hemispheric power from gaining acquisition of Latin American territory that could be used as a naval base or for other military purposes. The Lodge Corollary to the Monroe Doctrine passed the U.S. Senate on 2 August 1912 by a vote of 51 to 4. The resolution was prompted by efforts of a Japanese company to acquire Magdalena Bay in Mexico's Lower California. The Lodge Corollary declared that the United States disapproved of the transfer of strategic territories in the Western Hemisphere to any non-American company that might be acting as an agent for a foreign power. *See also* MONROE DOCTRINE (265).

Significance
The Lodge Corollary to the Monroe Doctrine was one of several efforts by U.S. political leaders to expand the scope and application of the "hands off!" policy first enunciated by President James Monroe in 1823. Magdalena Bay had long been of concern to the United States because, in the hands of a non-hemispheric power, it could threaten the security of the Panama Canal and California, as well as the lines of communication between them. As a result of aroused public opinion in the United States, the Japanese company that was attempting to negotiate the sale abandoned the project. The Lodge Corollary was important for two reasons: (1) it applied the principles of the Monroe Doctrine for the first time to an Asian country, even though Japan was not mentioned in the resolution; and (2) it applied the Monroe Doctrine to a private company that might or might not have been an agent for the foreign government. Although the resolution was not directly enforceable, the U.S. State Department accepted the Lodge Corollary and invoked it on several occasions to discourage U.S. citizens from selling their Mexican properties to the Japanese.

Monroe Doctrine: Olney Corollary | 268 |

A statement in 1895 by U.S. Secretary of State Richard Olney that sought to resolve the boundary dispute between Venezuela and British Guiana in favor of Venezuelan interests. Goaded by President Grover Cleveland, Olney delivered a diplomatic message to the British that took the form of an ultimatum. In highly jingoistic language, the secretary of state wrote that "the United States is practically sovereign on this [South American] continent, and its fiat is law upon the subjects to which it confines its interposition . . . because . . . its infinite resources combined with its isolated position render it master of the situation and practically invulnerable as against any or all other powers." The position laid down by

Olney was that Britain must submit the dispute to arbitration, with the United States ready and willing to use force to secure compliance. The U.S. public, Congress, and press rallied exuberantly to the support of Olney's position. Threatened with unwanted war in Latin America at the same time they were in a conflict with the South African Boers, the British gave in to President Cleveland's demands, and the dispute was submitted to an arbitration panel that divided the disputed territory. *See also* MONROE DOCTRINE (265).

Significance
The Olney Corollary action was typical of the new imperial mood that characterized U.S. relations with Latin America and much of the rest of the world as the nineteenth century came to a close. In invoking the Monroe Doctrine against Britain, Olney was clearly indicating that Latin America is a U.S. sphere of influence, a position that expanded upon the original doctrine. The action also served to thwart British expansionist aims, which had encouraged a progressive absorption of Venezuelan territory by the Guiana colony.

Monroe Doctrine: Polk Restatement | 269 |

A declaration by President James K. Polk in 1845 that he and the nation concurred with the principles of the Monroe Doctrine originally enunciated in 1823 by President Monroe. In his restatement, Polk emphasized that "no future European colony or dominion shall with our consent be platted or established on any part of the North American continent." Polk's restatement was occasioned by pressures applied by Britain and other European countries to win concessions in the Oregon territory, California, and Texas. In 1848, President Polk carried his position a step beyond both the original Monroe Doctrine and his 1845 restatement by claiming in the Yucatan case that the principle of the Monroe Doctrine prohibits not only colonial expansionism but the peaceful transfer of Western Hemispheric territory to a European power as well. *See also* MONROE DOCTRINE (265).

Significance
The Polk Restatement of the Monroe Doctrine was important because the Doctrine had remained virtually dormant since its 1823 enunciation. The 1845 Polk Restatement had the effect of changing a relatively minor policy statement that was aimed at a specific situation and at particular countries into a more general and enduring foreign policy position closely allied with national interest considerations. The further claim by Polk in 1848 was enunciated when the Yucatan peninsula tried to secede from Mexico, and, after fighting broke out between Indians and whites, the latter offered "dominion and sovereignty" over the peninsula to Britain and Spain in return for military protection. The Indian revolt ended and the territory returned to Mexico, but President Polk's restatements remained as an expansion of the Monroe Doctrine by challenging future incursions of European powers into the hemisphere even when invited by Latin states or peoples.

Monroe Doctrine: Roosevelt Corollary | 270 |

A new interpretation and application of the Monroe Doctrine enunciated by President Theodore Roosevelt that provided for U.S. intervention when required by "flagrant" wrongdoing of Latin states. The Roosevelt Corollary of the Monroe Doctrine was set forth in the president's annual message to Congress in 1904. In that message, President Roosevelt bluntly stated: "Chronic wrongdoing, or an impotence which results in a general loosening of the ties of civilized society, may in America, as elsewhere, ultimately require intervention by some civilized nation." In the Western Hemisphere, Roosevelt noted, that meant that the United States must, in such cases, reluctantly exercise an international police power. See also MONROE DOCTRINE (265).

Significance
The enunciation of the Roosevelt Corollary of the Monroe Doctrine grew out of the attempts by Britain and Germany to collect debts owed to them and their citizens by Venezuelan dictator Cipriano Castro. Although the European powers were initially supported by President Roosevelt in these efforts, public opinion in the United States turned against the European states when they tried to coerce Castro with a "pacific blockade." Roosevelt then began to view their actions as a threat to the Monroe Doctrine. Subsequently, the Roosevelt Corollary served as a direct or implied justification for U.S. actions in establishing protectorates in the Dominican Republic, Nicaragua, and Haiti. These interventions were justified by Roosevelt by anarchic conditions that prevailed in Latin America and by the refusal or inability of the Venezuelan government to pay its foreign debts. Roosevelt's main concern was that these conditions would invite interventions by European powers, leading to a serious threat to peace, and a nullification of the basic principles of the Monroe Doctrine.

Noriega Case | 271 |

The 1992 trial and conviction of the Panamanian dictator, General Manuel Noriega, following his overthrow and capture by the United States in the Panamanian intervention of 1989. After a seven-month trial in Miami, Noriega was found guilty on eight of ten charges of violating U.S. criminal laws pertaining to drug trafficking, racketeering, and money laundering. The major charges included conspiring with the Medellín drug cartel of Colombia to ship cocaine through Panama to the U.S. and specific acts pertaining to these shipments. The prosecution presented many witnesses to support the charges, some of whom were under indictment for drug trafficking. The defense argued that Noriega was a prisoner of war who could not be tried in a civilian criminal court; that he was taken illegally to the U.S.; that he had been an agent of U.S. intelligence agencies when the alleged acts were committed; that prosecution witnesses were given very generous reductions of criminal charges against them in exchange for testimony, which was therefore unreliable; that some of his conversations with his attorneys were recorded and broadcast; and that his assets were frozen, which limited the funds available for his defense. In July 1992, Noriega was sentenced to 40 years in prison; he still faced another trial in the U.S. on other charges, and possible extradition to Panama on charges of murder and corruption. See also PANAMA INTERVENTION (276).

Significance
General Noriega was seized in Panama in January 1990 when he voluntarily left the Vatican embassy where he had taken refuge during the U.S. military intervention called Operation Just Cause. Previous attempts to remove him from office by the Ronald Reagan administration through economic sanctions, promises of safe exile, and an attempted military coup failed. His nullification of the Panamanian election of 1989, assaults on U.S. military personnel, and declaration of a "state of war" with the U.S. galvanized President George Bush to order the intervention. The removal of Noriega to the U.S. was considered by some authorities as a violation of international law. The installation of Guillermo Endara as the Panamanian president was

also considered to lack legitimacy because, although he may have been the leading candidate, the election was suspended before all ballots were officially counted. Although Noriega's claim that he was a prisoner of war was denied, he was permitted to wear his general's uniform during the trial. His conviction greatly relieved the Endara government, who believed that this put an end to the Noriega era in Panama. In the U.S., President Bush believed that the conviction vindicated the military intervention, brought an international criminal to justice, and was a victory in the war against drugs. Drug trafficking through Panama continued after Noriega's capture, however. The Noriega case was the first time in U.S. history that a foreign head of state was convicted in a U.S. civilian court on criminal charges. The case also supported other efforts that called for prosecution of foreign nationals who were apprehended and brought to the U.S. under nonlegal methods.

Ostend Manifesto 272
An 1854 statement by the United States ambassadors to Great Britain, France, and Spain that declared if Spain refused to sell Cuba to the United States, the United States ought to take the island by force. The manifesto was immediately repudiated by the administration of President Franklin Pierce. *See also* SPANISH-AMERICAN WAR (281).

Significance
The Ostend Manifesto, first drafted in Ostend, Belgium, was an expression of the continuing interest of the United States to acquire Cuba. Earlier the U.S. ambassador to Spain had been instructed to purchase Cuba, but Spain rejected the proposal. Sentiment for annexing Cuba was especially strong in southern slaveholding states. The ambassadors who issued the Ostend Manifesto were pro-slavery Democrats. It aroused great criticism in northern free states and abroad. The rejection of the document by the government of President Franklin Pierce caused the political furor over Cuba to subside, but U.S. interest in acquiring Cuba or seeking its independence continued after the U.S. Civil War.

Panama Canal Neutrality Treaty of 1978 273
A treaty concluded between the United States and Panama that declared that "the Canal, as an international transit waterway, shall be permanently neutral. . . ." Under the treaty, both countries agreed that the canal will remain open and secure to ships of all nations. Officially designated the Treaty Concerning the Permanent Neutrality and Operation of the Panama Canal, it was negotiated, signed, and ratified as a companion agreement to the Panama Canal Treaty of 1978. The Neutrality Treaty specifically provides (1) that the two countries have responsibility to keep the canal open and secure for the ships of all nations at all times; (2) that each may take whatever action is deemed necessary to defend the canal against any act or threat of aggression; (3) that beginning with the year 2000 only Panama shall operate the canal and maintain military forces and bases within its national territory; (4) that war vessels of the two countries shall have the right to "expedited treatment" over others when necessary; and (5) that the treaty does not establish any right for the United States to intervene in the internal affairs of Panama. In a protocol to the treaty, all nations of the world were invited to agree "to observe and respect the regime of permanent neutrality of the Canal in time of war as in time of peace." Despite controversy in both countries over the wording of specific sections of the Neutrality Treaty

and interpretations and reservations of key words and phrases, the Neutrality Treaty was approved by Panama in a national referendum and by the U.S. Senate in a very close vote. *See also* PANAMA CANAL TREATY OF 1978 (275).

Significance
The Panama Canal Neutrality Treaty of 1978 was concluded to ensure that the canal would remain open to merchant and naval vessels of all nations, without discrimination as to transit conditions and tolls. Like the Panama Canal Treaty of 1978, the Neutrality Treaty evoked bitter debate, charges, and countercharges. Many Panamanians believed that authorizing the United States to undertake military action to defend the canal was providing an open invitation for employment of interventionist policies in the future. Many U.S. citizens, on the other hand, felt that the provisions were not tough enough to ensure the protection and uninterrupted operation of the canal. Basically, the negotiations involved a clash between a superpower and a small nation backed up by most of the world community, with especially strong support from other Latin countries. By attaching a protocol to the treaty, the two parties sought to secure the permanent neutrality of the canal.

Panama Canal Treaty of 1903 | 274 |

The treaty, officially known as the Isthmian Canal Convention, was signed in Washington in 1903 and provided the United States with the authority to undertake the construction of an isthmian canal. Under the Panama Canal Treaty of 1903, Panama granted the United States, "in perpetuity," the use of a ten-mile wide zone (five miles on either side of the proposed canal) and accorded it all the rights and authority within the zone as if the United States were sovereign. The United States was also granted the right to fortify the zone, defend the canal, and maintain order in the cities of Colon and Panama. In return, the United States was required to pay Panama $10 million and an annual compensation fee for the use of the territory, and to do whatever became necessary to maintain the independence of the Republic of Panama. The treaty was signed for Panama by Phillipe Bunau-Varilla, a Frenchman who had supported Panama's revolutionary breakaway from Colombia and was subsequently named Panama's first minister to the United States. He was also a major stockholder in the bankrupt French canal company that benefited greatly when the United States purchased its assets. *See also* PANAMA CANAL NEUTRALITY TREATY OF 1978 (273); PANAMA CANAL TREATY OF 1978 (275).

Significance
The Panama Canal Treaty of 1903 and the conditions under which it was concluded were highly controversial. Colombia charged that the United States had encouraged the Panamanian revolution and that its blocking of Colombian efforts to suppress the revolt constituted an intervention in violation of international law. These events were alleged to have resulted from the rejection by the Colombian Senate of a treaty with the United States, giving the latter the right to build a canal across the Colombian isthmus (Hay-Herrán Treaty of 1903). The treaty was rejected on the grounds that the $10 million initial price was too small and the limitations placed on Colombia's sovereignty were too great. The Panama Canal Treaty of 1903 was initially and continued to be highly advantageous to the United States. For Panama, it was a constant source of friction and an affront to the people's sense of national dignity. Although the treaty was modified in

1936 and 1955 to cancel the right of the United States to intervene in Panama's internal affairs and to provide for equal working conditions in the Canal Zone, by 1964 deep-rooted frustrations boiled over into rioting with many killed and injured. Panama briefly broke diplomatic relations with the United States and pled before the United Nations and the Organization of American States that its colonial status be ended and the canal and Canal Zone be turned over to Panamanian sovereignty. Thereupon, President Lyndon Johnson authorized the negotiation of a new canal treaty. Negotiations culminated in 1978 with the ratification of two new treaties that superseded the Panama Canal Treaty of 1903.

Panama Canal Treaty of 1978 (275)

The first of two treaties concluded between the United States and Panama that terminated and superseded all previous treaties relating to the ownership, operation, and security of the canal, and specified how the canal would be operated and defended until the year 2000. The second treaty, called the Neutrality Treaty of 1978, buttresses the first by providing for the canal's permanent neutrality and its defense by either the United States or Panama in case of aggression. Under the Panama Canal Treaty of 1978, the Canal Zone ceased to exist and the United States retained primary responsibility for the operation of the canal until the end of the century, but with expanding responsibilities placed in the hands of Panamanian citizens. The canal would be operated during this period under the direction of a Panama Canal Commission composed of nine directors, with five from the United States and four from Panama. Until 1990, the canal's chief executive officer, known as the canal administrator, was from the United States, with a Panamanian deputy; during the final decade of joint operation, the administrator is a Panamanian with a U.S. deputy. During this transition period, the United States will continue to set and collect tolls, turning over an increasing percentage of such income to Panama to promote its economic development. When the year 2000 is reached, Panama will assume full ownership of the canal, and the Panama Canal Treaty of 1978 will terminate. The two parties to the treaty also agreed to study the feasibility of constructing a sea-level canal in Panama. The United States affirmed that it will not negotiate with any other country in the Western Hemisphere concerning construction of a sea-level canal, and Panama agreed that no sea-level canal could be constructed on Panamanian territory without the consent of the United States. Finally, although not officially part of the treaty, the United States agreed to promote Panama's economic development through a program of loans, loan guarantees, and economic credits over a five-year period following treaty ratification, and to promote Panama's defense by providing military aid over a ten-year period. *See also* PANAMA CANAL NEUTRALITY TREATY OF 1978 (273); PANAMA CANAL TREATY OF 1903 (274).

Significance
The Panama Canal Treaty of 1978 consummated negotiations that had been carried on between the United States and Panama for almost 14 years. Long pent-up frustrations and a rising tide of Panamanian nationalism combined to produce major rioting along the Canal Zone border area in 1964, with many casualties. The dangerously escalating situation was calmed by President Lyndon Johnson's promise to negotiate a new treaty that would recognize Panama's sovereignty over its entire territory, including the Canal Zone. In addition to the rioting, the president was reacting to a rising tide of pressure generated through the United

Nations and the Organization of American States. Third World nations of Asia and Africa, other Latin American countries, and even the European allies of the United States strongly supported the negotiation of a new treaty. The 1978 treaty, therefore, was a product of Panamanian and world pressures, the diplomatic efforts of four U.S. administrations (those of presidents Lyndon Johnson, Richard Nixon, Gerald Ford, and Jimmy Carter), and the Democratic and Republican parties. The final treaty and the compromises it contained were the subject of controversy in Panama and the United States, but ultimately both countries ratified the final document. The Panamanian chief of government, General Omar Torrijos, obtained ratification support through a national plebiscite, and President Carter succeeded in winning a two-thirds vote (by a margin of one vote) in the U.S. Senate in support of the treaty's ratification. The treaty has helped to answer charges of colonialism and has changed the focus of U.S. interest in the canal from one of ownership to one of use. The treaty, together with the Neutrality Treaty of 1978, is based on the two nations' definitions of their national interests and is consistent with their respective national values.

Panama Intervention | 276 |

The U.S. military action begun on 20 December 1989, which aimed at overthrowing the dictatorship of General Manuel Noriega, bringing him to trial in U.S. courts on drug charges, and establishing a new government in Panama headed by Guillermo Endara. President George Bush ordered the invasion, dubbed "Operation Just Cause," to protect the 35,000 Americans living in Panama and to keep the canal functioning. Approximately 25,000 American troops participated in the action, with about 350 casualties. Panamanian military and civilian casualties numbered over 500. *See also* INTERVENTION (238); NORIEGA CASE (271); PANAMA CANAL TREATY OF 1978 (275).

Significance
The intervention was the thirteenth military action taken in Panama by the United States during the twentieth century. Reaction abroad to the invasion was mixed in Europe but almost completely opposed by Latin American governments. The Bush administration had tried to overthrow Noriega two months earlier in a military coup. The attempt failed, and Noriega, a onetime paid informant for the Central Intelligence Agency, ruthlessly executed more than 70 officers and men. Later, the Bush administration admitted that the coup attempt had failed because of poor "crisis management," an experience that perhaps led to the decision to invade. Noriega eluded American forces and took refuge in the Vatican embassy in Panama City. Several weeks later, he surrendered to U.S. authorities outside the embassy and was extradited to the United States, where he was convicted on drug-trafficking charges. Thousands of Panamanians were made homeless by heavy American firepower, leading to the provision of millions of dollars in economic aid to the new government.

Platt Amendment | 277 |

Limitations placed upon Cuban sovereignty by the United States when it ended its military rule carried on from 1898 to 1902. First attached by Congress to the Army Appropriations Act of 1901, the Platt Amendment was forced upon Cuba as a condition of U.S. withdrawal of military forces and the granting of independence to the island republic. The amendment was also added as an annex to the Cuban Constitution of

1901 and was incorporated into the treaty between Cuba and the United States in 1903. Under the amendment, concessions made by Cuba to the United States provided that Cuba (1) must permit the United States to retain the right to intervene in Cuban affairs to preserve its independence and to maintain a government in power that was able to protect life, property, and individual liberty; (2) cannot authorize a foreign power other than the United States to use its territory for military or naval purposes; (3) cannot contract any debts that cannot be paid from regular treasury sources; and (4) would sell or lease to the United States lands necessary for military or naval purposes. Under the last of these provisions, an area of Cuban land was leased by the United States at Guantanamo Bay, which in time was developed into a major military and naval base. *See also* GOOD NEIGHBOR POLICY (256); SPANISH-AMERICAN WAR (281).

Significance
The Platt Amendment made Cuba into a U.S. protectorate from 1902 until it was abrogated in 1934 by Cuba with the consent of President Franklin D. Roosevelt. During those three decades, the United States intervened politically and militarily on numerous occasions, supervising elections and sending in troops to quell disorders. From 1906 to 1909, for example, the United States ruled Cuba through a provisional military government. When Fulgencio Batista seized dictatorial power in 1934, the Roosevelt administration admitted that U.S. tutelage efforts had failed, and the new Good Neighbor policy was implemented by withdrawal from Cuba. Although the Platt Amendment was abrogated in 1934, the United States retained the right to maintain the Guantanamo base, which remains a matter of grave controversy between the two nations. The Platt Amendment and the interventions based on it have contributed to the growth of a strong antiyankeeism among Cubans, known as *Plattismo*.

Poinsettismo 278
A pejorative term used to characterize and condemn U.S. meddling in Mexican internal affairs. *Poinsettismo* is named after Joel R. Poinsett (1779–1851), the first U.S. minister to Mexico from 1825 to 1829. An active envoy who wanted to pattern the newly independent Mexican state on the U.S. model, Poinsett supported republican, liberal, and federalist forces against monarchist, conservative, and centralist forces in Mexico. He introduced the York Rite branch of Freemasonry to the country and competed for economic and political influence against the British envoy, who supported the Scottish Rite Masons. Poinsett promoted the idea that the United States should purchase Texas, and he encouraged Mexican liberals to take over the government after their loss in the close, but allegedly fraudulent, presidential election of 1828. He was expelled in 1829 when the conservatives came back into power. The poinsettia flower, which Poinsett popularized, was named in his honor. *See also* ANTIYANKEEISM (ANTIYANQUISMO) (51); FREEMASONRY (65).

Significance
As practiced by its namesake, *Poinsettismo* was not very successful, leaving a heritage of bitter feeling in Mexico against the United States. Poinsett lost out to the British in securing trade and economic privileges in Mexico, contributed to divisive Masonic rivalries, confirmed the suspicions of many Mexicans that the United States wanted to annex Texas, and gave the conservatives additional reasons for abolishing the federal system when they returned to power. *Poinsettismo* was one of the first of many episodes that engendered a long history of

Yankeephobia in Mexico. It became a convenient label that Mexican politicians used to condemn the programs and institutions of their political opponents, and the term is still used by nationalists to condemn any alleged U.S. intervention in Mexican affairs.

Puerto Rico: Commonwealth (279)

"Commonwealth" means a "self-governing territory associated with the United States of America." Congress in 1950 renamed the colony in Spanish as the *Estado Libre Associado de Puerto Rico,* which in English was shortened simply to Commonwealth. The law gave the people of Puerto Rico the power to draft an Organic Act, which, following adoption in a nationwide referendum vote, became the constitution of the commonwealth when it came into force in 1952. Under commonwealth status, the U.S. Constitution and federal laws continue to be binding except for those provisions that Congress or the federal courts determine not to be applicable to Puerto Rico. *See also* PUERTO RICO: OPERATION BOOTSTRAP (280).

Significance
Supporters of commonwealth status or statehood for Puerto Rico regard the adoption of the 1950 self-governing arrangements as a definitive declaration of the will of the Puerto Rican people. Opponents—especially Puerto Rican nationalists—regard commonwealth status as a fraud and have continued to agitate against it in favor of sovereignty and national independence. In the United Nations, Puerto Rico has been included among the non-self-governing territories that should be granted independence, and the U.N. has brought pressures on the United States to move toward that goal. Puerto Rico began as a Spanish colony but, following the invasion of the territory by United States troops during the war with Spain in 1898, Spanish sovereignty over the island was ended. It then became a U.S. territory, militarily occupied and economically exploited. Under the Foraker Act of 1900 and the Jones Act of 1917, Puerto Rico was brought under the U.S. Constitution and tariff and other federal laws, except for those held to be inapplicable by Congress. In 1917, Puerto Ricans were also accorded U.S. citizenship, and in 1947 the people received the right to elect their own governor, previously appointed by the president of the United States. A new economic policy, called Operation Bootstrap, was adopted by the United States in 1942 to help industrialize and modernize the island through favorable tax treatment and subsidies to attract capital. Some Puerto Rican nationalists have employed terror tactics to call attention to their independence cause. During the 1950s, for example, an attempt was made to assassinate President Harry Truman, and a terroristic shooting spree took place in the House of Representatives in which several congressmen were wounded. Numerous bombings also occurred in past years, especially in the New York City area. Options under discussion by Puerto Ricans are (1) maintaining the existing Commonwealth status with perhaps some modifications, (2) admittance to the Union as the fifty-first state, and (3) full independence and sovereignty. In December 1991, Puerto Ricans rejected a non-binding proposal that would have prevented a simple yes-or-no vote on statehood. By mid-1992, the U.S. Congress had yet to authorize a referendum on the three options. Most Puerto Ricans seem to be equally divided between statehood and commonwealth status, with only about 10 percent favoring independence.

Puerto Rico: Operation Bootstrap (280)

A U.S. policy aimed at helping Puerto Rico achieve economic development and modernization through an intimate political and economic relationship between the two. Established by the administration of Franklin D. Roosevelt, Operation Bootstrap was inaugurated in 1942 with the creation of the Industrial Development Company and a development bank to encourage the growth of local industry and to provide the means for financing that growth. Special tax exemptions and reimbursement of import duties and excise taxes were also instituted, and these continue to attract industry to Puerto Rico. Emphasis was placed in the early period on building an infrastructure on which industrialization could be based. Most of the capital to support the program has come from the U.S. companies and entrepreneurs that have been attracted by economic opportunities, tax incentives, and the relatively low-cost labor supply readily available. *See also* PUERTO RICO: COMMONWEALTH (279); TERRITORY (282).

Significance
The Operation Bootstrap program got off to a good start by the unparalleled economic opportunities provided by World War II. This economic growth and general progress led to post-war political changes, including the birth of a nationalist movement and concessions from the United States. The latter provided for the direct election of the governor by the people of Puerto Rico, and, in 1952, a change from colonial status to that of a self-governing commonwealth on the basis of a referendum vote by the people. Operation Bootstrap sought to turn Puerto Rico into a model of capitalist development success and a showcase for the United States, United Nations, and other international agencies. Per capita income rose from about $200 in 1950 to approximately $1,500 in the 1970s, and it continued to rise during the latter part of the 1980s. Rapid economic growth was explained in terms of free trade, open investment opportunity, government support for private enterprise, the adoption of social and technological norms based on those of the United States, and a stable political system with periodic elections. Puerto Rico became the free world's answer to Soviet-inspired demands for national liberation and socialist development for colonial peoples. By the late 1970s and early 1980s, however, Operation Bootstrap was in trouble because of the impact of inflation, the population surge in Puerto Rico, unemployment, and a general reduction in trade barriers that tended to diminish the favorable status enjoyed by Puerto Rican companies.

Spanish-American War 281
A conflict in 1898 in which the United States fought Spain primarily over the issue of Cuban independence. The Spanish-American War was the last and decisive phase of the longer War for Cuban Independence, which had broken out in 1895. The immediate cause of the U.S. entry into the war was the mysterious explosion on 25 January 1898 that sank the U.S. battleship *Maine* in Havana harbor, killing 266 men. A U.S. commission reported in March that the explosion was caused by an external mine that set off internal explosions, and not from an internal cause, as a Spanish commission had concluded. The *Maine* incident and the attendant battle cry, "Remember the *Maine!*," fanned war fever in the United States, which pressured President William McKinley to take action. Spain's offer of autonomy for Cuba was rejected in favor of demands for independence by Cuban nationalists and the United States, and war broke out in April. The U.S. declaration of war included the Teller Amendment, which disavowed any intent to annex Cuba. The fighting lasted only four months. American naval forces defeated the Spanish fleet at Manila in the Philippines and the Spanish Atlantic fleet

at Santiago, Cuba. U.S. forces invaded Cuba, fought several important battles, took Santiago, and also invaded Puerto Rico. An armistice was signed in August and the Paris Peace Treaty was signed in December 1898. Under the terms of the settlement, Cuba was granted independence, Puerto Rico and Guam were ceded to the United States, and the Philippines was ceded to the United States for $20 million. *See also* PLATT AMENDMENT (277); TEN YEARS WAR (42); VIRGINIUS AFFAIR (284); WAR FOR CUBAN INDEPENDENCE (46).

Significance
The Spanish-American War culminated a period of increasing U.S. support for a free Cuba and ushered in a new period of U.S. domination of the Caribbean. U.S. hostility towards Spain had been built up by a number of factors over a 50-year period: Spain's refusal to sell Cuba to the United States; the *Virginius* Affair, in which Spain executed U.S. citizens who were illegally running guns to Cuban rebels in 1873; the destruction of property of U.S. citizens during Cuban wars; Spain's failure to institute meaningful reforms in Cuba after the Ten Years War; the agitation of Cuban nationalist leaders in the United States; and years of "yellow journalism" by the U.S. press decrying Spanish atrocities in Cuba. The United States had developed strong economic ties to the island, and a strategic interest emerged when it became apparent that an interoceanic canal would be built somewhere in Central America. The *Maine* incident so aroused U.S. public opinion that nothing short of Cuban independence was acceptable. Spain relinquished its sovereignty over Cuba and the United States occupied the island for four years, making sanitary, health, education, and public works improvements and introducing political and administrative reforms. Although the United States did not annex Cuba, it imposed the provisions of the Platt Amendment as the condition for its departure in 1902. This made Cuba a virtual protectorate of the United States and led to a number of interventions. In addition, Puerto Rico became a U.S. colony, and the United States became more interventionist in Caribbean and Central American affairs. The war had other far-reaching consequences in the Pacific, with the United States entering the new century as a major world power. Spain lost its last possessions in the Western Hemisphere, and its former worldwide empire was ended.

Territory | 282 |

An area and its people under the jurisdiction of a sovereign state. In the United States, a territory is not part of any state of the union. In Latin America and the Caribbean, there are two territorial possessions of the United States—Puerto Rico and the Virgin Islands, both of which function under the supervision of the Department of the Interior. The Panama Canal Zone was returned to Panama under the provisions of the Panama Canal Treaty of 1978, although the canal itself is under joint administration until the year 2000. Various territorial courts along with some governmental agencies have been established from time to time by Congress for governing the territories, with no two territories having the same structure. *See also* PUERTO RICO: COMMONWEALTH (279).

Significance
The Latin American and Caribbean territories were acquired by the United States through purchase and conquest. Residents of Puerto Rico and the Virgin Islands are citizens of the United States, with Puerto Rico having the status of "a free commonwealth associated with the United States." Some members of Congress do not believe Puerto Rico, because

of its culturally diverse nature, should become a state, and they have delayed authorizing a referendum on the three options of statehood, independence, or continued commonwealth status. The Virgin Islands, formerly the Danish West Indies, were purchased from Denmark in 1917. They consist of three islands—St. Thomas, St. John, and St. Croix. To date, the Virgin Islands have remained prosperous, and there has been little agitation for political change in their status.

Veracruz Occupation | 283 |

The occupation of the Mexican seaport of Veracruz by U.S. forces in 1914. The Veracruz Occupation occurred during the Mexican Revolution following the arrest of some crew members from the *U.S.S. Dolphin,* which had landed on 9 April 1914 in Tampico to buy supplies. The U.S. naval commander, and later President Woodrow Wilson, demanded an apology from the Mexican government of General Victoriano Huerta in the form of various symbolic acts that Huerta refused to carry out. When a German merchant ship was about to land munitions in Veracruz on 21 April, the city was bombarded and occupied by U.S. forces. Nineteen Americans and about 200 Mexicans were killed in the fighting. General Venustiano Carranza, who led the Constitutionalist forces against Huerta, criticized the intervention but refused to rally behind Huerta's call for a national war against the United States. An attempt by Argentina, Brazil, and Chile to mediate this and other issues associated with the Mexican civil war was inconclusive, but their recommendation that Huerta be removed contributed to his fall from power in July 1914. U.S. forces remained in Veracruz until 23 November 1914. *See also* MEXICAN REVOLUTION (37).

Significance
The Veracruz Occupation was the natural consequence of the interventionist policy adopted by President Wilson following the overthrow and murder of Francisco I. Madero, the first elected president of the Mexican Revolution. Wilson used the Tampico incident to rally congressional support against Huerta in favor of the Constitutionalist forces led by General Carranza. Earlier, Wilson had lifted the arms embargo, which benefited Carranza. The Veracruz Occupation in turn had the effect of preventing war supplies from reaching Huerta and denying him the revenues of the Veracruz customhouse, which was his principal source of revenue.

Virginius Affair | 284 |

An 1873 international incident in the Cuban Ten Years War that involved the *Virginius,* a blockade-running ship. The *Virginius,* a Cuban-owned ship illegally flying the U.S. flag, was captured by Spain while it was carrying arms to Cuban nationalists. Spain executed the ship's captain and 52 crew members and passengers, among whom were U.S. and British citizens. The intervention of a British warship prevented more executions. The incident worsened relations between the United States and Spain, but a settlement was reached when Spain agreed to pay a $50,000 indemnity to the United States. *See also* SPANISH-AMERICAN WAR (281); TEN YEARS WAR (42); WAR FOR CUBAN INDEPENDENCE (46).

Significance
The *Virginius* incident almost caused the United States to declare war on Spain. It contributed significantly to the increasing popular sympathy for Cuban independence and for U.S. intervention in the Ten Years War. The episode, along with other incidents, fostered the buildup of a strong anti-Spanish attitude in the United States. The cumulative effect of these incidents was to strongly support U.S. policy when the Spanish-American War broke out in 1898.

Index

A reference in **bold** type indicates the number of a major dictionary entry. Numbers in roman type refer to dictionary entries within which additional information on that index term, person, or topic can be located. Index entries to terms or topics having English and foreign-language equivalents appear under both forms. Cross-references to dictionary entries are located in the text at the end of each definition paragraph.

Acción Democrática, 115, 127, 134
ACM. *See* Andean Common Market
Act of Chapultepec (1945), **233**
AD. *See* Democratic Action
Adams, John Quincy, 262
Adelantado, 27
Age of *caudillos*, 139
Agency for International Development (AID), 182
Agrarian reform, 10. *See also* Land reform
Agricultural production, 3
Agricultural systems. *See Ejido*; Hacienda; Land reform; Latifundia system; Minifundia system
Aldunate, Wilson Ferreira, 107
Alessandri, Jorge, 10
Alexander VI, Pope, 44
Alfonsín, Raúl, 84
Aliens, undocumented, 13, 260

Allende, Salvador, 10, 100, 185
Alliance for Progress, 182, **249**
Almagro, Diego de, 29
Alternation and Parity, **156**
Alternación y Paridad, **156**
Altiplano, 5
Amazon Basin, 5, 7, 198, 212
Amazon Cooperation Council, 212
Amazon Pact (AP), **212**
"American," 12
American Popular Revolutionary Alliance (APRA), Peru, **106**, 127
Americanismo, **49**
Amerinds, 18
Amparo, writ of, 171
Andean Common Market (ACM), **213**
Andean Development Corporation, 213
Andean Group, 213
Andean Pact, 213
Andes, 5
Anticlericalism, 30, **50**, 109

Index

Antiyankeeism, **51**, 277
Antiyanquismo, **51**, 277
Antofagasta, 47
AP. *See* Amazon Pact
Apertura, **85**
Appointment system, 156
APRA. *See* American Popular Revolutionary Alliance
April package of laws, Brazil, 85
Aprismo, 106, 127
Aprista parties, 106, 115, 118, 127
Arbenz Guzmán, Jacobo, 259
Arce, Manuel José, 24
ARENA. *See* National Renovating Alliance, Brazil
ARENA. *See* National Republican Alliance, El Salvador
Argentina
  caesarism, 138
  continuismo, 161
  corporatism, 61
  death squads, 82
  demography, 2
  Falklands War, **87**
  fascism, 64
  federalism, 167
  foreign debt, 197
  government system, 161, 167, 178
  guerrilla war, 91
  independence, 48
  LAIA membership, 227
  militarism, 138, 141, 153
  organized labor, 128
  Paraguayan War, 38
  Peronism, 64, 72
  political parties, 132
  political violence, 82
  population, 17
  Radical parties, 132
  slums, 20
  socialism, 78
  state of siege, 178
  trade unionism, 128
  unionization rate, 128
  urban guerrilla warfare, 91
  urbanization, 22
Argentine Anti-Communist Alliance (AAA), 82
Arica, 47
Armed forces. *See* Militarism; Praetorian army; Praetorianism
"Arms for hostages," 261
Atacama Desert, 7, 47

Audiencia, 27
Ayacucho, 101
Ayacucho (1824), Battle of, 35, 48
Aylwin, Patricio, 55, 112
Aztecs, 28

Baker, James, 197
Baker Plan, 225
Balboa, Vasco Nuñez de, 29
Bandung Conference (1955), 229
Barbados, 257
Barracks revolt, 141, 155
Barriadas, 20
Batista, Fulgencio, 57, 139, 141, 277
Batlle Ibáñez, José, 111
Batlle y Ordóñez, José, 52, 111, 159
Batllismo, **52**
Bay of Pigs Invasion, **250**
Belaúnde Terry, Fernando, 106
Belize, 24
Betancourt, Rómulo, 115
Bicameralism, **157**, 179
Bishop, Maurice, 257
Black legend, **23**
Black nationalism, 62, 71
Blanco, 18
Blanco party (National party) (Uruguay), **107**, 111
Bogotá, 80, 105
Bogotá Pact, **247**
Bogotazo, **80**, 105
Bolívar, Simón, 34, 35, 49
Bolivia
  Amazon Pact membership, 212
  Andean Common Market membership, 213
  Chaco War, 25
  exports, 200
  fascism, 64
  Fidelista movement, 89
  Guevara's defeat in, 90
  hyperinflation in, 199
  LAIA membership, 227
  land reform, 10
  nationalization of U.S. property, 245
  peasants, 129
  peonage, 16
  political culture, 75
  political parties, 127
  War of the Pacific, **47**
Bonaparte, Joseph, 48
Bonus election system, 117

Index

Bordaberry, Juan María, 91, 107, 111, 123
Borlaug, Norman E., 198
Bosch, Juan, 254
Botella, 74
Bracero, 13
Brady, Nicholas, 197
Brady Plan, 197, 225
Brazil
   Amazon Pact membership, 212
   caesarism, 138
   civilian governments, 145
   colonial system, 27
   continuismo, 161
   coronelismo, 162
   corporatism, 61
   death squads, 82
   distensão, 85
   election system, 117
   fascism, 64
   federalism, 167
   foreign debt, 197
   freemasonry, 65
   government system, 85, 170, 174, 176
   guerrilla war, 91
   independence, 48, 169
   institutional acts, 85, 170
   LAIA membership, 227
   militarism, 147
   monarchy, 174
   Paraguayan War, 38
   parliamentary system, 176
   peasants, 129
   political bossism, 158, 162
   political culture, 75
   political parties, 85, 137
   political violence, 82
   population, 17
   positivism, 76
   racial groups, 15, 18
   slums, 20
   Treaty of Tordesillas (1494), 44
   urban guerrilla warfare, 91
   urbanization, 22
Brazilian Democratic Movement (MDB), 85
Brazilian Democratic Movement party (PMDB), 85
"Bread or the club," 39
Brezhnev, Leonid, 252
Bribery, **74**
Broad Front (Nicaragua), 96
Broad Front (Uruguay), 123
Buchi, Hernán, 112
Buena Vista (1847), Battle of, 264
Bunau-Varilla, Phillipe, 274
Bureaucracy, colonial, 27
Bush, George, 197, 271, 276

Cabildo, 1, 27, 180
Cabildo abierto, 27
Cabinet, 173
Cabral, Pedro Álvares, 44
Cacique, 158
Caciquismo, **158**, 162
CACM. *See* Central American Common Market
Caesarism, **138**, 154
Caldera, Rafael, 134
Cali cartel, 86
Callampas, 20
Calles, Plutarco Elías, 30, 37
Calvo, Carlos, 242
Calvo Clause, **242**
Campesino, 56, 129
Campos, Roberto, 206
Canada, 235
Canal Zone, Panama, 274, 275
Candidato único, **108**
Candomblé, 79
Canning, George, 265
Capital cities, 9
Capitalism, 181, 186. *See also* Development strategies; Dependency—development theory; Multinational corporation; Neocolonialism
Capitalism development model, 280
Capitania, 27
Captain-General, 27
Captaincy, 27
Cárdenas, Cuauhtémoc, 125
Cárdenas, Lázaro, 16, 37
Caribank. *See* Caribbean Development Bank
Caribbean Basin Initiative (CBI), **214**
Caribbean Community and Common Market (CARICOM), **215**
Caribbean community secretariat, 215, 217
Caribbean Development Bank (Caribank), **216**
Caribbean Free Trade Association (CARIFTA), **217**
CARICOM. *See* Caribbean Community and Common Market

CARIFTA. *See* Caribbean Free Trade Association
Carranza, Venustiano, 37, 283
Carrera, Rafael, 24
Cartegena Agreement (1969), 213
Carter, James Earl "Jimmy," 275
Cartorial state, **53**
Castas, las, 18
Castelo Branco, Humberto, 141
Castillo Armas, Carlos, 259
Castro, Cipriano, 270
Castro, Fidel, 54, 89
    assassination plots against, 250, 251
    Bay of Pigs invasion, 250
    as *caudillo*, 139
    and Communist party of Cuba (PCC), 114, 165
    and Cuban Constitution (1976), 164
    development strategy of, 185
    economic policy of, 207, 210, 211
    and land reform, 10
    mass mobilization, 163
    moral incentives approach, 207
    and Organs of Popular Power, 165
    and Twenty-sixth of July Movement, 104, 114
    See also Castroism; *Fidelista*
Castro, Raúl, 114, 164
Castroism, 54, 100, 250
Catholic Church, 17, 30, 50, 109. *See also* Conference of Latin American Bishops
Catholic political parties, 55
Catholics, 30, 58, 109
Caucus Group of Seventy-seven, 226, 229, 230
Caudillismo, **139**, 154
Caudillo, 138, 139, 158
CBI. *See* Caribbean Basin Initiative
CDR. *See* Committees for the Defense of the Revolution
CECLA. *See* Special Latin American Coordinating Committee
CELAM. *See* Conference of Latin American Bishops
Center on Transnational Corporations (CTNC), 201
Central America
    anticlericalism, 50
    federalism, 24, 167
    filibusters to, 45
    regional organizations, 218, 236, 239
    unicameralism, 179
    United Provinces of, 24
Central American Bank for Economic Integration, 218
Central American Bureau, 236
Central American Clearing House, 218
Central American Common Market (CACM), 24, 203, **218**
Central American Court of International Justice, **239**
Central American Federation, **24**, 236
Central American Parliament, **219**
Central American Peace Conference (1907), 239
Central Intelligence Agency (CIA), 100, 250, **251**, 259
Central planning, 213
Cerezo, Marco Vinicio, 55
Césaire, Aimé, 71
César Turbay, Julio, 156
Céspedes, Carlos Manuel de, 42
Chacabuco (1817), Battle of, 35
Chaco Boreal, 25
Chaco generation, 25
Chaco War, **25**, 118
Chamorro, Pedro Juaquín, 95, 96
Chamorro, Violeta Barrios de, 81, 95, 133
Chamber of Deputies, 157
Chapultepec Conference (1945), 233
Charismatic leader, 185
Charter of Alta Gracia (1964), 228
Charter of Bogotá (1948), 247
Charter of San Salvador (1951), 236
Chiapas, 24
Chibcha, 28
Chicanos, 13
Chile
    Andean Common Market membership, 213
    anticlericalism, 50
    civilian governments, 145
    communism, 57
    corporatism, 61
    development strategy, 185
    election system, 117, 119
    exports, 200
    fascism, 64
    federalism, 167
    freemasonry, 65
    government system, 157, 176, 177, 180
    LAIA membership, 227
    land reform, 10

Letelier Affair, 83, 93
liberalism, 68
militarism, 147, 149
multiparty system, 24
organized labor, 128
parliamentary system, 176
plebiscite of 1988, 112
political parties, 55, 124, 132
political violence, 83, 93
positivism, 76
Radical parties, 132
revolution, 100, 185
secret police, 83, 90
slums, 20
socialism, 78
state security agencies, 83
suffrage, 136
unionization rate, 128
urbanization, 22
War of the Pacific, 47
Chilpancingo, constitution of, 35
China, 237
Chinese communism, 57
Cholo, 18
Christian base community, 69
Christian democracy, **55**
Christian socialism, 55
Christiani, Alfredo, 88
Christophe, Henri, 174
Church-state relations, 30, **109**. *See also* Catholic Church
CIA operations, **251**. *See also* Central Intelligence Agency
Cienfuegos submarine base, 252
Científicos, **26**, 39, 76
Cinco de Mayo, 36
Clark, J. Rueben, Jr., 266
Clark Memorandum of 1928, 238, 256, **266**
Cleveland, Grover, 268
Clientelism, **56**
Clientelismo, **56**
Climate—geographical factors, **5**
Cochrane, Thomas Alexander, 35
Colegiado, 52, 123, 159
Collective action, 233
Collective nonrecognition, 246
Collectivism
　Cuba, 211
　Mexico, 172
　See also Socialism, Communism
Colombia
　Amazon Pact membership, 212
　Andean Common Market membership, 213
　anticlericalism, 50
　civilian governments, 145
　demography, 2
　election system, 108, 117, 156
　exports, 200
　federalism, 167
　freemasonry, 65
　government system, 156, 167, 178
　"Gran Colombia," 34
　LAIA membership, 227
　liberalism, 68
　National Front, 126
　organized labor, 128
　Panama Canal Treaty (1903), 274
　political parties, 126, 137, 156
　political violence, 80, 105
　Republic of (Gran Colombia), 34
　slums, 20
　state of siege, 178
　Thousand Day War, 43
　United States of, 34
　urbanization, 22
　violence, 80, 105
Colonial Government, 27
Colonialism, 229. *See also* Internal colonialism thesis; Neocolonialism
Colorado party (Paraguay), **110**, 111
Colorado party (Uruguay), 68, 107, **111**
Columbus, Christopher, 28
Command for No, **112**
Commercial and industrial associations, **113**
Comintern. *See* Communist International
Commission on Human Rights, Inter-American system, **234**
Commission on Transnational Corporations (CTC), 201
Committee Organized for Independent Elections. *See* Social Christian party
Committees for the Defense of the Revolution (CDR) (Cuba), **163**
Commodity agreement, **196**
Common market, 213, 227
　Andean, 213
　Caribbean, 215
　Central American, 218
　Southern cone, 21
　See also Latin American Integration Association

Common protective policy (CARICOM), 215
Commonwealth, Puerto Rico, **279**
Communism, 54, **57**, 188
Communist International, 57
Communist party of Cuba (PCC), 104, **114**, 165
Compadrazgo, 56, **58**
Compadre, 58
Compadresco, 58
Comparative advantage, 186
Complementarity principle, 227
Comte, Auguste, 76
Confederation of Mexican Workers (CTM), 120
Conference of Latin American Bishops (CELAM), 69, 109
Conquest, **28**
Conquistador, **29**
Concientización, 69
Conservatism, **59**
Conservative modernization— development strategy, **181**
Conservative parties, 59
Consortium loans, 223
Constitution, **160**
  colegiado, 159
  continuismo, 161
  institutional act, 170
  judicial review, 171
  non-reelection principle, 175
  presidentialism, 177
  state of siege, 178
  unitary government, 180
  written, 60
Constitution, Cuban (1976), 117, **164**, 165
Constitution, Mexican
  (1857), 41
  (1917), 30, 37, **172**
Constitution, Soviet Union, 165
Constitution, Spanish (1812), 160
Constitution, Uruguayan (1918), 159
Constitution, Uruguayan (1951), 159
Constitutionalism, **60**
Constitutive recognition, 244, 246
Continental unity, 49
Continuismo, 119, **161**
Contras, **81**, 96, 261
Contreras, Manuel, 93
Cooperative, 10
Coparenthood, 58
COPEI. *See* Social Christian party

Cordillera, 7
Cordoba reforms, 135
Coroneis, 158, 162
Coronel, 162
Coronelismo, 158, **162**
Corporatism, **61**
Corregidor, 27
Corregidores de indios, 27
Corruption, political. *See* Political corruption
Cortés, Hernán, 28, 29
Cosmic race, 18
Cost-pull inflation, 199
Costa Rica
  in Caribbean Basin Initiative, 214
  Central American Common Market membership, 218
  Central American Court membership, 239
  Central American Federation, 24
  civilian governments, 145
  demography, 2
  exports, 200
  government system, 178
  legislature, 177
  ODECA membership, 236
  political parties, 127
  unicameralism, 179
Council of State (Cuba), 165
Council of the Indies, 27
Coup d'etat, **140**, 143, 145
Court of Justice (ODECA), 236
Creole (racial group), **1**, 18, 33, 35
Créole (language), **62**
Criollo, **1**, 18, 35
Cristero rebellion, **30**
Cry of Dolores, 35
Cuartel, 141
Cuartelazo, **141**, 155
Cuba
  Bay of Pigs invasion, 250
  Castroism, 54
  communism, 57, 114
  constitution, 164
  constitutional changes (1992), 117
  development strategy, 185
  economy, 210, 211
  election system, 117
  exiles, 250
  exports, 200
  Fidelista, 89
  freemasonry, 65
  government institutions, 165

guerrilla war, 90, 104
independence, 281
land reform, 10
mass mobilization, 163
migration, 13, 263
militarism, 141
missile crisis (1962), 252
moral incentives, 207
nationalization of U.S. property, 245
organized labor, 128
Ostend Manifesto, 272
peasants, 129
Platt Amendment, 277
political parties, 114
revolution, 100, 185
Spanish-American War, 281
suffrage, 136
Ten Years War, 42, 169
Twenty-sixth of July Movement, 104, 114
unicameralism, 179
unionization rate, 128
Virginius affair, 284
War for Cuban Independence, 42, 46
worker motivation, 207
Cuba, Communist party of. *See* Communist party of Cuba
Cuban Committees for the Defense of the Revolution (CDR), **163**
Cuban Constitution of 1976, 117, **164**, 165
Cuban missile crisis (1962), 237, **252**
Cuban Nationalist Movement, 93
Cuban Organs of Popular Power, **165**
Cuban Revolutionary Offensive of 1968, **211**
Cubans in U.S., 263
Cultural approach—development theory, **187**
Culture, Hispanic, 63
Culture, political. *See* Political Culture
Curaca, 158

D'Aubuisson, Roberto, 88
Damas, Léon, 71
Darwin, Charles, 262
De facto recognition, 244
Death list, 82
Death squad, **82**
Debray, Regis, 90
Debt-equity swap, 225
Debt peonage, 16
Debtor states, 229

Declaration of independence, 169
Declaration of Punta del Este (1967), 218
Declaration on the Establishment of a New International Economic Order (NIEO), 229
Declarative recognition, 244, 246
Decree-law, **166**
Decreto-ley, 166
Defense council (ODECA), 236
Demand-pull inflation, 199
Demarcation, papal line of, 44
Demilitarization, **142**
Democracy, **63**, 68, 77. *See also* Redemocratization; Demilitarization
Democratic Action (AD) (Venezuela), **115**, 127, 134
Democratic Revolutionary Front (FDR) (El Salvador), 88
Demographic Cycle, **2**
Dependency—development theory, **188**, 190, 191, 193
Desaparacidos, 84
Dessalines, Jean Jacques, 174
Destabilization—development theory, **189**
Detente, 252
Development Bank, 280
Development loans, 249
Development projects, 223
Development strategy: conservative modernization, **181**
Development strategy: import substitution, 204, 220
Development strategy: macro approach, **182**
Development strategy: micro approach, 182, **183**
Development strategy: progressive modernization, **184**
Development strategy: revolutionary approach, **185**
Development strategy: traditional approach, **186**
Development theory: cultural approach, **187**
Development theory: dependency, **188**, 190, 191, 193
Development theory: destabilization, **189**
Development theory: diffusion, **190**, 191
Development theory: dual society, **191**, 194

Development theory: impoverishment, **192**
Development theory: internal colonialism, **193**
Development theory: marginality, **194**
Development theory: political development, 146, **195**
Development thesis—militarism, **146**
Díaz, Porfirio, 26, 37, 39, 41
Dictatorship, 135, 138, 139
Diffusion theory, 190, **191**
DINA. *See* National Intelligence Directorate
Diplomacy, 243, 253. *See also* Dollar diplomacy
Diplomatic recognition, 244, 246
Directed economy, 203, 213
Dirigismo, **203**
Dirty War, **84**
Distensão, 82, **85**, 170
Distensão and *Apertura*, **85**
Dollar diplomacy, **253**
Dolphin, U.S. ship, 283
Dominant party system, **116**
Dominican party, 130
Dominican Republic
    in Caribbean Basin Initiative, 214
    civil war, 254
    civilian governments, 145
    election system, 117
    government system, 157
    independence, 48
    militarism, 139
    political parties, 127, 130
    suffrage, 136
    U.S. intervention (1965), 254
Dominican Republic intervention, **254**
Dominican Revolutionary party (PRD), 127
Donatario, 27
Donatary system, 27
Drago doctrine, 242, **243**
Drago, Luis María, 243
Drug war, **86**
Dual society thesis, 191
Duarte, José Napoleón, 55, 88
Duarte, Maria Eva, 72
Duvalier, François, 4, 79, 102, 139, 161
Duvalier, Jean-Claude, 161

East-West cold war issues, 229
Echeverría, Luis, 226
ECLA. *See* Economic Commission for Latin America
Economic Commission for Latin America (ECLA), 182, 184, 204, 220. *See also* Economic Commission for Latin America and the Caribbean (ECLAC)
Economic Commission for Latin America and the Caribbean (ECLAC), **220**. *See also* Economic Commission for Latin America (ECLA); Development strategies; Economic factors; Economic policies;
Economic factors: commodity agreement, **196**
Economic factors: foreign debt crisis, **197**
Economic factors: green revolution, **198**
Economic factors: hyperinflation, **199**
Economic factors: monoculture, **200**
Economic factors: multinational corporation (MNC), **201**
Economic factors: neocolonialism, **202**
Economic integration, 215, 227. *See also* Integration, economic
Economic intervention, 238
Economic policy: *dirigismo*, **203**
Economic policy: import substitution, **204**
Economic policy: *maquiladoras*, **205**
Economic policy: monetarists versus structuralists, **206**
Economic policy: moral incentives versus material incentives, **207**
Economic policy: privatization, **208**
Economic policy: Pronasol, **209**
Economic policy: rectification campaign, **210**
Economic policy: Revolutionary Offensive of 1968 (Cuba), **211**
ECOSOC. *See* United Nations Economic and Social Council
Ecuador
    Amazon Pact membership, 212
    Andean Common Market membership, 213
    demography, 2
    freemasonry, 65
    functional representation, 168
    government system, 168
    independence, 34
    LAIA membership, 227

OPEC membership, 196
peonage, 16
political culture, 75
political parties, 130
population, 17
suffrage, 138
Eisenhower, Dwight D., 250, 259
Ejidatario, 3
Ejido, **3**, 10, 37
El Salvador
    Bishop Romero murder, 88
    Central American Common Market membership, 218
    Central American Court membership, 239
    Central American Federation, 24
    civil war in, 88, 92
    demography, 2
    exports, 200
    Fourth World features, 221
    government system, 179
    Jesuit priest murders, 92
    ODECA membership, 236
    peace plan, 88
    unicameralism, 179
Election system, 108, **117**, 119, 156
Élite, **4**, 62
Enclave modernization, 192
Encomendero, 31
Encomienda, 8, **31**
Endara, Guillermo, 271
Enterprise for the Americas, 197
Equatorial zone, 5
Escalante, Aníbal, 114
Escoceses, 65
Esquipulas, 219
Esquipulas peace plan (Nicaragua), 81
Estado de sitio, 178
Estadounidense, 12
Estancia, 11
Estrada doctrine, **244**, 246
Estrada, Genaro, 244
European Common Market, 227
European community model, 215
European Convention on Human Rights (1953), 240
Executive powers, 177
Export-Import Bank, 256
Expropriation, **245**
"Extraditables," 86

Falklands War, **87**
Family farm, 10

Fanon, Frantz, 71
Farabundo Martí Liberation Front (FMLN), **88**
Farabundo Martí, Agustín, 88
Fascism, **64**
Favelas, 20
Fazenda, 8, 11
Febrerismo, 118
Febrerista Movement, 26, **118**
Federal district, 167
Federalism, 24, 157, **167**, 180
Federation of Central America. *See* Central American Federation
Ferdinand of Aragon, 40
Fidelismo, 89
Fidelista, 54, **89**
Figueiredo, João Baptista, 85, 147
Filibuster, **32**
First International Conference of American States, 232
FMLN. *See* Farabundo Martí Liberation Front
Foco theory—guerrilla war, **90**
Foquismo, 90
Foraker Act of 1900, 279
Ford, Gerald R., 275
Foreign debt crisis, 184, **197**
Foreign investment, 20
Fourth World, **221**, 229
France, 36, 41, 237
Franco, Rafael, 118
Free trade area
    Caribbean, 217
    Latin American, 227
Freemasonry, **65**, 278
Frei, Eduardo, 10, 55
Frente amplio, 123
Friedman, Milton, 206
Frondizi, Arturo, 132
Frustration gap, 189
FSLN. *See* Sandinist Front for National Liberation
Fuero, **33**
Fuero militar, 33
Fujimori, Alberto, 101, 103
Functional representation, **168**
Fund for Special Operations (FSO), 223
Furtado, Celso, 206

Gadsden, James, 255
Gadsden Purchase, **255**
Gaitán, Jorge Eliécer, 80
Gallegos, Rómulo, 115

Galtieri, Leopoldo, 87
García, Alán, 106
Garrison state, 154
GATT. *See* General Agreement on Tariffs and Trade
Geisel, Ernesto, 85
General Agreement on Tariffs and Trade (GATT), **222**
General Assembly (OAS), 235
General Motors, 201
General System of Preferences (GSP), 230
Generation of 1928, 135
Geographical Factors: climate, **5**
Geographical Factors: location, **6**
Geographical Factors: topography, **7**
Germany, 243
Gobernación, Ministry of, **173**
Godparenthood, 58
Golpe de estado, **140**, 143
Golpismo, **143**
Gómez, Juan Vicente, 139
Gómez, Laureano, 105, 156
Good Neighbor Policy, 51, **256**, 265, 277
Goulart, João, 161
Gran Chaco, 7, 25
Gran Colombia, **34**
Granada, fall of, 40
Granadine Confederation, 34
Granja del pueblo, 10
Grant of extraordinary powers, 178
Great Britain
    blockade of Venezuela (1902), 243
    control over Belize, 24
    in Falklands War, 87
    and Guiana-Venezuela boundary dispute, 268
    occupied Veracruz, 41
    ratified nuclear weapons treaty, 237
    rivalry with U.S. in Central America, 45
    support of Monroe Doctrine, 265
Green revolution, **198**
Grenada, 217, 238, 251, 257
Grenada intervention, **257**
Grito, 155, **169**
Grito de Yara, 42, 169
Grito de Ypiranga, 169
Grito do Dolores, 35, 169
Group of Seventy-seven. *See* Caucus Group of Seventy-seven
Guadalupe Hidalgo, Treaty of 1848, **258**, 264

Guantanamo naval base, 237, 277
Guardia rurales, 39
Guardian thesis—militarism, **147**
Guatemala
    Central American Court membership, 239
    continuismo, 161
    government system, 179
    ODECA membership, 236
    peonage, 16
    racial groups, 18
    unicameralism, 179
    U.S. intervention, 251, 259
Guatemala, Captaincy-General of, 24
Guatemalan Intervention, 251, **259**
Guerrilla movement, 89
Guerrilla warfare: *Foco* theory, **90**
Guerrilla warfare: urban warfare theory, **91**
Guevara, Ernesto "Che," 90, 207
Guiana (colony), 268
Guyana (independent republic)
    Amazon Pact membership, 212
    Fourth World features, 221
    government system, 174
    independent republic, 174
Guzmán, Abimael, 101
Guzmán Blanco, Antonio, 139

Hacendado, 8
Haciendas, **8**, 11
Haiti
    continuismo, 161
    Duvalier regime, 102
    élite, 4, 62
    Fourth World features, 221
    government system, 161, 179
    independence, 48
    language, 62
    monarchy in, 174
    negritude, 71
    political culture, 75
    religion, 79
    secret police, 102
    social classes, 4
    unicameralism, 179
Hamilton, Alexander, 181
"Have not" states, 229
Hay-Herran Treaty (1903), 274
Haya de la Torre, Victor Raúl, 106, 127
Herrara Campins, Luis, 115, 134
Herrara, Luis Alberto de, 107
Hidalgo y Costilla, Miguel, 35

Hispanic America, 12
Hispanic culture, 63
Hispaniola, 28, 48
Honduras
   Central American Common Market membership, 218
   Central American Court membership, 239
   demography, 2
   election system, 117
   exports, 200
   federalism, 24, 167
   Fourth World features, 229
   government system, 179
   ODECA membership, 236
   unicameralism, 179
Hoover, Herbert, 256, 266
Hot-line agreement, 252
Houngan, 79
Huallaga Valley, 101
Huerta, Victoriano, 37, 283
Human rights, 83, 229, 240
Human Rights Commission (OAS), 96, 235
Hyperinflation, 197, **199**

Ibero-America, 12
IDB. *See* Inter-American Development Bank
Illia, Arturo, 132
IMF. *See* International Monetary Fund
Immigration Reform and Control Act of 1986, **260**
Imperial city, **9**
Import substitution—development strategy, **204**, 220
Imposición, 108, **119**
Impoverishment—development theory, **192**
Inca Empire, 28
Independence, Wars of. *See* Wars of Independence
Indians
   abuse of, 23, 31
   adaptation of, 174
   conquest of, 28, 29
   racial group, 18
   soldiers in Chaco war, 25
Indigenismo, 18
Indio, 18
Indo-Hispanic America, 12
Industrial Development Company, 280

Industrialization, 2, 280. *See also* Development strategies; Development theories; Economic policies
Inflation, 197, 199, 206
Institutional act, **170**
Institutional Act No. 5, 85, 170
Institutional Revolutionary party (PRI) (Mexico), **120**
   defections in 1988 election, 120, 125
   dominant party system, 116
   electoral strength, 116, 120
   as heirs of Mexican revolution, 37, 120
   sector organization, 113, 120
Integralist party, Brazilian, 64
Integrated Revolutionary Organizations (ORI) (Cuba), 114
Integration, economic
   Amazon, 212
   Andean, 213
   Caribbean, 214, 216, 217
   Central American, 218, 219
   Latin American, 220, 227, 228
   lending agencies and, 223, 225, 231
   less-developed countries and, 221, 229
   trade conferences and, 222, 230
Integration, political, 219
Integration, racial, 18
Inter-American Commission on Human Rights, 235
Inter-American Conference, 232
Inter-American Convention on Human Rights, 242
Inter-American Council for Education, Science and Culture, 235
Inter-American Council of Jurists, **240**
Inter-American Development Bank (IDB), **223**
Inter-American Economic and Social Council, 235
Inter-American Juridical Committee, 235, 240
Inter-American Regional Organizations of Workers (ORIT), 128
Inter-American System, **232**
Inter-American System: Act of Chapultepec, **233**
Inter-American System: Commission on Human Rights, **234**
Inter-American System: Organization of American States (OAS), **235**

Inter-American System: Organization of Central American States (ODECA), **236**
Inter-American System: Treaty for the Prohibition of Nuclear Weapons in Latin America, **237**
Inter-American Treaty of Reciprocal Assistance (Rio Treaty, 1947), 233, **248**
Inter-American Treaty on Pacific Settlement (1948), 247
Interest Group, 113, **121**, 128, 129, 135
Internal colonialism thesis, **193**
International Coffee Agreement, **224**
International Confederation of Free Trade Unions (ICFTU), 128
International Conferences of American States, 80, 232
International Federation of Christian Trade Unions (IFCTU), 128
International law, 238, 271. *See also* Legal institutions; Legal policies
International Monetary Fund (IMF), 182, 199, **225**
International Telephone and Telegraph, 201
Intervention, 202, 233, **238**, 242, 243
Intransigent Radical party (Argentina), 132
Iran-Contra affair, **261**
Isabella of Castile, 40
Isthmian Canal Convention (1903), 273
Italy, 243
Iturbide, Agustín de, 24, 174

Jaguaribe, Helio, 53
Jamaica, 214, 257
Jesuit priest murders, **92**
John Paul II, Pope, 69, 109
John XXIII, Pope, 55
Johnson, Lyndon B., 254, 275
Jones Act of 1917, 279
Juárez, Benito, 36, 41
Juárez Law (1855), 33
Judicial review, **171**
Junta, **144**
Justicialismo, 72

Kennedy, John F., 249, 250, 252
Keynesian policies, 206
Khrushchev, Nikita, 252

La Prensa (Nicaragua), 96

Lacalle, Luis Alberto, 107
Ladino, 18
LAFTA. *See* Latin American Free Trade Association
LAIA. *See* Latin American Integration Association
Lamarca, Carlos, 91
Land redistribution, 10
Land reform, 3, **10**, 129
Landed oligarchy, 122
Las Casas, Bartolomé de, 23
Latifundia system, 10, **11**
Latifundio, 10, 14
Latifundismo, 10, **11**
Latin America, **12**
Latin American Confederation of Christian Trade Unions (CLASC), 128
Latin American Economic System (SELA), **226**
Latin American Free Trade Association (LAFTA), 203, 213, **227**. *See also* Latin American Integration Association (LAIA)
Latin American Integration Association (LAIA), **227**. *See also* Latin American Free Trade Association (LAFTA)
Legal institutions: Central American Court of International Justice, **239**
Legal institutions: Inter-American Council of Jurists, **240**
Legal institutions: International Court of Justice (ICJ), **241**
Legal policies: Calvo clause, **242**
Legal policies: Drago doctrine, **243**
Legal policies: Estrada doctrine, **244**
Legal policies: expropriation, **245**
Legal policies: Tobar doctrine, **246**
Legalism, 60
Legislative assembly (Costa Rica), 179
Legislature, 157, 179
Legitimacy, **66**, 67, 75, 244, 246
Legitimacy vacuum, 66, **67**
Lema election system, **123**
Lenin, Vladimir, 100
Leo XIII, Pope, 55
Leoni, Raúl, 115
Less developed countries (LDC), 215, 217, 221, 229
Letelier affair, **93**
Letelier, Orlando, 83, 93
Leyenda negra, 23

Liberal democracy, 63
Liberal Front party (PFL) (Brazil), 85
Liberal parties, 68, 132
Liberal party (Colombia), 68
Liberal Reformation. *See Reforma, la*
Liberalism, **68**
Liberation theology, **69**, 109
Liberators, **35**
Lima, 20
Limited government, 60
Limited voting, 117
Literacy requirement, 136
Llanos, 7
Lleras Carmago, Alberto, 156
Lleras Restrepo, Carlos, 156
Loa, 79
Loans. *See* Caribbean Development Bank; Inter-American Development Bank; World Bank Group
Location—geographical factors, **6**
Lodge corollary—Monroe Doctrine, **267**
Lodge, Henry Cabot, 267
López, Francisco Solano, 38
López Michelsen, Alfonso, 156
López, Narciso, 32
Lower California, 32
Lusinchi, Jaime, 115
Luso-American, 12
Luso-Brazilian, 12

Machete, 94
Machetismo, **94**
Machismo, **70**
Macro approach—development strategy, **182**
Macumba, 79
Madero, Francisco I., 37, 283
Madrinha, 58
Madrino, 58
Mahan, Alfred T., 262
Maine, U.S. ship. 46, 281
Malvinas, 87
Mambo, 79
Mameluco, 18
Manifest Destiny, 45, **262**, 264
Maquiladoras, **205**
Marginality—development theory, **194**
Mariátegui, José Carlos, 103
Mariel Boatlift, **263**
Marielitos, 263
Marighela, Carlos, 91
Martí, José, 46

Martial law, 176
Marxism, 57
Marxism-Leninism, 57
Masons. *See* Freemasonry
Matos, Hubert, 104
Maximilian, 36, 41, 174
Maximilian affair, **36**
Maya, 28
Mazombo, 1
McFarlane, Robert C., 261
McKinley, William, 281
Measures of security, 178
Medellín cartel, 86, 271
Meeting of Consultation of Ministers of Foreign Affairs, 235
Menem, Carlos, 84, 87
Mercantilist trade system, 67
MERCOSUR. *See* Southern Cone Common Market
Mestizo, 18, 41
Mexican cession, 258, 264
Mexican Constitution of 1917, 30, 37, **172**
Mexican Revolution, **37**
  and Institutional Revolutionary party, 120
  land reforms of, 3
  and Mexican Constitution of 1917, 172
  non-reelection principle of, 136, 175
  as revolutionary model, 185
  and Veracruz occupation, 283
Mexican War, 258, **264**
Mexico
  agriculture, 3
  anticlericalism, 50
  assembly plants, 205
  business-government relations, 113
  church-state relations, 31
  científicos, 26, 39
  civilian governments, 145
  commercial association, 113
  Constitution of 1857, 41
  Constitution of 1917, 30, 37, 172
  Cristero rebellion, 30
  demography, 2
  development strategy, 185
  ejido system, 4, 10, 37
  election of 1988, 116
  election system, 117
  fascism, 64
  federalism, 167
  foreign debt, 197

Mexico, *continued*
  freemasonry, 65
  fueros, 33
  Gadsden purchase, 255
  government system, 157, 167, 171, 177
  Guadalupe Hidalgo Treaty, 258
  independence, 48, 169
  judicial review, 171
  LAIA membership, 227
  land reform, 10
  liberal reform, 41
  Maximilian affair, 36
  migration, 13, 260
  militarism, 146
  monarchy, 174
  National Solidarity Program, 209
  nationalization of U.S. property, 245
  non-reelection principle, 175
  organized labor, 128
  peonage, 16
  political corruption, 74
  political party system, 116, 117, 125
  political violence, 135
  population, 2, 17
  porfiriato, 39
  positivism, 76
  presidentialism, 17
  revolutions, 30, 37
  student activism, 135
  trade unionism, 128
  undocumented aliens, 13
  unicameralism, 179
  unionization rate, 128
  urbanization, 22
  U.S. intervention in, 278
  Veracruz occupation, 283
  war with U.S., 264
Micro approach—development strategy, 182, **183**
Middle class thesis—militarism, **148**
Miel, 74
Migration, **13**, 20, 260
Militarism, 142, **145**. *See also* Demilitarization
  and caesarism, 138
  development thesis, **146**
  guardian thesis, **147**
  middle class thesis, **148**
  professionalization thesis, **149**
  renovation thesis, **150**
  and security agencies, 82, 83
Military intervention, 238

Military-civilian cycles, **151**
Minifundia System, 10, **14**
Minifundio, 14, 129
Minifundismo, **14**
Ministry of *Gobernación*, **173**
Ministry of Interior, 173
Minority representation, 117
Miscegenation, 18
Missile crisis. *See* Cuban missile crisis
MNC. *See* Multinational corporation
Modernization
  conservative, 181
  progressive, 184
  revolutionary, 185
  traditional, 186
  See also Development Strategies; Development theories; Economic policies
Monarchy, **174**
Moncado barracks, 104
Monetarists versus structuralists, **206**
Monoculture, **200**
Monroe Doctrine, 36, 238, **265**, 266
  Clark memorandum of 1928, **266**
  Lodge corollary, **267**
  Olney corollary, **268**
  Polk restatement, **269**
  Roosevelt corollary, 238, **270**
Monroe, James, 265
Montaña, la, 5
Montoneros, 91
Moral incentives versus material incentives, **207**
Morales Bermudez, Francisco, 106
Morazan, Francisco, 24
Mordida, 74
More developed countries (MDC), 215, 217
Morelos, José María, 35
Movimiento 26 de Julio (Cuba), 104
Movimiento democratico pradista (MDP) (Peru), 130
Mulatto, 18
Multinational corporation (MNC), **201**
Multiparty System, **124**
Municipal assembly, 165
Municipal government, 27

Nacistas (Chile), 64
Napoleon I, 48
Napoleon III, 36, 41
National Action party (PAN) (Mexico), **125**

National Assembly (Cuba), 164, 165
National Center of Information (CNI) (Chile), 83
National communism, 57
National Front (Colombia), **126**, 156
National Guard (Nicaragua), 96
National Intelligence Directorate (DINA) (Chile), **83**, 93
National Liberation Action (ALN) (Brazil), 91
National Liberation Movement (MLN) (Uruguay), 91
National Liberation party (Costa Rica), 127
National Opposition Union (UNO) (Nicaragua), 95
National party (Blanco party) (Uruguay), **107**
National Peasants Confederation (CNC) (Mexico), 120
National Renovating Alliance (ARENA) (Brazil), 85
National Renovation party (Chile), 112
National Republican Alliance (ARENA) (El Salvador), 88
National Republican Association (ANR) (Paraguay), 110
National Revolutionary Movement (MNR) (Bolivia), 127
National Revolutionary Movement (El Salvador), 88
National revolutionary parties, 118, **127**
National Revolutionary party (Mexico), 120
National Security Act of 1947, 251
National Security Council (United States), 251
National Sinarchist Union (Mexico), 64
National territory, 167
National War of Liberation (Nicaragua), 45
Nationalism, 185, 274, 275
Nationalism, black, 62, 71
Nationalization, 185, 245
Nazis, 64
Negritude, **71**
Negro, 18
Neo-Keynesian policies, 206
Neocolonialism, 48, **202**
Neomilitarism, 145, 146, 149, 151, **152**
Netherlands, 237
Neutralism, 229

Neutrality Treaty (1978), Panama Canal, **273**
Neves, Tancredo, 85
New Granada, Republic of, 34
New International Economic Order (NIEO)
 influenced by CECLA, 228
 and multinational corporations, 201
 and structuralist economists, 206
 and Third World countries, 229
New socialist man, 207
Nicaragua
 canal treaty case, 239
 Central American Common Market membership, 218
 Central American Court membership, 239
 Central American Federation, 24
 continuismo, 161
 contras, 81
 filibuster to, 45
 Fourth World features, 221
 Iran-contra affair, 261
 liberalism in, 68
 militarism, 139
 Nicaragua vs. U.S. case, 241
 ODECA membership, 236
 Sandinista revolution, 96
 War of Liberation, 45
Nicaraguan Democratic Force (FDN), 81
Nicaraguan election of 1990, **95**
Nicaraguan revolution, **96**
NIEO. *See* New International Economic Order
Non-reelection principle, **175**
Noriega case, **271**
Noriega, Manuel, 86, 271, 276
Nitrate war, 47
Nixon, Richard M., 275
Nonalignment, 229
Non-Proliferation of Nuclear Weapons Treaty (1970), 237
Nonrecognition policy, 246
"North American," 12
North American Free Trade Area, 205
North, Oliver, 261
North-South issues, 229
Nuclear-free zone, 239
Nuclear weapons treaty (1967), 237

OAS. *See* Organization of American States
OAS-UN jurisdictional conflicts, 235

Obregón, Álvaro, 37
ODECA. *See* Organization of Central American States
Odría, Manual A., 108, 141
Odriista National Union (Peru), 130
OECS. *See* Organization of Eastern Caribbean States
O'Higgins, Bernardo, 35
Oidore, 27
Oligarchia, 122
Oligarchy, landed, 122
Olney corollary—Monroe Doctrine, **268**
Olney, Richard, 268
OPANAL. *See* Organization for the Prohibition of Nuclear Weapons in Latin America
OPEC. *See* Organization of Petroleum Exporting Countries
Operation Bootstrap, 279, **280**
Operation Just Cause, 271, 276
Optional clause, 241
Organic law, 170
Organization for the Prohibition of Nuclear Weapons in Latin America (OPANAL), 237
Organization of American States (OAS), **235**
  Bogotá conference riots (1948), 80
  and Dominican intervention, 254
  and Guatemalan intervention, 259
  human rights commission of, 96, 234
  issues considered by, 235
  report on Nicaraguan atrocities, 96
Organization of Central American States (ODECA), 24, 219, **236**
Organization of Eastern Caribbean States (OECS), 257
Organization of Petroleum Exporting Countries (OPEC), 196, 224, 226
Organized labor, **128**
Organos de Poder Popular (OPP) (Cuba), 165
Organs of popular power (Cuba), **165**
Orinoco, 7
Ortega, Daniel, 95, 133
Ortega, Humberto, 95, 133
Ortodoxo party (Cuba), 104
Ostend Manifesto, **272**

Pacific blockade, 270
Pacific settlement procedure, 247
Pacific, War of the. *See* War of the Pacific
Pact of Bogotá (1948), 233, **247**
Pact of Zanjón (1878), 42, 46
Padrinho, 58
Padrino, 58
Páez, José Antonio, 139
Pampa, 5, 7
PAN. *See* National Action party
Pan-American movement, 232
Pan-American Union, 235
Pan o palo, 39
Panama
  canal, 273, 274, 275
  canal administrator, 275
  Canal Zone, 274, 275
  civilian governments, 145
  drug trafficking, 271
  elections, 271
  government system, 179
  independence, 34
  Noriega case, 271
  unicameralism, 179
  U.S. intervention in 1989, 271, 276
Panama Canal Commission, 275
Panama Canal Neutrality Treaty (1978), **273**
Panama Canal Treaty
  (1903), **274**
  (1978), **275**
Panama intervention, **276**
Papal line of demarcation, 44
Paracaidista, 3
Paraguay
  Chaco war, 25, 118
  continuismo, 161
  demography, 2
  election system, 108
  government system, 161
  independence, 48
  LAIA membership, 227
  Paraguayan war, 38
  political parties, 118
  Triple Alliance War (Paraguayan War), 38
  unicameralism, 179
Paraguayan War, **38**
Paris Peace Treaty (1898), 281
Parliamentary system, **176**
Partial Nuclear Test-Ban Treaty (1963), 252
Partido Aprista Peruano (Peru), 106
Partido Colorado (Uruguay), 111
Partido Communista de Cuba, 114
Partido de Acción Nacional (Mexico), 125

Partido Dominicano (Dominican Republic), 130
Partido Febrerista Revolucionario (Paraguay), 118
Partido Nacional (Uruguay), 107
Partido Radical (Chile), 132
Partido Revolucionario Institucional (Mexico), 120
Partido Social Cristiano (COPEI) (Venezuela), 134
Party of the Mexican Revolution (PRM), 120
Patrón, 56
Paul VI, Pope, 109
Pax Britannica, 265
PCC. *See* Communist party of Cuba
Peace Treaty of Guadalupe Hidalgo (1848), 264
Peasants, **129**
Pedro I, 48, 174
Pedro II, 174
Peninsular, 1, **15**, 18, 33
Peonage, **16**, 31
People's Revolutionary Army (ERP) (Argentina), 91
Pérez, Carlos Andrés, 115
Pérez Jiménez, Marcos, 115, 161
Pérez-Guerrero, Manuel, 230
Permanent Council of the OAS (PCOAS), 235
Permanent observer status (OAS), 235
Perón, Eva. *See* Duarte, Maria Eva
Perón, Juan Domingo, 72, 138, 139, 141, 161
Peronism, 64, **72**
Peronista parties, 130
Personalism, 56, 72, **73**
Personalismo, 56, 72, **73**
Personalist party, **130**
Peru
　Amazon Pact membership, 212
　Andean Common Market membership, 213
　constitution suspended (1992), 101
　cooperatives, 14
　corporatism, 61
　demography, 2
　government system, 176
　LAIA membership, 227
　land reform, 10, 14
　militarism, 153
　nationalization of U.S. property, 245
　organized labor, 128
　peasants, 129
　peonage, 16
　political bossism, 158
　political culture, 75
　political parties, 106
　population, 17
　racial groups, 18
　revolutionary forces, 101, 103
　slums, 20
　unionization rate, 128
　urbanization, 22
　War of the Pacific, 47
Peruvian Aprista party, 106. *See also Aprista* parties
Pierce, Franklin, 272
Piñerúa Ordaz, Luis, 115
Pinochet, Augusto, 83, 93, 112, 142, 234
Pizarro, Francisco, 29
Plan of Iguala, 174
Plantation, 8, 11
Platt Amendment, 46, **277**
Plattismo, 277
Plaza de Mayo, 84
Plebiscite
　Chile (1988), 112
　Panama Canal treaty (1978), 275
　Puerto Rico options, 279
Plural executive, 159
Poindexter, John, 261
Poinsett, Joel R., 65, 278
Poinsettismo, **278**
Point Four Program, 182
Political bossism, 139, 158, 162
Political corruption, **74**
Political culture, 40, **75**, 175, 187
Political development, **146**, 195
Political instability, 67
Political integration, 215, 236
Political intervention, 238. *See also* Intervention
Political modernization, 146. *See also* Political development
Political party, **131**
Political party system, 116, 120, 124, 137
Political violence, **97**, 98, 156
Political violence theory, **98**
Politicization of recognition, 246
Polk, James K., 269
Polk Restatement—Monroe Doctrine, **269**
Poll tax, 136
"Poor" states, 229
Popular democracy, 63

Index

Popular Front, 57
Popular Radical party (Argentina), 132
Popular Revolutionary Vangard (VPR) (Brazil), 91
Popular Social Christian Movement (El Salvador), 88
Popular Socialist party (PSP) (Cuba), 114
Population, **17**, 22
   densities, 17
   explosion, 2, 17
   growth rate, 2
   Indian, 28
Porfiriato, **39**
Portugal
   colonial system, 27
   discovery of Brazil, 44
   Treaty of Tordesillas (1494), 44
"Portuguese secret," 44
Positivism, 26, **76**
Power elite, 185
Pradista Democratic Movement party (Peru), 130
Praetorian army, **153**, 154
Praetorianism, **154**
Prebisch, Raúl, 206, 220, 230
Preferential trade agreement, 227
Presidencia, 27
President, 175
Presidente, colonial government, 27
Presidentialism, **177**
Pressure groups. *See* Interest groups
PRI. *See* Institutional Revolutionary party
Price-Mars, Jean, 71
Primary commodity, 196
Primogeniture, 14
Privatization, **208**
Professionalization thesis—militarism, **149**
Profit-pull inflation, 199
Progressive modernization—development strategy, **184**
Pronasol, **209**
Pronunciamiento, 141, **155**
Proportional representation, 117, 123
Protectionism, 204
Protectorate, 270, 277
Protocol of Amendment to the Rio Treaty (1975), 248
Protocol of Buenos Aires (1967), 235
Provincial assembly, 165
Provincial government, 27

Puebla Conference, 69
Pueblos jovenes, 20
Puerto Rico
   Commonwealth, 279
   Latin American culture, 12
   migration, 13
   Operation Bootstrap, 280
   options for plebiscite, 279
   Spanish-American war, 281
Punte del Este, 249

Quarantine policy (Cuba), 252
Quesada, Gonzalo Jiménez de, 29

Racial discrimination, 18
Racial group, 1, 4, **18**. *See also* Social group
Radical Civic Union (Argentina), 132
Radical parties, **132**
Radical party (Chile), 132
Radio Martí, 263
Rainforest dilemma, **19**
Ramírez, Pedro P., 141
Ranchos, 20
Ratification, 275
Rawson, Arturo, 141
Raza cosmica, 18
Raza, la, 18
Reagan, Ronald, 197, 214, 257, 261
Reciprocal trade agreements program, 256
Recognition of states, 244, 246
Reconquest, 40
Reconquista, 40
"Recontras," 81
Rectification campaign, 210
Redemocratization, **99**
Reforma, la, 39, **41**
Regidores, 27
Regional alliance, 248
Regional cooperation, 212
Regional court, 239
Regional economic integration, 215, 220
Regional system, 232
Reinois, 1
Relative democracy (Brazil), 85
Relaxation (Brazil), policy of, 85
Religion, 53, 79. *See also* Catholic Church; Catholic political parties; Catholics
Renovation thesis—militarism, **150**
Repartimiento, 31
Representation, 168

Republicanism, **77**
Residencia, 27
Revolution, **100**
  Chilean, 100, 185
  Cuban, 100, 185
  Mexican, 37, 136, 172, 175, 185
  Nicaraguan, 96
  rural guerrilla warfare, 90
  urban guerrilla warfare, 91
  Uruguayan, 52
Revolution of rising expectations, 186
Revolutionary approach—
  development strategy, **185**
Revolutionary Offensive of 1968
  (Cuba), **211**
Ricardo, David, 181
Rio de Janeiro, 20
Rio de la Plata, 7
Rio Magdalena, 7
Rio Treaty (Inter-American Treaty of
  Reciprocal Assistance), 233, **248**
Rivers, 7
Roca Calderío, Blas, 114
Rodríguez, Andrés, 110
Rodríguez, Carlos Rafael, 114
Rojas Pinilla, Gustavo, 105, 156
Romero, Oscar Arnulfo, 69, 88
Roosevelt corollary—Monroe Doctrine,
  238, **270**
Roosevelt, Franklin D., 256, 280
Roosevelt, Theodore, 253, 270
Rosas, Juan Manuel de, 139
Rule of law, 60
Rural police, 39

"Safe houses," 260
St. George's University School of
  Medicine, 257
Salinas, Carlos, 116, 125
San Luis Potosí, Plan of, 37
San Martín, José de, 35
Sánchez Cerén, Salvador, 88
Sanctions, 248
Sandinist Front for National Liberation
  (FSLN) (Nicaragua), 95, 96, **133**
Sandinistas, 81, 95, 96. *See also* Sandinist
  Front for National Liberation
Sandino, Augusto César, 96
Sanguinetti, Julio María, 111
Santa Anna, Antonio López de, 41, 139,
  255, 264
Santander, Francisco de Paula, 34
Santeria, 79

Santiago, 220
Sarney, José, 85
Scarcity theory, 192
Scott, Winfield, 264
Scottish Rite Masons, 65, 278
Security arrangements: Pact of Bogotá,
  247
Security arrangements: Rio Treaty
  (Inter-American Treaty of
  Reciprocal Assistance), 248
SELA. *See* Latin American Economic
  System
Semiparliamentary system, 176
Senate, 157
Sendero Luminoso, 86, **101**, 103
Senderos, 101
Senghor, Léopold, 71
Shango, 79
Shared election system, 117
Shining Path, 86, **101**, 103
Sin papeles, 13
Sinarquismo, 64
Single-member district election,
  117
Sistema Economica Latinoamericana
  (SELA), 226
Sitges Agreement (1957), 156
Slavery, 16, 31, 45
Slum neighborhoods, 20, 22
Smith, Adam, 181
Social Christian party (COPEI)
  (Venezuela), 115, **134**
Social Darwinism, 76
Social democracy, 63, 127
Social group, 18
  colonial, 1, 15
  creole, 1
  élite, 4
  laborers, 128
  landed oligarchy, 122
  peasants, 129
  peninsular, 15
  students, 135
  See also Racial group
Social reforms
  Cuba, 54, 211
  Mexico, 37, 172
  Nicaragua, 133
  Uruguay, 52
Social science, 76
Social theory, Catholic, 61
Socialism, **78**
  and Castroism, 54

Socialism, *continued*
   and communism, 57
   in Cuban Constitution (1976), 164
   democratic, 78
   and *dirigismo*, 203
   incentives for building, 207
   radical, 78
   See also Marxism
Socialist Falange, Bolivian, 64
Sodium nitrate, 47
Soft loans, 223
Somoza, Anastasio, 139, 161
Somoza Debayle, Anastasio, 96, 139
Sonora, 32
South America, 5
South Georgia Island, 87
Southern cone, **21**
Southern Cone Common Market (MERCOSUR), 21
"Southern" states, 229
Soviet communism, 57
Soviet Union
   and Cuban Constitution (1976), 164
   missiles in Cuba, 252
   submarine base in Cuba, 252
Spain
   Black legend, 23
   colonial system, 27
   discovery and conquest of America, 28
   treatment of Indians, 31
   Treaty of Tordesillas (1494), 44
   U.S. relations, 284. *See also* Spanish-American War
   wars in Cuba, 42, 46
   war with U.S., 46, 281, 284
Spanish America, wars of independence, 35, 48, 174
Spanish-American war, 46, **281**, 284
Spanish conquest. *See* Conquest
Spanish Constitution (1812), 160
Special Latin American Coordinating Committee (CECLA), **228**
Specialized conferences, 235
Squatters, 10
State farm, 3, 10
State government, 167
State of national emergency, 178
State of siege, 166, **178**
Stroessner, Alfredo, 108, 118, 154, 161
Structuralist approach, 183
Structuralists versus monetarists, **206**
Student Activism, **135**

Sublema, 123
Sucre, Antonio José de, 35
Suffrage, **136**
Suriname, 174, 212
Suspension of guarantees, 178
Syndicalism, 61, 168

Tacna, 47
Tacna-Arica controversy, 47
Taft, William Howard, 253
Tampico incident, 283
Taylor, Zachary, 264
Teller Amendment, 281
Ten Years War, **42**, 46
Tenochtitlan, 29
Territory, **282**
Terrorism, 82, 91, 102
Texas, 258, 264
Thatcher, Margaret, 87
Theology of liberation. *See* Liberation theology
Third World, 206, **229**, 230
Thousand Day War, **43**
Tlatelolco (1968), Battle of, 135
Tobar, Carlos R., 246
Tobar doctrine, 246
Tontons Macoutes, **102**
Topography—geographical factors, **7**
Tordesillas, Treaty of (1494), **44**
Torrijos, Omar, 275
Townley, Michael V., 93
Trade and Development Board (UNCTAD), 230
Trade union. *See* Organized labor
Traditional approach—development strategy, **186**
Transnational corporations, 201
Treaty Concerning the Permanent Neutrality and Operation of the Panama Canal (1978), 273
Treaty for the Prohibition of Nuclear Weapons in Latin America (1967), 237
Treaty of Central American Economic Integration, 218
Treaty of Central American Parliament, 219
Treaty of Chaguaramas (1973), 215
Treaty of Guadalupe Hidalgo (1848), **258**, 264
Treaty of Madrid (1750), 44
Treaty of Paris (1898), 46
Treaty of San Ildefonso (1777), 44

Treaty of Tlatelolco (1967), 237
Treaty of Tordesillas (1494), **44**
Treaty on Pacific Settlement, Inter-American (1948), 247
Trickle down theory, 181
Trienio, 115
Trinidad and Tobago, 174
Triple Alliance, War of, 38
Trotsky, Leon, 100
Trotskyite communism, 57
Trujillo, Rafael Leónidas, 130, 139, 254
Truman, Harry S., 279
Tugurios, 20
Tupac Amarú, 103
Tupac Amarú Revolutionary Movement (MRTA) (Peru), 101, **103**
Tupamaros, 91, 103, 111
Turco, 18
Twenty-sixth of July Movement (Cuba), **104**, 114
Two-party system, **137**

Ubico, Jorge, 161
UNCTAD. *See* United Nations Conference on Trade and Development
"Under-developed" states, 229
Underdevelopment, 191
Undocumented aliens, 13, 260
Ungo, Guillermo, 88
Unicameralism, 157, **179**
Unión Cívica Radical (Argentina), 132
Unión Nacional Odriista (UNO) (Peru), 130
Unions. *See* Organized labor
Unitary government, 167, **180**
United Fruit Company, 259
United Nations Conference on Trade and Development (UNCTAD), **230**
United Nations Development Program (UNDP), 182
United Nations Economic and Social Council (ECOSOC), 220
United Nations Industrial Development Organization (UNIDO), 182
United Nations Security Council, 257
United Party of the Socialist Revolution (PURS) (Cuba), 114
United States
   Antiyankeeism, 51
   attempts to purchase Cuba, 272
   Bay of Pigs intervention, 250
   Chilean relations, 93
   Cuban missile crisis. 237, 252
   Cuban wars, 42, 46
   Dominican intervention, 254
   expropriation of U.S. property, 245
   and Falklands War, 87
   foreign aid, 204
   Grenada intervention, 257
   Guatemala intervention, 259
   interventions, 238, 251, 270
   Mexican relations, 255, 278
   migrations to, 13
   Nicaraguan relations, 45, 96, 239
   Noriega case, 271
   Panama intervention, 276
   protectorates, 270, 277
   Puerto Rico, 12, 13, 279, 280, 281
   Spanish relations, 46, 272, 281, 284
   war with Mexico, 264
   See also Good Neighbor Policy; Inter-American System; Manifest Destiny; Monroe Doctrine; Organization of American States; Panama Canal Treaty
University autonomy, 135
University reform movement, 135
University students, 135
Urban guerrilla warfare, 91
Urban slums. *See* Slum neighborhoods; Urbanization
Urbanization, **22**
Uriburu, José Félix, 141
Uruguay
   Batllismo, 52
   civilian governments, 145
   demography, 2
   election system, 123
   executive system, 159
   government system, 157, 159, 177
   institutional acts, 170
   LAIA membership, 227
   liberalism, 68
   militarism in, 145, 146
   organized labor, 128
   Paraguayan War, 38
   political parties, 107, 110, 111, 123
   social reform in, 52
   unionization rate, 128
   urban guerrilla warfare, 91
   urbanization, 22

Uruguayan Constitution
    (1918), 159
    (1951), 159
Uruguayan round, trade talks, 222
Utilitarianism, 76

Vanderbilt, Cornelius, 45
Vargas, Getúlio, 138, 139, 161, 167
Velasco Alvarado, Juan, 106, 141
Velasco Ibarra, José María, 130
Venezuela
    Amazon Pact membership, 212
    Andean Common Market
        membership, 213
    blockade of, 243
    civilian governments, 145
    continuismo, 161
    demography, 2
    elections, 134
    election system, 117
    exports, 200
    federalism, 167
    foreign debt, 197
    freemasonry, 65
    governmental system, 167
    independence, 34
    LAIA membership, 227
    OPEC membership, 196
    organized labor, 128
    political parties, 115, 134
    population, 17
    slums, 20
    suffrage, 136
    unionization rate, 128
    urbanization, 22
Veracruz occupation, **283**
Viceroy, 1, 27
Villa, Francisco "Pancho," 37
Villalobos, Joaquín, 88
Villas miserias, 20
Violence, political. *See* Political violence

Violence, political, theory of. *See*
    Political violence theory
Violencia, la, 43, 80, **105**
Virgin Islands, 282
Virginius Affair, 281, **284**
Visitador, 27
Vodun, **79**
Voodoo, **79**

Walker filibuster, **45**
Walker, William, 32, 45
War for Cuban Independence, **46**
War of the Pacific, **47**
War of the Reform (Mexico), 41
Wars of Independence, 35, **48**, 174
Washington Conference of 1907,
    239
"Wetbacks," 13
WFTU. *See* World Federation of
    Trade Unions
White legend, 23
Wilson, Woodrow, 244, 253, 283
Women suffrage, 136
World Bank, 199, 231
World Bank Group, 182, **231**
World Federation of Trade Unions
    (WFTU), 128

Xangô, 79

Yankeephobia, 51
York Rite Masons, 65
Yorquinos, 65
Yucatan peninsula, 269
Yugoslav communism, 56

Zambo, 18
Zamora, Rubén, 88
Zanjon Pact (1878), 42, 46
Zapata, Emiliano, 37
Zedong, Mao, 100, 101